The Information Society in Europe

CRITICAL MEDIA STUDIES
INSTITUTIONS, POLITICS, AND CULTURE

The Information Society in Europe

Work and Life in an Age of Globalization

edited by Ken Ducatel, Juliet Webster,
and Werner Herrmann

ROWMAN & LITTLEFIELD PUBLISHERS, INC.
Lanham • Boulder • New York • Oxford

ROWMAN & LITTLEFIELD PUBLISHERS, INC.

Published in the United States of America
by Rowman & Littlefield Publishers, Inc.
4720 Boston Way, Lanham, Maryland 20706
http://www.rowmanlittlefield.com

12 Hid's Copse Road, Cumnor Hill, Oxford OX2 9JJ, England

Chapter 1 copyright © Rowman & Littlefield, 2000
Chapters 2–11 copyright © European Communities, 2000
The High Level Expert Group Background Reports were commissioned by the
Directorate-General V (Employment, Industrial Relations and Social Affairs).
They don't, however, express the Commission's official views: The
responsibility for the views expressed lies with the authors.

British Library Cataloguing in Publication Information Available

Library of Congress Cataloging-in-Publication Data

The information society in Europe : work and life in an age of globalization / edited by
    Ken Ducatel, Juliet Webster, and Werner Herrmann
        p.   cm.—(Critical media studies)
    Includes bibliographical references and index.
    ISBN 0-8476-9589-1 (alk. paper)—ISBN 0-8476-9590-5 (alk. paper)
    1. Information society—Europe.   2. Technology—Social aspects—Europe. 3.
Europe—Social conditions.   4. Europe—Economic conditions.   I. Ducatel, Ken.
II. Webster, Juliet.   III. Herrmann, Werner, 1941–   IV. Series.
    HM851 .I533   2000
    303.48′33′094—dc21   99-048272

Printed in the United States of America

♾™ The paper used in this publication meets the minimum requirements of
American National Standard for Information Sciences—Permanence of
Paper for Printed Library Materials, ANSI/NISO Z39.48-1992.

Contents

Illustrations

BOXES

FIGURES

TABLES

1

Information Infrastructures or Societies?

Ken Ducatel, Juliet Webster, and Werner Herrmann

INFORMATION SOCIETY POLICY: A PREHISTORY

The idea of an information society is hardly new. By the early 1960s Fritz Machlup (1962) had made a serious attempt to map out the production and distribution of knowledge sectors in the economy of the United States and to demonstrate their already great significance. In time, these observations developed into the notion that a transition was under way in the organizing principles of society from an industrial to a postindustrial model, and then to an informational model. Japanese efforts along these lines came as early as the 1960s (see Masuda 1981; Ito 1980). By the late 1960s and early 1970s, these ideas were gaining wider currency, especially through the ideas of Touraine (1969) in France and Bell (1973) and Toffler (1980) in the United States.

As the 1970s gave way to the early 1980s there was a growing recognition of the convergence taking place between computing and communications to form information and communication technologies (ICTs). On the one hand, the digitization of communications channels was heralding the possibility of "adding value" to radio, television, and telephony by offering computerized communications services. On the other hand, successful large-scale integration of circuits on silicon chips had created the possibility of a widespread computerization of society—the so-called microelectronics revolution (see Forester 1980).

During this period, a number of influential policy statements and initiatives were made on this anticipated "ICT revolution," which can be seen as launching a first wave of information society policies. In Japan there was the Fifth Generation Computing Initiative, as well as the Wired Cities and the HDTV programs. In Europe the specter of the American challenge to European competitiveness in high technology (Servan-Schreiber 1967) and the rising sun of Japanese high technology eventually gave birth to European programs to support precompetitive research capacities. These were launched in the mid-1980s with support for information technologies (through the ESPRIT Programme) and subsequently in support of a digital and later a broadband telecommunications infrastructure (Research in Advanced Communications for Europe, RACE).

Meanwhile, in France Nora and Minc (1978) launched the term "telematique" (English "telematics") to describe the coming computerization of communication services and even of society. The French state telephone authority (DGT) took up Nora and Minc's challenge by investing massively in telematics, most remarkably in the Télétel service that by the middle 1980s had already reached mass market proportions with one in five French households on-line with connectivity through Minitel terminals (see Berne 1997). Other countries picked up the challenge. For example, in Denmark the Hybrid Network Act was passed to stimulate the development of a broadband infrastructure that would unify television and telecommunications into a single infrastructure for the future. The Danes also launched a series of community-level social experiments to try to foster the take-up of the information services (Cronberg 1997). Likewise, in Germany, there was a plan for state telecommunications operators to invest DM 300 billion to provide broadband access to all subscribers over a twenty-five-year period (see Kubicek and Dutton 1997).

Similar "first wave" information society policies were also present in the United Kingdom and the United States during the 1980s but were colored by the rule of liberal politics. In contrast to the Danish, German, and French accent on public investment and leadership, the United Kingdom under Thatcher emphasized a market-led approach to the information society. Government efforts concentrated on raising awareness of the need to act early to capitalize on the United Kingdom's productive capacity in computing and software and to commercialize information services (e.g., ITAP 1983). Public relations were prominent, and in 1979 a minister for industry and information technology was appointed, with 1982 being declared the Year of Information Technology. There was also significant funding in precompetitive industrial research (such as the Alvey program), schemes for the use of computers in schools, and even funding for research into the socioeconomic aspects of ICT (through the PICT program). But it is hard to argue that an effective information society was established through these efforts. Rather, the real ICT item on the policy agenda was liberalization and competition in telecommunications services, involving both the privatization of British Telecom and attempts to stimulate a second communications infrastructure through the digitalization of cable TV systems. The second of these two initiatives stalled due to the short duration of franchises offered to operators and restrictions of the carriage of voice telephony. But the telecommunications liberalization policy became a prototype for subsequent deregulation efforts around the world.

The United States, also under conservative political control throughout most of the 1980s, had a similar emphasis on market-led development, and partly for this reason there was no overall political program aimed at the information society. This is not to say there was no debate and no action. Here also, despite the now obvious strengths of the United States in computers and communications, there was a keenly felt threat of a loss of competitiveness in advanced technologies, especially semiconductor, computer, and peripherals. For the Americans, though, the challenge emanated from the Far East and Japan and promoted a great deal of high technology trade disputes and diplomacy (Tyson 1992). We can see these worries in the tone as much as the substance of books such as *Made in America* (Dertouzos, Lester, and Solow 1989) and the *Competitiveness of Nations* (Porter 1990). The possible economic and social benefits from the wiring of society into digital broadband infrastructure were also discussed. But the idea of a single infrastructure (the hybrid network) was ruled out because the main policy focus was on liberalization and competition, following the breakup of AT&T. United States policy action operated mainly through public–private cooperation in areas of technology research such as high performance computing and communication (HPCC) and the semiconductor road mapping exercises of Sematech.

THE SECOND WAVE

It is now generally agreed that the current wave of "information society" policies was actually launched in the United States by Senator Al Gore during the 1991–1992 presidential campaign. This time the wave swept quickly eastward to Europe, with the establishment of the European Commission Action Plan on the Information Society and into national programs within Europe and subsequently globally, with the 1995 Summit on the Global Information Society.

With its U.S. origin, albeit from the Democratic party, it carried the North American conviction that private sector leadership is the way to get things done.

This is enunciated well in the four principles that Gore outlined for the Global Information Infrastructures in Buenos Aires in 1994 (see Gore 1996):

- Private investment and robust competition are the best ways to create growth.
- Regulation should be flexible, discarding the out-of-date while remaining true to the underlying ideals of that technology.
- Access should be open.
- Universal services should be guaranteed.

These themes—competition and business leadership balanced with accessibility—were echoed in European Commission documents, although the terminology shifted. Rather than talk about an information infrastructure or information superhighways, the documents introduced the much broader concept of an "information society." Whether this shift in terminology reflects any substantial change is debatable. Kubicek and Dutton (1997), for instance, suggest that from the U.S. perspective, reference to infrastructures and highways offered a more sympathetic hearing, thus avoiding, perhaps, the taint of governmental interference.

The European situation is rather different. At that time, most European governments were still in direct control of the telecommunication operators and were wedded to traditional interventionist policies in regard to industrial and technological affairs. But these were times of ideological change toward a more liberal political economy and greater political acceptance of market leadership. Also, on a very pragmatic level, the scope for expensive interventionist policies had been narrowed by the very tight constraints on public deficits associated with the convergence criteria for establishment of a single European currency: the Euro. However, the tradition of governmental leadership remained. The recession of the early 1990s had brought significant industrial restructuring, high unemployment, and general doubt and insecurity over the future of jobs and welfare. A stress on the softer side (society) rather than the harder side (infrastructure and highways) seemed to have political mileage.

Scratch the surface, though, and more similarities than differences appear between these programs. First, both policy frameworks were launched on the back of "challenge visions" that emphasized the need to seize the day or be left behind and, simultaneously, the enormous potential benefits to be gained by the nation from the information revolution (IITF 1993; CEC 1994a).

Second, the top issue for both approaches was the promotion of further reregulation of the telecommunications and media sectors. In the United States this culminated in the Telecommunications Act of 1996, which brought to a close the concept of a local monopoly in telecommunications provision, removal of barriers to market entry by operators, and relaxation on broadcasting licenses, cross-ownership and so on. In Europe, the Bangemann Report *(Europe and the Global Information Society),* the information society keystone document, was used to animate the sluggish progress toward communications liberalization, an agenda that was finally implemented at the start of 1998.

A third similarity lies in the subsidiary topics to be found in the early statements. Both U.S. and E.U. documents stressed the need to establish appropriate regimes for intellectual property rights, privacy, and security. The national information infrastructure (NII) program also placed strong importance on stimulating technological development and innovation (not least through a continuation of the high performance computing and communication program, which Gore had sponsored in 1988 while still a senator). In parallel, the European Union effectively rebadged under the banner of the "information society" much of its fourth research and technological development framework programs in the areas of computers (the ESPRIT program) and broadband communications (RACE and ACTS [advanced communications technologies and services]). This trend has continued to the extent that by 1999, with the launch of its most recent Fifth Framework Research Programme, the European Union has now even merged these activities under the term "information society technologies."

A fourth crucial similarity concerns the benefits of timing. In retrospect, it is clear that the NII and the information society initiatives were swept along by the rising tide of public and press interest in the Internet and the World Wide Web. The growth of the Internet has been something unique in the history of the information society but was not fully anticipated in the earlier policy statements of the second wave. The initial U.S. idea was a vision of high-speed infrastructures, now rather dated, offering five hundred channels of interactive television, video on demand, and multimedia. In this sense, the Gore plan was just a facelift of first-wave European information society policies, but with the private sector footing the bill. However, it turns out that the carrier of the second wave has actually been the commercialization of the already large Internet, with a supporting cast of innovations in the form of HTML and Web browsers that make the Web less difficult, more interesting, and highly graphical.

Finally, despite its "tangible as concrete" name, the NII did include a social and economic dimension, for instance, in the Telecommunication and Information Infrastructure Assistance Program, which provided support for community-level activities (NTIA 1995). However, it can be argued that, unlike the European information society, these structures were never a central part of the overall policy activities (Catinat 1998). By contrast, the European information society (CEC 1994a) stressed the development of services and usage through stimulation of content of information flows and applications (i.e., telework, distance learning, university networks, the use of telematics by small firms, air and road traffic management, health care, public administration networks, and urban information services).

LAUNCHING THE INFORMATION SOCIETY

The immediate follow-up to the Bangemann Report was the launching of an action plan including explicit social action lines, including the setting up of the High Level Expert Group on the Information Society, for which the chapters in this book were first developed (HLEG 1996, 1997). On the heels of the Gore and Bangemann initiatives, a series of national-level information society strategies were produced.

In Europe examples include the French *Information Autoroutes Report* (Théry 1994), the *Danish Information Society 2000* (Ministry of Research 1994), the U.K. Information Society Initiative (DTI 1996), and Info2000: Germany's Path to the Information Society (BMWi 1996), and the Irish Information Society Steering Committee (ISSC 1997). Meanwhile, in Asia there were antecedents such as Singapore's Intelligent Island strategy (which actually predated the NII Agenda for Action by more than one year) and Malaysia's Vision 2020 (dating from 1991). But there were also fast follow-ups in the form of Taiwan's NII 2005 (in 1994), South Korea's NII 2003 (1994), the Ministry of Posts and Telecommunications in Japan's launch of a high performance information infrastructure plan (1994), the Philippines's creation of a national information technology plan, Smart Philippines, for 2000. Even Vietnam had an IT 2000 plan (1995) and China a series of Golden Projects known as NII 2020 (see Wang 1997 for an overview of the Asian initiatives).

Most of these initiatives followed a similar format: establishing an expert group, producing a policy statement, and attempting to initiate an action program. There have been wide differences in how this process was managed (Moore 1998). The U.S. and E.U. model has external bodies of experts providing advice to the executive, which then formulates policy. At the national level Sweden, Australia, and Canada appointed external advisory bodies with the power to directly develop policies in an affected area. Other countries, such as Denmark, Finland, the Netherlands, Norway, Japan, and Singapore, have taken the process into the executive branch, with committees operating under ministerial (sometimes even prime ministerial) control.

Despite these operational differences there is a high level of commonality in the outcomes in terms of the definition of the general problems and issues and the kinds of solutions being offered. As noted above, core issues were introduced right from the start, including intellectual property rights, security and privacy, and decency. These issues continue to feature strongly in information society debates, as can be seen in recent E.U.–U.S. debates over the jurisdiction of international data protection rules, and access to and control over encryption technology (see the discussion in Ducatel et al. 1999). These debates time and again underline a difference in approach between the self-regulation philosophy in the United States versus the tradition of trying to lay down norms in Europe.

Also, and this is a key distinction from the first wave of information society plans, there was an immediate concern about a possible polarization of society into so-called information haves and have-nots. For instance, the U.S. National Telecommunications and Information Administration (NTIA) early on produced an analysis of access to rural services (1995, updated in 1998). This was also an issue that was signaled in the Bangemann Report and strongly taken up in some of the national-level reports, such as the *Danish Information Society 2000*. On one level, the polarization debate reflects the continuing struggle (still not resolved) to find a new formula for universal service provision (USP). Needed are new definitions of both universality and service. They should be written in a way that keeps faith with the underlying principles and is flexible enough to respond to rapid technological change and the wide variety of needs and services that are offered, while recognizing the consequences of greater competition (i.e., forbidding the cross-subsidy of services).

However, polarization and access issues are more than just USP. They also raise questions about who gains in the new market-led information society. To make headway on this on a North–South level was a theme for the so-called Global Information Society Summit of the G7 in Brussels during 1995. Relatively little progress seems to have been made in addressing the issue in the follow-up work on the global information infrastructure (GII). Rather the most productive follow up of the GII summit seems have gone into the arena of international trade, and into the ambit of organizations such as GATT (General Agreement on Tariffs and Trade), WTO (World Trade Organization), and WIPO (World Intellectual Property Organization) (Catinat 1998).

The list of direct GII follow-up projects is restricted to attempts to create a resource base for some types of global service and/or a new impetus to electronic or on-line public services. The "global" projects included a global marketplace for SMEs (small and medium-sized enterprises), global health care applications, and global emergency management as well as global interoperability.

The "electronic" projects were electronic libraries, museums, on-line education, and on-line government.

This listing is useful as it gives a rough guide to the types of rather limited aspirations of the social aspects of the information society. Very often, despite the armory of panels and action plans, most of the ground-level action has been confined to a limited range of applications of ICTs in the form of small-scale demonstrators and test beds plus so far mostly unenacted proposals for more far-reaching changes. This is particularly true in relation to areas such as on-line education in which the inertia of existing institutional formats seems very high. There have been many programs. Most countries have computers-into-schools programs. There are the so-called Net days (with central sponsorship in both the United States and Europe) to raise public involvement. National-level resource centers such as the Center for Technology Supported Learning in Denmark have been set up to support development and experimentation. There have also been changes in curriculum to try to introduce ICTs more centrally into school life. These piecemeal efforts, however, hardly add up to the revolutionary advances predicted in the challenge statements of Gore and Bangemann.

Similar accounts can be made of slow progress in other fields of application such as public administration. Some countries, especially the United States but also Finland and the Netherlands, have made outstanding efforts to put government information on-line and create a more open governmental structure. But mostly the developments are in providing information instead of introducing new relationships between the people and the state. In addition, the more ambitious plans for the electronification of government, the use of electronic data interchange, data sharing, and electronic filing have moved ahead much more slowly than many government plans had hoped (Friis 1997).

Actually, the global information infrastructure projects themselves turn out to be more an attempt to inventorize and thereby consolidate existing (mainly public sector) telematic applications efforts than to launch integrated policy initiatives. Moreover, the global information society remains organized at a national level (even within Europe). It can be argued the global rhetoric is an attempt to impose Western values on the rest of the world in order to open up communications and content markets to U.S. and European operators and producers (Masuda 1996).

The idea that communications technologies are propelling a convergence toward some common model of culture is hardly new but has reemerged as a key feature in the information society debates of the 1990s. We can see this in the observation that the Internet was and remains almost entirely a U.S. anglophone environment. Meanwhile, it also runs on U.S. hardware and software (chips, operating systems, servers, and routers) and is controlled by a corpus of mainly U.S.-based interests (e.g., the Internet Engineering Task Force).

Thus, despite the similarities, information society programs at the national level are often couched in terms that stress the importance of developing approaches that support national values (see, e.g., Friis on the Danish case). In addition, not all countries have completely bought into the hands-off approach to the development of the information economy.

PUTTING THE "SOCIAL" INTO THE INFORMATION SOCIETY

Overall, then, the challenge statements from the United States and the European Union that launched the new wave of information society activity display an axial tension between the vision of technologically driven progress and the supposed social and economic gains that will result from embracing change. Undoubtedly, the references to social and economic gains are well intentioned, but the inspiration was fundamentally technological (see Garnham 1997 for a skeptical view of the previous record and likely outcomes of such technicist policies). The creation of the European Commission's High Level Expert Group on the information society, from which this book stems, can be seen as an attempt to redress this balance. It aimed, as do the chapters in this volume, to place *social* considerations in the center of the frame and to devise social policy responses, which are more than just creative applications of ICTs to society.

This is not a simple task. The relationship between technological change and social transformation is now acknowledged to be a complex one, and the simple notion of technological changes having social effects, which in turn can be simply controlled by appropriate policies, has now been shown to be false. In particular, given that private and public sector organizations alike are under pressure to reduce their costs by restructuring their activities and the goods and services that they offer, the ways that ICTs are deployed tend to reflect these objectives and do not necessarily cause them. This brings an added complexity to policy making; it is not enough to develop and implement appropriate technology policies in isolation. Technology policies and social policies have to be developed in a complementary way and strive for complementary objectives.

It is necessary, if we want the "society" in information society to be more than a rhetorical device, to develop a more sophisticated appreciation of these social issues. To this end, while acknowledging the compelling rapidity of change in ICTs and their remarkable rates of diffusion in the past few years, we still have much to learn from consolidating the experience with previous attempts to introduce new ICTs. As Cronberg (1997) has argued, there is a tendency to reject the lessons—and especially the failures—of the past because of the feeling that "this time it really is different." In reality, it is different every time but also remains much the same. The social and economic milieu in particular provides a constancy from which even the greatest technological enthusiast could draw instruction.

The debate needs to be informed so that we can gain from our past investments and experiments in ICTs. To do this, to take stock of the existing socioeconomic knowledge about a range of the core social issues of the information society and to present them together, is the aim of this book. The chapters in this book can be grouped into three broad parts, each dealing with a different aspect of the information society debate.

Part I looks at the processes of economic development and job creation related to the adaptation to and adoption of ICTs. Chapter 2 by James Cornford, Andrew Gillespie, and Ranald Richardson and chapters 3–4 by Mark Hepworth and John Ryan pick up particularly on the geographical polarization of opportunities for economic growth and job creation in the information society. With the new wave of information society interest, the idea that ICTs mean the "death of distance" by shrinking time and space has experienced a resurgence (Karvonen 1997). In chapter 2 Cornford, Gillespie, and Richardson challenge this notion, showing that ICTs clearly affect spatial relations but do not dispense with regional disparities and may actually accentuate them. Some regions and cities may become even more favored because they are firmly ensconced at the head of the global league tables as global cities. Other regions have to scramble, as Hepworth and Ryan argue in chapter 3, to attract the investments of global firms, which are the carriers of the information society. But this is not easy. The global information society has had a strong sense of slash-and-burn to it. Global firms have considerable geographical mobility and seem to be adopting practices of permanent revolution, with large-scale downsizing being a feature of the new wave of ICT-led growth.

Meanwhile, a regional information society based on the growth of local firms is not an easy option. Mark Hepworth and John Ryan, in their second contribution, chapter 4, show that in terms of the polarization debate, disadvantages tend to multiply. Less favored regions often have more small firms that are lagging behind, with an inferior information infrastructure. These are the indicators of regional polarization in the information society. Chapters 2–4 all argue that the treatment for polarization depends crucially on building up innovative capacity in local institutions, managers, and workers. Such approaches are crucial both to develop indigenous growth and to attract and then "embed" global firms in the local economy. Overall, therefore, investment in socioeconomic networks is a necessary complement and may actually be more important as a policy instrument for the information society than investment in the information networks and applications.

Part II is concerned with consequences of the information society for workers. Here again evidence is provided of the uneven impact and socially mediated nature of the ICT revolution on different categories of worker. In chapter 5, Gerhard Bosch, Juliet Webster, and Hans-Jürgen Weißbach are particularly concerned with developments in flexible working in the widest sense as they are facilitated and promoted by the implementation of ICTs. They show how "flexible" systems of work organization such as teamwork, to work effectively, imply and must be closely linked to innovations in working hours. Rigidities in working hours are unhelpful to work systems in which the tasks being done are handled on a more variable basis; examples, particularly from Germany, show that flexible work arrangements can be negotiated that offer advantages to both labor and management. In this, they are picking up a set of concerns that are at the heart of much current European social policy thinking on employment and work.

In chapter 6, Juliet Webster considers the particular dynamics of women's work in the information society. Gender segregation in the labor force tends to be overlooked in discussions of work in the information society, yet women workers are often strongly affected by ICTs. Webster is particularly concerned about the evidence of increasing dislocation and what has been termed "temporization" of work, that is, the increasing use of employment contracts that are casualized (part-time, temporary, and so on). As another dimension of "polarization," will women in such casualized forms of employment be able to take advantage of the potentially positive aspects of the information society? In other words, how can policy ensure that the "knowledge society" is a knowledge society for all?

Meanwhile, access to jobs, and especially "good" jobs, increasingly depends on qualification levels. In chapter 7, Ken Ducatel et al. point out that even with the growth of new ICTs, the new skills that are in demand are not simply technical competencies. Indeed, with high rates of technological change, the skills needed to work with a specific technology quickly become outdated unless they are built on a strong platform of cognitive, analytical, and social-behavioral skills. The implication is that if we want to give workers good labor market chances and provide an adequate supply of workers to support the growth of industry, the answer is neither narrowly technical nor short-term and quick-fix ICT skill courses.

The trends toward "flexibilization," "casualization," and increasing knowledge intensity treated by these three chapters are three interlocking trends affecting the workforce of the information society. "Flexibility with security" is a central concept running through these chapters. It implies a radically different approach to work organization from the "hire-and-fire" approach to flexibility. It implies the need for investment in workers by their employers irrespective of the types of contract. It was suggested above that there is a need for a serious commitment to building innovative capacities to overcome the risks of "have" and "have-not" regions. This can be extended to the people and particularly the workers, implying a reorientation of labor market services toward a long-term aim of providing not just lifelong learning but lifelong employability.

It is clear that ICTs are implicated in these changes. In each of these chapters the discussion is careful to show that ICTs are often conduits of change rather than drivers of change in the workplace. This is one of the most important messages about the information society that should be transmitted to policy makers. It implies that the information society is an expression of the economic, social, and political drivers underlying it more than the exigencies of the technologies. These are issues of scope that need responsible policy decisions; to some extent we will get the information society we choose.

As noted above, there has been considerable information society policy interest in the promotion of ICT applications in areas such as health care, education, services for the elderly, teleworking, and on-line (or "open") government. Part III provides an account of the social reality in these policy "targets." The four chapters in part III tackle these areas one by one. First, in chapter 8, Jorma Rantanen and Suvi Lehtinen give a detailed and expert overview of what is known about health informatics. Their overall message is that the information society will be safer, cleaner, and healthier. They are also optimistic that ICT applications in the health area will support already existing moves toward better (i.e., more seamless) care services. But they caution against the hope that ICTs in health will lead to an overall cost reduction in health services delivery. They argue that, properly implemented, such services can raise quality and make health services more cost effective, but reaping these gains requires institutional change, not just bolting telematics onto existing services. In addition, the use of computer networks in the health sector raises significant new ethical and legal issues such as guaranteeing the privacy of patient records, especially once transborder data sharing takes place between administrations. Also, in what ways does telemedicine transform the doctor–patient relationship? Such issues clearly lie beyond the realm of technology push and require extended negotiation and dialogue among professionals in social and political circles.

In the area of education there are rather similar worries that exaggerated expectations about cost savings might be driving on-line teaching. It is true that ICTs provide greater flexibility as learning tools (e.g., allowing changes in the timing and location of learning, new modes of delivery, different forms of engagement with information, and even the possibility of improving people's ability to balance work and learning with, for example, family commitments). However, in chapter 9, Gill Kirkup and Ann Jones remind us that ICTs are not "magic bullets" that will overcome the traditional problems of distance learning. They are generally more expensive and complex to produce, and it is not yet clear whether these new media are actually more effective educationally. We have a long way to go to diffuse what is known about good pedagogic practice with ICTs out to the teaching professions. Although multimedia and hypertext-based learning materials are very attractive in that they permit self-pacing, as well as independent and exploratory learning, learners first of all have to have the ability to undertake self-paced and independent learning. These questions again point toward a lengthy process of social and institutional adaptation to the information society, in which pathways that build on existing experience are likely to yield better results than, for instance, saturation strategies with the sole purpose of building the mythical critical mass.

Kirkup and Jones also make some important points about the role of social processes in the take-up of on-line learning. They argue that for the present the ownership and control of ICTs lies in male hands in many households; one of the starkest examples of this is the gender bias of the Internet, which they regard as predominantly a globalized suburb of the male middle classes. As in chapter 6 by Juliet Webster, the information society emerges as strongly gender differentiated. This analysis is disturbingly absent from mainstream information society policies and rhetoric. This theme is also taken up in chapter 10, in which Leslie Haddon and Roger Silverstone show that the household is not a "neutral" territory but is actually a contested space with constant negotiation over domestic labor and the use of time. The integration of domestic ICTs—telephones, home computers, videos, and so on—into everyday life is a process in which the significance of the technologies changes, as do the routines of everyday life and patterns of social interaction.

Again, information society rhetoric and policy consistently fail to address the fact that the transformation of everyday life is highly uncertain and socially mediated. It often takes place over an extended period. For example, the fact that Europe's population is aging just as we are entering the information society is clearly a major challenge. Strategies for promoting learning about new technologies among older people are clearly important. Whether they are correctly targeted, however, is unclear. For example, in chapter 10, Haddon and

Silverstone make an important distinction between policies relevant to the *young elderly*, many of whom are very active and economically comfortable, and those relevant to the *older elderly*, who are often on lower incomes. The younger elderly generally acquire and use new technologies if they can be easily accommodated or seem relevant to their lives. For the older elderly, the main relevance of domestic ICTs is in their potential for supporting enhanced care services. Haddon and Silverstone suggest that the level of acceptance of ICT devices into the daily routines of the older elderly will be very low.

Similar distinctions could be constructed for other potential targets of ICT applications areas such as the disabled. However, it is vital that different technologies be specifically designed and implemented with the needs and requirements of different social groups in mind, if these groups are to gain meaningful access and thus confidence with the new technologies. People need to be able to exert their own needs over the technologies—and to have them met. Given the very different situations and requirements of different people, it is unlikely that "one size fits all" approaches to the development of ICT systems will be effective. The design of the systems, the way in which they are deployed, and the structure and timing of their availability can all exclude (or include) various social groups.

The final chapter in the book, chapter 11 by Pierre Chambat, reinforces much of the argumentation above while broadening its scope to the sphere of governance and political action. Chambat's analysis is all the more salient given that the emphasis in the new wave of information society policies on openness and accountability coincides with attempts to cut back on state-provided services. In the policy debates, ICTs figure prominently as solutions to both government transparency and performance. However, as Chambat reminds us, the technological revolution is part and parcel of wider processes of liberalization and privatization. We need to bear in mind that the market leadership—despite its claims to greater transparency and accountability—may erode the European tradition of public service and equal treatment. ICTs provide accounting tools that can monitor and measure performance and thus serve as instruments for efficiency drives and market substitutions for public services. But in many cases these efficiency gains have been chimerical; and the greater monitoring of our lives raises political questions in itself. For example, ICTs can contribute to the undermining of civil society by partitioning it, privatizing it, and fragmenting our shared experiences.

It is important not to overdraw arguments about the speed, scale, and direction of changes that new ICTs will induce. Each chapter in part III emphasizes that social change is slower and less decisive than it is portrayed by technological pessimists or optimists. For instance, Haddon and Silverstone stress the considerable time necessary to become "domesticated." ICTs are accommodated in the home in an incremental way, as some members of the household accept the technologies more rapidly and readily than others. Likewise, they argue that information and communication technologies have uncertain outcomes because of their "double lives." The same communication technologies have the potential to connect people or to isolate them. Arguably, as new technologies are incorporated into the social realm, new social ties are established to replace the ones that are withering away—another lesson for policy.

POSSIBILITIES FOR POLICY

The complexity and pervasiveness of the concept of the information society means that the policy areas involved are very diverse. As a result, it is often hard to discern a direct relationship between generalized policy-relevant research and concrete policy actions. Rather, research tends to contribute to an overall milieu in which certain policy approaches become increasingly feasible, and the policy-making process gradually shifts in its direction and orientation to incorporate new thinking.

It is to be expected, therefore, that the work presented in this volume will make an indirect contribution to policy thinking on the information society. But if a single message comes through this work, it is the necessity of understanding the social embeddedness of technological change. Social factors should not be viewed as "barriers to technological change" but as forces shaping technological development and use.

A recognition of the transformative power of the human and social relations of technological change underlies the emphasis that many commentators place on "knowledge and learning" as defining features of a European model of the information society. Well-educated and trained people, and people who have opportunities to develop their abilities and talents, whether they are employees, students, or citizens in general, are in a much better position to respond in a positive way to new technologies and to put them to work in their own best interests. As Bosch, Webster, and Weißbach, as well as Webster, argue in their chapters, contemporary developments in work and employment—and in the technologies that are applied in these spheres—could potentially be harnessed to ensure that learning, expertise development, and knowledge acquisition takes place. The potential for human development (and consequently economic growth) is very powerful; we would argue that it is absolutely vital that the information society be built with this objective. It is vital not only in terms of Europe's competitive position in the global economy but also in terms of the human and social sustainability of the information society it builds. If the information society is to be a "learning society" in a real sense, as opposed to a wishful rhetoric, then much more than computer training or multimedia educational software development is needed. A much more fundamental approach to our social institutions and social practices is required in order to handle the social and technological aspects of innovation processes more holistically and for people to be able to find avenues for self-development and therefore social development, which are supported and facilitated by these institutions.

The observation that our institutions, especially our public services, seem unresponsive to the risks and opportunities of the information society is surely a particular challenge for policy makers. Yet public services and public administrations are vast repositories of information, which makes them potentially major drivers of the European economy. Much of this potential is locked up because of unhelpful and rigid structures, departmental divisions, the constraints of bureaucratic procedures, and even entrenched attitudes. As a number of European administrations are discovering, addressing these problems is a process fraught with political difficulties. Clearly, as Chambat points out in his chapter, it would be wrong to sweep aside the public service ethos, the commitment to addressing social inequalities, and the needs of the marginalized in favor of the mechanisms of the market. Instead, we need to renew our efforts to find new public service models that are much more service oriented and much more responsive to real requirements than in the past. Indeed, policy initiatives to develop locally attuned forms of public service are necessities if the information society is to be built on a civilizing vision.

The consistent message that emerges from this collection is the need for social policy on the information society to privilege a "moral economy." Up to now the main information society discourse has been on competitiveness, efficiency, and economic growth, but there is a growing recognition that such growth has a qualitative as well as a quantitative dimension. A moral economy can be thought of as a renewed and updated European social model—with its emphasis on social protection, social dialogue, and participation—but designed to meet the challenges of the "information society in Europe." At the same time, we believe that there is a key challenge and role for Europe in the information society at the level of discourse and practical leadership. Rather than concentrate on how we can better develop and apply new technologies, what we really need is to develop a social model within which ICTs can be developed and applied so that these new technologies are pressed into the service of what we believe are essential civilizing social objectives.

If there is an opportunity here for European renewal and development, we would see it as less about making a quick dash toward an ever receding technological horizon and more about building a new social and political vision. Thus, we would agree with most of the authors of these chapters who take a broadly optimistic view of the potential for the European information society to be socially progressive. Undoubtedly, there are fundamental concerns about the future that need to be addressed, if lessons are to be learned and the best pathways identified. But the important thing is to build a humanitarian information society in which the key dynamics are those concerned with learning, social inclusion, community development, and democratic participation. Perhaps the best way of achieving this vision is by giving people the tools (ICT-based tools and more conventional ones) and the support to build their own future in a productive and creative European information society.

Part I

Space, Economy, and the
Global Information Society

2

Regional Development in the Information Society

James Cornford, Andrew Gillespie, and Ranald Richardson

THE INFORMATION SOCIETY AND REGIONAL DEVELOPMENT: VISIONS AND REALITIES

There is considerable interest in the potential of the information society (IS) to contribute to the economic development and greater integration of peripheral and less favored regions. The belief that underlies this interest is that the combination of increasingly information-based goods and services with widely diffused electronic networks will overcome the "tyranny of geography" that has previously ruled in a world of material goods and physical movement. Further, this will necessarily produce a major decentralizing influence on all aspects of economy and society.

This belief can be seen clearly within the development of the European Union's information society policy agenda (Nexus Europe et al. 1996). The white paper *Growth, Competitiveness, and Employment*, for example, stated that "the common information area is also a factor for economic and social cohesion: it will allow reconsideration of siting and make it possible to promote new decentralized methods of organizing work, for example teleworking" (CEC 1993, 109).

The Bangemann Report, *Europe and the Global Information Society* (CEC 1994a), also highlighted the potential of the IS to contribute to regional cohesion objectives:

- The Information Society gives Europe's regions new opportunities to express their cultural traditions and identities and, for those standing on the geographical periphery of the Union, a minimizing of distance and remoteness. (p. 5)
- The Information Society has the potential to . . . reinforce cohesion. (p. 6)
- Networking will also diminish the isolation of small and medium sized firms in Europe's less favored regions, helping them to upgrade their products and to find wider markets. (p. 9)
- For people in remote locations, the narrowing of distance will help cohesion. (p. 25)

This multifaceted appeal of the IS for peripheral and less favored regions can be summarized as follows:

- Enabling local businesses and professionals to overcome distance and gain access electronically to remote markets and sources of information.
- Providing electronic access to specialist business services supplied from central locations.
- Enabling information processing or information creation work to be decentralized from core regions.
- Improving remote access to services such as health care and education.
- Enhancing democratic processes by providing citizens with remote access to political decision makers or sources of information about these decisions.
- Facilitating cultural pluralism and wider media choice.
- Reducing social isolation by plugging remote areas into the "global village" of "virtual communities."

There is, we contend, nothing inevitable about the realization of this benign vision. We should be aware of a long-standing tendency to imbue a whole succession of new communications technologies with quasi-utopian qualities, which the American communications scholar James Carey has referred to as "rhetorics of the technological sublime" (Carey and Quirk 1989). A common feature of such rhetoric has been a belief that new technologies are necessarily liberating in the challenge they pose to existing centralized economic and political structures. Since subsequent realities have suggested that centralization can occur as often as decentralization, we should be skeptical of similar claims concerning the inevitability of the decentralizing nature of the information society. We have been here before, and it is not necessarily so, for two reasons.

First, there is a parallel (and almost equally deterministic) dystopian vision concerning the information society. It argues that information activities will become increasingly centralized in information-rich core regions and that the electronic highways will be used to control, rather than liberate, remote or peripheral regions (see, e.g., Hepworth and Robins 1988; Gillespie and Robins 1989). A version of this more negative vision of the information society from the perspective of peripheral regions was recently labeled as that of "subordinate incorporation" in Nexus Europe et al. (1996), in contrast to the more benign vision summarized above, which was labeled "active incorporation" (see table 2.1).

Even without invoking a Mr. Hyde counterpart to Commissioner Bangemann's nice Dr. Jekyll, the information society will not automatically and inevitably liberate peripheral regions. Such regions may display particularly severe barriers to embracing the opportunities created by the information society. The barriers might include a lack of access to the advanced networks, which are the sine qua non of participation in the information society; an inability to recognize the existence of the new opportunities until others have first reaped the benefits; or their failure to successfully adopt new practices, even if the potential opportunities are well understood.

For these reasons, we contend that the implications of the information society for regional development and regional cohesion in Europe need to be examined and investigated rather than assumed. Further, we argue that the possible outcomes of regional nonparticipation or participation, or of active versus subordinate incorporation within the information society, are not predetermined and are hence amenable to policy influence.

TELECOMMUNICATIONS INFRASTRUCTURE AND REGIONAL DEVELOPMENT

A strong positive correlation between the deployment and up-take of telecommunications and economic development (as indicated by indicators such as main telephone lines per 100 inhabitants and gross domestic product) is well established at a national level. A number of studies have also identified the existence of positive relationships of this sort at the regional level (Biehl 1982; Gillespie et al. 1984). In the United States, Parker and Hudson (1995), in an analysis of rural counties in Oregon and Washington State, found that more advanced telecommunications infrastructures, such as modern digital switches as opposed to electromechanical switches, are positively correlated with the level of economic performance of rural areas. Such analysis, however, fails to identify

Table 2.1 Forms of Incorporation into the Information Society

Information Society and Cohesion Issue	Active Incorporation	Subordinate Incorporation
Access to markets	Peripheral region enterprises gain access to core region markets	Core region enterprises gain access to peripheral region markets
Access to business services	Peripheral region enterprises gain access to remote specialist business services	Core region business service suppliers undermine peripheral region business service providers
Decentralization of information work	Creation of new "telework" opportunities in peripheral regions	Only lowest grade information work is decentralized, vulnerable to price competition from offshore locations
Access to health/educational services	Improved access to services via telemedicine and tele-education	Local provision of health care and education substitutes by remote access from core regions
Access to democratic processes	Remote access to political decision making and sources of information	Local democratic institutions undermined by external information control and manipulation
Cultural pluralism	Wider media choice and facilitation of cultural pluralism	Homogenization of media and under-mining of local cultures
Community	Reduced social isolation, plugging into the "global village"	Fragmentation of place-based communities

Source: Nexus Europe et al. 1996.

the direction and precise nature of the causal relationship between measures of telecommunications investment or up-take and economic growth: telecommunications investment could bring about economic growth or economic growth could, equally plausibly, bring about increased investment in telecommunications.

The first significant study to address this question (Hardy 1980) concluded that the evidence supported bidirectional causality: an increase in the number of telephones per capita caused economic growth and economic growth caused an increase in the number of telephones. However, he also noted the existence of diminishing returns, with the effect of increasing telephone penetration on economic growth being lower in the more advanced economies. The analysis by Cronin et al. (1991), using sophisticated statistical procedures to test for the direction of causality in a thirty-one-year time series for the United States, has confirmed the bidirectional causality first identified by Hardy. Even in the world's most developed economy increases in GNP or output lead to increases in telecommunications investment. But the converse is also true: increases in telecommunications investment stimulate overall economic growth, with the "causality" significant in both directions. In a follow-up study, Cronin et al. (1993) found a significant causal relationship between telecommunications investment and total personal income, although other evidence from the study was less clear-cut. Nevertheless, the authors concluded that their findings "suggest employing telecommunications infrastructure investment as a means to stimulate local economic development" (Cronin et al. 1993, 426).

In terms of the large corporate back office and call center type of operations discussed below, the major concern in terms of *regional* telecommunications infrastructure concerns the availability, reliability, and price of high bandwidth digital circuits (leased lines) provided by telecommunications operators. Although call center operations rely on the "intelligent network" functions of the Public Switched Telecommunications Network (PSTN)—such as local rate and free phone numbers—these functions concern the *national* network planning and the installation of switches (exchanges) in the *customer's* local call area. Provided that a leased line can be used to connect a site to the public networks, the quality and cost of the public networks in the region in which the call center is located is relatively unimportant. It is therefore the availability, quality, and price of leased lines that are the main issues for many of these firms.

Survey evidence from large companies suggests that telecommunications infrastructure is a significant location factor at the level of city regions. A survey of European business decision makers carried out in 1992 (Healey and Baker 1992), for example, found that 43 percent of (large) companies regarded the "quality of telecommunications" to be an "absolutely essential" factor in considering where to locate their business. Although "ease of access to markets, customers and clients" and "transport links with other cities and internationally" both emerged as more important, the quality of telecommunications was placed above the "cost and availability of staff" and the "availability of office space" in the ranking of important location factors. London emerged from the Healey and Baker survey as the best location in Europe in terms of the quality of its telecommunications provision. This is consistent with the finding that "the high quality and comparatively low cost of telecommunications in London have encouraged financial firms to make London a major hub for communications links into Europe" (Ireland 1994; see also DTI 1994).

The significance of telecommunications infrastructure and services varies widely by sector. A survey for the European Commission by Ernst and Young (Netherlands Economic Institute/Ernst and Young 1993) found that the quality of telecommunications was cited as critical to the choice of country in 27 percent of service companies, and for 20 percent of distribution and 15 percent of office location decisions. At the regional level, the quality of telecommunications emerges as critical to location decisions in 39 percent of office and in 27 percent of service activity locations. Only with respect to manufacturing plants do telecommunications fail to register as critical or important to location decisions to more than 15 percent of firms surveyed. The study concluded that the quality of telecommunications is a critical and increasing location factor for services, European head offices, and European distribution activities, and an important and increasing location factor for R&D and high-tech manufacturing (Netherlands Economics Institute/Ernst and Young 1993).

For the vast majority of small and medium-sized enterprises (SMEs) it is the quality, reliability, and costs of the *public* switched telecommunications networks (PSTN), rather than private leased lines, that are significant. Even in terms of the provision of these basic telephone services, a substantial gap exists between the prosperous core and the poorer periphery, despite efforts by the periphery to catch up. Although the number of main telephone lines in Portugal, for example, increased by over 75 percent between 1987 and 1992, it still had the lowest density of any European Union member state at 27 lines per 100 inhabitants. Ireland, Spain, and Greece, the other "cohesion" countries, also have telephone penetration below the Community average of 44 lines per 100 inhabitants (CEC 1994b). The same core-periphery pattern is also evident with respect to the quality of service measured in terms of faults per line per year. In the more developed member states, fault rates are below 20 percent (i.e., 0.2 faults per line annually). In the least developed member states rates vary from 30 percent in Spain to 50 percent or more in Greece and Portugal, despite intensive modernization that halved fault rates in these countries over the 1987–1992 period (CEC 1994b).

Although efforts have been made in recent years to increase the rate of investment in telecommunications infrastructures in the Community's less favored regions, helped by substantial support from the Community's structural funds, "the gap" still remains substantial. Recent estimates suggest that an investment totaling Euro 37 billion (US$40 billion) would be needed to bring about basic levels of infrastructure availability and quality in the Community's "Objective 1" regions (those with the lowest levels of economic development) (NERA 1993). To close the existing gap with more developed states Euro 67 billion (US$72 billion) would be required. When compared to planned investments by telecommunications operators to 2000, an investment shortfall was estimated at between Euro 14 billion (US$15 billion) and Euro 33 billion (US$36 billion) respectively.

Within the European Union, then, there are considerable and persistent disparities between regions in the level and quality of telecommunications infrastructure provision. These disparities are related, in a complex way, to the prospective regional patterns of economic growth in Europe.

The Impact of Liberalization

The liberalization of the telecommunications sector in Europe—a key component of E.U. information society policy—is interacting with technological change and the diversification of services to shape the uneven geography of telecommunications service supply (Cornford, Ó Siochrú, and Gillespie 1996). Although liberalization can be expected to increase overall investment, that investment will be highly unevenly distributed. Under state or closely regulated private monopoly regimes, investment decisions could be made on the basis of political or engineering imperatives, overriding commercial considerations. With the advent of competition in particular telecommunications markets, commercial considerations come to the fore, creating pressure on the operator to bring the prices charged for a service into line with the costs of providing that service.

Under these competitive conditions, telecommunications network operators will seek to minimize the costs of provision and to maximize the revenues gained from new investments. New competitive operators therefore tend to make their investment in the most profitable market segments by targeting large businesses' needs such as leased lines, virtual private networks, long distance and international voice telephony, and intelligent networks. Commercial pressures ensure that established operators are forced to reflect this strategy if they are to meet the competition (see Beesley and Laidlaw 1995). The largest and earliest benefits in terms of costs and functionality arising from the liberalization of telecommunications will therefore go to large service firms.

Such large business users have a characteristic geographical pattern of location, being concentrated in the central business districts (CBDs) of major cities and in business parks on the urban periphery. From the point of view of the telecommunications operators, targeting such agglomerations of aggregate business helps to lower the costs of providing services (fewer locations need to be serviced) and raises revenues received from new investments. Such locations therefore tend to receive new investments well in advance of smaller towns, residential urban areas, and rural areas.

The United Kingdom, for example, has one of the most liberal telecommunications regimes in the European Union and a highly differentiated "landscape" of telecommunications provision. In the city of London, firms are confronted with the most advanced services offered by a host of competing suppliers (including BT, Mercury, City of London Telecommunications, MFS Communications, Worldcom, and Energis) (Ireland 1994). In CBDs of other major cities, and on business parks and other concentrations of business activity, firms have a range of potential suppliers and access to most advanced services. In the remaining urban areas, firms have a more restricted choice of supplier, with direct connections usually available only from the incumbent service provider, British Telecom (BT), and, where infrastructures have been built, from the local cable operator. In many small towns and rural areas, customers are confronted with BT as a de facto monopoly supplier. Indeed in a number of areas, mainly rural, customers do not even have direct access to digital exchanges capable of providing services such as basic rate ISDN (integrated services digital network). The general pattern, then, is one of "hot spots" of intense competition and investment, surrounded by "warm halos" of duopolistic competition giving way in turn to "cold shadows" of de facto monopoly (Gillespie and Cornford 1995). Regions lacking a critical concentration of large sophisticated users in a major CBD are likely to find that their territory will remain in the cold shadow.

Telecommunications Policies for the Less Favored Regions

Evidence concerning the link between telecommunications infrastructure investment and levels of economic development, reviewed above, has been used within the European Community to justify investing in telecommunications infrastructure "ahead of demand" in order to stimulate the development of peripheral or remote areas and less favored regions. The main expression of this approach was the STAR program (Special Telecommunications Action for Regional Development). STAR ran between 1987 and 1991 and provided Euro 780 million (US$840 million) of funding from the European Regional Development Fund (ERDF) in order to accelerate the rate of advanced telecommunications infrastructure investment in the less favored regions in seven member states. The primary aim of the program was to "break the cycle by which demand for advanced telecommunications services (ATS) is too low to justify supply on commercial grounds, in which case lack of awareness of the benefits of ATS depresses demand still further" (CEC 1991).

Although the STAR program included measures to stimulate demand (considered below), 80 percent of the budget was spent on improving infrastructure, with the main thrust being toward network digitalization, public data networks, and cellular mobile radio. According to the community-level evaluation of STAR (Ewbank Preece 1993), the program was successful in bringing forward the investment plans of the telecom providers. It accelerated network digitalization in Greece by two years and brought forward the launch of a cellular radio network in Portugal, again by two years. These results are quite impressive given that the STAR's infrastructure funding amounted to only 2.2 percent of total telecommunications investment in the eligible regions over the period. Evaluating the contribution of STAR's infrastructure measures to regional development proved rather more difficult to achieve. Ewbank Preece were only able to conclude that "the type of infrastructure supported [by STAR] is important for regional economic development" and that "our opinion is that, in general, these projects have represented a good use of regional development funds" (Ewbank Preece 1993, S-17). They mentioned in particular in support of this statement that digital telecommunications infrastructure, on which most of STAR funds were spent, "can be a critical factor in attracting inward investment into a region."

Increasingly, the emphasis has shifted away from direct support for infrastructure and toward complex regulatory actions intended to shape the patterns of provision and to ensure widespread access to the core telecommunications services that underpin virtually all information society applications. Most attention in this field has been given to mechanisms to ensure the maintenance of universal service, that is, guaranteed affordable access to a defined set of telecommunications services for all users regardless of location (see, e.g., Hills 1993, 1989; Mueller 1993; Analysys 1995; Oftel 1995).

As it is currently understood, however, universal service specifies only a *minimum* level of service provision (currently restricted to little more than an analog telephone service) and does not guarantee any services above that level of competitive supply. Other regulatory actions have therefore been implemented or proposed in order to spread the benefits of competition more widely. Most directly, the costs of some services can be geographically "averaged," ensuring that the effects of competition in core areas are felt even in areas of de facto monopoly. Particular services can be mandated as universally available (although at prices reflecting underlying costs). Other approaches are geographical franchising, or the setting of coverage targets (e.g., for mobile services) and the promotion of new lower-cost technologies. All can play a part in extending the geographical areas benefiting from new services and from competitive pressures (see DTI 1995). Such strategies can certainly help to ensure that telecommunications infrastructures, including some advanced services, are more rapidly available in less favored and peripheral regions.

There have also been a number of proposals to mandate "public access" to advanced services in specified institutions (e.g., schools, training centers, hospitals and clinics, and libraries), the aim being widespread public availability without the major costs of universal domestic availability (IITF 1993; Nexus Europe 1995; Hudson 1995; Oftel 1995). Importantly, such proposals have begun to come to terms with the fact that, unlike basic voice telephony, such services often require the connection of expensive equipment (computers rather than telephone handsets) and new skills and capabilities. By providing public access in an institutional context, the costs of equipment can be shared and users can be guided or supported by expert help.

As the point above makes clear, the presence of telecommunications infrastructures and the availability of telecommunications services do not, in themselves, ensure regional development in the Information Society. To address that question we need to turn to the ways in which they are used, starting with some of the more sophisticated uses in the service sector, based on the process which we call the "industrialization of services."

BACK OFFICES, CALL CENTERS, AND RELOCATION

Information and communication technology (ICT) makes three major contributions to enhancing the mobility of work. First, ICT is a key element in the process of service sector "industrialization." ICTs allow the spatial separation of production and consumption. Finally, they enhance the capacity of firms to control and manage production at a distance.

The industrialization of services dates back to the early years of the twentieth century, with the progressive simplification, routinization, and division of many service activities. Technology has been a key element in this process (Zuboff 1988). The recent growth of ICTs potentially accelerates this process by allowing further codification of information and knowledge. This process diminishes the importance of "substantive knowledge" within the workforce as knowledge becomes systematized and embedded in technology (Richardson 1994). The full routinization of much service work has now penetrated a range of service sector activities. For example, in the financial services sector, the method for assessing applications for products such as mortgages and loans is now based on a number of standard criteria decided at the corporate level. Assessors merely "score" applications against criteria prespecified in the software and have little room to exercise discretion on individual applications.

This "industrialization of office work" has implications for where work takes place. First, there is a tendency to concentrate these semiautomated functions in a relatively small number of specialist sites in order to gain economies of scale. Second, as a result of the changing skills profile required, possibilities for relocating existing functions and for locating new functions open up and work becomes more mobile. Changing skill profiles (both *deskilling* and *reskilling)* can mean that a firm is not tied to a location, such as a large city center, where traditional skills are reproduced. What is more, workers in existing locations may be both less *willing* and less *able* to learn new skills, being trained in a particular set of techniques and well organized to resist having to change them.

Further ICTs can allow firms to enter remote markets cost-effectively by trading "over the wire," thus establishing a "telepresence" in a region without a physical presence. In doing so, production is separated from consumption, giving organizations greater mobility to seek sites with lower costs or higher quality inputs (particularly labor). The same technologies allow firms to retain control over the work process being carried out at a distance. For example, access to information on workers' activities in real time allows the monitoring of performance even to the level of the individual worker. Many firms engaged in service activities are now able to take advantage of the widespread availability of ICTs to (re)discover the basic principles of the (inter)national division of labor (Freeman and Soete 1994).

Back Offices

Back office work comprises those "corporate internal services that require little face-to-face contact with the corporate personnel they support or with the extra-corporate world" (Nelson 1986, 149) and are generally associated with routine, fairly low-level, and often bulk work, most notably data processing work. This type of work was the first office function to be subject to the industrialization process and was also one of the earliest forms to become footloose, as firms sought lower-cost locations (Nelson 1986; Moss 1992; Moss and Dunau 1986, 1987; U.S. Congress, Office of Technology Assessment 1995). Initially work traditionally performed in, or close to, the head office was relocated. Later, processing work was also removed from branch offices (e.g., in banking and insurance) and centralized in large back offices. ICTs have enhanced the mobility of these offices as processed work is sent "over the wire."

Empirical evidence is surprisingly thin, but it strongly suggests that the two main beneficiaries of this mobile work are suburban areas in core regions and peripheral towns and cities (Leyshon and Thrift 1993). Cities such as Newcastle in northeastern England, for example, have thus far benefited from attracting significant processing operations at a time of manufacturing decline. Back office work can be carried out in smaller units and moved into smaller towns. For example, New York Life established data-processing kinds of operations in the rural western part of Ireland. Hard copy data is flown into Shannon Airport and distributed to a number of small back offices where it is processed before being transmitted back to the United States by satellite (Wilson 1994; Pearson and Mitter 1993; Allan 1995). More recently, the French firm Telergos, which provides secretarial services mainly to firms in the Paris-Ile-de-France region, has established a number of small offices in rural villages in northeastern France and northeastern England, concentrating on word processing of mail and reports (Nexus Europe et al. 1996). The computer services company, Hoskyns, has established a "business out-processing center" in a small town in the Highlands of Scotland. The office is both a processing center and a call center for a range of bodies including the administration of parking fines for local governments in London (Gillespie, Richardson, and Cornford 1995a; Richardson and Gillespie 1996).

Teleservices and Call Centers

The 1990s have seen the emergence of a new form of work relocation, known as teleservices. Face-to-face customer service is replaced or supplemented by telephone-based customer service. Across a range of industries a number of functions are becoming "telemediated" including sales, banking, marketing, market research, technical support, reservations, appointment setting, order taking, lead generation, membership renewal, insurance, brochure fulfillment, and customer inquiries (Richardson 1997).

Once the face-to-face link is broken, service production no longer needs to be co-located with service consumption. Firms are able to concentrate operations into one or a few "customer service factories"—known in the industry as call centers (Richardson 1997). Although most call centers are relatively footloose, teleservices are far from homogeneous. The services delivered range from simple information (e.g., flight times) to fairly complex technical support (e.g., in computing). The different types of call centers require different types of skills and thus have different locational requirements.

Evidence from the United Kingdom suggests that teleservice firms that service a national market are tending to locate in large conurbations such as Greater Manchester, Leeds, Newcastle, and Glasgow (Richardson 1994). Wages in these cities are considerably lower than in the southeastern part of England. In 1995 call center agent salaries were, on average, £2,300 (US$3,700) lower in northern England and £2,000 (US$3,200) lower in Scotland than in southeastern England, while bonuses and commission, often a significant part of the pay packet, also tended to be lower outside the Southeast (Thompson 1995). Evidence shows that firms can save even more—£3,000 to £4,000 (US$5,000 to US$6,500) per employee—with cost savings made as a result of lower staff turnover (Richardson 1994). Grants for training, for property, and for capital investment are often available in certain locations within less favored city regions. In Tyne and Wear, for example, around half of all call centers are located in enterprise zones (Richardson and Marshall 1996). The tendency to focus on urban rather than rural areas seems to be explained mainly by the need for a large pool of labor from which firms can cherry-pick staff with particular attributes.

The importance of linguistic skills to Pan-European call centers leads them to generally exhibit somewhat different locational patterns. In the United Kingdom, most call centers with a Pan-European focus (or in one or two cases a world focus) tend to locate in the Greater London area, the industry perception being that a cosmopolitan population is required in order to attract sufficient people with the necessary linguistic abilities. A similar situation exists in the Netherlands, which is one of the leading locations for Pan-European call centers—most international centers are located within the Randstad. Pan-European call centers can be found on the periphery of Europe, for example, in Ireland where there were thirty overseas telemarketing companies with cross-border operations by spring 1996, although in the Irish national context they are located in the core region in and around Dublin (Richardson 1995).

Limits to LFR Benefits from Service Mobility

Empirical evidence suggests that most high value-added service activities remain in core regions and that it is generally the relatively lower value-added activities that are dispersed to less favored regions. Where *new* products and processes are developed, face-to-face contact is crucial for the transmission of ideas and knowledge. ICTs serve as a mechanism for enhancing the ability of central places in core regions to extend their spatial reach, both by controlling less sophisticated parts of the production process and by "exporting" their own products over the wire. ICTs do create opportunities for new growth locations in some nonroutine tasks (such as treasury and funds management) in areas such as financial services (Warf 1995; Langdale 1995), but this is the exception rather than the rule (Wheeler and Mitchelson 1991; Castells and Hall 1994; Sassen 1991, 1994).

What is more, although much routine work has become more mobile, not all Europe's less favored regions will be able to benefit from that mobility. Only those regions with a labor force with an appropriate set of skills can expect to attract the newly mobile activities. Furthermore, many core regions are realizing the importance of these new mobile jobs and are seeking to retain or attract them, thus increasing the competition for these functions. New levels of mobility facilitated by ICTs also mean that firms can also seek out production locations beyond Europe. There is some evidence to suggest that firms are relocating routine software (and in some cases more complex) activities to the Indian subcontinent, Southeast Asia, and Eastern Europe ("Sun Life Finds Success," 1993, "Passage to India," 1994; Keen 1991; Pearson and Mitter 1993; Wilson 1995).

Finally, although the volume of information processing is likely to continue to grow, the trend may have only a limited impact on employment growth in less favored regions. Existing data processing centers are tending to concentrate into even larger sites and thus fewer regions will attract this form of employment, although the ones that do will find proportionately greater benefits, at least in the short run (Gillespie, Richardson, and Cornford 1995b). The trend toward larger centers excludes rural areas without the critical mass of staff. Competition from lower-cost offshore locations is also intensifying as ICTs become more widespread (Pearson and Mitter 1993; Allan 1995; Wilson 1994; Warf 1995). The introduction of distributed processing means that many processing tasks have been reintegrated into front office operations; meanwhile, processing is likely to become further automated with the development of scanning, bar code, voice recognition, and other technologies (Marshall and Richardson 1996).

LOCALLY LED DEVELOPMENT:
NETWORKS FOR NEW MARKETS

The previous section has concentrated on an externally led route to regional development in the information society that is based on the new locational freedoms which ICTs have opened up to many firms and other organizations. There is, of course, another route that stresses the opportunities for locally led development. The externally led model places particular emphasis on the propensity of enterprises and entrepreneurs in core regions to use advanced communications networks to gain access to assets in peripheral regions (e.g., labor supply, property, or quality of life). The locally led model, however, emphasizes the way in which enterprises and entrepreneurs in less favored or peripheral regions can use advanced communications networks to gain access to markets, suppliers, or sources of specialist information located in core regions (Richardson and Gillespie 1996).

Existing policies toward advanced telecommunications and European regional development have been based largely on the locally led model. In particular, a succession of infrastructure, service, application, and demand stimulation policies have attempted to facilitate the adoption and use of telecommunications by SMEs in less favored regions (Ilbery et al. 1995; Richardson and Gillespie 1996).

There is, however, little evidence to suggest that the locally led model is working, to date at least. Levels of adoption of information and communications technologies remain much lower in less favored than in core regions, particularly among SMEs. Even more disturbing, the evidence consistently suggests that the ICTs are not put into effective use, even when adoption takes place. Thus a survey of over 2,000 businesses across a number of rural regions in Europe concluded that "there is considerable under use of equipment and telematics services. This failure to exploit potential suggests that the opportunities offered by telematics, especially for tackling business problems . . . are far from being realized" (Ilbery et al. 1995). Similarly, a comparative study of the impacts of telecommunications adoption by small firms in northern and southern Italy by Roberta Capello found that in the North there was a clear association between adoption of telematics and enhanced competitiveness. In the South no such relationship could be identified. She concluded that "backward regions . . . seem to be quite unable to achieve economic advantages from the use of these technologies" (Capello 1994, 220).

In part, however, these findings are explained by an overemphasis in much of the literature (and indeed in much of the policy making too) on *advanced* communications services, which may in many cases be inappropriate or unnecessary for small firms, even in instances when they are highly communications dependent. Evidence from firm surveys suggests that basic telecommunications, such as phone, fax, and basic data communications (modems and simple electronic data interchange), are often vital to the performance of small firms in peripheral and less favored regions. A survey of enterprises in food and drink, textiles and clothing, and computer services industries in twelve less favored regions across Europe found that for communications with suppliers and customers, nearly all surveyed firms identified both phone and fax as "very important" or "important" (Ó Siochrú, Gillespie, and Qvortrup, 1995). Further, and somewhat surprisingly, data communication was regarded as a very important or important means of accessing suppliers in 37 percent of the surveyed firms and of accessing customers in 39 percent of the firms. In terms of the contribution of telecommunications to overall competitiveness, all but 4 percent of firms believed voice communications to be very important or important, while even for data communications some 74 percent of firms categorized it in this way. Similar findings have been found elsewhere with widely diffused, basic (rather than advanced) communications services underpinning globally competitive firms in peripheral regions (Gillespie et al. 1994).

The promise of the information society, however, is that firms in peripheral or less favored regions can successfully use telecommunications to redefine their markets or to reposition themselves within existing markets. Williams and Taylor (1991) refer to the ability of telematics networks to bring about a new relationship between the geography of the firm and the territorial claims it is able to exercise. They term this a new "management of territory." There are a number of examples of such strategies in the literature (Goddard 1991; Dabinett and Graham 1994; Richardson 1996; Qvortrup and Bianchi 1996). However, there is little evidence to suggest that such examples are common, much less typical, of firms in less favored regions.

One other pattern of locally led development that is sometimes envisaged concerns the networking of SMEs in order to derive external economies of scale or to facilitate "flexible specialization." There is, however, very little evidence in support of such collaborative or cooperative developments within less favored regions. As Dabinett and Graham (1994, 615) note in the case of the United Kingdom, "the prime motivations for developing telematics linkages . . . were external pressures from large firms further down supply chains." They conclude that "for both manufacturing and services, the evidence overwhelmingly supports the thesis that telematics underpins processes of economic globalization rather than supporting the re-emergence of neo-Marshallian industrial districts" (p. 616).

Despite the opportunities within the information society for enhancing lo-cally led regional development (and excepting a few highly publicized counter-examples), the evidence we have reviewed suggests rather that the predomi-nant process is one of "subordinate incorporation" of peripheral and less favored regions into Europe's information society. Although this is providing develop-mental opportunities for some regions associated with the mobility of infor-mation-based work, it does not seem to be challenging the concentrations of economic power in core regions, as some have argued is likely. Parts at least of the periphery are undoubtedly becoming incorporated into the information society, though the terms of this incorporation are being largely determined by actors based in Europe's core regions.

Applications Development and Usage Stimulation Policies

A repeated criticism of telecommunications infrastructure-led initiatives is that they have assumed that firms and organizations will be able to use the new infrastructure effortlessly. Experience suggests that major efforts have to be made to educate, inform, and mobilize users in the effective use of new networks and services and, above all, in peripheral and less favored areas. Many of the European Community's policy initiatives have addressed the question of de-signing and launching appropriate services and applications with the goal of encouraging SMEs to adopt advanced communications in order to overcome problems of peripherality.

For instance, in addition to the above-considered infrastructure measures within the STAR program, considerable effort was devoted to the stimulation of new services targeted at firms, primarily SMEs, in the less favored regions. Although the evaluation of the STAR program reported a few relatively suc-cessful projects of this sort, the vast majority failed to reach the thresholds for commercial viability. Much more successful than these informational services were those that supported the transactional activities of the firm, notably elec-tronic data interchange services, or those that were integrated into other core business processes, such as computer-aided design (Ewbank Preece 1993).

Electronic data interchange services in particular appear to have proved rela-tively easy to diffuse among SMEs in less favored regions, often because there is an imperative for them to adopt these services if they are to participate in large firms' supply chains. Although electronic data interchange played only a limited role in STAR, it was much more prominent in the follow-up Com-munity initiative, the TELEMATIQUE program. An example of successful policy intervention at the level of an individual SME is that of a two-man salmon-exporting firm in western Ireland, whose main customer, in Germany, required them to link via electronic data interchange. With support from TELEMATIQUE, electronic data interchange links were established and the firm was able to maintain, and subsequently expand, its business. In Northern Ireland too TELEMATIQUE was considered successful in substantially increasing the number of SMEs trading through electronic data interchange links (Meharg 1994).

A number of initiatives have gone beyond the design and delivery of individual applications to provide gateways and interfaces between SMEs and a range of service offerings and applications. The rationale behind such initiatives is to provide an integrated package of services through a single (SME-friendly) user interface. Examples of such gateways include

- the videotext-based services funded under the STAR program, such as the Irish Minitel service,
- the Network Services Agency, established as part of the Highlands and Islands of Scotland Initiative,
- a program called SPRITEL established in the Basque region of Spain (also based on the French Minitel system), and
- the Manchester "HOST" system established to provide an integrated information and communication service for the city, with local SMEs intended as one of the principal beneficiaries.

The evidence that emerges from attempts to evaluate the effectiveness of such initiatives is not encouraging. All too often, the usage of these services by SMEs falls far below expectations. Information services in particular appear to have little utility to SMEs. Attempts to foster small firm networking are often frustrated by the lack of need for links between firms that are more often competitors than collaborators. In Manchester, for example, the usage of the HOST network by SMEs was extremely disappointing, and the initiative was refocused around social and community needs (Gibbs and Leach 1994; Tanner and Gibbs 1997). Similarly mixed results were found with the Service Centers developed under the STAR program (Ewbank Preece 1993, S-9).

Our brief review of noninfrastructural policy initiatives suggests firmly that substantial barriers exist to the realization of regional economic development benefits from information infrastructures. Not only is it clear that investing in high-grade information infrastructures is not in itself sufficient to bring about economic development, but even providing services and tailoring them to the (assumed) needs of indigenous enterprises often proves insufficient. In part, this is because the real needs of users are all too often taken for granted or misspecified in the initiative design process, as a recent review for the European Commission has demonstrated (Ó Siochrú, Gillespie, and Qvortrup 1995).

The same study went on to demonstrate, however, that the same application, even if designed to meet identical user needs, can have widely differing outcomes in differing organizational and socioeconomic contexts. It follows that both information infrastructure and demand stimulation policies need, if they are to be effective in meeting economic development goals, to be integrated with policies designed to mobilize and upgrade these other aspects of regional organizational and socioeconomic environments. This conclusion is not new or radical but is nevertheless valid.

The Participation of Local Firms in the IS

Even with respect to the relatively simple version of this model, in which firms in peripheral or less favored regions can use telecommunications to gain access to remote (i.e., core region) markets, suppliers, and sources of information, there are formidable usage barriers to be overcome. The success of telecommunications in stimulating this kind of development, then, "depends critically on how well individuals, businesses and communities use telecommunications networks to improve their economic prospects" (Parker and Hudson 1995, 161).

What then needs to occur for "effective use" to take place? In fact, a series of translations needs to take place (figure 2.1). Infrastructure investment needs to lead to the provision of *appropriate services and applications.* Service provision needs an *awareness by users* of what is on offer and what is possible. From this

Figure 2.1 Schematic Information Society Dynamic

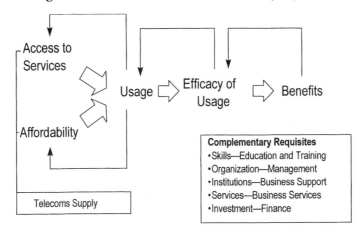

Source: Adapted from Nexus Europe et al. 1996.

awareness actual *adoption* and *effective usage* is needed. From effective usage a final translation is needed to achieve *competitive advantage*. If any of these translations fail to take place satisfactorily, the assumed causal link from infrastructure investment to regional development will break down (Gillespie, Richardson, and Cornford 1995b).

Significantly, from a policy perspective, none of these translations can be relied on to take place automatically, and even though they may take place in one region, they may well fail in another. Further, it would seem to be questions of skills, as well as organizational and institutional, capacities that account for the differing outcomes. Evidence from various European regions for the ACCORDE project, for example, found that the failure or success of telematics applications lay largely in the organizational and institutional contexts (Ó Siochrú, Gillespie, and Qvortrup 1995). In a similar vein, Capello (1994) attributed the lack of effective use of telecommunications by firms in southern Italy to the absence of various "micro-conditions," such as organizational flexibility and innovative capacity, which are necessary for adoption to lead to effective use.

From a slightly different perspective, a study for the European Commission carried out by Analysys Ltd. (Hansen et al. 1990) used econometric modeling techniques to estimate the costs and benefits of stimulating applications of telecommunications and information technologies across Europe. They determined that although benefits outweigh costs for most rural areas, the benefit is reduced for extremely rural areas. They interpreted this finding as supporting a "threshold hypothesis," meaning that a certain minimum level of general infrastructure or development is a prerequisite for a sustainable economic takeoff.

Such a threshold may need to be met across a wide range of infrastructures, both hard (e.g., roads, rail, airports, availability of suitable commercial and domestic property) and soft (e.g., schools and cultural and leisure facilities), and with respect to other issues (e.g., grants and fiscal incentives). Obviously, precise levels vary according to the characteristics of the region and the development model being pursued, although the basic minimum in all fields appears to be a necessary condition for development.

We have to conclude that telecommunications is unlikely to have particularly beneficial implications for indigenous enterprises unless these enterprises, and the broader regional contexts within which they are embedded, possess a number of complementary assets. These "complementary requirements" for effective IS participation have been summarized by Ó Siochrú, Gillespie, and

Qvortrup (1995) as skills and education, organizational capacity, institutional capacity, and investment resources (table 2.2).

CONCLUSION: LEARNING REGIONS?

The information society offers opportunities for some less favored regions to benefit from the increased mobility of routinized and codified work. But such opportunities are limited. Some regions, in particular those that can offer a large, differentiated, and underutilized labor force at low costs and have a developed basic transport and other infrastructure, have most to gain. But there are threats here too. The concentration of service activity in some regions can rob other regions of important service functions and employment. Some of these operations could be moved to lower-cost regions beyond Europe, and "customer service factories" face automation in the longer run.

Relying on externally determined location decisions might provide a short-term fix to some of the problems of unemployment or underemployment in less favored regions. But it does not provide the basis for a robust regional economy in the long run; in terms of the distinction introduced at the start of this chapter it promises mainly subordinate, rather than active, incorporation into the information society.

It is also clear that policies by less favored regions to support a more active form of regional incorporation into the information society face considerable barriers. *Some* local firms in less favored regions use telematics to reach out to new markets and suppliers or to reconfigure their patterns of operations and enhance their competitiveness. But there is little evidence that this is a widespread or systematic development or that telematics are supporting successful interfirm networking. If anything, the reverse seems to be the case. New technology adoption is generally lower in less favored regions and is often a result of pressure from larger firms (e.g., as for electronic data interchange).

In most cases the necessary chain of "translations" depicted in figure 2.1 simply fails. What is more, when one link in the chain is broken, the beneficial set of feedback loops that can generate an information society dynamic fail to materialize. As regional information society policies have developed, they have increasingly come to focus on the difficult task of supporting the successful completion of this chain of "translations" and on the role of the various complementary requisites for that process.

One way of approaching this task has been under the rubric of promoting a continuous process of "learning" within the regional economy—a "learning

Table 2.2   Complementary Requisites for Information Infrastructures

Skills and Education

Educated Workforce: Advanced communications, linked to the introduction of information technology generally, demand a relatively highly educated workforce. Otherwise, they tend to support only the low-value-added elements of the production chain.

Technical Usage Skills: The effective use of some advanced communications requires electronic engineers, technicians, and general computer literacy.

Entrepreneurial Skills: The ability to recognize and exploit new technologies, to spot opportunities, is a specialized skill, possibly requiring external support regarding the technologies. Advanced use of less advanced services may be an indicator of such skills.

Organizational Capacity

Organizational capacity refers to the ability of organizations to formulate objectives, develop effective plans, and implement them.

Access to Resources: Developing organizational capacity is difficult without access to the specialist resources required (hardware, software, business services, etc.).

Restructuring as Fostering Change: Restructuring of an organization, whether forced or voluntary, can often result in an openness to change that would otherwise be absent. Such openness can offer a good environment for the introduction of advanced communications.

Management Capacity: Managers must both identify clear objectives and develop and implement programs to realize them. Both tasks require specific skills (not necessarily the same ones).

Ability to Adapt/Adopt Technology: Managers and other employees require an ability to adopt advanced communications technologies and to adapt their organizations to them.

Institutional Capacity

Institutional capacity refers to the ability of institutions (generally public) within a region to devise, plan, and carry out programs of activities in an efficient and effective manner.

Institutional Adequacy: The basic necessity is a well-organized and robust set of institutions for economic and social development.

User Institutions and Organizations: "Intermediary" organizations, e.g., representative bodies of industry, sectors, workers, users, etc., might offer a significant asset to advanced service introduction.

Policy Integration Capacity: Successful implementation of advanced communication may require an integrated response from a range of institutions, and the development of policy instruments with cross-institutional boundaries.

Subsidiarity: Reacting quickly and efficiently to technological change tends to be supported by a territorially devolved system of decision making and administration.

Table 2.2   Continued

Supply of Services

Business Services: Complementary business services are essential to the effective use of advanced communications within a firm, including finance, accounting, marketing, advertising, transport, and logistic support. In general, where these are "pay-by-use" they are more accessible to SMEs and would therefore tend to support wider diffusion of services.

Advanced Communication Software and Systems Services: Consultancy and technical services in advanced communications software and systems may be needed for effective use. For SMEs, services should be available for purchase in "small units."

Physical Communications Infrastructure: Adequate physical infrastructures are necessary to exploit some advanced services. Only in a few cases can such services actually substitute for these, generally in social services rather than in the productive economy. This might include roads, railways, ports, and airports.

Investment Resources

Investment Funds: Adequate investment funding, local or external, is an obvious but necessary prerequisite, both for advanced communications themselves and for attendant adaptation and changes.

Source: Ó Siochrú, Gillespie, and Qvortrup 1995.

region" strategy. The concept of learning region is often little more than a trite application of fashionable business doctrines into regional development discourse (see Florida 1995) or a synonym for improvements in the education and training system. Individual-level learning is for the acquisition of appropriate skills (Morgan 1992) or learning associated with innovation within companies and industries (Lundvall and Johnson 1994). The concept of the learning region implies a focus on the issue of broad *institutional* learning both within the regional economy and from sources outside the region.

Indeed, from the perspective of regional development policy it may make more sense to focus on the concept of "the learning economy" than the "information society." Bengt Åke Lundvall, for example, has suggested that "we have entered a new phase of economic development," which he refers to as "the learning economy," in which competitive advantage is founded on the active acquisition and maintenance of knowledge rather than information. He characterized it as follows: "The learning economy is an economy where change is rapid and where the rate at which old skills get obsolete and new ones become in demand is high" (Lundvall 1996, 1–2). He sees the learning economy as distinct from the information society in that "the learning economy is affected by the increasing use of information but is not synonymous with what is often called 'the Information Society'" because "knowledge is something more than information" (p. 3). For Lundvall, the learning economy extends far beyond the formal research and development labs or education and training sectors of the economy. Rather, "learning is an activity going on in all parts of society and is an opportunity open for all citizens regardless if they are scientists or if they are workers engaged in simple tasks" (Lundvall 1996, 3).

Lundvall makes a useful distinction between four different kinds of knowledge: know-what (facts), know-why (principles), know-how (skills), and know-who (knowing who has know-what, know-why, and know-how). As he goes on to point out, "know-what and know-why can be more easily codified and transferred as information" (Lundvall 1996, 6), for example, using the kinds of technologies we usually associate with the information society. Know-how and know-who, the key forms of knowledge for supporting an information society dynamic, by contrast, are much more embedded in *social* networks that require repeated *face-to-face* interaction (Nohria and Eccles 1992; Boden and Molotch 1994; Storper 1995a, 1995b). The successful adoption and effective usage of information society services and applications to *transcend* distance, reach out to new markets, and overcome problems of peripherality paradoxically tends to rely on traditional face-to-face social interaction.

3

The Use of Information and Communication Technologies in Large Firms: Impacts and Policy Issues

Mark Hepworth and John Ryan

The strategies of large firms have a major influence on the evolution of the global information society. They not only dominate the markets for information and communication technologies (ICTs), but as major users they determine a large part of the future of work in the information society. In recent years new models of the large corporation have emerged out of so-called reengineering exercises, such as the networked organization and the virtual corporation. As Carroll points out, these models tend to be underpinned by ICTs:

> Much of the recent management literature has focused on organizational designs that allow firms to reduce employee size while increasing flexibility and output. The new type of organization has a flatter hierarchy because much decision-making is centralized. Prominent features of this new organizational design include the use of multifunctional, multi-unit teams and increased reliance on subcontracting and other joint-firm activities. Often the extensive use of information technology is essential to implementing the designs. (Carroll 1994, 35)

The employment impacts of ICT-linked transformations in large firms have caused political concern because of the scale and speed of the job cuts and the rising social and economic problems raised by greater job insecurity. The impacts on the local labor market of these organizational transformations have been most strongly felt in metropolitan cities in the form of social and spatial

Table 3.1 Shifting Economic Power in Asia, Europe, and North America (US$billion, constant 1987 prices)

	Asia	European Union	North America
GNP			
1970	1,600	2,320	3,220
1996	5,100	4,260	6,190
% Change	219	84	92
Per capita GNP			
1970	858	8,813	11,635
1996	1,704	14,632	15,934
% Change	99	66	37
Population			
1970	1,860	263	277
1996	2,990	291	388
% Change	61	11	40

Source: Adapted from World Development Indicators, World Bank 1998.

Note: North America comprises Bermuda, Canada, Mexico, and the United States; the European Union comprises Austria, Belgium, Denmark, Finland, France, Greece, Ireland, Italy, Luxembourg, Netherlands, Portugal, Spain, Sweden, U.K. (Germany is excluded because of the break in the data introduced by reunification); Asia comprises Bangladesh, China, Hong Kong, India, Indonesia, Japan, S. Korea, Malaysia, Nepal, Pakistan, Papua New Guinea, Philippines, Singapore, Sri Lanka, and Thailand.

divides that the information economy's rising skills and education demands are reinforcing (CEC 1996; Hepworth 1994a; Sassen 1994; Henley Centre 1996a).

At the same time labor markets are becoming more "global." Political concern has been provoked by evidence that new job creation in large firms favors Asia and the Pacific Rim countries owing to their higher growth rates, flexible labor markets, and an increasingly competitive base of skills and ICT infrastructure (see table 3.1; Freeman and Soete 1994).

By increasing the international "transportability" of information, computer networks allow large firms to shift "back office" and other information-processing work to low-cost, high-skill centers outside the European Union, such as India (Hepworth 1994a). Ironically, the job threats posed by corporate "transborder data flows" were originally raised by developing countries that saw the information society as potentially increasing global inequality (Hepworth 1989). The emergence of the "global firm" as an employer simultaneously operating in multiple local labor markets around the world has generated universal interest in the job implications of "transborder data flows" (Dunning 1993).

THE CONTEXT

From their emergence in the late 1960s, corporate networks have evolved as the main ICT infrastructures used by large multilocational corporations. By the end of 1993, about 1,000 digital corporate networks—carrying voice, data, and multimedia traffic—were being used by multinational companies to manage and coordinate their operations around the world (Interconnect Communications 1994). The liberalization of telecommunications markets, the relatively high costs of leased lines, the emergence of virtual private networks, and ISDN (integrated services digital network) services have been the main supply-side factors behind the growth of these private digital networks.

The diffusion of computer networking has taken place in all large firms across all sectors and in all corporate functions. A survey of 23,000 large firms in Japan found that in manufacturing and distribution 64.6 percent of companies were using intrafirm computer networks and 43.8 percent operated interfirm networks (OECD 1997a). However, the importance of different network applications vary across functions; for example, strategic management is less computer network–intensive than routine stock ordering and travel reservations. (See table 3.2.) Rates of adoption for different computer network applications also vary by sector:

- The adoption rate for ordering and production transaction systems is high in the automobile industry because of close linkages between assemblers and parts manufacturers (just-in-time production).
- The adoption rate for production control systems is high in the precision engineering of microelectronics parts, an electronics supply industry.
- The pharmaceuticals industry has high adoption rates in sales and inventory systems and customer information systems because firms have to manage diversified product lines and close links with institutional customers, such as hospitals.
- Wholesalers and retailers also show high adoption rates in sales and inventory systems and customer information systems because of the transaction-intensive nature of their core business.

Wider business philosophies and market trends have influenced the evolution of computer networking in large companies. In the 1980s, ICT was perceived as a cost burden and was outsourced as executives sought to refocus on core competences, as part of a broader trend toward "reengineering corporations" (Hammer and Champy 1993). The current trend is more toward selective outsourcing, with companies managing higher-value-added ICT applications internally and outsourcing lower-value-added tasks (Lacity, Willcocks, and Feeny 1996).

With companies now aiming to utilize information technology as a core competence, computer networks are beginning to support marketing strategies as part of business revitalization and organizational renewal (Henley Centre 1996). These strategies involve geographical expansion into emerging or new markets such as China and Russia, with corporate networks supporting this process of marketing-led globalization. Equally, networks are developing to enable large firms even more freedom to source products and components internationally (finance from Swiss banks, software skills from Bangalore, India, data processing from the Caribbean teleports, electronic components from Taiwan, and so on). In effect, global computer networks are being built to source assets or capabilities related to any part of the large firm's value chain. New systems of supply-chain management represent "virtual integration" rather than traditional vertical integration, with interorganizational computer networking—and now Intranets—being used to support more flexible, decentralized production systems and services (Axelsson and Easton 1992).

As computer networking becomes more sophisticated in large firms, there is a trend toward greater use of multimedia and other telematics applications. Progress in standards development and falling costs have led to much greater interest in videoconferencing by multinational corporations. According to a U.K. survey of two hundred top companies cited by Taylor:

Table 3.2   Taxonomy of Computer Network Applications in Large Japanese Firms

	Intrafirm Networks	*Interfirm Networks*
Business operation	Production control	Ordering system
	Sales & inventory control	
Business support	Accounting system	
	Human resources management	
Marketing	Customer information management	Reservation & guide system
Hub functions	Management planning	Technology information management
Other network uses		Distribution management
		Financial transaction
		General reference

Source: OECD 1997a, 71.

Nine percent (of firms) were already using videoconferencing, 70 percent said they would evaluate videoconferencing products over the next 12 months and more than half said they plan to implement at least one videoconferencing-based project by 1997. More than a half saw the technology as a means to cut travel budgets and time spent in meetings and said they plan to install units across multiple sites, both in the United Kingdom and overseas, while 12 percent saw videoconferencing as a way to improve internal communications. (Taylor 1996, xii)

An even more dynamic area of global computer networking is the use of the Internet by large corporations (and indeed small firms). Web sites continue to proliferate as global marketing platforms. For example, Fiat, Ford, and Volkswagen are using Web sites to advertise their new cars and gather market data by monitoring visitors logging on. Fujitsu and Mitsubishi use the Internet to send technical data to customers with microchip problems. Rockport, a U.S. shoe company, operates a Web site focusing on giving customers information on foot care and its products (Tringham 1996). Estimates vary substantially, but the Organization for Economic Cooperation and Development (OECD 1999) calculates a median current-day estimate of US$725 of commercial transactions (e-commerce) on the Internet, projected to grow to US$154 billion by 2000–2002. Of this revenue 75–85 percent is calculated to have gone to U.S. companies.

A newer development is the growth of so-called Intranets, or internal Internets, set up by large firms to facilitate global communications and transactions among employees, customers, suppliers, independent contractors, and distributors. According to market analysts, 22 percent of large U.S. corporations had internal Web servers in 1995, and 44 percent were investigating their installation (see OECD 1997b). By 1997 the *Durlacher Intranet Report* found 67 percent of U.S. firms already having or planning to have an Intranet, while an international survey covering Japan, the United States, Germany, France, and the United Kingdom found that average Intranet penetration rates across all firms had nearly doubled to 19 percent in one year from 1997 to 1998 (all data cited in Spectrum Strategies/DTI 1998). As a new component of large firms' computer networking infrastructure, Quelch and Klein (1996, 67) see three types of Intranet applications:

First, companies can use the traditional "one to many" or broadcast model to communicate corporate policies and product or market news to worldwide divisions. Similarly, companies can provide employees worldwide with immediate and up-to-date access to company databases, phone directories and reports. Second, in the "many to one model," multinational corporations can use the internal system to ask questions or collect information from divisions and individual employees.

Third, in the "many to many" model, perhaps the model with the greatest impact, multinational corporations can use the network to enable real-time, synchronous discussion amongst operating units.

In sum, the world's large companies are building a global information infra-structure to support their strategies for increasing market share and geographi-cally diversifying into market growth areas. The Internet and Intranet phenom-ena are accelerating this process of global "information highway" construction. In effect, large firms are less and less constrained by geography, time, and loca-tion in their business strategies.

The productivity impacts of ICTs in large firms with respect to employ-ment change are difficult to clearly identify and assess (Brynjolfsson and Hitt 1995; Loveman 1994). This is due to the public good characteristics and ex-ternalities associated with information itself as an economic commodity (Allen 1990). Added to this, the impacts of ICTs are more evolutionary than "over-night" owing to organizational inertia (David 1990). These points suggest that the productivity-enhancing, or transformatory, role of ICTs has been more apparent than real, being part of a more generalized cost-cutting drive based on the rationalization of corporate workforces.

The use of ICTs was linked to the drama of corporate downsizing in the recession of the early 1990s, which involved large-scale job losses and raised the new issue of white-collar and middle-class unemployment. If the reces-sion launched the downsizing trend, it was channeled and sustained by the erosion of middle management roles by ICTs. Tools such as e-mail, voice mail, and shared databases have increasingly taken over the routine collection, analysis, and transmission of information up and down the organization.

Corporate downsizing involved massive job cuts in a short period of time, the most advanced countries in this regard being the United States and the United Kingdom. In the United Kingdom these reductions numbered in the tens of thousands of jobs and affected large percentages of the workforce. (table 3.3). Large-scale layoffs were also a strong feature of the 1990s recession in the United States, although the head counts (normally in the upper thousands) and proportions of the workforce affected were not as severe, normally at around 10 percent (see Carroll 1994). However, there is evidence that in the United States this pattern of large layoffs has continued throughout the 1990s, despite the booming economy. Indeed, data on downsizing issued by U.S. outplacement specialists Challenger, Gray, and Christmas indicate that in 1998 head counts of 678,000 job losses topped the previous peak in 1993 of 615,000 (see Laabs 1999). In fact, the U.S. employment scene has exhibited high levels of turn-over, with announcements of both large layoffs and new hiring right through the 1990s. This seems to be attributable to a continual churning of the industrial structure with new industries emerging, old ones shuddering to a halt, a continuing search for efficiency and lean operations, as well as widespread mergers and acquisitions.

Although most European labor markets do not churn as much as the United States or even the United Kingdom, organizational transformations seem to have carried through into the rest of Europe. For example, in the case of the telecommunications sector:

> Job cuts on a large scale, like a sentence of execution, focus attention and concentrate the mind. So do tariff changes that substantially increase the cost of local calls and bring public discontent on the heads of politicians already bemused by the signs in Europe of economic downturn and a high general level of unemployment. The news of the swathe cut through middle management, first by British Telecom (whose downsizing is not complete) and more recently by AT&T, must have cast a somber shadow over workforces in such hitherto protected organizations as Deutsche Telekom and Telefonica in Spain (among others), who have yet to begin on major cost cutting programs so that they can compete in open world markets, and in the European Single Market once the 1998 free competition Directive applies." (*INTUG News,* April 1996, 3)

Corporate downsizing is partly driven by mergers and acquisitions, with large-scale employment losses obviously resulting from the elimination of duplication as several workforces are brought together "under one roof." Computer

Table 3.3   Early 1990s Job Losses from Corporate Downsizing in the U.K.

Company	Total Job Cuts	% Reduction
British Telecom	88,500	37
British Aerospace	71,500	56
Grand Metropolitan	58,351	48
British Petroleum (BP)	51,500	44
Forte	51,100	56
GEC	36,278	31
RTZ	30,926	62
Racal Electronics	27,133	71
Thorn EMI	24,276	42
BET	23,621	19
Rolls Royce	22,400	34
Pilkington	22,000	37

Source: Kennedy 1996, 68: © Hemmington Scott Ltd., London.
Note: Data for the U.K.'s top twelve companies, 1990–1995; the reduced head count is due to both divestments and core cuts.

networks provide, first, support for the transition to the new "information infrastructures" and, second, the greater coordination and control capabilities needed by the larger conglomerate (Kennedy 1996). The same forces of industrial restructuring that have driven recent U.S. downsizing trends are in Europe. Most tellingly, large-scale job losses can be expected with further high levels of merger and acquisition activity surrounding the full introduction of the Euro in 2002.

Merger and acquisition activity and computer network innovations have combined to bring about major rationalizations in information-intensive service industries like banking and insurance. In the first half of the 1990s, U.K. banks, building societies, and insurance companies rationalized their branch networks across the country and cut over 150,000 jobs. The enabling technological framework for rationalization was branch office automation (ATM networks), the creation of big data processing "factories" and call centers to centralize back office functions (e.g., accounts), and customer-facing functions (e.g., telemarketing), as well as "intelligent" corporate headquarters that allow senior management to monitor transactions and work processes "over the wire" (Sinden 1996; Richardson 1994; Hepworth 1994a). A similar pattern of centralization and decentralization within large firms has echoed through other sectors such as the telecommunications sector (Sinden 1995; Philips 1995), and in corporate information services across a wide range of manufacturing and service industries (Li 1995; Richardson 1994).

Distributional and policy issues emanate from the impact of these organizational changes on the international and interregional allocation of economic activity and employment within large companies. At the international level, large firms seem to be decentralizing and localizing more of their in-house or corporate services in order to enter and improve competitiveness in foreign markets. According to Dunning (1993, 270), global computer networks are driving more foreign direct investment and cross-border collaborative alliances:

> By reducing the cost of coordinating decision-making across national boundaries, these technological advances have tended to increase the scope for, and advantages of centralized control. This can be seen in such service industries as engineering and project control (through the increased use of computer-aided design and graphic systems) and in banking, insurance, airline reservation systems and hotel room bookings.

The emergence of the "global local corporation" (Mair 1994) is an integral part of the trend toward "mass customization": mass production of goods and services but customized to individual market segments, with ICTs providing the necessary flexibility throughout the large firm's operations (Pine 1993;

Hepworth and Ducatel 1992). The use of global computer networks is increasing the mobility of supplementary corporate services that enable multinational corporations to "localize" their products and services in foreign markets. These types of mobile services include customer information, consultation and advice, order taking and reservations, billing and payment. According to Lovelock and Yip (1996, 270),

> information-based services offer management greater flexibility to split the back office and front office, with opportunities to centralize the former on a global or regional basis. Production can thus take place at one location (or just a few), yielding economies of scale and access to global expertise, while delivery remains local. Banking, insurance, and other financial service products lend themselves well to delivery through electronic channels. Many forms of news, information and entertainment can also be delivered worldwide through public or private networks. Key issues in globalization include the constraints imposed by language, culture and government regulations.

A systematic assessment of which countries and regions are net gainers or losers from these trends in corporate services is both timely and necessary. Too much analysis and policy making is based on a few examples and anecdotes, such as the well-known cases of individual businesses using ICTs to exploit national and regional differences in comparative advantage; for example, the use of Irish and East Asian "telecenters" for claims processing by U.S. banks and insurance companies, or the use of Caribbean and Indian "teleports" by airlines for ticket data processing.

Regional trends in the information economy within Europe and the member states need to be assessed more systematically. A rational base is needed for the money and hopes that are being invested in information society policies covering issues such as the following:

- The net balance of employment change by numbers and types of occupation. For example, how many jobs have migrated to India's software industry or Jamaica's offshore data processing "teleports," when compared with the recentralization of IT operations in a few global "IT hubs"? (Phillips 1995)
- Changes in competitive advantage between regions and countries, especially the dynamic influence of ICT and nontechnology factors on large firm location decisions. For example, unfavorable exchange rates and "inflexible, high-wage" labor markets are cited as reasons for Japanese and German companies shifting production out of their home countries. (Gawith 1995)

- The role of national government and regional development authorities in attracting or indeed losing investment and jobs. "Host governments affect globalization potential through import tariffs and quotas, non-tariff barriers, export subsidies, local content requirements, currency and capital flow restrictions, technical and other standards, ownership restrictions and requirements on technology transfer. (Lovelock and Yip 1996, 75)

"GETTING THERE": LARGE FIRMS IN TRANSITION

Personal interviews were carried out with senior managers in seven large multinational corporations from manufacturing and services in early 1996 to shed fresh light on some of the key research and policy issues discussed above. The managers were asked, as experts in their sector and in the general field of corporate IT, to address the following questions:

- What is the new shape of the large firm and how do ICTs and telematics fit into the process of "reengineering" businesses?
- What are the impacts on employment and working conditions?
- What are the social implications and challenges for European policy makers?

Clearly, a large-scale survey or multiple case studies would be needed to determine the scale and depth of the developments reported here. It should be emphasized that the interviews do provide a broadly *consistent* view of current trends and issues with respect to overall responses and compared to the research literature.

From their own corporate situations and their knowledge of their sectors, the managers believed that the present trend toward "bureaucracy-free," flexible, information-based organizations is universal. In the interviews, they tended to use the term "lean and mean" to describe the transformation of the permanent corporate workforce into a smaller, more highly skilled core. Although all large firms were moving in this direction—involving rationalization and job cuts—the trend was thought to be geographically uneven because of fundamental differences in national economic cultures:

> We can restructure in Britain more easily than in Germany and France because of government labor market regulations, but not as easily in the United States where labor markets are even more flexible. It seems the further north one goes in Europe, the harder it gets to restructure. Italy and Spain are "softer" countries.
> The trend towards "lean and mean" is the same everywhere. Our market research for ICTs (the tools of restructuring) reveals different rates of change across

Europe. This reflects differences in national cultures as embodied in each country's unique institutions and in the national character of large firms, as employers and business organizations. Scandinavia is moving faster because it does not have entrenched hierarchical societies and there is more social mobility. (Anonymous interview with authors)

European companies have embraced the desktop computer, whereas U.S. business retains more of a centralized mainframe culture. Japanese firms have a different attitude toward information. They view it is a corporate resource and their culture supports information sharing between peers and management. This is a Japanese strength based on culture rather than technology. Supply chains are more clearly defined and maintained in Japan, so that creating EDI linkages is easier. National differences in European business culture have a divisive and retarding effect. For example, even on a mature product produced by European consortia, the partners will insist on individually stocking the same components.

The development of "information-based" organizations is certainly not seen as a smooth automatic process, nor does it follow the textbook model of business change. As emphasized by one manager, companies are not smart enough to use models in that way. Models tend to be followed or copied as competitors match each other's strategic moves. Multinational companies are also absorbing major trends on an international basis and on ever faster time scales. For example, in terms of new technologies, large firms all round the world had simultaneous access to Windows 95 because it was launched globally. The diffusion of the original Microsoft Windows from the United States to Europe and then Japan took five years. However, even with the technology available, organization change is a gradual process:

It takes 3 to 5 years to bring about cultural changes across the whole company, risk and commitment and trust and integrity. Since "networked" organizations are finely tuned they rely much more heavily upon teamwork. The big issue for us—as a global company—is how to create a shared vision. Even now, perhaps only 2 out of 10 of our factories located in different countries have absorbed this vision. Creating a global culture is very difficult. It has to cover countries, occupations or people within the firm and also the external networks of suppliers and customers on which we now depend. (Anonymous interview with authors)

The managers believed that there are limits to the "downsizing" trend, although it is not yet clear where the limits actually operate. At least one major consideration is the importance of maintaining the firm's human capital stock and achieving the right balance between costs and efficiency:

In Germany there is certainly a trend towards lean and mean, though not a very good one. This weapon becomes weaker the more often you use it. You can't go below zero staff.

The trend in retail banking is certainly towards lean and mean, however, the recognition that team working and employee satisfaction are powerful tools in achieving quality and efficiency is being addressed as major change processes are implemented.

On balance the trend is towards "lean and mean" and or "human-centered development" organizations with more worker involvement. We need both and have to find the right balance. After all "lean" and worker involvement are not necessarily conflicting targets. (Anonymous interview with authors)

The Dimensions of Change

The managers highlighted three main dimensions of change in the large firm, with the emphasis varying between sectors: supply-chain management, outsourcing, and rationalization through mergers and acquisitions. According to one manager, "all recent improvements in the company have been on the back of global computer network infrastructures."

Supply-chain management is a key dimension of change in the mass consumer goods industries, in which intense global competition and shorter product cycles have forced firms to reduce "time to market" from perhaps nine months to nine weeks. In the textile industry, this is supported by international computer network links for transferring "electronic" designs from the United Kingdom, say, to Hong Kong for engineering and production—printing and publishing has followed a similar trend. As a result, Europe has lost jobs in traditional occupations like drafting, tracing, tailoring, and typesetting but has gained new employment in graphics design, computer software analysis and design, fabric modeling, and other skilled ICT-based work.

At the national and global scales, large firms in the consumer electronics industry, for example, are introducing supply-chain management using ICT infrastructures. New methods of tightly coupled logistics (TCL) are reducing stocks or inventory with production capacity being sold "on demand." Telematics applications, specifically EDI (Electronic Data Exchange), enable orders to be processed and confirmed as they arise and customers "book" (reserve) production capacity, calling it off when required using ICT links. The job impacts are negative, involving losses in warehousing and purchasing departments, progress chasers (telephone-based clerks monitoring suppliers), planners and buyers, and a range of routine clerical support staff.

Moving toward information sharing as a corporate goal is a key prerequisite of supply-chain management. Although this is possible technically, it is dif-

ficult and expensive to implement, not least because of legal barriers. However, in industries such as aerospace engineering and manufacturing, ICTs will
play a crucial role in the future:

> The next stage in IT development will not be automating manual processes, but
> creating processes from an IT base. For example, a (European) aircraft is currently
> designed in pieces with individual elements being tackled consecutively rather
> than concurrently. This greatly extends "time to market." In future, information
> would be shared about design, production and development. The present supply
> chain would be encompassed in the process and IT would be a fundamental en-
> abler. The purchaser's requirements would need to be tightly defined and a more
> complex concurrent design activity would need careful management. The key is
> to create strong partnership consortia to protect intellectual property rights. We
> are introducing an Intranet, because it is difficult for the partners to work in global
> "virtual teams" owing to differences between European, Japanese and United States
> processing architectures, which hold back information sharing. Until now, video-
> conferencing has been held back by lack of common standards and old equip-
> ment. (Anonymous interview with authors)

All of the managers believed that large firms were monitoring opportunities for outsourcing services and production on a continuous basis. The following comments illustrate the increasingly global nature of outsourcing, particularly in highly mobile information services such as software programming:

> Most of outsourcing is local, such as office cleaning, security, PC deployment and
> maintenance. What we contract out and where depends on value and skills fac-
> tors. The lower down on the value chain, the more local the outsourcing; the
> higher up, the more international is the outsourcing. We have to look for the best
> and rarest specialists in Germany and the United States, for example. We can go
> around the world for the brainpower we need using computer nets—our own
> proprietary network and now the Internet. For example, we have an overall soft-
> ware development project co-ordinator in Germany, specialist contractors in San
> Francisco and Milwaukee and we outsource software engineering from India, an
> emerging global center for this type of information product building.
>   All European companies are looking at the future and monitoring global
> outsourcing opportunities. Flexible SMEs [small and medium-sized businesses]
> locally may clearly benefit from this, but large companies have increasingly glo-
> bal horizons. Looking into the 21st Century, it is plausible that Milan could func-
> tion as a global design center in fashion based on creative SME networks and
> multimedia links, while clothing and textile production would be done on the
> other side of the world, such as Chinese regions around Beijing and Shanghai
> again based on SME networks. (Anonymous interview with authors)

A third dimension of organizational restructuring is the rationalization that
comes with mergers and acquisitions. Informational economies of scale and

scope from computer networking have enabled the biggest companies to "upsize" their global markets while "downsizing" their workforce. According to the interviews:

> In the mid-1990s, international construction has seen big companies going through "refocusing processes" through mergers and acquisitions. They are actually swapping divisions with competitors to return to core competences. As several businesses are merged into one, big cuts are made in overheads involving the widespread elimination of duplicated functions. (Anonymous interview with authors)
>
> In the early 1980s, we thought computer nets could do the jobs of white-collar workers and we automated processes to eliminate jobs like draftsmen, accounting and production programming. From the mid 1980s to now, the emphasis has been on using technology to get rid of "overhead," and this converged with the "merger and acquisition mania" produced by global competition. So we can now use computer nets to run an organization ten times its original size, but with the same number of people in the core. You can see this everywhere. The rationalization of branch networks and regional processing centers in banking are the most obvious. (Anonymous interview with authors)

Several examples were cited to illustrate how ICTs in the context of "merger and acquisitions activity" contributed to major rationalizations and job losses. Eliminating duplication after concentrating multiple businesses "under one roof" could hit all types of occupations based in head, regional, and branch offices as well as factories and logistics and distribution. The challenge for big companies now was to shift away from a "copy-cat," cost-cutting mentality in their use of ICTs:

> We have gone through a painful process of de-layering, job cutting and divesting non-core businesses. But, our cost advantage over other European businesses could be eroded three years from now, as our competitors copy our strategies. Yes, our workforce has been slashed from 120 thousand to 45 thousand, but our turnover has risen by 10 percent. We have to now find a way of achieving sustainable competitive advantage that is not cost-based. (Anonymous interview with authors)

All of the managers reported this fundamental new direction in ICT use and the role of ICT services in large firms: searching for added value rather than simply cutting costs. A major implication of this shift is that IT departments themselves are "shrinking"—technical functions are being outsourced but being more closely integrated into the core of business activities. As expressed by one manager:

> The benefits of outsourcing ICTs were seen as cost-cutting, smaller head counts and less risk. The concern now is how to maintain the capability to develop new

applications to maintain competitiveness. Expectations that outsourcers will increase access to new developments have been unrealized. This is significant, as ICTs become more integrated into core business development. Then we have to ask, what is the optimum level of outsourcing? (Anonymous interview with authors)

The interviews suggest that cost cutting and job rationalization cannot go on indefinitely, at least in countries in which "downsizing" is already well advanced. Cost advantages tend to be temporary as firms copy each other's strategies in a global market context. The interviews also point to the fluid and uncertain nature of restructuring. "There is a danger of shapeless organizations which pull in different and opposite directions" (anonymous interview with authors). A new role for ICTs appears to be emerging, based on competing less through cost cutting than through finding new sources of value added. The "lean and mean" approach to corporate restructuring may, therefore, be a transitional phenomenon:

The attractiveness or differentiation of products will increasingly come from "humanized" characteristics based on personalized services—to offset the cold, inhuman product characteristics. This is a strong countertrend and goes hand in hand with the forced drive toward "lean and mean." "Lean and mean" as a central value governing an organizational model cannot survive in the long run. It is too meager, too mechanistic, too uninspiring an approach to attract creative workforces. For it to be successful it needs to be complemented with "human development values." (Anonymous interview with authors)

Employment and Work

The interviewees were extremely consistent in their views on the changing nature of work and employment. It was generally believed that models like "lean and mean" production and total quality management have led to a greater demand for highly skilled "knowledge workers," continuous investments in skills training, and innovative approaches to human resource management. The following trends and needs were highlighted:

- Broader multidisciplinary task definitions now require people to have wider educational backgrounds and to pursue lifelong/portfolio working and training paths.
- The emphasis on teamworking and networking is increasing, leading to greater demands for workers with communication and social skills.
- Higher educational standards are needed to carry out abstract and intellectual work for problem-solving approaches to decision making.
- There is less supervision and more independent responsibility. Progress is more closely monitored and "deliverables" are identified.

- Alternative payment systems and human resource policies are evolving to match with flatter and less rigid decentralized structures. Appraisals now become the job contract, so that everything is more individualized and customized.
- New roles of management are emerging with the emphasis on high quality, fewer errors, and less bureaucracy.
- There is greater attention to improving competitiveness through innovation and technology management, and measures to retain highly skilled "knowledge workers" call for a new management culture and new incentives.

All of the managers believed that employees in big companies are working harder and suffering higher levels of stress. This was mainly attributed to the pressures of making the transition to the "lean and mean" corporation—the challenges of survival and adapting to new responsibilities and new cultures. According to one manager, "the worst is over in our company, as we have gone from the 'down-sizing' phase to a new 'human-centered' phase of development." Another manager remarked that "people will have to work twice as hard, but further significant drops in head counts are unlikely."

As expected, work in large firms is becoming more ICT based and is carried out under a variety of arrangements—part-time, temporary, and other forms of flexible working. Home-based teleworking and dispersed "virtual teams" are predicted using videoconferencing and multimedia, groupware tools, networks (Internet/Intranet), and distance tutoring. Some existing practices were produced as examples of this ICT-supported working environment:

> We have "downsized" our IT department by 60 percent since 1990, and now applications are linked into core competences development. We use international resources as the communications infrastructure gets easier. We have triangulated videoconferencing systems worldwide—United States–United Kingdom–Switzerland—to enable global teamworking on projects. Have you noticed that the fastest-growing company is an Internet-based flower company that cuts out the middlemen? Virgin Cola has only 5 staff but it has 5 percent of the United Kingdom cola market. (Anonymous interview with authors)
>
> We use videoconferencing in training and presentations as an aid for team building. It supports global teamwork and is increasing throughout our worldwide operations. Teleworking is limited and we do not see it as part of the new "lean, human-centered" model we have introduced. We have a global electronic publishing system, where national product brochures are "peeled off" a central database and customized to local markets in each country. (Anonymous interview with authors)
>
> Half our workforce uses PCs and e-mail is widespread. More operational services are being delivered over the network—for example, health and safety in-

formation, work practices, human resources guidelines. This information will be CD-based and accessible over multimedia nets. Videoconferencing has started between London and Hong Kong using narrow band digital lines with desktop units. (Anonymous interview with authors)

The idea of global "teams" working over global computer nets has now emerged. The more extreme examples are the massive Mexican data-entry groups (more than 1,000 typists working in shifts to provide 24-hour services) that are wired into the U.S. administrative centers of credit card organizations. Or Indian software production facilities that take a design produced in Europe and deliver computer code back at high quality and 20 percent of the cost of European rivals. This model is here to stay according to the managers, and the ultimate net result is not clear: Technical jobs could migrate to India, but jobs in the European Union could be protected and increased for some occupations owing to the improved competitiveness of large E.U. companies using global teams.

Reflections on Policy Issues

All of the managers believed that new organizational models would result in greater social inequalities, marked by the emergence of a "knowledge worker" elite and a growing "underclass" of low-skilled and poorly educated people. Linked to this possibility is the further threat of increasing regional inequalities in Europe as new knowledge-intensive industries evolve around the advanced metropolitan centers. The following comments underline a new basis of labor market segmentation arising from the tensions between globalization and localization in a spatial context:

Regional inequalities will increase in Europe. Industry will be led by expertise in the advanced regions and look for proximity to software specialists, high-tech consultants and other professional skills. The low value, low-tech activities will go to cheap locations, like "call centers" and back office work. Telematics, by allowing outsourcing and remote co-ordination, is creating these regional divides in the information society. (Anonymous interview with authors)

There is an increasing threat of social divisions. Crossing the divides is the key policy issue. The elite "knowledge worker" is mobile and can work anywhere in the world. But global competition has forced large firms to become "virtual" and geographically spread. This means that they are less attached and committed to any particular locality. Telematics has killed off the "company town" and the influence for home states. The most vulnerable to these trends are, of course, the least mobile—that is, the less-skilled groups. (Anonymous interview with authors)

The managers thought that these trends made it incumbent on large firms to increase their social responsibilities, but solutions were not easy to identify. Corporate managers needed to understand local cultures and cultural differences based on trust and influence. New approaches to management should acknowledge the key concepts of "human capital" and "the learning organization":

> Human capital is often seen primarily as a cost factor and not sufficiently regarded as a solution to a problem. Some European countries are lagging behind in understanding to what extent the quality of leadership influences the engagement and motivation of the staff, and that in turn has a huge impact on the economic fate of the corporation. (Anonymous interview with authors)
>
> Education and training needs to adapt and keep pace. The role of formal training will decline because we need fast new ways of developing competences, skills, and knowledge. Knowledge is key to creating learning organizations and learning communities. The emphasis is shifting from delivering training locally to accessing knowledge globally. Thus, to be competitive locally, new infrastructures and services are needed, and there has to be global and local co-operation and partnerships between big companies and educational institutes. (Anonymous interview with authors)

The interviewees suggested that European policy approaches to these challenges should be balanced, realistic, and oriented toward managing change as a gradual evolutionary process. For example, in the case of large-scale job losses, one manager stated:

> We need to start with the basic premise that macroeconomic trends are beyond individual governments to manage. So, what can we do to ensure social stability? We need to encourage continuous change in small steps, rather than through legislative action that acts like a dam. For example, IBM cut 100,000 jobs overnight rather than 10 thousand over 10 years—the result is to explode a time bomb when the jobs are cut. We should not make restructuring harder than it is; we should be managing social change. (Anonymous interview with authors)

A number of more specific policy directions were suggested by the interviewees as a response to the socioeconomic issues raised by the job impacts of corporate restructuring. These included, for example:

- Improving the competitiveness of European industry by sector-based technology initiatives, with more emphasis on developing enabling standards and less on innovative research that has a commercial viability problem.
- Regional adjustment policies in specific sectors linked to defense and older

industries could involve supply-chain projects that benefit local economies and SMEs and contribute to job creation.

- European policies should ensure that new telecommunications infrastructure and services are evenly accessible across the member countries, so that all regions have a chance to compete for new investment and new jobs.

- Lifelong education and training needs to be a cornerstone of European social policy because everyone will need to change and adapt to new technologies, unfamiliar competences, and ever changing skills.

- Young people need to be encouraged to stay on in higher education— until they are perhaps twenty-three years of age—in order to develop a better knowledge base and avoid a future of deadend jobs and unemployment. Community service and more business experience could be woven into higher education.

- Small firms and start-ups are going to have to carry the burden of creating new jobs and absorbing the shakeout in large firms. There is scope for this from outsourcing, but new types of sectors and industries are needed for start-ups and growth on a wide front.

- Rising structural unemployment can create an underclass. We need to support our communities as people and places adjust to the new realities. Large employers should help with this by getting more involved in community development at the local level.

There seemed to be a common view that the European Union was falling behind the United States in terms of "information society" policies. One manager believed that Washington was able to exert more influence than Brussels and that Americans were embracing the new "wired society" more openly and rapidly than Europeans. For example:

> The wired world is coming true faster in the United States than in the European Union, where it is barely starting. For example, Europe led the way in the 1980s with the application of smart cards; now the United States is leading the way in secure payment capability over open networks such as the World Wide Web. (Anonymous interview with authors)

The economic transition to a twenty-first-century "information society" is clearly seen as a globally competitive process requiring political and cultural changes. It is necessary for "the European Union to develop more clever, sophisticated policies and implement them faster" if it is going to close the perceived gap with the United States.

Big Companies as Partners

It is generally agreed that large firms need to be actively involved as "partners" in shaping Europe's future "information society" (CEC 1994a). A number of policy questions surround the formation of effective partnerships:

- The "right" balance between worker protection and employer business imperatives is needed as workforces become more loosely coupled and firms adopt semipermanent arrangements of skills and tasks in emerging "networked organizations." Partnerships to achieve this balance will evolve at the enterprise level given the uniqueness of business challenges. This suggests that policies to strengthen the growth of works councils are necessary, with the European Works Councils Directive providing a framework for transnational consultation and information within companies.
- Policies to embed or deepen the embeddedness of large firms in the European Union national and regional economies are key to sustainable private–public partnerships. These types of policies, pursued as "after care" and inward investment services by many European cities and regions, range from securing the participation of large firm executives in local employer associations, economic development policy, and business networking initiatives that aim to improve local skills, small firm capabilities, community development, and infrastructure standards (Grabher 1993).
- With their global reach, large firms should be encouraged to "transfer" learning experiences and knowledge to the European Union from other countries. This knowledge of innovations and best practices can be useful also at the workplace level (works councils and employer–trade union meetings), as well as at the level of international and national employer associations. Partnerships to develop "learning organizations" and "learning communities" in Europe would benefit from these large firm contributions (which presently are developing inside global firms).

There appears to be a willingness on the part of employers, governments at different levels, and labor organizations to work together in partnership, perhaps driven by the common external threat of increasingly fierce global competition and its impacts on market share and profits, jobs and skills, and political stability and preferences. A new social economics of partnership is needed to reconcile these different stakeholder interests. This will need to be worked out from the European Union framework level down to the level of local economies, investment projects, and workplaces (Regular 1995).

Toward the "Human-Centered" Organization

Large employers are becoming more interested in human-centered models of corporate and work organization. In fact, "downsizing" has presented new problems: organizations may become "top heavy" in senior administration, tacit knowledge and experience may be lost, an aging labor force may result from seniority rules in dismissal, and, importantly, the workforce that survives may suffer from low morale and stress (Carroll 1994; Cappelli 1995). Recent business surveys indicate that large employers are skeptical about "downsizing," partly because of the lack of productivity payoff and partly because new pressures to develop markets through innovation, marketing, and globalization have underlined the need to build skills and capacity.

There is also little evidence of large firms moving toward "anthropocentric production systems" (APS) in Europe—advanced manufacturing based on the optimal utilization of skilled human resources, collaborative industrial organization, and adapted technologies" (Wobbe 1991). A survey of research by Penn and Sleightbone (1995) found no real shift toward either APS or Japanese-style "lean manufacturing," leading them to ask, "What is happening to skilled work in contemporary Europe?" (pp. 199–200). Similarly, outsourcing as a means of corporate downsizing has its limits. According to Chesbrough and Teece (1996, 65), "the virtues of being virtual have been oversold. The new conventional wisdom ignores the distinctive role that large integrated companies can play in the innovation process. Those rushing to form alliances instead of nurturing and guarding their own capabilities may be risking their future."

There is clearly a need for policies that exploit a small but discernible window of opportunity in the emerging debate about what comes after downsizing and the "lean and mean" movement (Millard et al. 1995). As Ducatel (1996) has pointed out, the time may be ripe for fresh thinking and experimentation as a basis for shaping future trends in large firms.

There clearly needs to be more R&D and systematic information based on organizational innovations in large corporations, given that ICTs will not lead to improved productivity and competitiveness without new workplaces, new organizations, and new institutions. Best practice and demonstration sites could showcase case studies of organizational innovations rather than only technologies (Van Eijnatten 1993).

A consistent European Union–wide approach toward creating new human-centered work environments in large firms would need to account for large differences between the member states in the resources allocated to R&D in this area. Common actions at the E.U. level are needed to reduce these differences, such as joint transnational programs on "organizational renewal" involve researchers, large firm managers, and employee representatives (European works councils and trade unions) (Hart 1995).

Large employers should be encouraged to think of innovative alternatives to upgrading skills and cutting jobs. A central E.U. repository of existing and possible schemes from within Europe and other parts of the world should be created for employers to refer to, validate, and possibly adopt. Multimedia links to this repository could be offered across Europe.

For example, a large Dutch bank created retraining and readjustment time by keeping redundant employees on the payroll but hiring them out to new employers. The bank still pays the difference between the market rate paid by the new employer and the person's old salary, which is still less costly than keeping such persons in the organization or forcing them out. The two-year period of this scheme can be used by the employee to retrain and increase his or her market value while under the income protection of the bank. In some cases this has worked so well that people came back into the bank at higher levels than before.

Education and Training

The interviews underline the importance of a highly educated workforce and continuous skills training for the European Union to compete successfully in the global economy for new investment and jobs. Computer networks enable large firms to "shop around" and draw on knowledge and advanced skills on a global scale. Even the "human-centered" organization of tomorrow requires highly educated, "self-starting," flexible employees rather than the old highly specialized, routine-dependent bureaucrats. Skills have to be constantly renewed as large firms develop new competences to compete in rapidly changing markets and adjust to new technological platforms. Large firms presently favor in-house, on-the-job training to keep pace with this moving skills frontier (Ducatel 1994). Some policy implications are outlined below:

- Investments in basic education, from school age to advanced college education, are essential for global competitive advantage and future job prospects in the European Union. Large firms prefer to employ highly educated, flexible generalists who can adapt to "learning organization" environments rather than "ready-made" government trainees with narrow occupation-specific skills.
- Similarly, the preference for "on-the-job, in-house" competence development that is process focused points to the need for training and education schemes based on placements in large employers for unemployed

people, college graduates, and senior schoolchildren. Employer participation will clearly require stronger business education and business–government training partnerships. Financial incentives may also be required.

- Large firms could be encouraged to open up (as far as possible) their emerging multimedia facilities for skills training and competence development. Access to these virtual learning organization environments could be negotiated with public training bodies and schools and higher educational institutes.
- This type of negotiated virtual learning organization environment could provide a platform for skills training and competence development in SMEs, perhaps extending the Intranet model to SME partners with sectoral and/or local links.
- New college training courses, business school education and "learning partnerships" could be set up for large firm managers to increase their knowledge of local economic development as a social and economic environment for new business strategies.

Localization Strategies

Stopford and Strange (1991) argue that "the power of the individual firm may be regarded as having fallen as (global) competition has intensified. New entrants have altered the rules and offer governments new bargaining advantage. One needs to separate the power to influence general policy from the power to insist on specific bargains" (pp. 215–216). Clearly, for powerful multinational corporations (MNCs), the geographical term "regional" can refer to a foothold in North America or Europe as a whole rather than individual countries or regions within countries. The geographies of markets and marketing strategies will determine, in each case, what "local" means to the global firm. Four areas can be identified in which public authorities could improve competitive advantage and possibly influence MNC localization strategies:

- Deregulate and simplify administrative procedures (eliminate "red tape") to remove unnecessary constraints that reduce MNC competitiveness and the freedom to innovate and create jobs.
- Maintain globally competitive standards of ICT and other infrastructures, workforce skills, supplier networks, and technology/innovation resources.
- Maintain general conditions of social, economic, and political stability that MNCs can use as a referential framework in making long-term investment and human resource development decisions.
- Ensure that MNCs are embedded in the "host" economy both technically,

in terms of business linkages and infrastructures, and socially, in terms of personal and corporate membership of local institutional networks.

The different ability of regions to attract inward investment, with more favored regions able to attract more mobile international investment, should be noted. As such, localization strategies will need to be differently formulated and sensitive to the ground-level reality of the virtual economy.

The practical implications are unclear, although a bottom–up approach is clearly favored by the emerging political trend toward regionalism. For example, Riegler (1995, 11) suggests that support institutions need to be designed according to the following principles:

- The development of organizations and work roles is foremost a matter of local-level processes to which the principle of participation of everyone involved or affected must apply.
- The public infrastructure should be sufficiently widespread in social and geographical space to allow, at least from time to time, a direct dialogue with the enterprises.
- It is important that the enterprises organize themselves from the bottom up in systems of certain size, organizations for cooperation, networks, industrial regions, or other systems.
- Public enterprise support programs—training, grants, technology, and so on—need to be "integrated primarily at the local and regional levels, but must be linked to initiatives at the national level."

As Blankaert (1995) emphasizes, the local availability of skills, training, and R&D links, as well as the embeddedness of the large firm in local production/ industrial networks, may limit the real mobility offered by the technical potential of ICTs. Similarly, Lorentzon (1995) has shown that logistics and favorable environments are important locational factors in Swedish large companies, even with the shift toward just-in-time production and global computer networking. Embedding global firms in local industrial networks is the new orthodoxy of local economic development, even if there is some evidence that model regions like Germany's Baden Württemberg are struggling with maintaining its networking assets in the face of globalization (Braczyk, Schienstock, and Steffenson 1995).

A bottom–up approach is clearly beginning to emerge as a cornerstone of regional policies for the information society. Such "local" frameworks for E.U. policy might be based on:

- Linking large firms into "regional systems of innovation" that encourage technology transfer, public–private sector collaboration in policy, and strategic ICT projects and networking among all local stakeholders in the information society, including employers, unions, educational, and training institutions. (Cooke and Morgan 1993; Braczyk, Cooke, and Heidenreich 1996)
- Similarly, large firms need to play a central role as mentors and catalysts of technological innovation in local networks of SMEs that may be suppliers of services and components, or targets of local economic development policy in which the large firms are contributing as community-conscious employers and investors. (Kanter 1995)
- Local strategies to promote the rural information society with large firms—individually and through industry associations—supporting the development of telecenters, training, ICT networks, and telematics services. (Millard 1995)
- Urban strategies for Europe's metropolitan centers, focusing on localizing information society policies for training, SMEs, infrastructure, and large firm partnership activity in the most problematic communities and areas.

CONCLUSION

Uncertainties over the capacity of large firms to act as the major creators of employment in the global information society is causing considerable political concern, particularly in light of doubts as to the true job-creation capacity of SMEs. This decline is partly attributed to the job impacts of ICTs in large firms, in which technological innovation and the trend toward so-called lean-and-mean organizations have been linked. In fact, both in theory and on the basis of empirical work, this link is not easy to identify and even more difficult to quantify. Computer networks are certainly being used to support strategies to shift production and information work outside the industrially advanced countries to low-cost countries. But policy makers have to rely on ad hoc evidence rather than systematic assessments of who wins and who loses from transborder data flows within and between MNCs. It must be concluded that more and better research is needed to support industrial and employment policies in the information society, particularly with the aim of building partnerships between large firms and regions.

There appear to be three areas of policy opportunity in the development of this partnership role. First, there is a growing recognition among large employers and economic and social policy makers that downsizing, and other aspects of corporate restructuring that involve massive job losses, have negative consequences for consumers and markets, staff morale, as well as the skills base and the economy and society more widely. Interest in business ethics, new options for corporate governance, the role of large firms in their communities, and in improving the environment has grown over the last few years. Clearly, this interest needs to be translated into the development of an active partnership role for large firms to play in the information society.

Second, there is a tremendous international governance challenge to manage the political issues and dilemmas for policy harmonization that result from the international geography of organizational change. The turbulent employment situation in the United States and the United Kingdom seems to be in transit to other parts of the developed world, where national systems of industrial relations and employment legislation are perceived to be less "flexible" on workers' rights and job protection. Will political and social pressures to bring down unemployment lead to fierce competition between cities, regions, and countries for new investment and new jobs? Or will reregulation and social protection come first? Clearly, international-level policy has a crucial intermediary role to play in minimizing the negative economic and social impacts of such potential territorial competition.

Third, access to ICT and information superhighways are necessary but not sufficient conditions for large firms and economies to improve growth, competitiveness, and employment. As the *Fifth Periodic Report on Competitiveness and Cohesion* (CEC 1994b) shows for Europe, less favored regions are catching up on the infrastructure side but are falling further behind on innovation or using the ICT infrastructure. "Learning" communities and organizations are needed to create and exploit the new knowledge bases required for successful exploitation of ICTs. As large firms innovate and develop technological capabilities, can the associated skills be shared with external training and educational providers through business–community partnership schemes? In the context of information society partnerships, large firms should be persuaded to share their knowledge and knowledge-creation processes with those groups outside the walls of the corporation—the unemployed, college students, SMEs, community and voluntary groups, and possibly the government sector.

The partnership role of large firms in the information society needs to be elaborated. What types of partnerships exist already? What is the nature and form of these partnerships? What factors facilitate successful partnerships? Which ones actually undermine them? Large firms do contribute to the development of the information society as employers, investors, and global competitors. These contributions are well documented and understandable. But so far our knowledge of the social economics of such partnerships is very limited.

4

Small Firms in Europe's Developing Information Society

Mark Hepworth and John Ryan

Instead of being competed out of existence in the era of advanced monopoly capitalism, small firms have moved to political center stage. Large firms can no longer be directly relied upon as new job creators, as they rationalize their workforces in the context of organizational and technological change. Policy attention has therefore increasingly focused on the role of small firms in job creation. All of the evidence on new job creation in industrialized countries clearly shows that the momentum of employment creation has shifted decisively toward microfirms (OECD 1995).

If present employment trends continue, job opportunities in Europe's future information society will depend on the economic and technological dynamism of small firms (less than 100 workers). This point is emphasized in the Bangemann Report (CEC 1994a) on the global information society and the Delor's Report (CEC 1993) on growth, competitiveness, and employment. These reports indicate that:

- for a *mass market* in information and communications technologies (ICTs) and telematics services to evolve in Europe, small firms, as 99 percent of Europe's 16 million businesses, need to adopt the new technologies and services, and

- for *mass job-creation* in Europe to become a reality, ICT and telematics innovations need to strengthen the small firm sector in terms of its growth, competitiveness, and employment.

Meanwhile, European SMEs (small and medium-sized enterprises with fewer than 500 employees) still lag behind in their use of telematics and even personal computers. The increasing economic importance of small firms draws attention to the potential social costs of the slow innovation of small firms, especially in the context of large firm–small firm network relationships.

THE ECONOMIC IMPORTANCE OF SMALL FIRMS

Methodological and data issues dominate research reports on employment and job creation in small firms (see, for example, OECD 1994; Storey 1994). First, most self-employment involves earning an income rather than enterprise growth. In Germany, home-based businesses are normally counted as waged employment (ENSR 1995). This type of "business" comprises 72 percent of the United Kingdom's 3.8 million enterprises; 62 percent of Spanish and Portuguese enterprises were "0-employee" businesses in 1986 (Bannock and Daly 1994). More than half of Europe's SME population would be wiped out if "0-employee" enterprises (self-employment) were deleted from the official figures, the greatest changes being in countries like Italy, Greece, and Portugal. In the United States, meanwhile, self-employment figures are rendered unreliable indicators of enterprise activity because many such jobs are part-time.

Second, many enterprises are included as legally independent firms in official national statistics, whereas they are really subsidiaries or franchise operations of large companies. This would include many thousands of retail and fast-food outlets and thousands of subsidiaries, all of which are de facto parts of large European, American, and other foreign multinational corporations. According to Sengenberger, Loveman, and Piore (1990), these types of enterprises should be excluded or at least clearly separable from national "business counts," since their economic and technological dynamism reflects their true status as extensions of large enterprises.

Third, there are fundamental differences between national data collection systems and institutional regulations concerning the formation and dissolution of enterprises. In Germany, for example, a *Meister* certificate is required by individuals wishing to start up a craft business; in the Netherlands, a permit is needed in 110 different enterprise activities. Regulations differ greatly and thus the quality of new start-up enterprises, as well as their potential job-creation role, also varies. The general implication is that measuring the scale and performance of the SME population is problematic (OECD 1994).

These technical issues notwithstanding, the role of small firms is extremely impressive. In 1992, SMEs (firms with fewer than 250 employees) made up 99 percent of Europe's 15.8 million (nonprimary) businesses, 66 percent of employment, and 65 percent of business turnover (CEC 1996a). In turn, 93 percent of all enterprises were microfirms employing less than ten people, and these accounted for 42 percent of E.U. jobs and around 33 percent of business turnover. By comparison, the 30,000 large firms (employing 500 or more) in Europe reveal their economic clout by accounting for about 33 percent of jobs and 33 percent of turnover. Nevertheless, the *collective* importance of small firms as generators of employment is indisputable in Europe and the United States (table 4.1).

The typical European SME employs six people, but there are wide regional variations. The average size of business ranges from three to thirteen employees across Europe. In southern European countries (such as Greece and Portugal), the average SME employs three to five people, compared with northern European averages of ten employees or more (the Netherlands and all of the EFTA-4 [European Free Trade Area] countries). As Van den Horst (1995, 3) emphasizes, these data on the limited scale of SME businesses point to the

Table 4.1   Employment by Firm Size

Sector	Percentage of employment in				Total employment (millions)
	Microfirms (0–9)	Small firms (10–99)	Medium firms (100–499)	Large firms (>500)	
Extraction	7	17	15	61	4.3
Manufacture	15	28	21	37	27.4
Construction	44	34	11	10	8.8
Wholesale	34	35	22	9	7.6
Retail trade	58	20	9	14	12.1
Transport & communications	19	6	9	56	7.1
Producer services	28	20	15	37	11.3
Personal services	49	23	13	15	15.8
E.U. (12) 1990	32	25	15	28	94.6
U.S. (1992)	25	22	12	40	101.1

Sources: Data adapted from ENSR 1994 and U.S. Census Bureau 1998.
Note: The figure for microbusiness in the USA is inflated because of the inclusion of the nearly three-quarters of U.S. businesses that have no payroll; an unknown number of these provide only part-time employment.

need for realistic expectations when developing policy measures: "It will be clear for instance that it is not very realistic to expect that the majority of European SMEs will be able to sell their products and services abroad, nor that high-tech products can be produced by the average European firm."

THE REALITIES OF ECONOMIC POWER

The issue of "myths versus realities" lies at the center of current debates on the economic and technological dynamism of SMEs. A balanced perspective is clearly needed. In the ICT industries, in which small firms are expected to stimulate innovation and competition (Club de Bruxelles 1995), markets tend to be *polarized* between a few dominant large multinational companies and large numbers of SMEs. For example, in European IT manufacturing, SMEs make up 99 percent of all enterprises but only 97 percent of the workforce. Similarly, two manufacturers account for 55 percent of the European telecommunications equipment market, although only 90 of the 4,390 enterprises in the sector employ more than 900 workers. Globalization in the software and systems integration markets is also leading to new patterns of market concentration, with small firms relying on niche strategies to compete and survive (EITO 1995).

The enormous presence of SMEs is a key feature of the ICT industries. Indeed, governments have actively attempted to promote innovation by SMEs through funding science parks, technology transfer, and regional innovation networks, and by involving technology-based SMEs in R&D. Such initiatives have met with mixed success in terms of SME business performance and new firm formation (Innovation and Employment 1992; Andreasen et al. 1995; Club de Bruxelles 1995).

A major criticism of high technology–oriented industrial policies is that they tend to be divisive socially and geographically, excluding the vast majority of less innovative small firms and less educated entrepreneurs (Massey et al. 1992). Most SMEs "slip through the net" of high-technology sector policies, as Michel Coomans of the European Commission comments on "SMEs and global electronic trading and commerce":

> It's not just about reaching the 1 per cent of SMEs involved in developing these technologies, nor even the 10 per cent who are already high-tech companies, but rather how the remaining 90 per cent can benefit from the telematics services, starting with basic services such as fax or e-mail, and eventually including more sophisticated technology. (Club de Bruxelles 1995, 45)

The need to look beyond SMEs in the ICT industries is strongly emphasized by Freeman and Soete (1994, 144), who argue that "only a minority of the new jobs needed would actually be in the ICT industries and services themselves, or indeed in ICT occupations in other industries and services."

About 75 percent of European SMEs are in the service sector (table 4.2). While the medium-sized *Mittelstand* engineering companies have traditionally been seen as Germany's major job generators, their leadership role in job creation has declined, overshadowed by the rise of the "micro" service business. In 1995, only 1 percent of newly founded German firms were defined as industrial. Most were in services, crafts, and trade ("Mittelstand Meets the Grim Reaper" 1995). The majority of European SMEs in the service sector tend to be family businesses with limited growth ambitions, low survival rates, and local consumer and business ties (Curran et al. 1994). Small shops in cities are threatened with extinction by the ICT-based distribution systems operated by large retail conglomerates (Hepworth and Ducatel 1992). Further, small intermediary firms in the distributive trades face the new competitive threat of relationship marketing and new business uses of the Internet and other media to create "virtual value chains" (Sheth and Parvatiyar 1995; Benjamin and

Table 4.2   Size and Sectoral Distribution of Enterprises

Sector	Percentage Share of All Enterprises[a]		Average Enterprise Size		Number of Enterprises (thousands)	
	EU15	*USA*	*EU15*	*USA*	*EU15*	*USA*
Extraction	1	1	29	4	158	164
Manufacturing	11	4	16	30	1,844	690
Construction	12	10	5	3	1,945	1,916
Wholesale trade	10	4	5	7	1,575	772
Retail trade	22	15	4	7	3,656	2,848
Transport & communications	6	4	8	8	946	778
Banking, insurance & finance	9	12	91	4	1,570	2,272
Business services	11	11	5	4	1,851	2,007
Hotels & catering	9	4	3	19	1,444	1,649
Other Services	16	37	4	4	2,596	6,829
All Sectors	100	100	6	6	16,348	18,363

Sources: Data derived from ENSR 1995, table 1.3, pp. 50–51 (1990 data) and U.S. Bureau of the Census 1997 (1992 data), table 1, pp. 7–8; includes nonpayroll enterprises (see table 4.1).
[a]May not add up to 100 because of rounding errors.

Wigand 1995). The distributive trades are not expected to generate new jobs in the "information age," due to vertical integration along the supply chain by retailers and producers, productivity gains due to logistical innovations, and competition from e-commerce services (CEC 1997), all trends related to the deployment of ICTs.

The large personal services sector covers a wide variety of microenterprises, such as hairdressers, garage repair shops, private nurseries, old people's homes, and other miscellaneous services. These services partly overlap the nontradable "informal sector" and the nonprofit "social economy" and could generate many job opportunities in semiskilled and unskilled occupations. As Freeman and Soete (1994) argue, in the new era of global competition and rising skill demands, personal services could be "pillars of a sheltered economy offering a wide variety of new employment opportunities, related to local needs and circumstances" (p. 167). But the real contribution of personal services to new business formation is difficult to assess, owing to the intervention of government enterprise start-up programs in E.U. countries. The overall policy aim of reducing unemployment tends to conflate SME business development objectives with job-creation objectives, with numerous microfirms created by subsidies for social rather than economic reasons (CEC 1994c; Storey 1994).

As a source for new enterprise development, especially among vulnerable groups, service industries are still expected to lead the way. The future is likely to be more uncertain due to unfavorable political trends and financial pressures on the public sector. Commenting on the U.S. situation, Ghaffari (1995) points to a reversal of trends and a future of more growth in a harsh climate:

> Most of the real growth during the past few (stagnant) years has come from the small business sector. Women enterprises, even more so than ethnic or racial minority business enterprises, have been the fastest growing sub-sector by most measures. Contributing factors include corporate downsizing, outsourcing and early retirement programs sending major numbers of experienced professionals into limbo. Other factors include major frustrations with the corporate glass ceilings, family-unfriendly policies, plus the sheer numbers represented by aging Baby Boomers moving toward their "mid life reassessment of values." Major growth is expected to continue for several years. Local and national public policies which in the past supported "affirmative action" and other equalizing contract practices are going away. Reasons include a white backlash against perceived "preferential treatment" of ethnic, racial and gender small business competitors. Even more important are the greater financial pressures on national, state and local budgets, which are forcing public-contract people to get the lowest possible bid. Today, there is much more cost-consciousness than social-consciousness in economic development strategies.

"SMALL IS BEAUTIFUL BUT BIG IS BETTER"

The economic importance of SMEs needs to be assessed in terms of the balance of power between large and small firms. According to some influential observers (see Naisbitt 1994; Piore and Sabel 1984), small firms are "drivers" of economic development in the post-Fordist era of flexible production and global market-based capitalism. Implicit here is the belief that the strategic influence of large firms is declining as multinational companies continue to replace hierarchical relationships with "alliance" relationships in expanding networks of interfirm cooperation. However, as Dunning (1995) emphasized, the evolution of SME networks (e.g., Japanese "keiretsu" networks) is driven and shaped by the dominant strategies of large industry leaders. Many small firms "are either spin-offs of large firms, or owe their prosperity to the fact that the latter are frequently their main clients and suppliers of critical assets" (p. 472). In Van der Horst's (1995) summary of national policies to promote SME subcontractors, the chief "targets" for procurement schemes in Greece, Portugal, Ireland, and the Netherlands are large multinational companies. Policies to develop local innovative capacity in some European less favored regions (LFRs) are aimed at building up SME supply chains for "new generation" branch plants, in the hope of levering multinationals' investments in knowledge-based production (Morgan 1995).

In his book *Lean and Mean,* Bennett Harrison (1994) also argues that the rise of decentralized "networked" production does not signify a new balance of economic power between large firms and small firms. He highlights the emergence of big firm–led, core-ring production networks in which small firms are no more than dependent suppliers and subcontractors operating at the margins of business survival. According to Harrison (p. 145):

> The emerging global economy remains dominated by concentrated, powerful business enterprises. Indeed the more the economy is globalized, the more it is accessible only to companies with a global reach. The spread of networking behavior signifies that the methods for managing that reach have changed dramatically, not that there has been a reemergence of localism, as others have argued.

Regional development provides a related context for looking at the economics of SME networks. According to Piore and Sable (1984), local networks of SMEs can function as globally competitive regional economies. Evidence on apparently dynamic local economies—including "industrial districts"—has been somewhat patchy. The most publicized examples of these dynamic regions include Emilia-Romagna in northern Italy, Baden-Württemberg in Germany, and the Silicon Valley in California (Pyke 1994; Saxenian 1991).

Clusters of related industries drive regional development in such "industrial district" models, for example, the specialization in watch making in the Swiss Jura (Coriat and Bianchi 1995). The creation of local interfirm cooperation networks in Denmark and Germany is a more general phenomenon. SME "clubs" and alliances engage in joint solving of technical problem or marketing to secure contracts (Karlsson, Johannisson, and Storey 1993; Andreasen et al. 1995). Indeed, local economic frameworks for SMEs exist in all regions of Europe, whether based on institutions like local chambers of commerce or agricultural cooperatives.

A REVIEW OF THE EVIDENCE ON THE USE OF ICTs

A major argument of the Bangemann Report is that Europe's successful transition to an information society depends on the growth of *mass markets* for ICTs and telematics services. As small firms make up 90 percent of all European businesses, their adoption of the new technologies and services is critical to the evolution of mass markets. Intense global competition means that these Pan-European mass markets need to develop rapidly.

Key Factors: Size and Sector

Although the use of PCs now seems to be very widespread in small firms, the majority of Europe's small firms still do not use telematics services. Within these generic statistics size and sector are the main factors that influence the adoption and use of ICTs and telematics services in small firms. Investigations into the usage and uptake of ICTs by SMEs across twelve European countries found that in 1997 only 16 percent of microbusinesses had Internet access, as opposed to 41 percent of firms with fifty to ninety-nine employees. Likewise, although as many as 80 percent of microbusinesses now have computers, penetration rates among the larger SMEs were 97 percent (data cited in Spectrum Strategy Consultants/DTI 1998).

Market penetration rates for small firms highlight the influence of national economic contexts. PC and modem adoption rates across the richer parts of Europe, the United States, and Japan are now roughly equivalent, running from 70 percent to 90 percent and higher. However, in the United States and Japan small firms still have a substantial lead over Europe in terms of Internet access and e-mail use (table 4.3). In addition, less recent data from 1994, but covering a wider range of European countries, indicated a considerable lag within

Table 4.3 Use of Information and Communication Technologies in Small Firms for Selected E.U. Countries, 1998 (small firms with IT equipment by country, %)

Type of Equipment	France	Germany	Japan	U.K.	U.S.
Computers	99	97	100	89	95
PC with modem	65	75	73	70	78
Internet access	17	35	65	37	52
External e-mail	26	30	53	45	51
Internal e-mail	19	27	53	24	37
EDI	13	28	25	15	16
Videoconference	2	1	6	4	7

Source: Spectrum Strategy Consultants/DTI 1998.

Europe (EITO 1995). At that time, modem penetration in U.S. small offices had reached 32 percent as opposed to 9 percent for Italian homes and 20 percent in West Germany (EITO 1995).

Adoption rates for ICTs have also been shown to vary considerably among sectors (Fundesco 1994; CBS 1995). A survey of small firms in London found that 0–3 percent of mechanical engineering firms used e-mail, EDI, or external databases, versus 18–33 percent of electronics engineering firms (table 4.3). In professional business services, e-mail was used by 23–31 percent of firms. Electronic data interchange and on-line databases were more widely used by ICT and engineering consultancies (Hepworth 1994b). Results of the European Network for SME Research Survey for 1996 corroborated this finding, indicating that industrial firms tended to lag behind trade and services in terms of adoption of data communications. Respectively, 40 percent versus 53 percent and 63 percent used at least one: e-mail, electronic payments, or electronic ordering (ENSR 1996).

The same survey showed that ownership structure and the extent of international cooperation also seem to play a role. Subsidiaries are ahead of independents; 69 percent versus 49 percent were adopters. Internationally orientated firms are ahead of those with a national orientation 60 percent versus 44 percent (ENSR 1996). Overall such results indicate the need for ICT innovation policy to be sensitive to specific conditions at the industrial and even subindustrial level.

Similarly, peripheral or core location also affects the take-up of ICTs. Except where telematics programs have boosted adoption, a survey of over 2,000 firms in seven rural regions across Greece, Germany, and Spain found generally limited use of any form of telematic service (Ilbery et al. 1995). By contrast,

Table 4.4   Telematics Use in Small Manufacturing and Producer Service Firms in London, 1993 (percentage of sample using application)

Sector	E-mail	Public Database	Electronic Data Interchange	Public Data Networks
Mechanical engineering	3	3	5	5
Electrical & electronic engineering	33	14	46	36
Advertising & accounting	31	15	19	15
Computer & engineering services	23	15	46	36

Source: Hepworth 1994b.

in London by 1993 already 92 percent of small firms in manufacturing and business services were using public data networks and 63 percent of firms were aware of their availability (Hepworth 1994b).

As noted above, the inherent difficulties of studying small firms leads to fragmented and often ad hoc knowledge about small-firm ICT adoption. We can do no more than draw rough indications of the state of play of such survey results. This problem is of course vastly exacerbated by the takeoff of the Internet and the transition of many business-to-business transactions from proprietary electronic data interchange systems to Internet commerce (OECD 1999). Trends in the use of public-data networks by small firms seem finally to have followed the common S-curve pattern of innovation diffusion—acceleration from a slow start and a spread to the rest of the economy from lead sectors. These developments lend credence to the idea that the Internet is a growth platform for SMEs (see Industry Canada 1995; CEC 1994d). The CEC-funded EBNET project argued that the most plausible explanation for the Internet's explosive growth is its increasing use by SMEs worldwide. Anecdotal evidence points in the same direction. For example, membership of the SME-dominated New York New Media Association grew to nearly 2,200 firms in its first 18 months of operation, with about 1,500 businesses being Internet-based software and content producers (*Financial Times,* 18 March 1996, p. 9).

Barriers to Adoption

Although ICTs may be considered essential to their business operations, small firms tend to rank the new technologies below other "critical success factors" in explaining their performance. For example, in the Europe's 500 project, it was found that dynamic entrepreneurs tend to view "soft competences"—marketing and human resources—as more critical to business performance than "hard competences"—production and technology (EFER 1995). These findings confirm the role of ICTs in enabling business tools and infrastructure and show that adoption behavior needs to be understood in the wider context of small firm development.

This broad approach is illustrated by Fundesco's (1994) highly informative research on the impact of ICTs on small firms located throughout Spain. Based upon large-scale surveys, the project report identified a range of factors that influence SME innovation behavior:

- Available technological options do not match up to SME needs in terms of costs and functionality.
- Cultural barriers, especially in family businesses, prevent SMEs from introducing the changes to operating strategies and organization needed for ICT innovations.
- Where large customers (e.g., electronic data interchange in the case of international food distributors and tourism companies) impose ICT, technology investments and business problems diverge.
- Most SMEs lack the technical personnel to develop, implement, and maintain ICT applications—for example, computer-aided design in clothing and footwear.
- Wider economic and market conditions have led SMEs to reduce total capital investment, thus restricting the scope and scale of new ICT investments.
- SMEs are not well informed on the technological options available, how to gain access to them, how to use them, and what the benefits of using them are.
- The lack of a well-informed, strategic approach to ICT leads SMEs to specify modest technological demands that may only increase short-term profitability.
- The adoption of different ICTs is strongly related to SME size, the extent of its market, its presence in international markets, and current growth trends.
- Most telecommunication services are viewed positively, but fixed and mobile telephone services are considered too expensive.
- Videotext services are seen as too slow and not relevant to concrete and immediate business needs (e.g., market and industry data).

The major contribution of the Fundesco study, covering a range of regions and sectors in the Spanish economy, is its comprehensive assessment of the complex influences on ICT adoption and diffusion in SMEs. These influences operate at the macrolevel (global and national economy), the mesolevel (region and industry), and the microlevel (the individual enterprise). The study report placed a special emphasis on structural barriers to innovation and technological change in the sectoral and regional milieus of SMEs (Camagni 1991).

Small firms adopt ICTs according to their view of how the new technologies will change "bottom line" profitability and its contribution to specific problems—for example, meeting short delivery times, searching for new customers and suppliers, or improving product quality. Innovation in SMEs tends to be problem-orientated rather than a part of a formal strategy, as in large firms and government.

Most research emphasizes the skill and training barriers to ICT adoption and innovation in SMEs. The Bangemann Report envisaged telematics' strengthening technology transfer links between SMEs and sources of technology, such as universities, R&D centers, equipment suppliers, and consultants. Increasing adoption levels through this type of networking activity will be constrained by well-known barriers that prevent or retard innovation in SMEs. As noted by Bessant (1995, 253):

> SMEs often lack the capacity for such technology transfer because of a lack of resources and capability. Typically they have little spare manpower for the necessary search and scanning activities for identifying emerging technological trends, they lack internal experience in project management and implementation and have little capacity for absorbing costly failures. Resource limitations extend from financial and technological constraints to what may often be a serious gap in managerial capability in areas like firm strategy and project management.

A key issue raised by Bessant's comments relates to the management of change and ICT innovations in SMEs. SME strategies for organizational and technological innovations are rarely discussed in the management literature, except in the context of large company trends. Models of ICT implementation and advice, therefore, surround large firms. Few small firms have these choices or, in any case, the resources to implement them. For example, Antonelli and Marchionatti's (1996, 18) research on the Italian cotton industry concluded that

> the effective adoption of complex technologies such as new information technology (NIT) requires an organization different from the existing one: firms need to be larger, more vertically integrated and run by professional managers. . . . Successful diffusion of NIT in the Italian cotton industry risks being delayed by its traditional structure, characterized by the small size of firms and the centralized and functional organization of family-owned companies.

If effective use of ICTs and telematics in small firms is to develop, models of learning and innovation need to evolve in parallel that match directly with the idiosyncratic needs of small firms (Andreasen et al. 1995). Emerging patterns of large firm–small firm relations are crucial to the formation of these "innovation milieus" (Camagni 1991). In a local economic development context, there is considerable potential for "mentoring" of small firms by large companies, involving know-how and technology transfer between the partners. A major success story that has been replicated in other E.U. countries is the Belgian "Prato" scheme. Eight years following its setup in 1988, four hundred companies had been involved with large firm "mentors"—collectively generating 1,400 jobs and an average increased sales of 15 percent a year (*Financial Times,* 6 February 1996, p. 10).

In a market context, the innovative capacity-building potential of large firm–small firm relationships appears to be more limited, given trends toward "virtual integration." In the consumer goods sector, powerful large retailers that control the entire supply chain (e.g., Benetton in woolens/clothing and IKEA in furniture/interiors) have driven the adoption of electronic data interchange by small manufacturers. A major trend in supply-chain management is for large firms to rationalize their supplier and customer networks (Axelsson and Easton 1992). For example, Xerox reduced its suppliers from 5,000 to 300 in the process of both selection and development of the remaining firms' innovative capacity. Trends in the automotive industry are equally dramatic. A two-tier system of SME networks has emerged, with first-tier suppliers working closely as partners with large firms and second-tier subcontractors supplying parts to the subassemblers. Large manufacturers often force small suppliers to adopt electronic data interchange, leading to "dependent" innovation (see the chapter by Bosch and colleagues in this volume). A similar two-tier system is emerging in distribution as large firms such as Philips are reducing and consolidating their base of direct customers. An elite set of customers is selected for business development and innovation while smaller and less significant customers are forced to buy through distributors.

The general implication of trends in ICT-based "virtual integration" is that an "industrial divide" is opening up *within* the small business sector, creating not two but three "tracks" in the information society. There are core-periphery relations between SMEs in different sectors, with SMEs lagging behind large companies as dependent suppliers and customers. A different scenario, requiring changes in economic and business culture and public intervention, is to understand large firm–small firm networking in the context of local economic milieus (Harrison 1994; Porter 1990). New approaches to regional development are leading policy makers in this direction. Learning by interacting, regional innovation milieus and policy integration are the cornerstones of new SME policy thinking for the information society (Malmberg 1996; Maskell and Malmberg 1995).

WORK AND EMPLOYMENT

As emphasized in the Delor's Report (CEC 1993), the European Union faces a jobs crisis and the threat of rising structural unemployment. Having created 80 percent of new European jobs in the 1980s, small firms are understandably perceived by policy makers as key actors in the labor market. The *OECD Jobs Study* (1995, 32) concluded:

> The full benefit of science and technology cannot, however, be realized without complementary changes in the organization of work and production. Such changes appear to shift the balance of advantages toward smaller operating units. This has reinforced interest in the role of new, mainly small and medium-sized enterprises in employment creation. Policy can foster an environment supportive of the success of such firms by *inter alia* encouraging regulatory reform; greater entrepreneurship; open markets; and the diffusion of technology and innovation throughout the economy.

But identifying and quantifying the links between employment change and ICT innovations is difficult. As the *OECD Jobs Study* (1995, 32) concluded, "More extensive assessment of the linkages between technology and jobs is needed to inform policy choices."

Services and the Incredible Shrinking Economy

The reemergence of SMEs over the last twenty-five years is an integral part of industrial development in the information economy, marked by a fundamental employment shift from manufacturing to services (Beniger 1986; Hepworth 1989). Baumol (1989) found that between 1960 and 1980 the growing share of "information occupations" in the U.S. workforce was mainly due to two productivity-related effects: the substitution of white-collar workers for blue-collar workers within production sectors and interindustry shifts of labor from manufacturing into office-based services. In line with Jonscher (1983), Baumol concluded that ICT innovations had their biggest impacts on the manufacturing workforce, with widespread rationalization and overall decline in job numbers. There were, at that time, no signs of the information society. "The rising share of the labor force in information-related occupations is the result of two distinct forces, both of which may be considered the ingredients of unbalanced growth, *leaving relatively little to be attributed to an autonomous explosion in demand for information"* (Baumol 1989, 158).

These employment trends in favor of white-collar work and service industries continued throughout the 1980s in all industrialized countries (OECD 1994). A major factor in these employment changes was the "big bang" in world capital markets, made possible by the use of ICTs in financial services. The "boom" period of the 1980s encouraged large numbers of professional people to set up their own businesses, encouraged by emerging trends toward outsourcing services by large companies. Self-employment in Europe rose during the 1980s led by financial and business services and linked to the property development boom, where self-employment is predominant. About one-third of the 1980s increase in self-employment (70 percent of the United Kingdom's enterprises) in the United Kingdom was concentrated in construction. The "epicenter" of the "IT revolution" was in financial services (ENSR 1995). The boom conditions of the 1980s also led to favorable market conditions in retailing and consumer services, areas populated by large numbers of microfirms.

By 1990, there were 16.4 million SMEs in Europe, and only 11 percent of these businesses were manufacturing firms. Factory automation and outsourcing have "shrunk" the manufacturing enterprise over time. The average European manufacturer now employs sixteen people. Only three out of sixteen production industries in Europe have an average workforce of more than fifty (motor vehicles, office machinery, and chemicals). Employment prospects in this post-Fordist industrial economy are not good. Europe's major corporations are now using global computer networks to coordinate more decentralized production systems, shifting plants to low-cost locations around the world and leaving behind regional networks of SME subcontractors. Advances in logistics and supply-chain management permit large multinational companies to take advantage of global sourcing and two-tier subcontracting networks, exposing Europe's SMEs to worldwide competition. Long-range employment forecasts point to a continuing decline in the manufacturing workforce across most sectors. On the whole, small manufacturers are unlikely to compensate for this decline, even though "industrial districts" and science parks may evolve as local economic platforms for global companies and their SME "satellites" (Dunning 1995; Harrison 1994; Amin and Thrift 1994; Porter 1990).

The great majority of workers in the information society will be in service industries as ICTs reinforce the job shift out of manufacturing. In Europe and the United States, employment growth is predicted in producer services, such as business, computer, and financial services, and consumer services, covering leisure and tourism, personal care, and environmental protection (e.g., BLS 1997; DRI Europe 1997). Notably, the job-generating power of the distributive trades (14 percent of Europe's labor force) is expected to weaken. Small shops cannot compete with ICT-based supermarkets, "teleshopping," and out-of-town superstore developments. In distribution, like other sectors, small firms can only compete by finding profitable niche markets. New technologies and services become valuable as process innovations only after small firms have developed new knowledge, market intelligence, and contact networks through personal, face-to-face meetings with customers and distributors (MacPherson 1995; Cornish 1995).

As noted earlier, small firms in the ICT and electronic information service sectors are concentrated in niche markets. Outsourcing trends in the large corporate sector and the public sector have generated market opportunities for SMEs, but competition is fierce and global computer networks allow multinational companies to draw specialist and standardized skills from firms and locations all around the world (Gillespie et al. 1995c). SMEs face competition from not only foreign firms but also from SMEs and specialist information businesses (e.g., call centers and telemarketing companies) located in LFRs, second cities, and rural areas (Phillips 1995; Richardson 1994). The net impacts of such ICT-based competition in tradable information services have not been systematically assessed. Is Europe a net loser or winner? Which cities and regions are net job importers of "wired work"? Probably European SMEs will compete with one another for a smaller piece of the jobs cake, implying that global competition will lead to fewer firms and fewer jobs, as well as some decentralization to lower-cost regions and cities within the European Union, but not necessarily to designated LFRs and remote rural areas. Telecottages have proliferated across Europe on the back of public sector funding, not market demand. It is premature to appraise their contribution to local business development and sustainable job creation, but few telecottages could survive without public subsidies (Denbigh 1994). More fundamentally, what are the net effects on small business development of displacing opportunities from the city to the country? Intuitively, the net effects would be zero, but research on teleworking has not looked at the job impacts from this perspective.

Large numbers of microfirms are based at home, but only a minority are teleworkers, or users of business data communications. According to EITO (1998), of the nearly 4 million estimated teleworkers in Europe, there are perhaps about 500,000 self-employed teleworkers in Europe (plus about 1.4 million working in local telecenters). If this estimate were reliable, self-employment would add up to only about 3 percent of the European Union's 16 million enterprises. But home-based telebusinesses should grow as microfirms increase their share of total employment and larger employers continue to outsource office services. A significant proportion of Europe's "0-employee" enterprises fall in the "portfolios" of part-time work available as an alternative to unemployment or working in big organizations (Wedderburn 1995).

Government policy and social changes will heavily influence the impacts of ICTs in growth-oriented consumer services. For example, environmental telematics could generate new SMEs in Europe's environmental goods and service industries (1–2 percent of total employment), if supported by appropriate legislation and wider changes in business and consumer attitudes (Innovation and Employment 1995). Another dynamic socioeconomic trend in Europe and the United States is the growth of women entrepreneurship:

> Up to 20 years ago women entrepreneurs were exceptional. They are now an important phenomenon, both socially and economically. According to national estimates, in 1992, women created 33 percent of new firms in North America (75 percent of new United States firms in 1993) and 40 percent in the new German *länder*. Women account for a substantial portion of non-agricultural self-employment: from 17 percent in Greece, to 22-25 percent in Germany, Italy and the United Kingdom to 34-39 percent in Japan, Canada and the United States. In Spain, 16 percent of entrepreneurs are women, as against 1984 when they comprised only 9.7 percent. (Innovation and Employment 1995, 3)

Clearly, the growth of women entrepreneurship raises the issue of gender inequalities in ICT skills training and telematics use. They will benefit indirectly from government decisions to invest and promote telematics in the female labor–intensive sectors of personal care, environment, and other human services. New business development and job creation arising from these innovations will depend on how SMEs are integrated into private-public partnerships and government programs. The Bangemann Report (CEC 1994a) argues that small firms have to be "partnered" into economic development plans for the local information society. Although small firms are increasingly involved in the CEC telematics programs, as producers and (trial) consumers, it is not clear to what degree small business development has been helped by over a decade of investment and effort. Instead of counting up the number of small firm participants (in R&D, demonstrations, trials, information and awareness exercises, etc.), the European Commission and its partners should calculate new firms and new jobs created as a *result* of their investments.

The 1990s recession was a watershed for small firms. Characteristically, they grow and multiply at great rates during economic booms, but contract and disappear at the same rates in recessions (OECD 1994). For most of Europe's SMEs, the impacts of telematics and ICTs do *not* derive from their own use or assessments of technology. Most small firms are innovating as a side effect of global market competition among big firms. The resulting impacts on employment and work are hard to judge because researchers spend less time on SME deaths. The marginal impact of these deaths on local or national labor markets render them too small to be noticed (Storey 1994).

The Political Economy of Small Firms

Public policies to improve SME growth, competitiveness, and employment are evolving rapidly in Europe, the United States, and other regions of the world. Some key issues surround these policies. The first set of issues relates to the true capacity of small firms to create jobs. According to Storey (1994) and Hall (1995), less than 5 percent of new firms actually develop into sustainable job creators, most simply failing or never growing. The policy issue is whether SME support should be targeted at a small group of winners, as opposed to a shotgun approach that does not discriminate between new start-ups and potential entrepreneurs. The obvious problem is that picking winners is no more than a lottery (especially if done by the public sector). And, far more importantly, the losers will be many millions of aspiring entrepreneurs from society's more vulnerable groups—the unemployed, ethnic minorities, and women. These groups will be left out of the information society if their skills and entrepreneurial capacities are not improved through enterprise-support policies including ICT skills training schemes. In addition to social reasons, the rationale for maintaining a nonexclusive approach to business support is that increasing rates of new firm formation are needed to replace job losses in existing firms (OECD 1994). In the inner cities, rebuilding the economic base and communities is impossible without enterprise policies (Innovation and Employment 1993).

The second set of issues relates to the quality of jobs in small firms. Research shows that, compared to large private and public sector employers, small firms pay lower wages and offer fewer nonwage benefits (pensions, health, sick, and maternity leave, etc.). There is also less job security and less worker training, and workplaces tend to be inferior. Indeed, the present trend toward smaller firms and more service employment should be looked at with some concern. Wages councils may protect the rights of big-firm workers, but union representation is weak in small firms. In 1993, only 12 percent of British workers in firms with fewer than twenty-five employees (85 percent of all British enterprises) were represented by trade unions, compared with 49 percent for firms with more than twenty-five employees and 72 percent for small workplaces in the public sector. Small firm workforces in service industries, such as hotels, catering, and distribution, tend to be worse off and less protected by unions. In the distributive trades (employing every one out of seven European workers), workers are poorly paid and suffer from job insecurity; union density ranges from 2 percent in some parts of the French industry to 15–20 percent in the United Kingdom and Italy.

The key point is that "small is not necessarily beautiful." In fact, policies and resources that encourage small firms as employers may result in a poorer, less-skilled, and more insecure European workforce. This scenario is the big black cloud hanging over Europe's transition to a twenty-first century information society.

SMALL FIRMS AND THE INFORMATION SOCIETY

As shown earlier, the size of the business is a key factor influencing ICT adoption rates in small firms. This size influence is reinforced in the case of low-value, labor-intensive service industries. The 1990s job-creation trend in favor of microfirms and services may, therefore, lead to slower rates of market development and innovation. Most European SMEs do not believe that information is a source of market competitiveness. Very few are prepared to pay for information in the form of specialized business services, and only a small minority appear to be interested in electronic information services (ENSR 1995; IMO 1995). It follows that public intervention to build an information society is essential if small firms are really going to form mass markets for ICTs and telematics services and generate new jobs by innovating and exploiting information as a source of competitive advantage.

Current thinking on the nature of public intervention favors a decentralized policy on SMEs. This is consistent with E.U. policy toward not only SMEs but also the local information society in urban, rural, and LFR contexts (CEC 1995a). Local policy frameworks for encouraging "growth by innovation" and "innovation by growth" are highlighted in the OECD's (1994, 103–104) report on job trends in firms:

> In analysing the policy experience of the last two decades, one major message does emerge. This is the need, in many OECD countries, to create a network of local strategic resources—business services, access to universities and centers of technological expertise and good physical infrastructure—to increase the chances of new firms surviving and prospering. Corporate networking and encouraging

close interaction between large and small firms do seem to facilitate access. . . . Institutions promoting a network of partners among local, national, public and private actors, including small and large firms can help to raise the quality of small firms and their workers, perhaps leading to some reduction in the flows from jobs to unemployment.

A local approach to building the information society could help resolve key policy issues raised by small firms as innovators, wealth creators, and job generators. First, a local economy focus keeps the door open for all small firms and all aspiring entrepreneurs to enter a future information society. Second, it offers more flexibility in building a wide variety of interfirm cooperation networks, including large firms. These networking models, so prominent in Denmark, Germany, and Italy, take different forms but generally allow small firms to "borrow size," or obtain external economies of scale through cooperation and collaboration. Joint ventures, collective bids for government contracts, closed user-group training schemes, sharing of R&D and market intelligence, and so on, are examples of practical network activities (Andreasen et al. 1995; Pyke 1994).

If they do become significant drivers of economic growth and development, these local networks of interfirm cooperation would certainly generate market demand for ICTs and telematics services among SMEs (for Swedish and Finnish initiatives, see NUTEK 1995; TEKES 1995). Have the hundreds of networks created in Denmark and Germany generated higher rates of ICT and telematics use among the small firms involved? If the answer to this question is yes, then local innovation systems based on technology and institutional cooperation are essential to European information society policies aimed at creating a strong, dynamic base of small firms.

THE POLICY CHALLENGE

Our analysis leads us to highlight two basic dimensions of SME-centered information society policies. First, a coordinated approach is needed in which a wide range of policy initiatives pursued by different parts of the policy machinery have a direct or indirect influence on the role of SMEs in the information society. Second, to implement this integrated approach, a local framework at the urban or regional scale is needed to complement overall policy initiatives.

European Union policy toward SMEs reflects the highly fragmented nature of research and policy that adopts the information society as an explicit focus. What exactly is the information society envisaged in the Bangemann Report?

Opinions differ from one sector to the next (IBM versus the garage repair shop), from one discipline to the next (electronics to geography), from one policy area to the next (technology to social services) and from one region to the next (Silicon Valley to rural Greece). In fact, if experts differ on what the information society is, why should small business managers have a good idea? Let's say a small business owner wants to obtain a loan to invest in ICTs or telematics services. What matters more to the bank manager: Whether the owner has a successful business with no PC or whether he or she has an ICT-intensive but problem-ridden business? The basic point is that mainstream SME policy tends to keep in step with small business trends rather than attempt to get in front of small business demands and needs (the logic of technology) and push information society policies. There is actually very little futurism or information society debate in the small firm research area (Storey 1994).

In terms of the SME component of overall "information society" initiatives, it is important to note that strengthening the small business sector depends on a large matrix of program areas and policy actors cutting across different areas of policy such as education and training, research and development, and regional development. To make these different instruments operate in concert requires appropriate performance targets and some idea of how these targets translate into real progress in small business development. Given the plethora of initiatives in the past, should we not already be in a better position to find out what have been achievements so far in terms of new firm formation and job creation?

Promoting the economic performance of SMEs—including their capacity and propensity to innovate—needs to include a strong local dimension to policy development and implementation. The case for this local dimension is supported by the following characteristics of the small business sector:

- Small businesses and microbusinesses in the service industries—that is, the majority of European SMEs—are still tied to local urban-regional consumer and labor markets.
- In manufacturing, there is evidence of success with extensive networks of technology transfer centers organized regionally but decentralized as close to the business user as possible.
- The last decade of SME policies has built up local institutional capacity and public-private investments in partnerships between local firms, development and training agencies, local authorities and other actors.
- For start-up enterprises, where training and other support is needed in the birth and first year of the business, there needs to be close and intensive interaction between SME support agencies and the fledgling firm.

- In the case of large firm–small firm relations, there is evidence to support the argument that local innovation systems for technology or know-how transfer are favored by a joint interest in local economic competitiveness.

There is a need to develop a coordinated approach that links with local economic strategies—pursued at the regional or urban scale—being pursued to improve competitiveness through partnership. In this context, ICT-centered information society policies tend to be one component of local economic strategies that extend to transportation and land use planning, the environment, education and training, inward investment and marketing, tourism and culture, and a variety of business-related initiatives that are not necessarily ICT related. Reflecting this policy spectrum, the private and public partners involved in these local strategies will have different levels of interest in the information society, depending on their market and policy backgrounds. Finally, because these strategies reflect local economic and social contexts, they will differ from region to region and between urban and rural areas.

The prospects for localizing information society policies are favored by growing political support for the notion of a "Europe of regions." As partners in local economic (competitiveness) strategies, central policy should be to support, develop and monitor the impacts of locally orientated SME policies, by

- setting realistic ICT adoption targets for SMEs by size and sector based on wider assessments of the local economy's competitiveness in the information society; size, sector, and location should be jointly considered in target setting in order to contextualize E.U. policies and make them more meaningful to local SME networks and policy makers;
- monitoring and publicizing the targets through the appropriate lead agency on local information society policies—this one-stop responsibility for policies is both desirable and valuable;
- assuming the first two measures are in place, innovation, intensity, and market growth could be monitored for SMEs, and local economies and partnerships (rather than individual SMEs) could be rewarded for their competitive performance based on information society policy success criteria.
- At an early stage, telematics policies and projects need to be linked into local financial, investment, and marketing strategies if they are to develop beyond the R&D stage and make a real economic and social impact. This requires forming partnerships with a range of local private and public sector stakeholders, including large companies and governments operating on a local basis (e.g., British Telecom's new marketing strategy for SMEs is based on regional innovation sales teams).

These four types of measures—local targets, local one-stop agencies, local competitiveness, and local investments—are suggestions for innovations in policy infrastructure. They are intended to provide a basis for localizing information society policies based on the argument that successful coordination requires institutional compatibility and that, for SMEs, these public-private partnerships need a strong local dimension.

CONCLUSION

Policy makers in the European Union, the United States, and other regions of the world are looking at small firms in a completely new light. They are expected to drive future economic development alongside large multinational corporations. Since the European Union's future is defined in terms of an information society, it is incumbent on policy makers and researchers to promote the role of SMEs in the economic development context of the twenty-first century. How can SMEs contribute toward the challenge of creating new sources of wealth and jobs across the European Union? What support is needed at European, national, and local levels?

Major improvements in the quality of relevant data—supported by empirical and theoretical research—are needed if policy makers are to be properly informed about trends, issues, and options. Areas of SME research and policy, telematics, and the information society are new topics of interest, obviously reflecting the current state of innovation in small firms themselves. The available evidence suggests that the diffusion of telematics innovations in small firms is following the normal S-curve: slow rates of adoption and uneven growth by leading versus lagging sectors against a rising level of general awareness. However, if effective adoption of ICTs is to evolve in the European Union, the innovation performance of SMEs will have to improve enormously and rapidly, given that global economic competition is increasing.

Current thinking in formulating information society policies for SMEs calls for the *decentralization* and *integration* of support measures and service delivery to make them cost-effective and sustainable. A decentralized approach would involve framing policies in terms of sectors and regions and local subregions, thus allowing an interactive, user-driven model of SME innovation and policy development. Complementing this would be an integrated approach to SME needs and requirements that includes a package of measures covering finance, marketing, training, and other business functions, with technology and innovation being part of this overall package. Clearly, integration means partnerships between different service providers—not only public sector organizations (including higher educational and research institutes) but also private companies, especially large firms and networks of SMEs.

The basic conclusion is that information society policies for SMEs need to be decentralized and integrated if they are to reach out to and matter to 16 million enterprises of ten or fewer workers. This policy approach is, of course, much easier to recommend than it is to implement. It involves major institutional changes to make the idea of effective interdepartmental, central–local collaboration a reality. Public–private sector partnerships too are easier to espouse than create as sustainable economic institutions. Going local may be the only way of building the necessary institutions required for Europe's transition to an information society.

Localizing E.U. policies should be based on an understanding of the institutional networks partnerships and strategies for territorial economic development that exist in the many different regions and localities that make up Europe. These networks, partnerships, and strategies vary geographically in terms of their economic power and political influence. As such E.U. information society policies need to be flexible and localized while maintaining an overall consistency and coherence. For the great majority of SMEs, as the statistics on the size and sector characteristics show, the localization of policies is essential if they are to be genuinely involved in driving the information society from a bottom-up rather than a top-down direction. This reversal of policy direction, building on the growth of local competitiveness strategies and local partnerships throughout Europe, is needed if the SME sector is to effectively be relaunched as an engine of growth in Europe's developing information society.

Part II

Work and the European Information Society

5

New Organizational Forms in the Information Society

Gerhard Bosch, Juliet Webster, and Hans-Jürgen Weißbach

THE FLEXIBLE FIRM

According to the E.U. white paper on growth, competitiveness, and employment, internal flexibility in firms requires "staff versatility, the integrated organization of work, flexible working hours and performance-related pay. Tailored to the European company model, it should be central to negotiations within the company" (CEC 1993, 17). Internal flexibility in firms cannot be increased simply through isolated modifications to work organization on the shop floor or to wage systems. They are embedded in the broader structures of the firm, and only changes that are consistent with the overall context make sense. In past decades, many experiments with the introduction of semi-autonomous groups failed because the technological and organizational environment remained unchanged. Moreover, many European firms have been unable to significantly improve their competitive position, despite considerable investment in the hardware of new technologies, because they were unable to exploit the potential of those technologies to the full because of inadequate work organization and skill shortages. By ensuring better collaboration between men and machines, Japanese companies have succeeded in achieving considerably higher productivity with the same technology. As a result, the technology fixation of many Europeans has been called into question and their attention directed much more forcibly to the renewal of organizational structures within the firm. This requires a more holistic approach to company structures.

Equally, Europe's competitiveness problems are not caused by insufficient expenditure on research and technological development, including information technologies. "If we bear in mind that European expenditures on R&D in this sector are significantly larger than those of Japan ($15bn as opposed to $12bn), it is clear that we have identified the core of a paradox that requires fuller explanation" (Andreasen et al. 1995, 17). Obviously there are problems in Europe with putting scientific discoveries and technological innovations into practice. These problems are related to (1) the highly fragmented structures characteristic of European companies, (2) the inadequate links not only between science and industry but also (3) between production and development departments within companies. We shall confine our comments here to this last aspect, which relates directly to company structures. Research, development, and production have to date been organized sequentially within firms. Communication between departments has been poor and specialists in R&D departments have had little interest in the problems of production departments. Communications between development and marketing departments have also been poor, and consequently consumer preferences have not always received sufficient attention in the innovation process. Simultaneous engineering has enabled the Japanese to organize this in an iterative way, with permanent exchanges of information between actors (Womack, Jones, and Roos 1990). As a result, they have been able to shorten innovation cycles and reduce production problems during the start-up period for new products. This requires completely new internal organizational structures (Aoki 1988). Provision must be made for a constant exchange of information along the innovation chain. A flow of personnel among departments is also necessary. Finally, project managers must manage the interfaces between manufacturing and research. Many European firms have now begun to restructure their innovation processes, although they have not yet caught up with the Japanese innovations in company structures. Organizational competences are now seen as the determining factors for the future competitive strength of European enterprises. Exaggerating somewhat for the purposes of simplification, the traditional model of European and North American firms can be summed up in the key terms *complex organization* and *simple jobs*. Flexibility is accomplished by designing a complex work organization including simple jobs with short learning times in which workers can be replaced easily. The complexity of the organization is grounded in the radical split between "thinking" and "doing." The organizational memory is based on formal procedures, strong hierarchies, and a professional elite at the top of the firm. This type of organization is well suited to mass production in a stable environment. However, if products become more diverse and markets more turbulent, if quality requirements increase and the pace of technological change quickens, such organizations lack flexibility. What is required is a *simplified organization with more complex jobs*. Flexibility can be achieved by the re-integration of tasks and the introduction of teamwork. As a result, a considerable proportion of a firm's coordination and communication problems can be resolved at lower levels of the organization, with a corresponding reduction in organizational complexity. In order to achieve such a modern *flexible firm*, decentralization at all levels of the organization is required. Top-down control in corporate organization has to be replaced by a continuous dialogue with business units.

The flexible firm means a radical change for companies; it is intended in the short term to safeguard the existing core business and offers in the longer term a new perspective on job creation (Lehner 1993). The organizational principles underlying the flexible firm are not restricted to large manufacturing plants. They are also emerging in large and small public and private service organizations, as well as in small and medium-sized industrial firms. Of course there is no one generally applicable patent remedy for all types of firm. Any attempt at reorganization has to be tailored to suit the particular firm in question. Examples of successes as well as exchanges of experiences between firms and across countries are valuable here. This applies in particular to small and medium-sized firms that have at their disposal only limited resources for development. In Denmark, where there are only a few large firms, the Confederation of Danish Industries (DI) and the counterpart trade union organization, the Central Organization of Industrial Employees (CO), have agreed to issue six small publications providing information on experience with the introduction of organizational change and new wage systems. In other European countries, the state has supported company restructuring through national programs in which experiences are evaluated and the reports made publicly available, for example, in the Swedish LOM program or the German Humanization of Work program (Den Hertog and Schröder 1989).

Changes to organizational structures will have the desired effects only if they are consistent with other elements of companies' social structures. This applies to in-firm training and further training, career structures, and wage systems. For example, some wage systems date back forty years to a time when payment was made for a specific job in a strongly hierarchical organization with a rigid division of labor. Such wage systems, rooted in hierarchies and antithetical to cooperative working, are now obstructing the introduction of more flexible company structures. Moreover, they frequently discriminate against groups of employees whose work within the company has increased in importance. It is precisely in the most up-to-date companies that traditional pay differentials between manual and white-collar workers, between men and women, or between members of the same team are often no longer workable. Not only firms but also employees benefit from new payment structures, since it is only in this way that they can develop their skills and improve their long-term opportunities in the labor market. Consequently, there is a basis for a common enough agenda to make reform of wage systems a feasible topic for management/labor.

New wage systems that are more compatible with the flexible firm have already been introduced into many firms in Europe and North America, in both manufacturing and services and in large, medium-sized, and small firms. These new payment systems involve broader job descriptions and fewer pay grades, training incentives, a higher premium on competences (such as cooperation, responsibility, decision making, problem solving, etc.), pay supplements for results or for continuous improvements, status equity for blue- and white-collar employees, for time and piece-rate workers and for part-timers and full-timers, and equal pay for men and women. Simplification of payment systems and consequent reductions in bureaucracies can also have a positive effect on firms. The Ford Motor Company in Great Britain, for example, has reduced the number of job titles from over five hundred to around fifty.

OUTSOURCING

The term "outsourcing" is used when services or products previously provided or manufactured by a firm are transferred to outside suppliers.[1] Particularly in the case of new investment programs and the development of new production sites (so-called green-field plants), make-or-buy decisions may be made at an early stage. At existing sites—so-called brown-field sites—firms are more likely to switch to outsourcing. To a certain extent at least, we are clearly dealing here with two processes that impact employment and work organization in completely different ways. In the case of outsourcing, existing jobs may be threatened while at the same time employers' maneuvering room is limited, since existing production sites are designed for traditional, vertically integrated manufacturing processes. In the case of make-or-buy decisions, particularly in conjunction with the development of green-field sites, firms have more maneuvering room, since they can recruit only workers who are actually required. In this respect, multinational companies seek to create a sort of ping-pong effect. They define the factory of the future as a green-field site and set up liaison departments at such sites already operating within the group. Then, by calling for internal tenders for new investment projects, they place existing brown-field sites under pressure to adapt. There are many examples of this in the automotive industry. Mercedes has such new-model plants in Rastatt and in France (Smart) while General Motors has Cammi/Canada, Saturn/Tennessee, and Opel/Eisenach.

The reasons for outsourcing are numerous and varied and may be briefly summarized as follows (Bliesener 1994; Fischer, Späker, and Weißbach 1994; Knolmayer 1994; Knüppel and Heuer 1994):

- more rational organization through concentration of company resources on the core activities essential for survival
- exploitation of cost differences between in-house and external production
- development of strategic alliances with reliable suppliers/partners
- introduction of greater cost variability and the avoidance of costly investment programs
- the development of instruments for creating and managing cooperative structures at plant level even between plants operated by different companies

These various factors influence individual decisions on outsourcing to very different extents. In many cases, the sole objective is to transfer jobs from large firms with strong trade unions, good rates of pay and social benefits, and regulated working conditions to either small and medium-sized firms in the same country with worse conditions or firms abroad. In other cases, the principal objective is to tap into the specialist skills and know-how of a supplier or partner. This diversity of motives suggests that reductions in the range of in-house activities will lead to the development of a variety of different relationships among firms and that the consequences for employees will also vary widely.

The new information technologies are certainly not the cause of the current trend toward outsourcing but are the instruments that support its implementation. It is true that some of the new sourcing arrangements are being implemented through conventional supplier relationships. This applies particularly to the outsourcing of peripheral activities, such as catering or cleaning services, and to the transfer of the production of simple parts to low-wage countries. However, a considerable and rising share is being implemented through the use of new information technologies that provide an efficient means of coordination. Decisions on outsourcing are made easier for firms if they do not communicate with suppliers through the market but rather integrate them into internal company activities and treat them as departments within the firm. This integration can be seen to be taking place through the incorporation of suppliers into manufacturers' information systems via electronic data interchange systems and associated just-in-time agreements. Information systems make it possible to go beyond traditional organizational boundaries without disrupting established internal coordination mechanisms.

This process of outsourcing is altering company structures in Europe in a quite fundamental way. Large firms are employing fewer workers than in the past. At the same time, they are reducing the number of direct suppliers in order to cut back on the costs of coordination and reduce the number of firms with which they have to maintain contacts. Between 1990 and 1993, the number of automotive suppliers in the Europe decreased from 16,000 to 11,000 (excluding Japanese transplants). Manufacturers were aiming for a further reduction of about 6,400 suppliers (Heim 1994). Direct suppliers are now delivering not just individual parts but whole modules or subassemblies. Firms have to establish themselves as module suppliers if they are to avoid demotion to the role of subcontractor. Manufacturers or end customers, particularly in the automotive industry and the retail sector, are forcing their suppliers to install electronic data interchange systems (Webster 1995). In the automotive industry, one survey found that the introduction of electronic data interchange systems was initiated by the business partners in 77 percent of all cases (Picot et al. 1995, 71). Inability to introduce electronic data interchange systems can lead to the demise of suppliers. Electronic data interchange standards are also often forced upon suppliers, which creates one-sided dependencies. Market power is one of the central mechanisms of electronic networking and is associated with the emergence of "electronic hierarchies" (Malone 1987; Webster 1995).

Suppliers who find themselves downgraded to mere providers of parts find themselves under immediate threat of extinction. They are in competition with low-wage countries, for which they are no match. Suppliers can survive only if they develop expertise as partners in production, development, or the value-added process. The range of activities of such firms differs from that of mere parts suppliers. Suppliers can also develop such strategic expertise through cooperative relationships with other firms. They may then be able to free themselves from the "electronic hierarchies" by building up their own networks. The term "virtual firm" has been coined to describe such situations. J. Bryne takes this to denote a "temporary network of independent firms—suppliers, customers, even former competitors—linked to each by information technology in order to share costs, complement each other's skills and to develop new markets together. . . . each firm brings with it its own expertise" (Bryne 1993, 37). Firms take this step either because electronic networking is imposed on them by "market power" or when it becomes economically worthwhile to have "lasting commercial relations" with other firms. Many economic obstacles have to be overcome before the investment required can be considered advantageous for firms, and many small and medium-sized firms still do not know what electronic trading or electronic data interchange actually is.

Governments in many European countries are seeking to support suppliers in their efforts at restructuring, particularly in the automotive industry. Their objective is to prevent the downgrading of suppliers to mere producers of parts and thus to save at least some of the jobs at stake. The government of the German federal state of North Rhine-Westphalia, for example, is supporting projects involving cooperation among suppliers as part of an initiative it calls "project cooperation in the automotive industry." And the European Union, with its Objective 4 and Adapt programs, is supporting cooperative projects between suppliers and small and medium-sized firms.

Outsourcing and Labor

Outsourcing has serious consequences for employees. It is true that in legal terms suppliers are independent firms; economically, however, they are completely dependent. To a certain extent at least, downstream manufacturers dictate working conditions in supplier firms. Production or work cycles in supplier firms are increasingly closely linked to their customers' production schedules. In extreme cases, production schedules on both sides are fully synchronized and suppliers lose any autonomy they may once have had in organizing night and weekend working, overtime, or flexible annual working hours. This undermines codetermination or collective bargaining at plant level, since the actual decisions are no longer made at that level.

Outsourcing is also changing industrial relations in many countries. One reason for shifting activities out of firms is differences in rates of pay between firms or industries. On the one hand, the "industry," which in many countries has until now been the reference point for collective bargaining, is becoming less important. On the other hand, in industries in which there are comprehensive collective agreements that also cover small and medium-sized firms, demands are now being made for special conditions to be agreed for smaller firms. In some European firms, therefore, there are already employees working alongside each other who are paid very differently. Pay depends on whether they are covered by the agreements concluded in the engineering, chemical, or textiles industries and whether they are employed by the manufacturer or by a small or medium-sized firm supplying the manufacturer. As a result, the principle that all employees working at the same site should be covered by the same payment arrangements is being undermined. This has led to heightened competition between SMEs that are covered by collective agreements and those that are not, as has been the case in the United States for a long time.

In some outsourcing arrangements, certain activities are not transferred to other firms; rather, members of the core firm's workforce are offered the chance to carry on those activities as self-employed consultants or contractors. If a nucleus of new firms is created in this way, innovation may be promoted. However, creating a self-employed workforce is a completely different matter when employees are faced with a choice between dismissal without compensation and acceptance of their new self-employed status. In these cases, such self-employed status is merely illusory, since workers are unable to organize their working time and means of production as they see fit. Such employment relationships are found, for example, in the insurance industry. Insurance representatives are increasingly "self-employed" in name only and are not able to become their own bosses. Their employment status is merely a means for insurance companies to circumvent the provisions of collective agreements and social protection legislation. Virtually all of it (legislation on working time, health and safety at work, and employers' social insurance) rests on the premise of dependent employment and can be avoided by creating the illusion of self-employment. The consequence is a very considerable deterioration in working conditions.

ICTs are, however, an important element in the reduction of market entry barriers for SMEs or microbusinesses. For example, consultants can go into business with the help of PCs and other ICT tools. Thus a growing range and number of value-added services can be offered by smaller providers. The continued outsourcing of such services will be mainly caused by two mutually reinforcing trends: the demand of big firms and the ever growing range of cheaper and better external service providers.

The emergence of many new services such as software, computer services, and logistics is closely linked, therefore, to the development of outsourcing in "traditional" industries. These new sectors, emerging as autonomous areas of economic activity, rest both on the reorganization of work and on technological developments. The longer-term efficiency and stability of these new service sectors is also dependent upon broader socioeconomic structural changes, including

- the loss of importance of economies of scale and the increasing importance of economy of time,
- the importance of knowledge resources that can be dealt with worldwide,
- blurred intersectoral boundaries,

- the development of a large number of microbusinesses and an increase in self-employment (Dostal 1995),
- the need for global presence on markets,
- the development of service clusters (e.g., highly qualified and experienced financial, consulting, media services, etc. in global cities),
- networklike structures of cooperation (Mill and Weißbach 1992), and
- the dominance of new types of management: management by objectives replaces management by rules or by hierarchy (see Weißbach 1997).

Knowledge-Intensive Services?

Within sectors that require intensive technical know-how, the work prospects for the self-employed seem to be good. In technical and business services, there was a rise of 80-100 percent in the number of employees between 1980 and 1995 (Kerst 1995; Dostal 1995). Many small business services were initially established as single-person enterprises and subsequently developed into larger companies. Companies are increasingly dependent on the availability of external services for their global and decentralized activities (Stanback 1981). The existence of high-expertise "intelligent" service providers is reinforcing this process (Kerst 1995, 138).

Effective services cannot be provided solely by individual professionals, and larger service providers are often required. There has always been a market for technical and commercial services like consultancy and R&D. As lead times become more critical, large vertically integrated firms may increasingly rely on external development or design services; these can often work more rapidly than internal R&D departments because less information is lost at the communicational interfaces. They may also be more innovative where internal company departments are engaged in a great deal of routine work. Outsourcing can also secure access to innovation potential by raising the knowledge base and contributing to the expertise development of both partners (in, for example, a strategic partnership). This practice has been reported in the chemical and pharmaceutical industries when large enterprises seek to compensate for their internal weaknesses by buying licenses; research and development results from smaller innovative partners, which may even be bought out completely. (This may of course also be done partly for reasons of image management.) In many industries, however, such practices are regarded as damaging to innovation, undermining the synergies achieved through outsourcing. Schneider (1995, 18) shows that there may be a connection between outsourcing and the reduction of the innovation rate.

Yet with some notable exceptions, specialist service providers, particularly of communications services, tend to be concentrated in urban areas—a direct result of the uneven development of telecommunications and its superior provision in urban areas (Stanback and Noyelle 1982). It is only recently that firms in other areas have been able to make use of these services via telecommunications. The tendency for firms to move toward global purchase of knowledge-based services, and therefore the potential for improved regional employment prospects, may well increase because of the possibilities afforded by telecommunications (Ernst and Young 1996).

On the other hand, the creation of certain outsourced service jobs may only be transitory. Routine jobs, such as data processing and some software development, may be automated by ICTs or may be relocated among different parts of the developing world according to changing wage and other operating costs, creating recurrent patterns of uneven development. Furthermore, for reasons of control, large, vertically integrated companies often decide to keep core service functions in-house. That need for control then presents an obstacle to the emergence of new regional centers of expertise or excellence, and thus to employment growth in less favored regions, as Cornford and his colleagues show elsewhere in this book.

As product variety, customization, and customer-centered delivery become increasingly central to firms' competitive advantage, the balance of emphasis on routine versus customer-related functions, and thus decisions on whether to outsource these functions, become more critical. Routine work can be outsourced if continuing to manage it in-house is unhelpful to the core firm's development of a stronger customer orientation. Equally, nonroutine activities may be outsourced where external suppliers can be more easily forced than internal company departments to abide by time and cost agreements. But the distinction between routine and nonroutine customer-services functions is not always a clear one. In some industries, such as financial services or telemarketing, much of the work of customer representatives is both routine and yet critical to the competitive advantage of the company. Here, some very radical decisions are being made to outsource apparently central core functions involving high levels of customer interaction. In these cases, recruitment and training of outsourced labor becomes critical: the employee's role is to provide the customer with an aesthetic experience of the company and service being provided (Witz 1992), to act as the company's ambassador (Frenkel et al. 1998), and to perform "emotional labor" (Hochschild 1983). In this context, the personal qualities of the employee are of paramount importance. Companies that make use of outsourced labor nevertheless have to ensure that this conforms to the ethic and aesthetic which they wish to present.

There may, therefore, be grounds for optimism about the creation of knowledge-intensive outsourced services in the information society, but little is known about the future of such routine service functions that are outsourced. These are services typically associated with the information society—information processing, retailing services, and telemediated financial services, for example. They are also, of course, disproportionately performed by women (Webster 1998; Belt, Richardson, and Webster 1999). In these circumstances, outsourcing does not on the face of it seem to offer prospects for expertise development or career improvement but may serve to confirm the routine nature of these types of work and to isolate outsourced employees from core organizational processes and potential learning opportunities. Analysis of the conditions of routine service employment in the information society still remains to be carried out, but the indications are that the gender relations of work in the information society are in this respect little different from the gender relations of work in general. This issue is the central concern of the chapter by Webster in this book.

Of course, outsourcing is only one strategy for reorganizing work and the location of its performance, only one element among a broad range of tools for achieving organizational flexibility. Its implications are nevertheless critical for the identity of the firm and its products, and for the motivation and loyalty of employees. Other strategies include "insourcing," which has increased recently, mainly in the use of research and development services of universities and in public research bodies. An organizational practice that has attracted particular policy attention in Europe and in the United States is "teleworking," in which functions and employees are retained in-house but relocated away from the traditional workplaces. It is to this development that we now turn.

TELEWORKING

Teleworking is an organizational innovation, or, more accurately, a series of innovations, that has received considerable attention from policy makers and analysts concerned with the development of the information society. Teleworking follows on the implementation of ICTs, which make it possible to establish direct and immediate communication between individuals and organizations that are often located a very great distance from one another. The term covers a range of phenomena. "Telework" and "teleservices" refer to the spatial distancing of service work (at the customer's premises, at the central or regional office, at home, in the car). "Telecooperation" refers to the establishment and improvement of interfirm communications systems. "Telemanagement" refers to the management and control of processes being supported by new technologies.

Of these, "telework" (with which we are concerned here) encompasses very different types of work that can be divided into six broad categories:

1. the employment of people on remote sites controlled by the employers
2. the development of telecottages or telecenters
3. the development of telecommunications links between organizations
4. fully home-based teleworking
5. part-time teleworking, in which home-based work is combined with some working time spent on the employer's premises
6. mobile work—work at different locations (e.g., building sites) in which costings and data gathering and transmission are facilitated by telecommunications and work routines are changed as a result

The economic and social significance of these various forms of teleworking is very heterogeneous. Some teleworkers are employees while others are self-employed. Some of the self-employed work exclusively for one company while others work for several companies. Some workers are mainly teleworkers while others only telework occasionally or temporarily. The only common elements of these different forms of telework are the use of computers and telecommunications, which substitute for physical travel and reduce the need to commute to work or to transport a product (e.g., a written text) to a head office.

> At its broadest, such a definition could be extended to cover a majority of white-collar work as currently practiced in Europe. For instance, it could include work carried out in branches of banks or insurance companies which are linked electronically to head-office databases, or work carried out in shops where there is an electronic link from the point of sale to a central stock control unit. (Huws 1994, 7)

In the past, analysts thought that teleworking would spread very quickly. It was maintained, for example, that "all Americans could be home workers by 1990" (AT&T, cited in Huws 1984) or that by the end of the century some 10–15 percent of the labor force in developed economies would be teleworkers (Korte and Wynne 1996, 11). These expectations have not been fulfilled, and more recent forecasts are less ambitious. Against this background, in 1994 the European Commission supported a project known as the TELDET study, the aim of which was to investigate the diffusion of teleworking and its potential for development in the five largest EC countries (Germany, the United Kingdom, France, Italy, and Spain) (Korte and Wynne 1996). In the four countries investigated, teleworking, defined broadly, was used in about 5 percent of European organizations, and the number of teleworkers was approximately 1.1 million. For the European Union member countries as a whole, it was estimated that the figure would be about 1.25 million. Teleworking is far more widespread in France and Great Britain than in the other countries, partly due to their greater social acceptance of technological developments and to the establishment of a facilitating infrastructure (Minitel in France).

But these are not 1.25 million new jobs. A considerable number of these jobs already existed. The location of some jobs has changed from conurbation to peripheral areas or into private houses. Other people are now working occasionally at home and no longer solely at their employer's premises; in other cases only the form of communication with the employer has changed. Many self-employed people and even employees who have always worked some or all of the time at home, such as translators, academics, or journalists, are now merely using different tools to do their work. It remains unclear whether additional jobs are being created by teleworking, but the location of work is certainly being shifted. Telework is used in particular by large organizations in cities, since by relocating work they are able to reduce operating costs.

The TELDET study estimated that the number of teleworkers would potentially reach 10.4 million by the year 2000. This estimate was based on surveys of employers and employees who were asked whether they were interested in the introduction of teleworking. In cases where the interests of both parties overlapped and the jobs were also suitable for the introduction of teleworking, a realistic potential for telework was identified (see table 5.1). This estimate contrasts sharply with the cautious approach to the introduction of telework adopted hitherto by firms.

The survey found that firms seek to introduce telework for a variety of reasons. At the top of the list is cost reduction, although reasons related to human resource management are also of considerable importance. Some firms wish to create an image of themselves as "good employers" or even seek to secure the loyalty of skilled workers by offering them more flexible forms of work. This contrasts with the "popular notion that competitive reasons are either the sole or the prime motivation for telework" (Korte and Wynne 1996, 54). The main obstacles to the introduction of telework cited by the firms surveyed were insufficient knowledge (51.4 percent); difficulties of managing and supervising teleworkers (45.7 percent); problems of communicating with teleworkers (38.9 percent); expense of computing equipment and telecommunication services

(36.7 percent); lack of pressure to change current practice (35.2 percent); and reasons relating to productivity or work quality (31.3 percent). The easiest problems to solve are those related to information. The others are all connected with the management and cost of telework. They indicate that firms can profit from telework only if they select appropriate activities and workers, ensure that these workers have the means to communicate personally with their employers, and are successful in adopting a more task- or goal-oriented style of management and working.

However, if firms do decide to loosen some of the ties that integrate workers so closely into company organizational structures and allow them to work all or part of the time at home, considerable problems have to be overcome. First, the home workstation must be designed in a way that guarantees adequate productivity. In the case of high-grade work, one criterion adopted by companies is that teleworkers are able to provide "a suitable work area in their home, free from any major distractions" (British Telecommunication Teleworking Guideline for managers, quoted in IDS 1994, 12). A frequently cited advantage of telework is that it offers a means of combining family responsibilities with paid work; this is clearly irreconcilable with such requirements. Telework is not a substitute for public child care provision. Whether and how teleworkers can be integrated into company culture, which is taking on an increasingly important role in management thinking, has yet to be established. Many companies, with their new, decentralized organizational structures and cultures, are

Table 5.1   Tasks Considered Suitable for Teleworking

Task	% of Responding Firms
Data entry or typing	44.6
Programming or specialist computing	31.6
Secretarial or administrative work	29.3
Translation	27.9
Financial services, bookkeeping, or accounting	25.8
Ordering, information, or booking services	24.8
Sales, marketing	22.3
Editing	21.3
Research, consultancy	19.7
Design, architectural work	16.5
Training, education	14.3
Management	10.4
Repair, maintenance	10.0

Source: Korte and Wynne 1996.

increasingly reliant on direct personal communication and continuous on-the-job training. They tend to offer part-time teleworking only to employees who have already worked for several years on the same team, who have been socialized there, and whose work is individualized and requires long periods without interruption (like Digital Equipment in the United Kingdom; IDS 1994, 14). The U.K. Department of Employment publication *A Manager's Guide to Teleworking* refers to the high demands placed on teleworkers (see also Moorcraft and Bennett 1995). The qualities that are seen as important for teleworking are maturity, trustworthiness, self-sufficiency, self-discipline, good time management skills, good management skills, and good communication skills.[2] Case studies show, however, that even in companies where teleworking is carefully thought out, only a limited number of employees can work at home some of the time. At the Harris Trust and Savings Bank in Chicago, which is sometimes cited as an example, this applies to only 38 out of a total of 4,000 employees. These thirty-eight employees have average seniority of 1.5 years, have been teleworkers for 2.5 years, and work 1.3 days per week at home (Firpo 1995).

Telework is not likely to create permanent jobs if only simple, repetitive activities are moved from company premises. In the short run, such a transfer of jobs from workers in the primary labor market to home workers with little bargaining power, low wages, and no guarantee of work leads to a deterioration of working conditions. In the long run, particularly when only low-skilled repetitive tasks are involved, there remains a continuing danger that a "downward spiral of competition" from parts of the world in which labor costs are lower and social protection poorer will operate. Indeed, there is evidence that simple jobs are now being transferred to the Third World.

> Studies which have been carried out on data entry workers in the developing countries . . . have found that they are characterized by high intensity of work, shift working involving unsocial hours, health hazards and wage levels which are extremely low by international standards although often slightly above local minima. (Huws 1994, 34)

If jobs are to be created by teleworking in the medium term as well, there should not be a return to the classic forms of home working, with their poor working conditions. Rather, the quality of the goods or services, and of the jobs, offered by firms will have to be improved as a result.

Nevertheless, we should not ignore the disadvantages of teleworking, which may include isolation, extra costs for heating and lighting, expenditure on additional living space, the nonpayment of supplements for unsocial hours, the circumvention of health and safety guidelines, the involuntary change of status from employee to dependent self-employment and inadequate access to further training opportunities and internal promotion. There are numerous examples of such disadvantages, and several trade unions have established guidelines for the protection of teleworkers (table 5.2). They have also modified their hitherto negative attitude toward part-time teleworking. Like BIFU, the English Banking and Finance Trade Union, some trade unions see advantages in it for employees. Some employing organizations (e.g., the London Borough of Enfield) have drawn up exemplary rules for part-time teleworking that seek to organize this form of work in a way that is attractive both to the employees involved and to their often skeptical superiors.

One serious implication of teleworking for both working conditions and firm competitiveness is the extent to which it allows employees to develop new skills. In conventional working arrangements, employees have access to a considerable amount of training on the job. In teleworking situations, training provision and employee skill development will need to be conceptualized and addressed differently:

> With workers increasingly dispersed on separate sites, the kinds of tacit learning practiced in the past become impossible. Although the first cohort of teleworkers have come from a generation of workers who have learned their skills in this traditional way, there are no mechanisms in place for the training of their successors since few enterprises have developed policies for training new teleworkers or designed ways in which people on remote sites can upgrade their skills or can gain access to the corporate culture. (Huws 1994, 50)

Thus one of the biggest risks for teleworkers is that without adequate access to in-house training, which is becoming increasingly important as the pace of change quickens, they will become deskilled and thus forfeit their career opportunities. This is particularly problematic for women teleworkers, who are already disadvantaged in their access to training and skills and are disproportionately concentrated in low-grade teleworking functions (Stanworth and Stanworth 1989). The gender dimensions of teleworking are critical and should not be underestimated in the process of developing an understanding of its implications for employees.

This is not to say that there are no social advantages in the implementation of teleworking. One of its major potential benefits is that traffic flows may be reduced. Another is that service activities will develop even in peripheral areas. So-called telecottages or telecenters have been established in a number of

Table 5.2   List of Trade Union Demands Concerning Telework

1. Equal pay and benefits.
2. Two days a week at the central office.
3. Managers visit homes no more than twice a month.
4. Proper equipment and furniture supplied by employers, reimbursement of all costs, and union rights to inspect home workstation.
5. Equal right to promotion information and opportunities, with union contacts given daily on teleworkers' computer screens.
6. Limitation on monitoring of teleworkers.
7. No preferential treatment for teleworkers.
8. Equal training and extra training.
9. Recruitment of teleworkers only from existing personnel; no direct hiring from the job market.
10. No change of status from employee to subcontractor or "out-sourcing supplier."
11. All teleworkers must be volunteers.
12. An automatic right to return to the core team.
13. Teleworkers' workstations in a separate room in the home.
14. Regular meeting between teleworkers and core team personnel.
15. Rights to use equipment to communicate with colleagues (reducing isolation).
16. Specified "mentor" for each teleworker.
17. Specific health and safety officer visits and reports with teleworkers represented on health and safety committees.

Source: Bosch 1995, 11, citing Noel Hodson, *Telework and Employment in Europe* (1994).

regions (such as the telecenter set up by Jämtland county council in Sweden). The supply of available labor in such areas consists to a large extent of less highly skilled workers. The most successful strategy for creating high value-added employment in those areas is to persuade highly skilled workers to move in. Such incomers would bring to the region not only their knowledge and skills but also their contacts.

The European Commission has in recent years undertaken a range of activities in the sphere of telework, and several proposals for action have been put forward:

- The measures taken to date to foster telework in disadvantaged regions should be examined and proposals developed for creating high-skill jobs in such regions.
- The skill structure and skill requirements of teleworkers should be investigated and models developed for the training of teleworkers.
- The numbers of men and women currently involved in telework should

be ascertained, together with the activities they are engaged in, and proposals drawn up for preventing women in particular from being concentrated in low-skill activities.

• Company and collective agreements on teleworking should be drawn up and evaluated and support should be provided for innovative forms of collective organization of self-employed and home-based workers.

CONCLUSION

Some of the changes currently taking place in European organizations, as in organizations elsewhere in the world, represent very radical departures from past methods of organizing work. Many of them are critically dependent on the implementation of ICTs. Others are forms of organization that, arguably, could well have emerged regardless of technological developments and of the development of the information society. ICT dependent or not, organizational changes are ultimately driven, not by technological imperatives, but by social choices and particularly by managerial programs and strategies for change. Because of this, they are amenable to social intervention and to negotiation. No innovation in the organization of work and workers is inevitable or nonnegotiable. More than this, evidence from across Europe suggests that the involvement of employees, through employee participation in organizational change, produces by far the most efficient and competitive outcomes in organizational development (EPOC Research Group 1997). Acknowledging the positive role of negotiation between all groups in industry may help us to ensure that organizational changes are designed to meet both the requirements of competitiveness and the needs of employees as social partners and that they are ultimately pursued to the benefit of all members of the information society.

NOTES

1. The National Association of Purchasing Management (NAPM) has suggested the following definitions: "Make-or-buy: a determination of what products or services a firm should manufacture or provide in-house, as opposed to purchasing from outside sources. Outsourcing: a version of the make-or-buy decision, in which a firm elects to purchase an item that previously was made in-house; commonly utilized for services" (NAPM n.d. 16–17).

2. The guide continues: "For instance, a young, single person, not yet fully trained, may need the social stimulus of the office and the presence of more experienced colleagues. Five or ten years on, he or she may be more mature and settled with a young family and grateful for the chance to work from home for a few years. In another ten years, this teleworker might be ready for a change back to an office environment."

6

Today's Second Sex and Tomorrow's First? Women and Work in the European Information Society

Juliet Webster

The European information society would seem, on the face of it, to hold out the possibility of far greater gender equity than its predecessor societies. First, it is, we are told, a society with an economy that will be dominated by services and service industries. The decline of manufacturing and the growth of services are very long-run processes that began, in many European countries, after the Second World War. The information society characterized by the production and consumption of immaterial commodities (data, information, communications products, and services) takes this process to its limits: services now become the bedrock of economic life. Those working in service industries, whether in the private or public sector, are no longer marginal to the conduct of such an economy; they are at its very center and would seemingly stand to gain considerably in terms of economic and social inclusion as their job prospects grow and their work becomes more critical to the economy.

Services are, of course, the locale for the great majority of women at work throughout the European Union. Women have historically been concentrated in services, particularly in public services and, by contrast, somewhat peripheral to manufacturing employment, where they have largely been concentrated in semiskilled areas such as assembly work and auxiliary functions such as packaging and clerical support.[1] This concentration persists and is a feature of all European Union member states. The highest concentrations are evident in Luxembourg, the Netherlands, Sweden, the United Kingdom, Belgium, and

Denmark—all countries with generally high rates of female labor market participation (CEC 1996c). All visions of the information society (IS) place great emphasis on the increasing importance of services (e.g., CEC 1993; CEC 1994a; HLEG 1997). The High Level Expert Group on the social aspects of the information society regards public services as particularly critical, indeed, as the "engine of growth" in the emerging IS. Perhaps their female employees will be among the major beneficiaries of this development.

It is also becoming an article of faith to say that in the developing information society, the learning done by individuals, firms, regions, and even nations will be critical to their ability to participate fully in social life. For individual members of society, social inclusion will be predicated on the deployment of knowledge and competences gained throughout life—in the education system, in the world of work, and in wider civic society. As a number of chapters in this volume make clear, education, training, and learning are emerging as the central defining features of the European information society vision—central to individual, social, and economic growth and central to the policies that aim to promote that growth.[2]

If this vision becomes reality, women should again be strong beneficiaries of this development. Women and girls are casting off their former status as mediocre educational achievers who rank equally with boys until puberty and then slip down to second-class status as their attention turns away from educational and career aspirations. Today, they are maintaining their strong performance in the education system beyond puberty and across the range of subjects rather than simply in traditional areas—arts, languages, and social sciences. Indeed, because of the dramatic way in which girls have begun to outstrip boys at school, it has been variously argued in France, Britain, and the United States that "the future is female" and "tomorrow belongs to women."[3]

What is the likelihood of this promise being fulfilled? What are the factors promoting the improved social inclusion of women in a future information society? What exclusionary factors operate and how persistent are they? How may women of different ethnic groups fare in the emerging information society? And are the improvements in girls' educational performance sufficient to secure them all a more equal place in the workplace and in other areas of social life? Finally, what policy initiatives—in addition to those already under way—would contribute to greater gender equity?

The position of women in the labor market is interesting in this regard because work remains one of the key areas in which women are currently excluded from full social and economic enfranchisement and from the opportunity to develop to their full potential as members of society. Moreover, the world of work is at the center of other forms of gender-based exclusion—from trade union activism, from political involvement, from culture and the arts, and from scientific and technological endeavor.[4]

GENDER DIVISIONS IN EMPLOYMENT

Despite attempts to open up opportunities for women beyond the spheres in which they have traditionally been employed, women remain concentrated in relatively limited areas of the economy. This concentration has been described by the concepts of horizontal segregation and vertical segregation, which refer, respectively, to the segregation of women within certain economic sectors (e.g., financial services, retailing, health care, education) and at the lower levels of occupational hierarchies (e.g., clerical work, cashiering, nursing, and lower- and middle-level teaching jobs). The concentration of women's employment in a few industry sectors—and particularly in service industries—persists. Indeed, in some industries and occupations, segregation of women and men appears to have *increased*, with women withdrawing from some manufacturing sectors (such as textiles and footwear) and becoming more concentrated in office work. Though in some countries women are becoming more visible in the higher echelons of economic life, they are still in a small minority at these levels. In the most gender-equal European Union country (Finland), women still make up no more than 38 percent of legislators and managers; in other countries their representation is less than 20 percent (CEC 1996c).

This pattern of employment segregation is the context within which women's place in the information society is being shaped. It has a number of implications for women's prospects for labor market and wider social inclusion, irrespective of the role of ICTs, which I discuss below. First, however, it is worth noting that because of their concentration in particular industries and at low levels of occupational hierarchies, women are particularly vulnerable to the effects of organizational restructuring, one important effect of which has been redundancy and unemployment. For example, downsizing, coupled with high levels of capital investment in ICTs, has for the past decade been a key strategy by which many organizations have sought to maintain their profitability (in the short term at least). It has been particularly popular in labor-intensive white-collar industries such as financial services, where the impact has been felt disproportionately by routine clerical employees, the majority of whom are (still) women. Where women continue to be concentrated in relatively routine and unskilled activities, they will be particularly vulnerable to employment shakeouts and associated programs of automation and "informatization" (Zuboff 1988).

Second, because of their underrepresentation in particular types of work, especially work that is defined as "skilled" or requiring "know-how," women do not stand to benefit equally with men from current employment growth trends (Council for Economic Advisers 1996; OECD 1996a). It has been argued that in the emerging growth sectors of the European economy (e.g., telecommunications, multimedia, and audiovisual industries, as well as services such as health care and business services), the key forms of employment will be knowledge based and predicated upon sustained education and training. On the other hand, it is feared that the unskilled will be increasingly excluded from the labor market on a long-term basis (CEC 1996d). Yet much of the work that women do is considered unskilled, women are underrepresented in "knowledge-work," and their access particularly to training (especially on-the-job training) remains poor. At the same time, there is evidence that long-term unemployment is rising among women and affects women to a greater extent than men.[5]

Third, coterminous with the development of the information society has been a growth in "atypical" (or "flexible") forms of employment in all the member states of the European Union—such employment forms as part-time work, temporary work, self-employment, and subcontracting.[6] Part of the explanation for these developments lies in an absolute growth in employment in sectors in which atypical employment is more prevalent (e.g., in the retailing sector, which relies on a variety of different part-time working arrangements), and this development particularly affects female employees (Rubery, Smith, and Fagan 1995). However, there has also been a relative growth in atypical employment compared to full-time, lifetime employment. These developments are facilitated by the implementation of ICTs (information and communication technologies) by organizations. Apart from direct employment displacement, ICTs allow organizations to schedule labor requirements and to outsource functions to other areas of the value chain. Chapter 5 in this volume, "New Organizational Forms in the Information Society," explores these developments and their relationship to the IS in more detail.

Some forms of atypical work are more characteristic of women's employment. Part-time work, for example, is very prominent in certain occupations and industry sectors that are female dominated (e.g., cleaning, catering, retailing, and retail financial services). Temporary contracts are also more frequently held by women than by men. Other forms of atypical work, such as self-employment and freelancing, are more likely to be done by men. This is, of course, an oversimplification of what is a very complex picture. The extent and significance of atypical work for women and men varies across the European Union. Women hold over 80 percent of part-time jobs, but the importance of this fact differs among countries. Part-time work has become particularly significant in the Netherlands, Germany, Denmark, and the United Kingdom but not in others, particularly in southern Europe (e.g., Spain and Italy). In some countries (e.g., the United Kingdom) there is a labor market demand for part-time workers. In others (such as Denmark), the demand comes from labor market supply issues, particularly school hours arrangements that compel women to finish work in the middle of the day.

Different employment patterns have therefore developed in different ways in the member states, and within different contexts of social protection, labor market regulation, and other factors shaping women's labor market participation. Indeed, as Rubery et al. (1995) show, understanding the dynamics of flexible employment in a country requires considering not only developments in work organization and working time but also the social systems for sharing income within families and through the state. Nevertheless, it is clear that across the European Union and the OECD countries, atypical work, particularly part-time work, is steadily growing as a proportion of total employment, in some countries to well over one-third of total employment (OECD 1996a).

THE ROLE OF ICTs IN WORKING TIME CHANGE AND WORK RELOCATION

It is clear, therefore, that the effects of ICTs *specifically* on women's work are extremely hard to isolate and assess. Most of the employment dynamics that are discussed below are functions of restructuring and work reorganization within industries. The introduction and application of ICTs are a part of, as much as the consequences of, technological change. The application of ICTs should not be considered in isolation from the wider dynamics of organizational restructuring. But it is clear that ICTs are profoundly implicated in changes in work organization and work location in particular industries that are central to the IS. It is this role within a total picture of innovations—and their implications for women's work in the IS—that this chapter addresses.

What, then, are the key patterns of technological change and therefore the dynamics of women's work in the IS? One industry sector that employs women in very large numbers, and is also a rapidly innovating and restructuring sector, is the retailing sector. The sector is increasingly dominated in some European countries, the United Kingdom and Ireland in particular, by large multiples and by chains of specialist shops. In other countries, especially the Nordic countries and southern Europe, the sector retains a large proportion of small retailers and worker cooperatives. However, the sector is also becoming increasingly internationalized with many retail companies (e.g., Sweden's IKEA, Britain's Marks and Spencer) now operating across national borders.

ICT systems and networks are critical to the innovation strategies of the larger retailing firms. First, they allow these companies to integrate what were previously separate functions. Electronic points of sale (EPOS) systems monitor sales of all product lines by customer and by time of day and week. Computer systems perform inventory management. Electronic data interchange networks transmit electronic orders for stock replenishment to suppliers. Computerized "scheduling engines" generate rosters of staffing requirements by fifteen-minute time slots (Neathey and Hurstfield 1995). Additionally, many large retailers are now experimenting with customer-held scanners that hold personal customer information, read the bar codes of the goods selected from the store, and charge the customer accordingly. Personal loyalty cards with credit units are used for payment, and these technologies decrease the need for checkout operators. Teleshopping and mail order shopping over the Internet are becoming established in all countries and in some, such as Sweden, are already strongly established, partly because of local climate and conditions.

What implications do these innovations have for the organization and experience of work in this sector? Just as the larger retail organizations may now use the facilities offered by ICT systems to plan and anticipate their requirements of every type of material resource necessary to meet customer demand, so they are also able to plan their human resource requirements in very great detail. The large retail multiples are progressively adopting atypical employment contracts that allow them to vary their labor utilization in response to the circumstances of the market and to periods of high demand (Freeman and Soete 1994).

Retail outlets in the countries of the European Union are staffed overwhelmingly by women, and part-time contracts are the most common form of contract under which they are employed. Over the last decade these contracts have been progressively refined to cover a plethora of different requirements. For example, some of the major retail multiples in the United Kingdom operate more than one hundred different types of contract per week (Neathey and Hurstfield 1995). These include "zero hours" contracts, in which employees are on call all the time but may only be employed for brief interludes to cover busy periods; Saturday contracts, in which employees work Saturdays only; and permanent part-time contracts, in which employees work for set periods during the working week. In highly capital-intensive companies with integrated computer systems, computerized scheduling engines monitor the customer footprint (the profile of customers passing through the store at any one time), assess level of sales staffing required, and thus allow the companies to plan their labor requirements down to fifteen-minute time slots. They then employ part-time staff only for the exact periods when they are needed—as fill-in labor where contingencies require it.

These innovations are having "knock-on effects" on employment patterns throughout the retailing supply chain, right back to the agricultural industries that supply raw materials to the food industry. Quick response (a form of just-in-time supply specific to the retail industry), an increasing intervention by retailers in suppliers' production practices, and on-line ordering (Frances and Garnsey 1995) reverberate across organizations in the retailing sector. Suppliers are often called upon to produce goods at very short notice, and their contracts with their customers may be very tenuous. In food retailing, the agricultural sector is having to modify its employment arrangements, now hiring its largely female employees on a casual daily or part-daily basis through agencies when supermarket orders intensify.

This is one dynamic affecting the retail industry and its supply chain in Europe, and it is arguably a strongly Anglo-Saxon dynamic. At the other end of the spectrum there is of course the continuing presence of the small, privately owned or cooperatively owned company, in which the deployment of labor and the nature of the work done by the women who are employed in them runs along very different lines. Here, the work is much more labor-intensive and much more variable. There is also much greater opportunity for the women who work in smaller shops to have some social interaction with customers, to use their discretion in the course of their work, and to make decisions autonomously. At present, women's experiences of working in the retail sector are very much conditioned by the type of firm in which they are employed. To what extent, however, is this form of retailing likely to remain in the IS? Will pressure develop toward increasing "industrialization" of retailing, with greater concentration of ownership, standardization of work, and informatization of a wider and wider range of retailing functions? Or will the physical shop disappear altogether, to be replaced by mail order or teleshopping, so that the assistant behind the counter is replaced by the voice at the end of the phone or is done away with altogether? Teleshopping has a number of advantages and benefits. It can help people who are housebound, have young children or elderly relatives to care for, or lack transportation. What does this mean for the women who work in the retail sector? The same women who benefit from increased convenience as consumers may well suffer as employees, either by becoming subject to greater casualization and routinization of their work or by being made redundant altogether. This is an area in which policy makers could intervene to promote developments in retailing that aim to meet the needs not only of consumers but also of employees—who very often may be the same people.

The retailing sector is not alone in having made dramatic transformations in working hours and working arrangements with the gradual development of the IS. The garment industry is also renowned for its volatility and rapidly changing markets, and for its dependence on ICTs to help it meet the demands of these markets. Clothing companies use quick response systems, together with computerized market information systems, barcode readers, and electronic data interchange (EDI) networks, to monitor the turnover of particular product lines at point of sale, to transmit the information back to the manufacturer, and to make it possible to gauge the market with speed and accuracy. Consequently, a U.K. textile company director can produce T-shirts with Mickey Mouse on them today and Donald Duck on them tomorrow, if that is what the market demands (Mitter 1991, 58). The clothing industry is a major employer of women throughout the European Union. Following the lead of Japanese retailers, it is now subcontracting its manufacturing processes. This has been taken up widely in Europe, most famously by Marks and Spencer in the United Kingdom and by Benetton and Pronta Moda in Italy (Elson 1989; Belussi 1991; Mitter 1991). Small batch production, subcontracted to small firms, allows the industry to respond flexibly and rapidly to changes in market demand of this sort. In some companies, such as Benetton, the final machining is subcontracted to family networks of female machinists working in small factories or at home; the skilled parts of the production process (designing, cutting, and final presentation) are retained by the main contractor. In other companies, such as Marks and Spencer, the entire process of production is subcontracted. In both cases, the rationale is to hold down overheads—the costs and complexities associated with employing small and dispersed workforces—while at the same time achieving the quickest response possible to market fluctuations.

The financial services sector is another area of work that is held to be central to the IS and which depends strongly on female labor. The sector has witnessed substantial changes in work organization over the past decade, changes that have taken a number of forms and have radically affected the work of all employees in the sector. First, there have been significant reductions in employment across the countries of the European Union, particularly in the northern European countries. This is attributable to a combination of ICTs and business process reengineering, a managerial technique that has been imported into Europe from the United States. Business process reengineering (BPR) represents a fundamental overhaul of all the internal processes undertaken by a company in the course of its business. Its implementation has helped the sector to overcome the so-called productivity paradox that beset many European industries during the 1980s (OECD 1996a) and thus to achieve significant productivity gains from the use of ICTs.

The two central elements of the BPR philosophy are, first, downsizing the staff complement of an organization and, second, delayering it, which involves removing the need for entire categories of staff, mostly at clerical, junior, and middle management levels.[7] In the United Kingdom, these methods have been adopted very keenly, and linked to them has been a restructuring of working time arrangements and work location. In terms of working time arrangements, the sector has been making increasing use of part-time and temporary contracts for staff, in order to correct for persistent understaffing; it also makes permanent employees redundant (Neathey and Hurstfield 1995). In particular, these arrangements are used for the employment of people in clerical positions, the majority of whom are women. Temporary contracts often define these employees as "seat warmers" to fill in for jobs that are being readied for complete automation. At one credit card processing center in the United Kingdom, an employment agency has been established on the premises to provide for the center's temporary labor requirements on an immediate basis. Part-time contracts, by contrast, are often used to employ staff in suburban areas, many of whom are married women, for work in back office processing centers. In the United States, these twin forms of numerical flexibility are already widespread in the sector. The Bank of America has estimated that only 19 percent of its employees will be employed full-time in future years (Bridges 1995).

This is not the situation in all the member states of the European Union. In some countries, such as Spain, part-time work barely exists; in others, such as the Nordic countries, it is prevalent but is not necessarily associated with low pay and poor career prospects as in the United Kingdom. Nevertheless, it is not clear to what extent women across the European Union are subjected to increasing work casualization in this sector. In order to fully understand women's experiences of the IS at work, we need a serious comparative study of the dynamics of working time arrangements in the economic sectors, such as financial services, that are central to it.

ICTs have played a very important role in restructuring and relocating the work done by women in service industries in the IS. The implementation of ICTs allows the retail, financial and other service industries of the IS to separate customer service functions from information processing functions and to situate them in different locations, sometimes in different cities. Information processing activities no longer need to be situated in city centers or handled face-to-face with the customers; instead, information can be transmitted to customer interfaces via telecommunications networks.

Information processing work itself has historically been the province of women clerical workers. In many service industries, this work is now being relocated and centralized in dedicated back offices away from the physical point of contact with the customer. For companies such as financial services that have especially high-volume data processing requirements, centralized back offices located in less favored or suburban areas tend to offer lower labor and overhead costs. Sometimes, the work is also outsourced to subcontracting organizations, with one organization serving as a processing agency for a number of different companies. For example, the outsourcing of check processing from banks to separate information processing agencies is an increasingly common strategy. Alongside the relocation and outsourcing of this work has been the introduction of ICT-based systems that can handle all aspects of information processing and customer servicing. The application of such systems has, however, removed many of the discretionary or expertise-based elements of work, making them amenable to decision making based on expert systems. For example, in the newly emerging "telemediated" remote information processing centers, the work is usually very routine. The banking representative or salesperson adheres to a tightly prescribed series of operations and interacts with computer systems and customers in a predetermined manner. There is substantial evidence of increasing routinization of both back office and front office work in European financial service companies as a result of the use of ICTs (Smith and Wield 1987; Richardson 1994; Arvanitaki and Stratigaki 1994).

It is not only the "back office" information processing tasks that are being relocated and automated in the IS. Even work that formerly seemed to necessitate face-to-face contact with customers is increasingly being performed remotely. The introduction of home banking and telebanking and telephone-based insurance services has allowed these companies to serve their customers directly by telephone (often at the cost of a local call) and thus to obviate the need for street branches or city center premises. ICTs are particularly critical to the new services being offered in the financial services industries and, therefore, to the type of employment that is emerging in them. Telephone banking has been introduced in a number of European countries. Virtual banking, in which bank staff are located either in an office or at home and interact with customers via multimedia computer terminals, is currently under development. In the insurance sector, computerized call distribution systems have been installed to handle customer business, allowing companies to locate their information processing operations at any site. They can route customer inquiries from a central control point so that the service to the customer is identical regardless of where the staff are physically located (Richardson 1994).

First Direct (the United Kingdom's first branchless bank) used freephone and local call rates to offer cheap, convenient phone banking to customers. These services, together with their geography-free tariff structures also allowed First Direct to service their target market *from a single site in a different region.* The services offered over the intelligent network allowed First Direct to locate at the most suitable site, in Leeds (where there was a large labor catchment area and cheap labor), and still serve the target market in the southeastern part of England. All the other major banks have launched (or are about to launch) some form of telebanking. In a few cases (e.g., the Banks of Scotland and Ireland) this can be seen as a branchless and therefore cost-effective way to gain market share in England (Richardson 1994).

We know little as yet about the skills and experiences of the women who work in these environments. Cornford, Gillespie, and Richardson's chapter in this volume is one of the very few to explore these issues. They suggest that telemediated back office developments are often welcomed because they offer employment opportunities to women in less favored or declining regions. However, the opportunities for skill development and thus for personal development within organizations may in fact be limited because of the routine and systematized nature of much of the work. The work of the telephone banking representative is controlled through automatic call distribution systems that route calls and by computerized scripting systems that dictate the conversation between customer and clerk. Any "skill" or discretion in the job may lie in being the "welcoming" voice at the end of a telephone, something for which women are supposedly well suited. Much is made of the importance of interpersonal skills as components in overall life skills that are deemed necessary for working in the IS. But there has been little debate about whether and how, if at all, these skills can be acquired or whether they simply come naturally to certain people—women in particular. In the past, essentialist notions about the skill that women possess (such as nimble fingers) have often been used to justify their employment in particular kinds of extremely rapid manual and usually menial work. If it is similarly to be asserted that women have a particular aptitude for handling customers because of their interpersonal skills, then perhaps these skills should be recognized and rewarded as having a particular value, and mechanisms for transmitting them explored. This is an issue to which policy makers must turn their attention in their examination of the skills that workers need to adapt to the IS. It is also necessary if the skill requirements of the IS are not to be construed in a sexist manner that discriminates against both men and women in different ways.

As Cornford, Gillespie, and Richardson point out in their chapter, the relocation of work can have significant benefits for the regional development of less favored regions if combined with policies that are designed to enhance the overall competence of the region—its ability to learn and to develop autonomously. The difficulty lies with inward investment patterns in which capital is simply footloose and there is no opportunity for real learning transfer into the region so that it may begin to develop a coordinated approach—involving local institutions and actors—to local innovation and economic development. The same may be said of the relocation of women's work in the IS. Too often, it is predicated on inward investment that is not geared to transferring lasting expertise to the women who work in the industries that relocate. Rather, work relocation strategies are based on, among other things, the employment of women with suitable skills at suitably low costs. ICTs are generally critical to these strategies and allow companies to reorganize and relocate work in very efficient ways, but without attending to the long-term human development prospects of their female labor force.

For example, in the clothing industry, as we have already seen, ICTs are critical to the marketing, production, and employment strategies of the manufacturers and therefore to their use of female labor. ICT networks are used to monitor market demand and enable companies to coordinate international production based on this intelligence. Some companies coordinate production through the use of dedicated satellite links that maintain electronic and video-conferencing links with suppliers and customers. Other global players use computerized systems to keep track of work in progress in all of their factories and to control the overall volume of production on a global basis. In highly automated companies, computer-aided design, computer-controlled cutting technologies, robotics, and systems of conveyors automate the process of design, making and cutting patterns and handling and cutting materials.

The example of Benetton is now well-known, and its subcontracting practices have already been considered in this chapter. ICTs are also vital to the Benetton operation in marketing, distribution, designing, and pattern laying and cutting—rather than assembly operations. At the Italian headquarters is a computer that is linked to an electronic cash register in every Benetton shop; those at a great distance (e.g., Tokyo and Washington) are linked via satellite. Every outlet transmits detailed information on sales daily, and production is continuously and flexibly adjusted to meet the preferences revealed in the market. Benetton produces entirely to the orders received from the shops.

These innovations mean that companies like Benetton can improve the efficiency of subcontracting or locating their operations overseas and, at the same time, improve the cost-competitiveness of their domestic operations. The location of their operations can be very finely organized according to the imperatives of the market and the type of labor required. The result has been to reduce their reliance on the female labor of the Third World, with new factories there showing a decrease in employment due to "modernization." Garment companies have now begun to reverse the international sexual division of labor and stay close to their markets. Western and Japanese companies alike are disinvesting from the Third World and shifting to domestic producers. Even offering cheap labor, it would seem, provides no guarantee of employment security for women.

Indeed, the move back to the West has served to reproduce the conditions of work traditionally associated with the "rag trade." The labor force employed in European garment manufacturing is predominantly female and largely from migrant and ethnic minority groups—African, Tunisian, Moroccan, Cypriot, Turkish, Indian, Pakistani, Bangladeshi, and Vietnamese women. In Europe, these women are concentrated in particular regions within individual countries and in congested inner-city areas, or garment districts. They usually live in the immediate vicinity of the factories and may do subcontract work in their own homes at very low rates of pay. Despite the high levels of capital investment in the industry, and the application of advanced technologies throughout the production and support functions of firms, there seems to be little by way of IS expertise transfer to the women who work within the industry. Their work remains very insecure and poorly paid. They endure poor working conditions, and there seems to be little interest in enhancing their position or skills. On the face of it, many are working in the microbusinesses (very small companies of one or two people) that are held up to represent one of the major engines of growth in the IS. The reality, however, is that these are often simply their own front rooms that serve as their workplaces. Social policy for the IS certainly must recognize the importance of the small firms sector. But it must also recognize that the promotion of small firms for their own sake is not a sufficient condition to ensure a vibrant form of human and economic development characterized by learning, innovation, and entrepreneurship. Policy also has to attend to issues of dependency, expertise transfer, and pay and working conditions if some small firms are not simply to be sweatshops for the marginalized groups in European societies.

The relocation of women's work also takes place across national boundaries, and this is one of the most obdurate challenges facing European social policy for the IS. Clearly, frontiers cannot be thrown around the European Union as

far as capital investment is concerned, and, in any case, international companies have little respect for the boundaries of nation–states. However, the export of jobs out of Europe continues to exercise policy makers concerned with
the 18 million and rising registered unemployed in the fifteen member states
of the European Union. With the development of the IS, not only are manufacturing jobs moved overseas but so too are white-collar, professional, and
clerical. The software industry is a noteworthy example. It is one of the industries of the IS that were hoped would represent a major source of new employment generation. In software production, the recent tendency has been to
export jobs to the developing countries, particularly India, China, Mexico,
Hungary, and Israel. As in textiles and clothing, outsourcing to software development centers in these countries has allowed the industry to cope with fluctuating markets and labor requirements. (The industry refers to this strategy as
"smartsourcing.") Company management in Europe and the United States
continues to control the conduct of software development projects but uses
employees overseas as programmers working to their own requirements and
design specifications. The use of "offshore" labor for data entry in CD-ROM
development and updating is common (Probert and Hack, n.d.). Telecommunications technologies facilitate the transmission of specifications and completed
work between Western client companies and their overseas subcontractors.

In this industry, there is widespread use of female programmers; women are
deemed extremely suitable for this work. They are attractive because (1) the
price of labor power is much lower than in the West, (2) productivity is often
higher than in Western companies, and (3) they are excellently qualified at the
same time. Countries like India have a ready pool of female labor available for
software work, consisting of workers who are well educated, English speaking,
and technically proficient. Here again, in an industry in which the timely delivery of work is becoming increasingly critical to the maintenance of market
share, offshore programming labor compares very favorably with Western labor.

Offshore processing has also been adopted by a wide variety of service industries and affects a range of clerical functions performed largely by women.
For many years the publishing industry has been sending manuscripts overseas
for typesetting and printing. This has been greatly facilitated by ICT networks,
which allow material to be transmitted very rapidly and reliably. The
Anglophone publishing industry tends to use typesetters and printers in Southeast Asia because of their English-language skills. The Francophone industry
sends work to the Maghreb countries of northern Africa, equally because the
requisite language skills are to be found there.

Benefits from the relocation of work accrue to any company whose business has a high information processing content. Automatic call distribution (ACD) systems route customer inquiries to regional processing centers that are centrally controlled—a virtual single office. The service to the customer is identical regardless of which site answers the customer's call, and national staff rosters detail the number of staff required at any site at any time.

The relocation of clerical work done by women is not limited to the private sector. Locating administrative offices in out-of-town settings, and sometimes outsourcing their functions, is now widespread within public sector administrations. Tax and local government functions have been relocated in the United Kingdom, most notably to sites in northern England and Scotland. The work in these offices, entering information into a computer database, is often routinized. In some offices the work is a little more varied, as staff also deal with telephone queries and handle inquiries from members of the public, again by means of automated telecommunications routing systems. But, in relation to similar developments in Australia, Probert and Hack argue that the application of new technology, in combination with the back office nature of the work and the division of labor, means that most workers do not need to understand the significance of their tasks or their place in the overall process. Although tasks have been automated, this has not been done in a way that expands the knowledge and skills of the workforce. In addition, there is a considerable degree of temporary contracting that is reducing job satisfaction there. However, the women employed in such environments are often grateful for the employment opportunities provided, usually because of the lack of alternatives in their local economies.

Finally, any discussion of the relocation of women's work must address the much discussed phenomenon of teleworking. Teleworking has been at the center of the debate about the European IS, perhaps because it provides such a clear example of the way in which work could develop under the IS. The case of teleworking seems to make the IS—in other ways still very notional and abstract—a tangible reality. It is perhaps for this reason that teleworking has also been at the center of European policy making for the IS. It was emphasized in the Bangemann Report (CEC 1994a) as one of the key developments needed to bring about the European IS, and the Commission has supported a range of teleworking pilot actions to this end. Despite this, teleworking, particularly teleworking from home (with which I am concerned here), remains in its infancy in the European Union. It is often jokingly remarked that there are more people researching the teleworking phenomenon than there are actual teleworkers. Nevertheless, it has important potential implications for what we can expect of women's work in the IS, for two reasons. First, it, like other forms of labor, is characterized by sexual division. Across the European Union, there is a conventional pattern of occupational segregation in teleworking: women who telework are mainly secretarial and administrative workers while men who telework tend to work in occupations like consultancy and computing (Huws, Podro, and Arvanitaki 1996). The only work that is equally divided between men and women is translation. Otherwise teleworking preserves the sexual division of labor prevalent in the wider society.

Second, teleworking is sometimes promoted as if it offers people the opportunity to participate in the labor market who might not otherwise be able to do so. It is often suggested that social groups like women with domestic responsibilities and the disabled will gain better access to the labor market by dint of teleworking. In their *Final Report,* the High Level Expert Group (HLEG 1997) question the viability of this approach to teleworking; from the point of view of efficient working, they argue, it is not feasible to have women teleworking and child minding at the same time. From the point of view of this discussion, we might also question whether it is good for women personally or for their families if they use teleworking as a means to combine employment with child care.

Men and women are propelled into teleworking for very different reasons. Men often become self-employed teleworkers after having been made redundant from their jobs or in order to increase their productivity; women take up teleworking in order to combine child care with work, since affordable child care is not available in many European countries. Survey after survey reports child care as women's central motivation for taking up teleworking, whereas it is simply not a motivation for men. And due to these differing motivations, teleworking is experienced differently by men and women because of the gender identity of the domestic sphere, which makes women's presence at home seem "natural." Women mention domestic responsibilities as a prime consideration in working from home, whereas men treat the home as a place to be used exclusively for work during working hours.

As chapter 10 by Haddon and Silverstone in this volume shows, teleworking confirms men's and women's different relationships to the domestic sphere. Teleworking also fuses women's domestic labor with their paid labor. It is often promoted by employers as allowing women to assume the double burden of paid work and domestic responsibilities. Yet the double burden is not eliminated, nor is the domestic division of labor undermined in any way. Women would bear the two types of labor every day of their lives anyway, and teleworking appears at first glance to ease this burden. However, the matter is less straightforward than this. Many women find it very difficult to separate their paid labor from their domestic labor when they telework; they are constantly torn in several directions as they try to juggle the demands of home, children, and work that do not neatly dovetail with one another. There is evidence of self-employed teleworkers silencing crying children by locking them out of the workroom when potential clients telephone and keeping their mobile telephones nearby even at mealtimes in case someone calls with new business. A study conducted among a group of German women found that teleworking precipitated personal crises for most of the women, who were struggling vainly to balance work and home life. To cope with this double burden, teleworking women with children work extremely diverse and unpredictable hours, as they seize opportunities when their children are at school or in bed to work without interruptions.

IMPLICATIONS FOR WOMEN IN THE IS

What implications do these developments hold for the work of women in the information society? What are the gender dynamics of contemporary IS developments? What will be the prospects for female employees—fast becoming the most significant group in the labor markets of the European Union—to benefit from these developments? Will they be able to develop the skills and expertise that, we are told, will be central to work in the information society and will separate the haves from the have-nots, the "knows" from the "know-nots"?

In relation to teleworking, the central concern of E.U. social policy is to ensure that self-employed teleworkers do not fall through the net that protects the employment conditions and social security status of employees. The policy priority is with harmonizing the rights of all teleworkers, regardless of employment status. But how relevant is this priority to the needs and requirements of female teleworkers working from home and coping with the juggling acts described above? Perhaps teleworking policy should also focus on child care arrangements for teleworkers and on the sites in which teleworking is carried out. If women are not to be forced into teleworking for lack of child care provision, then proper child care has to be provided. Similarly, if teleworking is to be done effectively away from domestic demands, then proper teleworking environments have to be developed. And if female teleworkers are to have access to a wider choice of employment opportunities, then training is vital to keep them from being marginalized by the remoteness of their work status.

In general terms, European policy approaches to work in the IS emphasize the importance of flexibility—in organizations, in working, and in skills. Flexibility is of paramount importance in helping organizations respond rapidly and innovatively to external circumstances, and it is critical to the development of Europe's competitive strength in the information society. The challenge is for European companies to develop *appropriately flexible* patterns of work organization; to offer their staff security and allow them to acquire expertise on the job, to benefit from training, to have access to promotion opportunities and careers, and thus to contribute in a sustained way to the continuing competitiveness of their companies (CEC 1996c). This issue is of particular salience for female employees, who form the majority of staff working in these conditions and for whom the acquisition of knowledge, as well as the provision and take-up of training and career paths, has traditionally been much more problematic than for their male counterparts.

Although there are some shining exceptions, it would seem that to date, flexible patterns of working have not on the whole offered women (or, for that matter, many men) the kinds of benefits in terms of employment security and skills development so often held up as important concomitants of flexibility. Flexibility for organizations has not generally been translated into security for employees but all too often signals the casualization of their work and their marginalization within the labor force.

There is no intrinsic objection to flexibility and its associated innovations. Indeed, when correctly formulated as a policy for social inclusion rather than solely for economic competitiveness, it could generate positive benefits to women workers. For example, flexibility of working time is a development that could very well benefit many employees, particularly women. In this society of "work-rich" and "work-poor" those who are in employment are working longer and longer hours than ever before. For both sexes, the arguments for reducing the time spent at work are compelling. These arguments are particularly compelling for women, given the amount of unpaid labor in the home that they continue to perform without a matching effort from their partners.

Moving away from full-time work to other working arrangements could therefore be extremely helpful to people, women in particular, who wish to organize their paid employment to fit in with their domestic demands or reconcile their working lives with their private lives in a better way. The German automotive industry is currently experimenting in some very promising ways with working hours. Although not addressing female employees directly, they show how working hours and shifts could be radically readdressed in the interests of employers meeting fluctuating patterns of customer demand on the one hand, and employees reconciling home and work on the other hand. Bosch (1995) has similarly proposed a system of annualized working hours in which work is organized in a variety of different ways in order to offer, for example, a four-day week or blocks of time off distributed over the year. The dominant pattern of nonfull-time employment for women in many European countries today is, however, part-time work. There are a number of challenges to be addressed by policy makers and employers alike to keep part-time work from becoming work casualization.

First, it is important that part-time staff do not forego the levels of remuneration and employment protection that full-time workers enjoy. Women, who dominate part-time and precarious jobs, are currently concentrated in the low-paid jobs in the European Union; a woman is three times more likely to be poorly paid than a man. Although regimes of employment protection are steadily being extended from full-time to part-time work, pay for part-time work remains comparatively low, and part-time workers are relatively poorly represented in negotiations between the social partners. Increasingly, wages are being determined by individual performance rather than by collective agreement, which carries risks for part-time workers. Even though some member states have statutory minimum wage levels, there is no European Union–wide agreement on this. There is a very urgent need for policy makers to address ways of protecting part-time workers from poverty, so that women do not suffer disproportionately from workplace developments in the IS but can take up these forms of employment where they offer real benefits to employees and employers alike. It may be that setting a minimum wage is the most appropriate way of ensuring this.

Second, there may be difficulties inherent in ensuring the same career and personal development for part-timers as for full-timers, unless explicit attention is paid to this issue. This arises partly from the lack of work continuity that part-timers have and partly from the fact that in many organizations, career development rests upon being visible, making contacts, and being available. These networking activities are not straightforward for part-time workers, and there is a danger that they are excluded from the career paths open to full-time employees. Access to training and promotion prospects needs to be provided to part-time employees. As employers develop human resource development strategies for them, they need to be aware of the more subtle ways in which they may lose out in the career stakes.

Despite these provisions, part-time work is often by its very nature not work in which there are prospects, for in some organizations it is reserved for routine work requiring little skill or expertise. Much checkout work in the large retail multiples has become very routine, simply passing goods over barcode readers as rapidly as possible. The sole training component of such work involves increasing the speed at which the operator is able to process items, and some organizations train employees in precisely this area. The expertise component of this work is therefore very slight indeed, and, in the longer term, with the development of self-billing by customers and teleshopping, much of this work may be eliminated altogether. In smaller retail outlets and independent companies, the level of expertise and knowledge required for the work is much greater, as the employee may be involved in a much greater variety of tasks, with some responsibility, for example, for ordering stock, dealing with suppliers, and balancing accounts. The options that exist for human resource development within this sector are therefore unclear but will ultimately depend on the patterns of work organization that come to dominate in the sector. This of course also varies across the European Union. In some member states, this type of low-grade work offers employees few prospects for personal development. In others, particularly the Nordic countries, where the systems of social protection are very advanced, the status and prospects of women working in these type of jobs, whether part-time or full-time, is no different. Part-time workers are therefore less likely to forfeit their earning power or career prospects.

Given that various forms of flexible employment are both growing and being positively promoted by E.U. policy makers, the policy challenge is to ensure that in the IS, women workers benefit from its growth in career and human resource development terms. Systems of work organization and working time that simply fracture the contact between employee and workplace should be avoided. All forms of work, whether full-time or not, need to be designed to offer human development prospects. The same issue is raised for women in relation to the relocation of work in the IS. The outsourcing of activities and the delocalization of jobs involve the danger of separating jobholders from the organizational context in which they work and preventing them from gaining the expertise and personal contacts necessary to progress within their organization.

The best illustration of this point is the call center. Call centers represent a growing organizational form in the European IS that is used by many different industries for many different types of work, ranging from routine financial information processing to skilled language work and information technology advice. As we have seen, the industries that utilize female labor tend to be those in which delocalized work in call centers and back offices is very routine. What are the prospects for expertise development and career enhancement in these settings? Aside from progressing to the position of call center supervisor or manager, where are the opportunities for undertaking a variety of tasks, as multiskilling discourse suggests employees must do? Are there prospects for call center staff to learn and undertake a range of activities, to use their initiative in the course of their work, and to come into contact with colleagues and other staff over substantive work issues through which they might learn?

This issue touches at the heart of the information society discourse most prevalent in the European Union. To what extent does women's work in the information society offer the opportunity for expertise development and for on-the-job learning? Both of these are important elements of policy thinking on the IS, and much effort has been devoted to articulating ways of effecting lifelong learning. What role does work play in this process? Is there any contradiction between the routinization of work in sectors in which women are strongly represented, resulting in little opportunity for skill development, and the exhortation upon employees to engage in lifelong learning? As Ducatel and colleagues argue in chapter 7 in this volume, lifelong learning and employability are not simply the responsibility of the individual employee in the abstract. Surely it is also incumbent upon organizations to promote the learning of their employees?

If the information society is really to be a learning society for workers as well as organizations, work needs to be designed and organized in a way that offers opportunities for training, inside and outside the organization. There should be opportunities for learning on the job and developing expertise that can be transferred between different functions and activities. Employing organizations, together with training agencies and educational providers, have a major responsibility to ensure that these opportunities exist. Public policy makers have a responsibility to attend to the social protection and wider social policy aspects of the IS. They can do this by legislating where appropriate (perhaps on minimum wage levels) and providing for social security, welfare, and child care systems to support women so that they are not ghettoized in low-paid work for want of other opportunities. The opportunities for women employees themselves to develop their skills and prospects as members of the IS at the moment do not seem very widespread. But the potential is great and there are many ways in which flexible forms of work organization could be used to their advantage. Whether or not they will be so used depends on social policy decisions, not on technological trajectories.

NOTES

1. They have been much more central to agricultural activity, though the importance of this sector in the economies of most European Union countries is greatly reduced from the importance that it had in the past.

2. See, for example, the OECD conference paper *Employment and Growth in the Knowledge-Based Economy* (Paris: OECD) and the E.U. 1996 conference, Lifelong Learning for the Information Society. The year 1996 was designated European Year of Lifelong Learning.

3. See "Tomorrow's Second Sex," *Economist*, 28 September 1996.

4. Equally, the position and experiences of women in the employment sphere are derived from wider social relations—of the family, of the state and its policies (e.g., on child care and welfare benefits), of the education system and the provision of training.

5. Fifty percent of unemployed women are long-term unemployed, compared with 48 percent of men (CEC 1996c). Given the disparities in their labor market participation rates, this presents a disproportionate unemployment burden on the female workforce.

6. "Atypical work" is something of a misnomer, suggesting that nonfull-time, nonlifetime employment is the norm from which other forms of employment diverge. In the case of women's employment, this is not an accurate representation, since women have historically been much more likely than men to work in a variety of nonfull-time arrangements, usually in order to reconcile their domestic responsibilities with their paid employment. "Flexible employment" is equally problematic because it is a highly ideological term that implies a neutrality in these developments and conceals the fact that, to date at least, they have predominantly been implemented to the benefit of employers and to the detriment of employees (Pollert 1988).

7. Downsizing as a strategy is now being seriously questioned, particularly where it results in a slash-and-burn approach to the organization. The hemorrhaging of expertise leaves the company unable to grow or to respond innovatively to new circumstances. In chapter 3 of this volume Hepworth and Ryan show that management is beginning to recognize that the accumulated knowledge held in a company is one of its most important assets and that downsizing can seriously hamper its ability to operate effectively.

7

Toward the Learning Labor Market

Ken Ducatel, Hanne Shapiro, Teresa Rees, and Claudia Weinkopf

It is now widely recognized that traditional passive labor market measures (such as income supplements for the unemployed) can do little to solve the structural mismatches that underlie Europe's chronic unemployment problem. Thus, European policy makers have increasingly looked toward more active labor market policies (ALMPs) such as training, help and guidance services, job placement, and subsidies. ALMPs are seen as especially important in combating long-term and structural unemployment because they help the workforce adapt to structural change, one of the key drivers of which currently is the introduction of new information and communication technologies (ICTs). These technologies are associated with fundamental changes in sectoral structure, with the emergence of new products and processes, and associated changes in work organization skill requirements. The sheer scale and pervasiveness of these changes have led to a widespread belief that we are entering a qualitatively different system of industrial organization in which ICTs are a defining feature of the new economic paradigm—the information society (IS). Whether or not we accept this belief, the scale of adoption of these new technologies merits examining these active labor market policies to see how they might be deployed to meet the structural economic and occupational changes associated with the IS.

ACTIVE LABOR MARKET POLICIES: WHAT WORKS?

Active labor market policies are programs or initiatives, usually funded from governmental sources, that actively promote the labor market position of unemployed people. In the European Union, the most significant of these measures, in terms of the proportion of total spending, is training (CEC 1996e). Such training aims to increase or adapt the skills of unemployed people (and, in some cases, people at risk of unemployment) in order to help them meet changing skill demands in the labor market. The second main form of intervention is wage subsidies, which encourage employers to take on extra staff and so enable unemployed people to stay in contact with the labor market. The longer anyone remains unemployed the lower his or her chance of getting a job. Job placements or work-based internships have a similar function, except that the employer may not have to contribute a top-up wage at all. Job guidance (or job search assistance) tries to improve the efficiency of the labor market by helping employers find appropriate workers and vice versa. In many cases these services attempt to "match" the labor pool to employment demands by recommending a battery of training or work experience measures to job seekers.

ALMPs, therefore, are directly relevant to policies that aim to modernize the labor market for the IS. The emphasis on training and retraining in such measures would seem to upgrade the general qualification level of the workforce. Work experience and job subsidy programs may allow people to get hands-on experience with the new technologies that otherwise would have been unavailable to them. Public employment services (PES) can direct job seekers toward opportunities for training in the new technologies, place trained workers in work, and help educators and training providers meet emerging skill demands. At the same time, the application of telematics to job matching services should lead to higher efficiency on the part of PES and therefore in the labor market overall. ICTs might also be used to reach out to groups in society that are at a disadvantage in gaining access to jobs. For instance, ICTs can be used to provide training, work experience, and, ultimately, new forms of work to disabled people. ICT-based skill development programs might attract demotivated youths who are put off by traditional classroom training because of its similarity to school. ICTs offer flexible opportunities for autonomous learning, which allow people to study at a time, place and pace appropriate to their individual needs. They open up a much large range of learning options to people in remote areas.

High hopes for the implementation of ALMPs for the IS furnish the backdrop for an examination of the impact of ALMPs and to gain some perspective on the role and effectiveness of ALMPs in overall terms.[1] We are concerned about studies (mainly based on evaluations of programs in the United States, Canada, the United Kingdom, and Scandinavia) that show training, work experience, and job subsidy schemes to have poor or negative effects on the employability and wages of participants (Fay 1996; OECD 1993a, 1996b, 1996c; Robinson 1996).

Regarding training measures, the OECD (1993a) noted, "For the broadly targeted subgroup of programme, the overall impression is most troubling. . . . it gives remarkably meagre support of a hypothesis that such programmes are effective" (p. 58).

Similarly, wage subsidies and work experience schemes have been found to suffer from heavy "deadweight" (participants would have found a job anyway) costs of up to 90 percent (OECD 1996b). In the Irish Employment Incentive Programme deadweight was found to be as high as two-thirds of participants (OECD 1993a). Also, subsidy schemes need careful formulation and control. In Finland, for example, employers systematically laid off workers at the end of the subsidy period, and the scheme now only applies to permanent hires (OECD 1996c). Furthermore, in some E.U. countries there has been a shift of policy from training to work experience, following concern that much of the training being offered was not really used for skill acquisition but merely as a means of renewing entitlement to benefit (OECD 1996c).

Overall, the only ALMP intervention that appears to produce consistently positive results is job search assistance (sometimes combined with other labor market measures) (Fay 1996; OECD 1996b). Job Search Assistance (JSA) comprises a battery of techniques to help unemployed people find, apply for, and get into work including initial screening, activation interviews, reemployment bonuses, and so on. Such services might be expected to increase in significance as a result of a turbulent labor market in which employment contracts have become more uncertain and of shorter duration and in which there is the ongoing technological change associated with the information society. In such circumstances JSA may be increasingly important in assisting a smooth passage through more and more common transitions between periods of education, training, employment, and unemployment. An efficient labor market will depend on job seekers being able to make informed choices based on personalized advice and guidance as well as the provision of information on job vacancies, training opportunities, and so on.

For these reasons, JSA, and especially guidance services, might be seen as a core component of labor interventions. In this context, it is interesting to note that JSA is also often seen as a relatively low-cost type of ALMP. For instance, an evaluation of the U.S. Employment Service (Jacobson 1994) indicated that such assistance can aid equity because it concentrates on applicants less able to find jobs on their own. It can also be very cost-effective, as each placement costs only $80 and saves on average 1.25 weeks of unemployment benefit payment of around $200. Similarly, P. Robinson (1996) calculated the battery of measures used by the U.K. Public Employment Service (PES) to aid placement. Jobclubs, Jobplan, and Restart are not only low cost at £100–200 (US$150–300) per head as opposed to £2,000–3,000 (US$3,000–5,000) for more expensive measures (table 7.1) but, he argues, seem to carry no risk of any adverse side effects.

It has to be said that the benign nature and relative low cost of JSA depends on how targets for JSA services are set up and the balance of activities that such service undertakes. For instance, if job advisers are presented with placement targets, there is a risk that they will engage in "cream skimming," that is, selecting the easiest-to-place job seekers in order to raise their own performance. By contrast, counseling and advising a very hard-to-place unemployed person may require long-term, intensive counseling, as well as customized support measures from more expensive interventions such as training, job placements, and so on. Counseling, where there is a commitment to transforming the labor market position of an unemployed person, contrasts starkly to the other end of the spectrum, where there is a one-off interview to control access to benefit or to channel a claimant into a low-cost mass program of "labor market activation." Nevertheless, simple screening interviews certainly can save a lot of wasted time and search if the counselor is able to find the counselee a quick way back into the labor market (for an elaboration of these points, see Rees and Bartlett 1996; Rees, Bartlett, and Watts 1996).

Overall, these results do not mean that ALMPs offer few potential benefits but that they should be approached with care and realism. First, all the reviews we have seen underline the need to get the role of ALMPs in perspective. For instance, "the underlying hypothesis is not that, once their effectiveness has been enhanced, ALMPs on their own would be able to cure unemployment" (OECD 1996b, 3) or "labor market programs have a role to play, but a modest one" (Robinson 1996, 4). In particular, ALMPs have to take their place within a coherent policy framework of labor market regulation, vocational education, and training systems and complementary and supportive passive benefits systems. Second, as a result of these recent reviews of evaluation studies across a range of OECD countries (especially the United States, Canada, the United Kingdom, and Scandinavia) some important lessons are emerging (table 7.2). At least some of the poor performance of ALMPs can be tackled through better design and targeting of programs and for their performance to be assessed against

Table 7.1   Costs of Active Labor Market Policies in the U.K.

Intervention	No. of places (000s)	Cost/place £ (US$)	
Employment Service programs			
Job clubs	257	196	(317)
Job finder grants	5	181	(293)
Job interview guarantee	300	6	(10)
Job plan	250	127	(206)
Job review workshop	40	80	(130)
Job search seminar	65	75	(121)
One-to-one	10	no data	(no data)
Restart courses	144	98	(159)
Travel to work interview	55	40	(65)
Work trials	20	110	(178)
Workwise	10	no data	(no data)
Training programs			
Training for work	280	2,475	(4,012)
Work programs			
Community action	50	1,860	(3,015)
Recruitment subsidies			
Workstart	1	2,340	(3,794)
Youth programs			
Youth training	232	2,831	(4,590)

Source: Calculated by Robinson 1996 from Employment Department Group, Departmental Report.

appropriate targets that do not encourage "cream skimming" or other perverse outcomes (box 7.1).

It is against the background of these recent results on ALMPs that the rest of our argument will be played out. First, careful targeting, monitoring, and control are emerging as fundamental design features for all categories of ALMP. These design criteria seem especially important in the context of training for the IS. Our understanding is that there is a good deal of unsystematic innovation taking place in the provision of training courses in telematics that relates rather weakly to employer and job seeker needs. In effect there is a need to look in detail at the ways in which these forms of provision are designed and implemented (targeted, monitored, accredited, etc.) as part of making sure that they have an optimal longer-term impact on employment.

Second, the requirement to target labor market policies more accurately implies the need for a careful process of matching job seekers to an appropriate

Table 7.2 What Works and What Does Not in Active Labor Market Policies

Policy Type	Helps	Does Not Help	Observations
Job search assistance	Most unemployed, especially women and single parents	Employed, people in a good labor market position	Needs careful control
Formal classroom training	Women re-entrants	Youth (unless supported by other interventions) Mature workers with low qualifications	Course should be highly related to labor market needs and give a signal that they are of high quality
On the job training	Women returners, single mothers	Youths (unless supported by other interventions)	Must meet labor market needs
Subsidies	Long-term unemployed Women returners	Youths (unless supported by other interventions)	Needs careful targeting and controls Few long run benefits
Direct job creation	Severely marginalized labor market groups		Mostly creates low-value added-jobs
Business start-up support	Men, better educated, aged 35–55		Only a few can be helped

Source: Table constructed from information in OECD 1996b.

Box 7.1 Key Program Features for Success in ALMPs

Training Courses
- Better where the courses are rationed and lead to formal qualifications that indicate quality and real attainment to employers.
- Combining measures tends to produce better outcomes.
- Payoffs for women, especially women returners, are better than for men.
- Young people tend be helped least, except in the case of the Job Corps (USA), in which success seems to be related to high-intensity counseling and a controlled environment for the intervention.
- Courses that teach technical skills tend to produce better results.
- Employer perceptions of the training are important.
- Clients and courses may be poorly matched, indicating a need for complementary support such as guidance and counseling.
- The timing of the evaluation is important, as payoffs may occur long after the training.

Subsidies
- Can be very successful if targeted at certain types of disadvantaged workers (long-term unemployed reinstated in the labor market, single mothers) especially as in these cases shuffling the queue of job seekers could be a legitimate policy goal.
- Needs careful design and targeting as well as close monitoring and adequate contact with employers to make sure that there is additionality.
- Wage subsidies can lead to the creation of dead-end jobs.

Start-up Grants
- Highly successful for a narrow segment of unemployed (well-educated men aged 35–55 seemed to benefit in one study).
- Need a pool of highly motivated individuals with good ideas.
- Involves lots of support and monitoring.
- Are better targeted at the short-term unemployed.
- May be susceptible to variations in the supporting financing systems.

Public Sector Job Creation
- Typically only really useful to the hardest-to-place job seekers.
- Can help to develop work-related skills.
- Can be a counter-cyclical policy when unemployment is not too severe.

Job Search Assistance
- "Profiling" may help target interventions more accurately, which might be important in countries with very high rates of turnover among the unemployed.
- Individual action plans have not been fully evaluated yet.
- Tends to work well for single mothers, especially with other ALMPs.
- Young people need more than JSA.

Source: Adapted from Fay 1996.

intervention (whether it be training or work experience). Given the relatively strong performance of job search assistance (as a form of ALMP), it would seem to us that a greater emphasis on labor market brokerage could yield considerable benefits. It could improve the matching of job seekers to jobs, identify gaps in the labor market, and work with job seekers to help them transform their skill profiles in order to improve their employability. Surely, information systems can support the labor market intelligence needed to achieve such labor market transformations?

SKILL NEEDS FOR THE IS

The ideal content for this section would have been a review of impact evaluations of ICT training and work experience programs that have been delivered as part of active labor market policies. Unfortunately, we have not been able to find such publications. We do know, however, that considerable resources are being pumped into such training schemes. Nevertheless, we think it is possible to identify some major strands of argumentation in the broader literature on skills. A key point is that technical competences are more easily and more effectively built upon with an already established base of education and learning. Moreover, the application of technical competences usually depends upon aptitudes and behaviors that can only be acquired directly in the workplace. In short, therefore, our argument will be that narrow technical training in the use of ICTs is probably not enough on its own. For this reason, we have serious doubts about whether technical training *on its own* should be supported by public funds as part of an active labor market policy.[2]

There are a number of dimensions to this core insight. First, in order to mobilize technical skills people need to acquire a broad educational base. Reorientation of initial education and training around the development of these broad competences is a crucial preparatory step for the IS. We consider this issue in more detail in the next section. Second, it is clear from these debates that training that is abstracted from the working environment is a lot less effective than training that takes place in a hands-on environment.

This does not mean that the existing working environment should be accepted as correct or desirable. One of the major failings in the traditional craft apprenticeship system is that it can cement working patterns that are out-of-date in terms of their technical approach and lead to the transfer of organization practices and attitudes that exclude some members of society. Such embedded practices, for instance, perpetuate systems of gender inequality in access to work opportunities.

Training measures need to make sure that trainees have a sufficiently developed grasp of the broad capacities necessary to do a job that can be extended through specific training through exposure to real-work experiences. If people receive narrow, specific training without the broad understanding of principles provided by a good basic education, then their skills will be "brittle" and they will have a limited ability to respond to technical changes, new products, new organizational patterns, and other features of the dynamic IS. At the same time, an understanding of broad principles often has no salience unless people are able to apply their learning in the workplace. Skills exist in application, not in the abstract. The most effective forms of learning include interplay between developing broad competences and understanding, specific technical knowledge, and direct experience. The aim is to promote people's ability to learn how to learn and to open up opportunities for them to actually put these capacities into practice.

A Broad Base of Education for the IS

The relationship between skill and new ICTs is complex and hotly disputed; for example, the debate over whether ICTs have an inherent tendency to drive up skill demands (see Howell and Wolff 1992; Howell 1996; Krueger 1993; Wolff 1995). Nevertheless, ICTs are associated with a shift in the balance of skills required of workers, if not a direct upgrading or deskilling. Skill is a multidimensional concept requiring the integrated deployment of a range of abilities from physical abilities (hand-eye coordination, dexterity, strength) and cognitive abilities (analytical and synthetic reasoning, numerical, and verbal abilities) to interpersonal skills (communication, supervision, leadership, team working, etc.) (Wolff 1995).

Skill is also a social construct. For instance, the wages that a group of workers can demand will depend on their claims to social status as much as to the actual cognitive complexity, dexterity, and so on, needed to complete the tasks. Many low-paying jobs actually demand highly developed and complex competences. The low rate of pay represents the relatively low status of the people who possess these skills and/or the fact that the skills have been acquired through informal mechanisms, for instance, mothers teaching their daughters to cook and sew at home. This line of argument is clearly presented in feminist critiques of concepts of skill (see Phillips and Taylor 1980; Webster 1996).

Changes of technology are not neutral in these social processes of skill transformation but tend to reflect existing power and status structures in society. Thus, whether a technology is enskilling or deskilling will to some extent depend on the social status of the main groups of users and their ability to use the new technology to enhance their status.

Nevertheless, social structures are not unchanged by new technologies. The technologies have their own characteristics that tend to replace certain components of skill more than others. For instance, tools have always provided assistance in transferring and transforming materials. The level of skill is not so much diminished but transformed as new skills evolve around the use of the new tools. In the same way, new ICTs can be seen as transferring the locus of skill requirements away from direct action into controlling the systems that perform the direct processes. Zuboff's (1988) insightful analyses into these transformations identify an increasing abstraction of work. Zuboff sees this as a shift from intuitive and experiential skills (or "sentient" skills) to "intellective" skills, which rely on codified, formal models of the processes taking place.

In terms of skill requirements, then, new ICTs reinforce demands for the ability to engage in formal reasoning and symbol manipulation. This implies a shift in the composition of skills, with physical skills losing place to cognitive skills. As formal education tends to concentrate upon developing cognitive skills rather than physical skills, an association between new technologies and increasing demands for more highly qualified people is hardly surprising. Formal education has become an increasingly important signal to employers that an employee has the cognitive ability to perform well in the work environment, whereas physical attributes are likely to decline in importance. However, cognitive abilities are not enough by themselves for a worker to work effectively. The ability to do a job depends upon an effective integration of a wide range of abilities that go beyond the immediate requirements of the technologies being used or the task in hand. For instance, in a recent synthesis of findings from Eurotecnet (1995) competencies required for work included the following:

- visualization—the capacity to mentally manipulate models
- understanding of a process—how machines function and the interaction between machines and the product
- statistical deduction
- verbal, oral, and visual communication
- individual responsibility for the product and the process
- the ability to make judgments
- the ability to combine business and technical issues.

This list includes a mix of both cognitive and interpersonal abilities that relate to a willingness to take responsibility, problem solving abilities, the ability to work with others, and the willingness and capacity to learn. Several of the categories emphasize synthetic abilities that comprise abstract cognitive abilities and interpersonal abilities.[3]

The increasing value of broad abilities (especially the ability to learn) is, perhaps, best exemplified in the continuing growth of higher education in Europe during recent years. Both students and potential employers greatly prize the broader range of abilities that students develop as undergraduates. For instance, Mason (1996) found that a degree is an indicator of above average intellectual capacity and creative problem solving, in combination with good interpersonal skills, teamworking, and communication skills. Many employers also think that increased recruitment of workers trained to a higher level will increase industrial performance. Consequently, graduates are often recruited over and above people with lower-level but more directly related technical qualifications because they offer a broader range of personal and business-related skills and the ability "to move with the times."[4]

In addition, there are good reasons to believe that a mix of competences across these broad categories will be increasingly necessary as ICTs continue to diffuse and develop, first, because the rate of change in the technological base means that each hot new area of technical skill has a relatively short life cycle. For instance, in the computer industry there have been distinct cycles of skill demand, which Virgo (1995) argues correspond roughly to the following schema:

1970–1980: batch/mainframe skills
1980–1990: transaction processing mainframe skills
1990–2000: low bandwidth network system skills
2000++: broadband networks and multimedia skills

As each new wave of technology has swept over the industry, there have been rapid changes in the technical skills required of professional staff in the industry, indicating that specific technical skills can have a relatively short shelf life. Also, the growth of networks and decentralized computing (client-server systems) increases the integration of systems in ways that cut across existing professional disciplines. Yet the cultural backgrounds and disciplines of computer professionals remain disparate. Network engineers understand the effects of delay, the need for resilience, the need for reliability. IT and software engineers believe in error correction. Neither has the ability to use intelligently the results of data mining techniques because it requires the operational/business skills of midmanagers. The trend toward integration means not only new forms of cross-skilling but also different patterns of work that that bring together different specialists. Decentralized computing also weakens the demand for narrow specialists in favor of those who can work with end users. "Ex-users," who combine technical competence with an understanding of the business, may be more valuable in many user support roles than technical specialists.[5] As Virgo phrases it, "juvenile cybernerds" have less value in a client-server environment than people with good interpersonal skills.

If these trends are true for computer professionals, they are even more likely to hold in less technical occupations. Work involves the mastery of abstract cognitive competences in combination with interpersonal skills in order to make the person valuable in a real work situation! Training for specific tasks (such as the use of a particular software program) *only makes sense once it is clear that the trainee has the basic competences necessary to undertake that training and that the training is relevant to the work environment to which it is applied.* However, since constant change in technical specifications is one of the defining features of the IS, there will be a constant skills gap problem that cannot be resolved by direct, specific technical training on its own. Attempts to fill that gap through narrow training are only likely to work with people who already have a broader understanding of the principles.

Learning and Skill Acquisition by Experience

Despite the long-term rise in educational levels across Europe and the rising demand for graduate-level educational achievement, there is a feeling that the educational system is inadequate to prepare people for life and a lifetime's work in the IS.[6] Nor do current systems of provision meet the growing need for retraining and requalification. In particular, the different arenas of learning (general education, specific training, and direct experience) remain poorly integrated. Evidence of this abounds; for instance, the transition to work is still one of the major periods of risk of unemployment for young adults (CEC 1996e). This is true even for graduate recruitment, since many employers remain concerned by the lack of communication skills, business awareness, leadership, and teamworking skills (Connor 1995).

One key component of building a labor market that assists smoother and more efficient transitions between the stages of education, training, employment, and unemployment (at least for younger people) for the information society is to provide ladders and bridges between vocational education, generally regarded as lower status, and academic education (OECD 1996d). Clearly, the ambition is to "future proof" trainees by accompanying specific vocational education with the broader set of competences outlined above. This provides both the opportunity to "upgrade" to an academic qualification later and a higher chance of successfully keeping up-to-date as technologies change by referring to first principles.

But links between education and work are also needed to complete the triangle of learning. For this reason many vocational programs now seek to provide work-based learning in combination with continuing general education or, at least, vocational education with a larger general component.[7] For example, various patterns of business and education partnerships that aim to ease the transition to work have also been tried, such as workplace visits, work shadowing, teacher placement, mentoring of students by employees, adopt-a-school programs, and enterprise-in-school initiatives (OECD 1992).

ICTs open up many attractive options to link the spheres of education and work in support of more effective processes of learning (see the examples in box 7.2). The Connector Project provides a means by which highly qualified unemployed people can learn practical skills to the mutual benefit of trainees and employers. Netjob opens a door to work for people with disabilities. The home economics example shows that lack of computer experience is not a bar to using ICTs to overcome problems of access to training. It is evident from these three cases, however, that such initiatives require careful planning, high levels of support for the trainees, a close working relationship between the trainers and the sponsoring firms, well-developed procedures to ensure quality control, and very careful content design to ensure that the learning and the work experience are mutually reinforcing.[8] In each case, also, the technology certainly allows new activities and forms of training to happen, but the value of the learning is critically dependent upon the fact that real skills are developed because the learning takes place in a context of use!

The difficult balancing act between the three main arenas of learning (academic, vocational, and experiential) is clearly a crucial component of developing the skill base of the IS for new entrants to the labor market. However, it is equally clear that we face the even greater challenge in helping the existing labor force to meet the challenge of the IS. Workers will have to be given the chance and the motivation to learn (and to learn how to learn), and the engagement of enterprises will be crucial to achieving this transformation. It is worth considering some recent ideas on the nature of learning through experience (or learning by doing).

Employee training often has disappointing results. It may not be clear to employers whether their investment in training is optimal in achieving higher productivity, higher quality, or even higher worker motivation and loyalty. At the extreme, in smaller firms and in many traditional sectors there is a well-documented underinvestment in training. But even in technology-intensive environments where there is a recognized need to continually upgrade worker know-how there is often underinvestment in training for new technologies and new staff. These trends are especially true in down cycles in the economy, and consequently severe "skill shortages" appear during the next upswing (for the computer industry, see the arguments in Virgo 1995; for engineering, see Senker 1992).

We do not intend to rehearse well-known discussions of the effectiveness and barriers to worker training. Our intention here is simply to pick out some key features of importance to the development of our argument:

- Employers are often reluctant to invest in training because they are not sure that workers will remain long enough for them to recoup their investment. Underinvestment in worker training is higher for people on temporary or fixed-term contracts. Higher qualified workers tend to receive more training than less well-qualified and lower-status workers.
- Lower-qualified workers and workers with lower social status (such as women) tend to receive less training; what training they get is more likely to be short-term and narrowly cast, for instance, only dealing with the direct task or changes in health and safety legislation.
- It is difficult to devise objective criteria for the measurement of success in training outcomes, since often these are the subjective responses of individuals or their immediate supervisors.
- Much formal worker training is inefficient at developing skills as it mimics educational practices, using classrooms to engage in the transfer of codified factual information. The transfer of information under these circumstances is highly incomplete because much of it is not relevant and much is simply not absorbed.
- Training courses are often static packages with little customization to meet the needs of the individuals being trained and little attempt to develop learning through experiencing the ideas that are being conveyed.
- When the workers return to their post, often nothing has changed in their work environment to allow them to put their new knowledge into practice; thus much of the training effect dissipates quickly.

Recent U.S. literature on training shows interest in "high performance workplaces," establishments that try to commit their workers more fully to the objectives of the firm so that more of their creativity, ingenuity, problem solving abilities, and energies are given to the firm. To motivate their workers in this way, firms are encouraging greater participation by the workforce in decision making, providing information, extra benefits, and so on. Kling's (1995) review of the research in this area suggests a positive relationship between the use of

Box 7.2 Training, Learning, and Working with IT

Case 1: The Connector

The Danish project connector aims to get 25 unemployed masters of arts into work as project managers in the areas of information management and human resource management in small firms. The project is a cooperative effort between the public employment service, some small firms, and two training providers-one public and one private.

A period of training is followed by a six-month placement in a firm. The training builds knowledge of strategic management and innovation and ICT use in small businesses. Students explore business start-ups using a PC simulation, groupware, and access to external databases. They can draw on training providers and managers as resource persons, but the trainees also function as consultants when they have specific skills relevant to the process. In the placement they work on a project specified with the firm's manager. The firms and the trainees have access to on-line communication tools, so that the trainee and the company can access the training providers and other trainees for advice.

Case 2: Netjob

Netjob prepares disabled people for work in multimedia, Web, and database designer or information brokerage. The trainees either have a background in computing— but no formal qualifications, or qualifications in other subjects—but no job. Through project-based learning they acquire technical, conceptual, and design expertise on the new media.

The course runs for sixteen months with training and internship in private companies. The trainees work in close cooperation with the host firm to specify a project for their internship, and acquire specific expertise needed in this project. Parallel to Netjob, Netjob Agency has been formed to act as private employment agency where companies can contract Netjobbers to carry out specific ICT tasks either as teleworkers or on their premises.

Case 3: On-Line Home Economics

Local community home economics counselors need to know about changes in regulations and food production methods. Distance, family, and work obligations make it difficult for many (mainly women aged 30–55) to attend an on-site course.

A course ran over two and a half months that was action orientated and involved the completion of a project in the community; for example, working with a school catering service on a new nutritional policy. To make the course accessible to the students, computer conferencing and on-line databases were used from home and from work. The students worked on-line in project groups, with assignments and on-line guidance.

Although none of the counselors had prior computer experience, evaluations were good compared to traditional courses. The course had been accessible and convenient. The training was directly relevant to their work. And the use of the media forced the trainees to be more reflective and articulate when they formulated questions or answers in their work group or to a teacher.

Source: Adapted from case studies undertaken by the Center for Competence Development and Media Integration, Danish Technological Institute, Aarhus, Denmark.

these new work practices and productivity, especially where they are used in a mutually reinforcing manner in the form of work systems (see also Osterman 1994; Frezis, Herz, and Harrigan 1995; Johnson, Baldwin, and Diverty 1996; U.S. Department of Labor 1993). It is interesting to note that there is no systematic development of a "model of high performance workplace." Different firms are putting the different practices together in different ways with variable, if largely positive, outcomes.

The high performance workplace debate indicates that this is a complex area with no single or easy solution. However, it does indicate very strongly the value, if not necessity, of a combined approach to technological innovation, training, and work reorganization. Firms that do well are those that integrate these three managerial disciplines; it may also be that they are just generally well managed.

On the other hand, good management seems to imply success in building bridges between training, personnel, and technology strategies. Thus examining the literature on the learning organization, which arguably is an attempt to provide an overall concept for these three aspects of organizational success, seems worthwhile. The learning organization is of interest here because it implies that a key locus of learning is above the individual level among teams, departments, plants, and organizations. It also implies that organizations should look beyond reacting to or coping with changes in technologies or markets and look toward strategies to regenerate themselves and to expand as part of their philosophy (Senge 1990). Learning organizations are places "where inventing new knowledge is not a specialized activity. . . . it is a way of behaving in which everyone is a knowledge worker" (Nonaka 1991, 97).

Much of the literature on the learning organization operates at a rather abstract, even rhetorical, level. More practical approaches tend to stress the need for frameworks to systematize efforts to improve the organization's performance by converting experience into knowledge and skills for the benefit of the organization. As more of the workforce is drawn into this knowledge net, the organization benefits more from the experiences of the staff. This implies a set of practical strategies for helping workers to acquire new skills[9] such as

- carrying out the new tasks (90 percent of company managers thought this activity was of great or some importance in employees acquiring new skills)
- being given time for coaching (78 percent)
- organizing work in teams (60 percent)
- supporting cooperation across departments (59 percent)
- tailoring education and training (57 percent)
- long-term educational planning (51 percent)

- conventional classroom courses (43 percent)
- planned job rotation (31 percent)

There are several key lessons here. First, the fundamental point is that organizational learning (and therefore skill development) does not merely take place at the individual level but among groups. Second, skill development across an organization takes place in a wide variety of ways (traditional formal training playing only a minor part). Third, skill development can only be effective if it takes place in context. Fourth, the employers' approach to work organization and realization of the many different ways in which skills are acquired will affect how effective they are at mobilizing any training their workforce has already had, as well as the value employers gain from the experiences of their workers.

Summary

Recent concerns about the effectiveness of ALMP training programs are almost certainly relevant to ICT training that takes place under the banner of the information society. We know that a large amount of effort has been put into such training courses, but we do not know of any systematic attempt to evaluate their outcomes. The absence of this sort of impact evaluation is a general weakness of ALMPs, and we greatly emphasize the need for such evaluations in the case of ICT training, and for such evaluations to be widely circulated so that lessons can be diffused in this rapidly growing sphere.

In the absence of systematic published evaluations in this area, we have sought to draw on some general ideas about learning and skill acquisition that might provide guidelines for policy formation in the area of training for the IS. First, we have argued that training should take account of the need for broader competence development in order to provide a platform for the technical skills that people acquire as part of their ICT training. In particular, we argue that any training measures should take account of the need to develop complementary abilities in general level cognitive skills, interpersonal skills, and the broader understanding of general principles that underlie specific technical skills, which people acquire as part of ICT training.

We have seen that generalized (one size fits all) labor market training is not very effective. As individuals vary a lot in the degree to which they need reinforcement in complementary skills, as we discuss below, matching people to opportunities through high-quality personal guidance is likely to be a crucial step for improving the value for many of these services.

Before moving on, however, we have to note an apparent paradox in the value
of ICT access courses for participants. Such courses provide the first experience of using ICTs for many; our theory is that these courses are unlikely to
have a major positive impact in the absence of complementary skills. In some
ICT training, however, there may not be such a simple cause and effect. Such
courses have been observed to have an important positive effect on labor market
chances for certain groups, such as women returners, for a number of reasons.
Because ICTs are seen as up-to-date, progressive, and difficult, they have a more
positive image than other courses. This golden halo of ICT training is perceived
by both participants and potential employers, and it may be more important
than the actual substance of the training. Although women taking such courses
may not use ICTs directly at work, the course distinguishes them from other
job applicants and increases their self-confidence. This issue merits further investigation as it implies that there is a balance to be struck between the attractions of the technical halo of ICTs, the practical skills acquired, and the fact
that, being capital intensive, ICT training is a relatively expensive form of training provision.

Our second major point concerns the implications for ALMP training as the
compartmentalized structure of learning is rethought in response to the need
for lifelong learning. Changes here are crucial not least because most of the
workforce that will be available for work in the IS has already completed initial education. This involves nothing less than changing the culture of employers
and workers and reforming existing patterns of work organization. An essential step here is integrating ICT training into direct work experience, which is
an important way of making sure that effective learning takes place. Our next
requirement, then, is making hands-on use of ICTs in the workplace a design
criteria for ALMP training programs for the IS.

Meaningful work experience requires the active cooperation of employers.
And many employers are coming to see the need to build learning into the
routines of the organization, especially in the context of the IS, which is expected to be increasingly knowledge based. Many firms have attempted to create
high performance workplaces, but few are striving to become "learning organizations." There are three key insights here. First, learning, or skill acquisition,
takes place in social settings and is not just an individual activity. Second, learning
is an ongoing process. Third, there are many different ways of learning, of which
traditional formal training represents only a small portion. If ALMPs are to be
effective, both policy makers and employers need to embed these features of
effective learning into their practices. For employers this means finding ways
to transform work organization in order to encourage learning and human

resource development as a source of competitive advantage. It also challenges employers to rethink their views on the value and potential contribution of different types of worker, and to transform patterns of work organization so that in-built gender and race biases, which ultimately reduce productivity, can be eliminated. For policy makers, it means reexamining the systems of benefit control and administration, the guidance services, and the structure of training and work experience measures so that they support these different levels of learning.

For ALMPs there are two immediate issues from this discussion. First, it implies that for the future prosperity of Europe, policy makers should examine the scope of ALMPs in the area of training beyond remedial aid for the unemployed or "at risk" workers to a broader cross-section of those currently employed. Given the relatively high cost of effective training interventions, any policy developments in this area clearly need very close scrutiny in terms of their cost-effectiveness. Second, it implies that to be effective, training-based ALMPs need to comprise three integrated components: an impartial training needs analysis and personal action plan, well-targeted and developmental training, and directly relevant work experience. This inherently requires a close integration of action between job guidance services, trainers, and employers. Is this a tall order to achieve? One that implies a high cost per participant? Maybe so, but perhaps one that will produce higher-quality results in the longer term for individuals, enterprises, and the economy as a whole.

LABOR MARKET COORDINATION AND INFORMATION

Employment services, particularly the public employment service (PES), play a central role in any model of active labor market policy for the information society. As we have seen above, job search assistance (JSA), one of the main roles of the PES, has been found to be the one form of active labor market policy (ALMP) that produces consistently positive results. In turn, a key part of JSA, job placement, is increasingly the subject of applications of ICTs. Clearly, here is an aspect of ALMP that is directly affected by the information society. However, there are trends toward liberalization taking place that affect not only job placement and job search assistance but the whole arena of action of the PES in Europe. This also relates to the information society because it will affect the way that information flows within and between labor market institutions and because of the importance of the PES in making sure that labor market policies are delivered effectively. In this section we look at these two sides of the changes in information flows through the labor market. First, we examine the emergence of on-line job vacancy systems. Second, we treat the potential threat to the PES as the central conduit of information on the labor market that is formed by the process of liberalization.

Computer-Based Job Search Systems

As Weinkopf (1997) notes, this is an area in which there are no conclusive answers. In some countries such as Italy and Greece the systems are just being implemented while others such as Sweden have been operating computerized systems since the 1970s. In most countries, they are undergoing development; for instance, the German Stelleninformations-system (SIS) was still being diffused nationally in 1996. Computerized systems have not yet been subject to systematic cross-national inquiry. Most attention has focused on the development of vacancy information systems operated for internal use by the public employment services (PES) (e.g., OECD 1993b, 1996c, 1996e; Weinkopf 1997).

At the moment, we can see quite a wide variety of practice and philosophy from place to place centering on how open the systems are to job seekers. Access can be open, self-service systems; semiopen systems that require support from employment service staff; or closed systems that are accessible only to staff.

Closed systems are attractive to the PES because they can retain control over the placement process. This is important in controlling applications to employers so that people do not waste time applying for posts for which they are unsuited and so that employers are not inundated with applications. It means that the PES staff can provide help and advice to applicants (and employers), especially where they are trying to support people who face disadvantages in getting jobs. It also means that information flows back to the PES from staff about the situation in the labor market and the performance of the service in achieving job placements.

Semiopen systems have similar advantages in that job seekers can self-select types of jobs for which they would like to apply. But they have to go through the staff to make the application because names and addresses of employers are not revealed. Open systems are being introduced in some countries in Europe, such as Germany, where traditional adherence to equity of access and a reliable and robust guidance service have dictated that the service remain closed. Other countries, such as Norway, have a long history of self-service techniques that were developed because of the need to facilitate long-distance access of job seekers to placement services. These include a PES newspaper, free of charge telephone services, and computer terminals with occupational information. The information is accessible not only in the PES offices but also in schools, libraries, shopping centers, military bases, and so on. This sort of openness is also a political tradition in Scandinavia (OECD 1996c, 1996e). For instance, Denmark has a variety of open systems, with vacancies on billboards at local offices, TV and radio, job phone lines, and smaller "job shops" with a few staff and computers to search through vacancy lists. A recent innovation is an unmanned "job box" located in large shopping centers that has touch-screen computers for job seekers to search for positions by geographic area, occupation, and so on. It permits the printing out of details on specific vacancies. These tend to be semiopen vacancy displays that require an inquiry at the local PES office. Such open facilities are not as widely developed in Finland, but TV advertising and job kiosks in main shopping areas are used to some extent.

Irrespective of whether the information system is open or closed, job-matching systems can be operated to improve the performance of labor market policy. The spin-off benefits of such systems is considerable in terms of making the operation of the local labor market much more transparent. It also provides an opportunity to track demand and supply of skills, which in turn may be useful in designing the vocational training and on-the-job training offered in the locality. Another example of integrating labor market procedures through the use of ICTs is the practice of "profiling." A job seeker's characteristics are entered into a computer model that identifies those who are at risk of prolonged unemployment and thus qualify immediately for intensive aid (Fay 1996). A study by the U.S. Department of Labor (DOL 1995) found that this system increased placement speed by about one week. Such systems imply a proactive approach by placement staff. These "active brokering" techniques are widely used in countries such as Denmark and Finland. In Denmark the AF-MATCH database is used to select suitable candidates for vacancies on the basis of occupation, qualification, age, and experience, according to employer specification and the placement officer's judgment.

The mode of access to self-service employment systems also warrants further investigation. Most of the services are in PES offices. Others are in places where nonspecialist advice is at hand, for example, libraries, career offices, and colleges. But there are also moves to make such vacancies available via information kiosks in unsupported environments such as shopping malls, bus stations, and leisure facilities, and even on dial-up databases that can be accessed from home. It could be argued that such systems reach people who would be put off by the formality of the public employment services. It might also mean that the complementary advice and guidance services of the employment office are not accessed, with perhaps poor job matching in the labor market overall.

However, this remains to be seen, as we know of no serious attempt to examine the outcome of such different access policies.

Similarly, the relative value of on-line job services has not been adequately measured, despite the large resources that have been given to their development by the PES. The little information that does exist gives a mixed picture. User surveys in Sweden show that printed sources are more heavily used for self-service than computer terminals (500,000 consultations per week versus 50,000 computer accesses). The experience of EURES, the Pan-European system developed by the European Commission, similarly seems to attract small numbers of users, probably in this case because the number of internationally mobile job seekers is relatively small (see Weinkopf 1997 for more details). In Germany, though, the SIS tends to be used 1,500 times in a week against 5,000 visits to a typical PES office. But use can be expected to rise as computer systems become easier to use, better known, more widespread, and more efficient.

Open and semiopen systems seem to be a more natural form for private-sector on-line employment services. We are not aware of a systematic survey

Box 7.3   Private Sector On-line Recruitment of IT Professionals

The use of the Internet for recruitment is growing rapidly but from a very small base and is still mainly concentrated in the information technology sector. The main advantages are immediacy, 24-hour accessibility, the ability to link into more information than can be offered in an advertisement, and the relative low cost of wide distribution (compared to trade advertisements). Often recruitment can be linked to other information on the Web, which attracts the attention of people who are not actively searching for a new position. Costs can be low. JobServe, formed in 1995, now issues daily electronic bulletins to 22,000 subscribers, to whom registration is free, on behalf of 550 job agencies who pay £5 to £10 per day for each vacancy advertised.

On-line recruitment, though, is strongly self-selecting. This can be positive for some employers in that people using the Web to search for jobs are regarded as dynamic and up-to-date. E-mail filing of CVs also seems to be used most heavily by IT professionals with "newer skills" rather than traditional skills. The fact that access to the Net is still limited inherently limits the pool of candidates. Perhaps because of its new wave image, even in the IT sector the Net is simply not seen as appropriate. For instance, recent research by IT recruiters Delphi found that less than 7 percent of a sample of 276 organizations use the Web to recruit IT professionals, and of these only one-third thought it was a success. As with most experiences on the Internet, one of the major problems is finding the information. Job searchers often need a "trigger" to visit a site, especially if the employer is less well-known.

Source: Adapted from J. Kavanagh, "Job-Hunt in Cyberspace," *Financial Times Information Technology Supplement,* February 5, 1997, 8.

of job match databases, but several widely advertised services have been launched recently, such as People Bank (owned by the U.K. Daily Mail Group), Cyberdyne, InterWeb, Price Jamieson, Reed Personnel Services, the Danish Job Index, and Monster Board Driveway. Recently there has been much interest in the use of the Internet for recruitment. Many companies now include their Internet address in job advertisements, which offers extra information on the firm. These Web sites often include vacancy pages. Quite a few trade journals and magazines and some general circulation newspapers post situations-vacant columns on their Web sites; sometimes this information goes up ahead of the physical publication of the journal. In addition, computer systems are now used widely to locate educational opportunities across Europe and beyond (this may reflect the extensive and pioneering use of Internet and e-mail in the college and university sector). Private employment agencies are also increasingly looking to the Web as an extra avenue for recruitment. This expansion appears to be taking off from a very low level; most of the vacancies filled in this manner are IT related (see box 7.3). Nevertheless, as the example of JobServe indicates, traditional job ads and agencies may eventually find themselves under pressure because of the low cost of on-line services.

Self-service job searching on the Internet will undoubtedly continue to grow in importance and in time will be embraced more widely by the PES. In 1996 the German PES launched T-Online, which permits access to vacancy information from home computers (Weinkopf 1997). Such developments raise major challenges both to the traditional role of the PES and to the equity of access to job offers.

In many member states the PES still plays a central role in filling vacancies in a formal sense at least. This role has been important not least because it has allowed policy makers to gain some feel of the local labor market situation. With the growth of the Internet, which is both informal and internationally oriented, the traditional role of the PES as gatekeeper to the labor market may well diminish. Then its ability to signal to policy makers what is happening in the labor market will decline.

The increasing incursion of private agencies or self-service on-line via the Internet into these areas could destroy any hope of retaining an integrated public job service. For instance:

- Marketization could lead to cream skimming by private job placement agencies of more highly qualified workers while the PES becomes ghettoized as a service for harder-to-place job seekers.
- The growth of third sector agencies providing services for certain target groups of disadvantaged people could fragment the coverage of services,

making it harder to monitor quality and performance of job services at an overall level and excluding job seekers who are not defined as "target."

- The specialization of the overall guidance and placement function into separate functions (recruitment and placement, training advice, career guidance, counseling, labor market program management, benefit control, etc.) could lead to a maze of poorly articulated services rather than a one-stop service.

Our fears are not relieved by the unbalanced growth of the new on-line job information systems, concentrating on the relatively easy tasks of automated job vacancy databases and placing high-tech professionals using self-service kiosks or home based search. To what extent can such trends be extrapolated? Will these systems further advantage the already advantaged, thus institutionalizing exclusion? Such issues are of central importance to the debates on the reform of the PES and other labor market institutions and are, therefore, the final issue to which we now turn.

LABOR MARKET INSTITUTIONS FOR THE IS?

Current institutional structures and trends toward liberalization of employment services will undoubtedly have a major influence on the transparency of the labor market and the effectiveness of the PES in administering labor market policies. Here we examine three aspects of this issue: the institutional structure itself, the ability of the PES to coordinate labor market information, and its role in providing job guidance.

Internal institutional barriers in the PES, and even PES offices, can be a source of problems. For instance, German job brokerage functions have tended to be very specialized. Large offices may have as many as twenty teams covering different client groups or occupations. There is evidence that this leads to an inflexibility that restricts mobility across occupational boundaries—potentially a major problem in a labor market that is undergoing the structural changes associated with the IS. These divisions mean that the job vacancy databases are not available on the same terminals as the vocational guidance systems, nor are staff generally trained to help job seekers to move from one system to another. Similarly, relations with other institutions can create difficulties; for instance, in Italy a nominally national service is really operating under the auspices of regional authorities. Undoubtedly, the fragmented structure of the PES in Italy has contributed to the nonemergence of national job vacancy systems.

These sorts of problems help illustrate the rationale for the recent liberalization of job placement services, which has traditionally been the preserve of the PES in most European countries. In practice this monopoly was far from effective, in some cases with so many exceptions that the system was largely ignored in practice. The effect of private agencies on the development of ICT-based labor market services, however, is unclear. At the moment, relatively few job seekers seem to use the growing private agency sector (the highest recorded figure is in the Netherlands at 7 percent). There are also wide variations in how people find jobs, with informal methods being used more often in southern Europe (CEC 1996e).

In time, private employment agencies may become more important, but at the moment their main effect is arguably to promote innovation. The PES realize the need to build market share and becoming more customer orientated by providing better levels of service for job seekers (including the development of job vacancy systems). Most importantly, they are more active in getting employers to register vacancies.

Another issue is whether, with liberalization, we will have to guard against a fragmentation of labor market intelligence caused by job placement data becoming commercially valuable. The PES already has a far from complete picture of what is going on in the labor market. Most job seekers (70 percent) do use the services of the PES; often they are obliged to in order to claim benefit. But levels of use vary from 90 percent (in Denmark, France, and Sweden) to 5 percent (in Greece). And there are a wide variety of other sources of information on vacancies such as newspaper advertisements (used by 10 percent of job seekers), direct applications (9 percent), and informal contacts through family and friends (5 percent) (CEC 1996e).

Likewise, employers tend to use a wide variety of different sources to gain information about the labor market, employing a mixture of formal (routine scanning of publications, etc.) and informal strategies (" keeping an ear to the ground") (Boddy et al. 1995). Much of this intelligence function appears to be rather ad hoc, stimulated by specific pressures to examine the external labor market such as large expansion of production, relocation or new investment, acquisitions, or major technological changes. Given the intermittent nature of recruitment, it might be difficult to establish sustained contact with labor market organizations based around the job placement function alone. Moreover, U.K. evidence shows a PES not really oriented toward providing information to employers; such requests were often referred elsewhere and regarded as a disruption of PES officers' work routines (Boddy et al. 1995). Often the information provided was not found to meet the employers' needs, thus perhaps leading to a mutually reinforcing lack of information exchange, which undoubtedly limits the effectiveness of labor market coordination.[10]

Clearly, these issues merit consideration in any future model of labor market institutions. We should expect neither that the PES nor the PES on-line databases will be completely comprehensive in their coverage of labor market information. But there is room for improvement. And, surely, the PES has an important role to play in labor market coordination. Within this role computerized information systems could be offered as a service to job seekers and employers, with the possible triple effect of raising job matching efficiency, increasing employer satisfaction, and helping to maintain the central role of the PES as a provider of labor market information.

Finally, it is arguable that in the past too much PES staff time (in some countries as much as 50 percent) has been taken up in administering entitlement to passive benefits. With liberalization and the new complexity of career choices that will face people in the information society, a shift toward personalized guidance provision has great attractions as part of a new role for the PES. The ability of the PES to fill this role, however, will vary dramatically from country to country because of different traditions, roles, and even recruitment practices. For instance, in Finland there is a heavy emphasis on the role of occupational psychologists who seek to match workers to jobs for which they have aptitudes. In Germany, the emphasis is on vocationally related guidance. In Italy, PES staff tend to be trained in public administration or law and are admitted to the administration by entrance competition. This has directly affected the innovativeness of the service: "a lack of appropriate qualifications was cited as one factor behind the delay in introducing electronic data-processing systems in local offices" (OECD 1996c, 59). And local employment offices in Italy (Sezioni Circonscrizionali per l'Impiego—SCIs) tend to be too bureaucratic. "To make more room for brokerage work, SCIs need to cut out bureaucratic procedures which have become obsolete and computerize those which are to be retained" (p. 67).

For practical reasons, controlling access to benefits is likely to remain a major role of PES staff, not least because it provides a check on whether unemployment claimants are available for work. However, an emphasis on supportive and developmental employment guidance helps to eliminate the impression that a PES is concerned with administering unemployment instead of providing employment services. This, for instance, is a key feature of the Danish IHP (Individuel Handlingsplan) and represents a fundamental shift in the orientation of job guidance. In the past guidance was only called for if something had gone wrong. Against the background of the information society, there has been

Box 7.4   The Many Variants of Guidance

Places that offer guidance
Schools, colleges, universities, training centers, job centers, the workplace, private employment agencies, job placement services, etc.

Guidance is provided to
Schoolchildren, high school dropouts, college entrants, enrolled students, job seekers, people with learning difficulties, long-term unemployed, women returners, workers facing redundancy, etc.

Guidance is given by
Mainstream teachers and educators, specially trained counselor-teachers, occupational or educational psychologists, qualified therapists, public employment service bureaucrats, family and friends, firm recruiters, professional bodies, peer guidance, etc.

Guidance is given in
One-on-one interviews, small seminars and workshops, large-scale presentations, recruitment fairs, written materials (self-help books, brochures and prospectuses, publicity, etc), on-line information.

The orientation of guidance can be toward
Job placement, identification of aptitudes through psychometric testing, helping people map out employment pathways, helping people develop employability skills, tangible support to develop contacts, help in filling out applications, counseling for psychological and/or social problems.

Guidance activities include
Providing information, assessment, advice, counseling, career education, placement, advocacy, follow-up, and controlling access to benefit.

Source: Adapted from OECD 1996f.

a slow realization that guidance can be an effective "lubricant" to labor market policies (Watts 1991). However, job guidance is already split across a range of different labor market actors and involves a wide range of activities (box 7.4). Thus we can hardly expect the PES to absorb the roles of all the other actors currently involved in providing guidance.

On-line information systems will play a part in the job guidance function, but they should not be seen as a cheap technological fix that can replace the "personal touch" of counseling. Computer tools will help to indicate that the service is modern, dynamic, and in touch, but the proliferation of services providing guidance in most E.U. countries means that there are substantial institutional barriers to putting guidance on-line. Here too liberalization is taking place with many new private and third sector guidance services emerging, many cofunded by the EC. In this area as well, marketization leads to concerns about cream skimming, quality, and equity. Especially with the growth of ICT-based tools, there are concerns that the complex process of guidance could be reduced to a checklist exercise.

Given the nature and uncertainties of the IS, the policy effort should if anything be on increasing the quality, depth, long-term scope, and professionalism of guidance. Self-service modes of accessing information will certainly have an increasing role to play, but most people will need chauffeurs to guide them through increasingly complex training, qualification, and job structures. If ICTs have a role, then, it is to free staff to concentrate on providing in–depth advice based on professional expertise.

A ROLE FOR THE PES IN THE IS?

To meet the challenge of the information society, we need a higher performance labor market than we have at present. ICTs can undoubtedly help us achieve this challenge by increasing the transparency of labor market information, especially in regard to the outcomes of ALMP interventions, the structure of demand for skills, and patterns of job vacancies, as well as helping provide job search assistance, especially job counseling and guidance.

The liberalization of labor market placement services creates a need for careful evaluation of the emerging agency structure for the labor market. Competitive pressures on the PES are stimulating a customer orientation as it strives to retain market share, and on–line job vacancy information plays a part. However, there is a risk that as the new private agencies gain in strength the effectiveness of the PES as an instrument to enact ALMPs will decline. Our fear is that flows of information on the labor market will become fragmented among many different labor market agencies, all of which regard this information as commercially confidential. The result could be a drought of information for policy making in the midst of the Information Age! There is, then, a need for a robust strategy to guarantee the collection of labor market information from the various agencies involved. Such strategies should be built into the new institutional structures from the start and should lay the foundation for an upgraded system of job guidance and counseling, supported where appropriate by ICT-based labor market information services.

A more immediate threat is that on–line job vacancy systems are used to cut staff. We regard that as shortsighted. On–line systems can only do part of the job of job search assistance and guidance. The range of activities that fall under the heading of job guidance is broad and often, especially in the case of disadvantaged groups, requires high levels of interpersonal and complex professional skills. These systems, also, are not yet fully diffused, completely accepted, or clearly reliable. Their most effective use at the moment is supporting PES staff and, in this role, could be put to good use as part of an overall development of the job search assistance aspect of ALMPs (which by all accounts is the most effective form of ALMP). We believe that much may be gained in using ICTs to develop the guidance function of PES, especially as part of widening the JSA to support other aspects of ALMPs. For instance, is there potential to use ICT-based techniques to attract certain groups (such as demotivated youths) into active programs?

Finally, the new institutional structures in employment placement services should reflect the need for equity, longer-term development of employability, and transparency of labor market patterns. Efforts to achieve a greater integration of different areas of job guidance should be supported by the development of widely available computerized information on careers, vocational education, and training opportunities as well as current employment opportunities. The liberalization of employment placement markets should be seen as an opportunity for innovation in the use of ICT applications to support labor market services. But care should be taken to ensure that new regulatory systems governing these markets provide for the collection of high-quality information on labor market conditions, not only to aid in the design and delivery of labor market policies but to help employers in analyzing recruitment needs and educators in designing training courses.

CONCLUSION

Surprisingly little work seems to have been done to find out how the transition to the IS can be supported and eased by active labor market policies and, conversely, what the IS means for active labor market policies. This is unfortunate, given the considerable sums that are being poured into such policies and into ICT training schemes.

In particular, though, it is worth recalling that we should not expect too much. Labor market policies can only make a relatively small contribution to unemployment. They work best as part of a long-term approach to employability throughout life. This would require adaptations of learning opportunities and behavior throughout education from early school age onward and in employment from apprenticeship to retirement and beyond.

The full elaboration of such a system of lifelong learning and employability is beyond the scope of this chapter, but we cannot help feeling that a period of structural change in the labor market brings forth great opportunities for

change and progressive policies, if we can only grasp them. A key example relates to the increased participation of women in the labor force. Women now
represent the majority of new labor market entrants. ICTs are purportedly more
"women friendly" because of their association with the reduction of heavy
physical labor and an increasing emphasis on social skills at work and on the
advantages of computers.[11] Yet women are still more likely to have higher rates
of (long-term) unemployment, are more likely to have fragmented careers, are
less likely to go into technical occupations, and so on. The headline story may
spotlight the failure of our labor market policies to get people to work, but
there is a persistent failure also to deal with structural inequalities in the labor
market. While we are engaged in the task of transforming and renewing our
labor market institutions and policies, perhaps we should take the opportunity
to embed within them a commitment to progressive and equitable treatment
of all people in the labor market. The alternative is a lost opportunity. Driven
by the crisis of unemployment, we grasp at jobs at any cost—hardly the way
to build "an information society for us all" (HLEG 1997). The European community needs a bolder and deeper policy vision of the information society in
this area.

NOTES

1. We start with these general reviews because (despite the large sums committed
to ALMPs) general impact evaluations themselves are relatively scarce and the impacts
of ICT-related ALMPs are worryingly absent from the literature.

2. We should make it clear that we are not against technical training per se, merely
that we are against simplistic "skill gap" policies that only respond to an apparent mismatch between new technologies and existing skills in the workforce. These sorts of
responses are still highly influential in the rhetoric and actions of policy makers confronted by the information society. In our view, these policies are misplaced even though
their intentions may be good. Many of the outcomes may indeed be positive, but we
argue that indirect actions to improve the integration of ICT use into a broader program of training and experience is more likely to be effective, since there is a context
for the "skills" that have been acquired.

3. Similar lists have also been recently produced by Clematide and Ager-Hansen
(1996), European Round Table of Industrialists (ERT 1995), NACFAM (1996), and
SCANS (1991). It is interesting to note that some of these are derived from working
parties of industrialists who are normally accused of short-termism (although it might
be argued that the views of employers are different from their behavior; Williams 1997).

4. The issue of whether the rising demand for graduates is really driven by increased
skill demands or whether it is "qualification inflation" that is taking place due to a
graduate glut is a matter of debate. Mason (1996) finds that both effects are present
but to different degrees in different industries and occupations. He finds that the en-

hanced cognitive and social capacities of more educated workers in itself helps to transform jobs. Having hired someone for a lower-status role, employers slowly begin to extend the work to absorb more of his or her capacities. However, this results in a contradictory outcome that mixes enskilling and a social deskilling. If such patterns persist, the result is to upgrade the skill demanded from the occupational role (enskilling?), but this would increasingly exclude less qualified workers. On the other hand, the worker loses the status normally accorded to people with that level of qualification (deskilling?).

5. The shift toward a greater focus on user services has been accompanied by a feminization of the task and, disappointingly, a simultaneous downgrading in terms of status and pay.

6. Although the information society is currently seen as a force driving the need for a reform of educational provision, we should recognize that the idea of a "learning society" has been around for a long time. The term "lifelong learning" was used as long ago as 1964 by one of the pioneers of Swedish educational reform Torsten Husen (see Husen 1974, 1986) and in other countries, such as Denmark, from the early 1970s (e.g., Himmelstrup and Stjerne 1972).

7. The dual training systems in Austria and Germany, of course, have always offered such integration. But dual training is now often regarded as too inflexible to meet the challenge of the increasing multiskilling of jobs, the blurring of occupational distinctions, and the need to respond to technological changes, all changes that are associated with new ICTs in the workplace. Young people are opting for academic higher education or for jobs in high technology and service sectors that do not have these well-defined apprenticeship patterns.

8. This level of support does not give us confidence that such schemes can be "rolled out" rapidly and on the broad scale that might be needed to meet the high level of demand which may actually exist. For instance, when the Danish Ministries of Social Affairs and Education posted fourteen new jobs specifically aimed at handicapped, it received 1,000 applicants (*Politiken*, December 1996).

9. Derived from a survey of 2,000 Danish firms (Lund and Gjerdling 1996; Gjerdling 1996).

10. This information is based on the U.K. case study undertaken as part of a wider CEDEFOP-funded investigation into labor market information flows.

11. This point is important, but we would distance ourselves from the essentialist assumption that some kinds of technology or some kinds of skills are inherently feminine (see chapter 6 by Juliet Webster for a more detailed examination of this point).

Part III

Life in the Information Society

8

Health and the Information Society

Jorma Rantanen and Suvi Lehtinen

Overall, we expect information and communication technology (ICT) to impact the health of the population through the improved performance of public health authorities and health service (see below and Ministry of Social Affairs and Health 1996). The ICT will have a profound effect on the conditions of life and the time budgets of computer users, as well as on the daily routines and work of citizens. Special concerns include the sedentary lifestyle, the ergonomic aspects of ICT, and the risk of information overload.

THE SEDENTARY "SCREEN LIFE"

There have been very few studies on the lifestyle impact of the ICT and thus analysis must be based on indirect information. The use of ICT primarily implies communication with a computer through video display units (VDU), keyboard, and mouse. This communication is time-consuming, requires concentration, and excludes contacts with other social and physical environments. As the use of these technologies becomes more widely diffused, there is a real risk that behaviors will emerge that are detrimental to health, at least among certain users.

For instance, Finland has the highest density of users in the world, with an annual growth rate of 100 percent (Taloustutkimus Oy 1996). The average user of Internet services in Finland spends 2.3 hours per week on the Net, or about

175

2 percent of waking hours. However, 6 percent of the users reported spending more than twenty-one hours a week on-line, which is half a working week and almost one-fifth of the time they are awake. Heavy users tend to be students or young or middle-aged men who use Internet at work. Elsewhere, substantial proportions (9–56 percent) of eleven- to fifteen-year-old boys have been found to spend at least twelve hours a week watching videotapes or TV or playing computer games; similarly aged girls reported one-tenth to one-half the rates of the boys (King et al. 1996). Some users are even deviating from normal diurnal rhythms in order to take part in on-line activities (Salmela 1996). As a result other activities can be squeezed out and sleeping patterns can be disturbed, with the same health effects that have been found with shift work (Härmä 1995).

Such behavior can also promote a sedentary lifestyle, which is surprisingly common in many countries. This is of concern because physical activity constitutes an important tool for modern health policy and for the prevention of the most important lifestyle-related diseases in society (WHO/FIMS 1995), such as cardiovascular disorders, musculo-skeletal disorders, obesity, hypertension, diabetes, colon cancer, osteoporosis, psychological depression and anxiety, and age-related decline of certain psychomotoric and cognitive capacities (Spirduso 1995).

Virtual Reality and Mental, Psychological, and Psychosocial Health

Virtual reality (VR) applications are increasingly used in areas such as aviation training and testing and medical treatment; with many new applications also emerging in public and private entertainment and education and training. Attention has been given to potential adverse effects (called cyberpathology) of the new virtual environments (Gupta, Wantland, and Klein 1996; Igarashi, Noritake, and Furuta 1996; *What Is Wrong* 1993; Crow 1996).

Numerous physiological, psychological, and biological factors and mechanisms are at play, including the overstrain of visual sensory systems—the mismatch of visual cues and the balance and proprioceptive senses; psychological stresses; and physiological and psychological dysfunctions in the real environment caused by gaps between real and virtual space (Gupta et al. 1996; *What Is Wrong* 1993). Very little empirical research data are available, except in the case of cybersickness, which is a real and frequent condition among aerospace simulator users and seems to be a variant of common motion sickness with systemic, visual, neurological, and psychological symptoms. Nor do we understand the behavioral problems that might arise from poor socialization of young people who are excessively exposed to cyber-reality and not the real world.

Physiological Impacts and Usability

The fear of new technology is likely to have similar origins and cures in its general use as in occupational settings (see below). Insufficient training, as well as the introduction of technology changes without sufficient preparation, has been found to increase user stress and frustration, including a strong feeling of incompetence. This affects the acceptance of change from "old" to "new" technology and leads to dissatisfaction or withdrawal (Huuhtanen 1985).

At a deeper psychological level, Frankenhaeuser (1994) and Cox and Ferguson (1994) point out that once-meaningful stress responses become inadequate in the new technology environments. Humans have not had time to develop meaningful responses for the new stress factors, possibly leading to negative health impacts (Frankenhaeuser 1994).

Computer stations should be set up in ways that are easy to use and are ergonomically efficient, for example, by building user-friendliness into the systems themselves and instructing users on potential health impacts and how to set up and use a computer station. Particular attention is needed for computers that are used in community centers and for some special user groups such as children, the elderly, and handicapped people. The knowledge and experience accumulated from workplace computer use should provide a basis for such instructions and arrangements, although the intensity and duration of use may be lower (Van Offenbeek and Koopman 1996). However, direct research efforts are needed regarding ICT use in the home including patterns and conditions of use and impact on family life.

Adequate training, information, and usability could be brought together to increase the acceptance and take-up of the new ICT. For instance, for ICT-based services, such as bank and shopping services as well as health services, user-friendly support services and the development of user competences are critical to wide service provision and acceptance by clients.

Finally, a totally new phenomenon from the health point of view is the potency of misinformation in the information society. International networks, such as the Internet, transcend traditional policing measures. Sales of pharmaceuticals and drugs with strong biological or psychological effects are available beyond the control of pharmaceutical services. Devices are sold and alternative health practices and lifestyles promoted on the Internet, often without appropriate information and control by consumer protection bodies. The health impact could be similar to the antivaccination movements of the early twentieth century, which led to significant loss of life. The potential risks and possibilities for control need to be studied in this new area, and it is likely that new regulatory and control actions will be needed.

IMPACT OF THE INFORMATION SOCIETY ON
OCCUPATIONAL HEALTH

Introduction: Implementation of ICT and Change at Work

New ICT is used first at work, is used by the most people and in the most intensive way. About 38 percent of European workers use ICT on a daily basis and the percentage is climbing (in some European countries topping 50 percent). There are numerous positive effects of these changes, but there are also a number of new health and safety problems that have been relatively well researched.

The Human-Technology Interface

The human-technology interface (HTI) is becoming crucial to information-intensive work, not only its usability and the well-being of workers but also productivity and quality of work. A good match between technical and physiological, psychological and social aspects has to be sought for technological systems (Kern and Bauer 1995; Leventhal, Teasley, and Blumenthal 1996; Mantovani 1996). Further research is needed to achieve this good match because of the complexity of the human systems that are involved. On the human end alone it involves visual, auditory, cognitive, and psychomotoric systems.

Indeed, the user's whole personality is involved—intelligence, competence, experience, and skill—in performing tasks with the help of new technology (Mantovani 1996).

Good user interface design involves a vast number of factors from the technological, human, and organizational perspectives. As many as seventeen ISO standards or draft standards have been prepared to guide the design of visual display units (VDUs) (Dul, deVlaming, and Munnik 1996; Harker 1995; Stewart 1995). A similar number of issues have to be considered regarding interfaces between VDU work and other aspects of the work process. For instance, the guideline on the implementation of the EC Directive on Visual Display Terminals contains more than twenty special points that need to be checked. Each of them contains numerous individual aspects of user interface (CEC 1990; Finnish Institute of Occupational Health 1995). All these checkpoints carry potential health risks and have to be optimized to ensure healthy and productive use of VDUs.

For the majority of workers the overall impact of ICT on work is positive (Hukki and Seppälä 1993; Dul et al. 1996), but both technology and the hu-

Figure 8.1   General Outline of the Human–Technology Interface (HTI) in Computerized Information Work

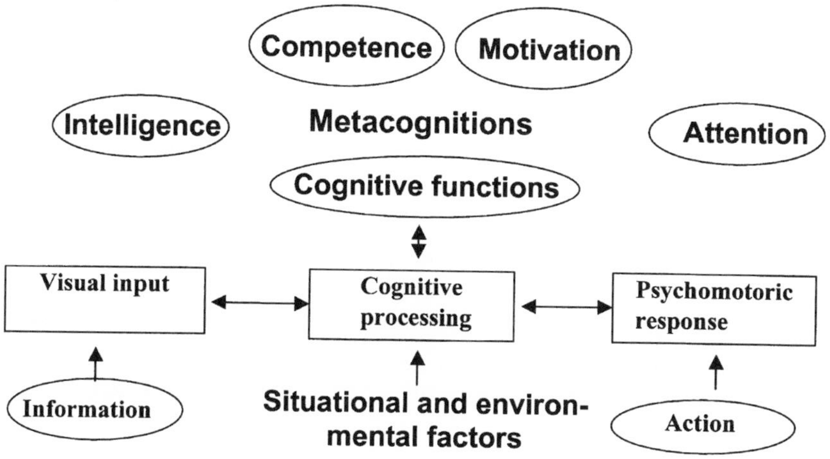

man element may exhibit structural, functional, or psychological incompatibilities that could affect the usability and acceptability of ICTs. Discomfort and physical or psychological strain leading to lower quality and productivity are the result. Some of the key aspects of user interface are discussed below in the light of the health and safety of information-intensive work

Vision, Hearing, and the Use of ICT

Vision is the sense mainly used in information work, particularly in connection with VDUs. A large number of the technical and physiological aspects of video screens have been researched, and well-established standards are available (Dul et al. 1996; Stewart 1995; Bergqvist 1984). Some of the visual problems can be controlled by more ergonomic design of workstations. Others are technology dependent (contrast, stability, etc.). Recent developments in screen quality have substantially improved the visual ergonomics of video screen work, but the health effects of these technologies are still uncertain. For instance, more research is needed on the impact of invisible flickering on fatigue rates (Finnish Institute of Occupational Health 1995; Dillon 1994).

One less well understood area is the interaction between video screen use and poor vision. (Luck, Vogel, and Shapiro 1996). Sufferers include a small proportion of people who have congenital anomalies of the eye and the large number of individuals over forty-five years of age. Both groups can be treated with corrective spectacles, although this creates issues of viewing distance, accommodation, and visual field. Spectacles can also affect the position of the neck, adding muscular strain of the shoulder-neck region (Piccoli et al. 1996; Horgen et al. 1995).

Yet ICT can also improve visibility and presentation of information work and often make work processes easier. ICT can even enable individuals with extremely poor vision or blindness to participate in working life (Den Brinker and Beek 1996).

The auditory senses have a growing role in ICT. So far, however, keyboard-mouse systems are superior in performance and better accepted (Damper, Tranchant, and Lewis 1996; Murray, Jones, and Frankish 1996; Molnar and Kletke 1996). Even relatively slight hearing loss substantially diminishes the ability to understand speech, particularly machine-generated speech.

Cognition

In using computers, the human brain is confronted with a technology that has a degree of intelligence. In evolutionary terms this is a new departure and relatively little is known about the effects of computer use on human intelligence, particularly in the longer term. The cognitive functions of information work are, therefore, a priority for experimental psychology, work physiology, and ergonomics (Whitefield 1990). The complex interactions among technologies, work, and the great number of individual (internal) factors are not yet fully understood, despite several models that aid analysis and experimental research (Dillon 1994; Whitefield 1990; Ziegler, Vossen, and Hoppe 1990; Falzon 1990). Available research information on cognitive functions and user interface supports the following conclusions (Spirduso 1995; Falzon 1990; Westerman, Davies, and Glendon 1995; Rosenbrock 1989):

- Technologies, hardware, software, work site design, and work organization affect cognitive functions.
- There is great interindividual variation in cognitive capacities.
- Cognitive functions can, to a certain extent, be learned and are supported by competence and training. More time is needed to train older workers.
- Aging slows the simpler cognitive functions that are typical for mechanical routine information work (see below).
- Sensitivity to disturbing factors varies greatly and increases with age.
- The cognitive performance of aging individuals, though slower, may be better in accuracy than that of younger individuals.

Among external factors (technology and work organization), the ergonomic design of the workplace is very significant for cognitive performance. An unergonomic work site, such as a poor chair or a tiring position, promotes fatigue and lowers cognitive performance and alertness. Although these effects are quite well-known, treating them is often difficult. For instance, shared offices may provide little scope for improvements in individual workstations. It is not surprising that noncompliance with the existing standards or guidelines on video screen use is widespread (Westlander and Viitasara 1995). This is unfortunate, since poor work design almost certainly lowers productivity, increases errors, and lowers the quality of life of the workers. By contrast, organizing work in an ergonomically optimal way can increase worker performance to about the same degree as task-specific training (Huuhtanen 1985; Huuhtanen et al. 1995).

Software design has a major impact on cognitive functions. The structure of hypertext topology has a significant effect on speed, accuracy, orientation, and navigation of the worker, as well as on sensitivity to disturbances and rates of comprehension of material (McDonald and Stevenson 1996). There are also significant differences in the performance of users of different ages (see below), genders, and levels of education. All users, however, prefer and perform best with simple, easily accessible interfaces (Leventhal et al. 1996).

Ergonomic Aspects

The requirements of manual psychomotorics are not highly demanding in information work and do not substantially differ from the demands of conventional typing except in the use of the mouse. Usually, visually guided movements of the hand-arm system are highly adaptable (Clower, Hoffman, and Votaw 1996). However, some individuals have coordination problems when using a mouse that affect their work performance (Marteniuk, Ivens, and Brown 1996). A new element is hand-arm musculo-manual activity in virtual reality systems.

Motoric responses primarily depend on cognitive and other central processes that vary with the constitution of the worker, age, psychomotoric abilities, training, and psychological environment. A number of acute or chronic diseases may also affect psychomotoric performance (Spirduso 1995). Also, ergonomic design of the work site, screen, keyboard, and mouse affects motoric responses (Hahn et al. 1995). Once again, environmental factors, such as lighting, organization of the work site, and basic physical design of the keyboard, affect performance (Dul et al. 1996; Stewart 1995). But screen and mouse technologies are tending to improve. For example, flat screens could have a major impact on ergonomics and could offer more flexibility and opportunities for ergonomic improvements.

Overall, in contrast to the situation in cognitive ergonomics, manual ergonomics is well supported by research. The issue is to apply existing research knowledge and standards (Westlander and Viitasara 1995).

Aging

The effects of aging on the comfort and performance of ICT users deserves special mention, given the aging of the European workforce and the particular difficulties older workers face.

First, older workers often become farsighted and wear glasses, which makes using video screens more difficult. Although the rate at which visual information is transmitted by the optical nerve to the central nervous system is not severely affected by aging, progressive presbyopia and a lowered ability to monitor the environment can affect comfort and performance (Ilmarinen et al. 1996). Aging individuals have more problems discriminating between blue and green (Spirduso 1995) and are particularly sensitive to glare and poor contrast and lighting. This requires close attention to the design of the workplace. For instance, recent guidelines propose 100 percent more light for aging workers to support their visual performance.

Second, although aging slows total cognitive ability and nonverbal functions, verbal abilities and general intelligence remain unaffected. The so-called liquid intelligence needed in the mechanical operation of a computer is based on short-term memory and declines with age. But higher cognitive functions, such as verbal reasoning, logical reasoning, and evaluation functions tend to remain unaffected by advancing age or may even improve. It is worth noting that good physical fitness, competence, and general intelligence seem to strengthen some cognitive functions (Spirduso, MacRae, and MacRae 1988). The general slowing of cognitive functions implies that the aging worker should be given more time to perform cognitive tasks. Aging workers may be much more susceptible to a poorly lit, noisy, or hectic work ambience but can perform more accurately than younger ones in calmer situations.

Information processing speed as well as simple and complex short-term memory and the processing of information declines substantially after fifty (Suvanto et al. 1991; Nygård, Eskelinen, and Suvanto 1991; Goedhard 1992). Most software is constructed so that short-term memory functions are crucial, especially in the use of hypertext and the Internet, where nonhierarchic, non-linear (networked) data structures abound (Westerman et al. 1995; Lansdale 1990). This leads to a relatively weaker performance of older individuals and increases stress at work. One challenge therefore is the development of software and interfaces that provide support for the reduced short-term memory and visual performance of the aging individual.

Summary

All facets of HTI—visual interface, human-computer interface, and environmental and ergonomic factors—affect the productivity of information-intensive work. Most of the ergonomic issues can be improved with the help of existing research knowledge. The main demand for new research concerns the cognitive effects of ICT, especially in the longer term.

Overall, thanks to the rapidly developing standardization of ICT, psychomotoric ergonomics will undoubtedly improve. The main focus will remain on the visual and cognitive ergonomics of the technology interface. Planning and design need to be consistent with emerging evidence on human physiology, ergonomics, and psychology. Individual variations should also be given a higher priority, especially in respect to the aging workforce (Stewart 1995; CEC 1990; Fernström and Ericson 1996).

ICT and Healthy Work: Satisfaction, Stress and Competences

The effects of ICTs on the quality of working life is dealt with elsewhere in this volume (chapter 5) and thus will not be treated in depth here. It suffices to point out that ICT enables and often requires changes in the work organization, teleworking being the extreme example (table 8.1). It brings changes in the nature and frequency of interpersonal contacts, possible stresses associated with the removal of support services, and greater difficulty in monitoring health and safety standards. Many efforts are being made to overcome these problems through the publication of guidelines and new legal obligations (e.g., Pekkola and Ylöstalo 1996; Huuhtanen 1996).

Many health problems associated with ICT at work relate to the mismanagement of its human, social, and political aspects rather than technology. Research on organizational psychology strongly emphasizes the association between work organization and culture and the health, safety, and job satisfaction of workers. This insight will gain importance because productivity and quality are more dependent on psychosocial aspects in information-intensive work (Juuti and Lindström 1995).

Table 8.1   Positive and Adverse Occupational Health Aspects of Telework

Positive	Adverse
Avoidance of commuting traffic/saving time, lower accident risk, less pollution	VDU ergonomic problems/ visual and and musculoskeletal stress
Autonomy in work tasks and work organization/control of stress	Role conflicts; work vs. family/stress
More time for family/fewer role conflicts, less stress	Psychological stress by several work-related factors/time pressure, competence demands
More degrees of freedom/more self-steering and job satisfaction	Disturbance of work by family/stress
Often at least esthetically good work-place/better quality of life	Risk of self-committed overload/ burnout
	Social isolation/depression
	Lack of developmental and social stimuli from the working comm-unity/dropping out from the collective development process

Sources: Aronsson and Sjögren 1994; Huuhtanen 1996; Moorcraft and Bennett 1995; Huws, Podro, and Arvanitaki 1996.

ICT-based automation usually makes work lighter and cleaner, and it reduces exposure to hazardous substances (Rantanen 1996a; Hukki and Seppälä 1993). In principle, work can also be better managed to avoid stresses and overload. On the other hand, increasing abstraction in information-intensive work using computers and ICT creates difficulties. The key issue is to organize work to optimize both production processes and visual, cognitive, and manual ergonomics (Aronsson and Sjögren 1994; Eason 1996).

Worker Satisfaction and Stress

Although most workers assess ICT positively, there are problems associated with the manner of implementation. A Helsinki city study (Hukki and Seppälä 1993) found that 82 percent of the administration and service units considered the implementation of ICT to be a positive change that enriched their work but simultaneously increased competence demands and time pressure. More than 60 percent of workers over forty reported too few opportunities for training and practice before implementation. A significant minority suffered "some" stresses during the implementation, often caused by time pressures, organization problems, and insufficient competence rather than the technology itself. Difficulties centered on ICT jargon and understanding the manuals (often in a foreign language). Anxiety was caused by a fear of making errors, unexpected breakdowns, and difficulties in navigating complex software.

Stress and Competence

A healthy workplace requires the renewal of the competences of workers. The new demands on our sensory systems, particularly cognitive skills but also visual senses and some psychomotoric abilities, may be quite new, especially for older workers who thus risk exclusion from the workforce (Hukki and Seppälä 1993; Huuhtanen et al. 1995; Kinnunen and Parkatti 1993). The profile of skills needed seems broader than in the past, encompassing a good overall understanding of the principles of the work processes and materials used, specific technical and general computing skills, and social skills such as teamworking and communication ability (Westlander and Viitasara 1995; Leppänen 1995).

Knowing computer terminology, concepts, acronyms, and symbols is important in ICT competence and in "verbal" ability in the computerized world. Learning computer talk may be easy for younger people, but it is often hard for older and less-trained workers. The widespread use of English creates barriers for many. The abstract nature of computer use may also create barriers for workers who lack a good educational background.

People may need help adjusting to networked ways of working, which require self-motivation and self-direction. Many tasks are carried out individually and independently (often in some isolation). Simultaneously workers have to join networks, share information, and interact with other workers. These are conflicting demands and may cause dissonance for some individuals, cultures, and professional groups.

To some extent all of the above demands can be met through training. The effect of training on overall performance, stress control and productivity of the workers has been found to be positive (Leppänen 1995). Good working conditions also raise work performance. In particular, productivity in information-intensive work rises in a good psychosocial environment (Rantanen 1996b). Competence, meanwhile, increases work rates and lowers stress levels (Toppinen and Kalimo 1996; Leppänen 1995). Overall, work ability, working conditions, and competence are closely interdependent variables in information work that affect the workers' performance in a complex way.

THE INFORMATION SOCIETY AND HEALTH SERVICES

There are many potential applications of ICT in the health sector. ICTs may help health services meet expanding demands while increasing cost-effectiveness (Rantanen 1996b; Kajander and Konttinen 1996; Gott 1995). It is not surprising, then, to find public policies on health telematics in the European Union, the United States, and elsewhere (e.g., CEC 1994e, 1994f, 1995b, 1996f; U.S. Congress OTA 1995).

The development of health telematics varies widely across Europe, with the United Kingdom, the Netherlands, Norway, and Sweden being frontrunners (CEC 1996f). Finland has recently established a national strategy and an action plan for health and social services in the information society that aims at nationwide introduction of ICT in the health and social sector via municipal governments. Health care telematics, including appropriate instruction, services, follow-up, and self-care activities, are growing and experience with their usability in widescale practices is accumulating (CEC 1996f). However, the number of patients served is still relatively small (McLaren and Ball 1995).

Possible applications of health telematics (Perednia and Allen 1995; SatelLife 1996) include the following:

- communication of information between health care systems
- transfer of diagnostic information in digital form obtained from radiological, electrophysiological, clinical biochemistry, and other diagnostic methods
- two-directional and interactive communication of information needed in therapeutic services, including consultations and advised surgical and other operations
- telematic information and training of health personnel, students of health professions, patients, and the public
- compilation, storage, processing, and transfer of administrative and operational information on the activities of health systems
- collection and communication of information in health promotion and rehabilitation, as well as training where needed
- compilation, processing, and storage of information needed in health research, including evaluation of health care systems
- collection and communication of information needed in preventive health services, providing health services to remote areas and areas without other communication systems (satellite services)
- better quality of services with better cost-efficiency and better information on the availability of services (Kajander and Konttinen 1996)

ICT use in health and social services cannot be seen solely as an issue of technology. It is also an issue of managing change that involves new tools, competences, ways of organizing services, and the work practices of health professionals and social service providers. Services for patients should improve (Rantanen 1996f; Willcocks and Currie 1996; Kaplinsky 1995).

Health Service Systems

Although similar in their overall mission, health services differ widely across Europe. There are substantially different legislative, financial, and institutional traditions and practices. Demands vary according to demography (e.g., age structure, occupational structure, social structure, geographical distribution of the population) and the structure of demands for health services (e.g., maternity and child care for young families versus geriatric care of elderly populations).

Most European health services are being pressured to provide better public health and hospital-based services as cost-effectively as possible, without compromising availability, quality, or safety of the services, and without unreasonably overloading health care workers (Willcocks and Currie 1996; Andreasen et al. 1995). The analysis of cost-effectiveness requires extensive data on costs, performance, outcomes, and impact of health service systems to meet present and future service needs. Thus further developments in collection and analysis of such information is a key feature of the EC Programme on Public Health (CEC 1995b, 1996g).

Raising Health Service Performance

We can expect to see a growing role for evidence-based medicine that uses ICT to track treatments, promotes efficacious and effective treatments and methods, and eliminates unnecessary, inefficient, or harmful ones. The challenge is to bridge the gap between the scientific evidence and health care practices (Kaplinsky 1995; Davidoff et al. 1995). Properly implemented, such evidence improves the accountability of health service systems.

If well implemented, information tracking should lead to better planning as well as to better organization of work at each level and in the system as a whole. Better transfer of relevant information at the right time to the right place in the right form is likely to be the key factor in the development of cost-effectiveness and quality of services (so-called "seamless care"). This requires integration between services as well as within them, vertically and horizontally and at European and international scale (fig. 8.2). Such experiments offer convincing

Figure 8.2   Multisectoral Information Network and Seamless Health Care

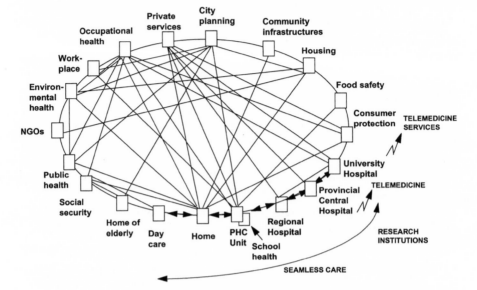

evidence that even large and complex health service systems can achieve substantial savings and shorten the queues without reducing the quality of care (Kaplinsky 1995).

Telemedicine

Telemedicine is still mostly experimental in Europe (Williams et al. 1994) and the United States (U.S. Congress OTA 1995). It includes teleradiology, telepathology, telepsychiatry, teledermatology, and other services that can make use of digitized data or visual information. Numerous other parameters can be recorded and transmitted with the help of telematic monitoring and recording. Videoconferencing is also used for oral and visual communication.

Network operators and industry have promoted telemedicine heavily, probably leading to overestimates of health gains and cost containment (US Congress OTA 1995; McLaren and Ball 1995; Consultation on Health in the IS 1996). However, empirical evaluations of telemedicine are still in short supply. An exception is a telemedicine service in northern Norway that has been studied for fifteen years (Rinde, Nordrum, and Nymo 1993). This service is seen as fully positive and is now being integrated into the Norwegian health service. The main impacts are a better availability of services to people in remote areas and better possibility for health personnel in front-line services to get diagnostic and specialized consultations (Rinde et al. 1993). But the structure of the Norwegian health care system is exceptionally "ambulatory care" oriented. In other cases the impact remains to be evaluated (U.S. Congress OTA 1995; Kajander and Konttinen 1996) and benefits may be less evident in more hospital-based systems (Agdestein and Roemer 1991). Analysis of the overall health and economic impact at individual, community, institutional, and national levels is needed. There is also a need for critical technology assessment from the perspective of both health systems and health workers and clients (e.g., estimates of the costs of process changes needed for telemedicine).

Information for Health

The WHO/EURO Health for All Strategy (WHO 1993) proposes a shift from institutionalized curative health care to prevention and promotion-oriented community services, implying that health will no longer be considered an issue concerning the health sector alone. Rather, it will involve social services, training and education, community planning, housing, traffic, industry, agriculture, and media, which are all called upon as equal partners for health (see fig. 8.2). Planning and decision making should be shifted to frontline services and citizens. This implies that more and better information will be needed for coordination and communication among actors in different sectors and levels of the system. Similarly, the E.C. strategy on public health emphasizes two aspects as key strategic elements: the importance of preventive community care and the development of information systems in the health sector as a prerequisite of preventive actions (CEC 1995b, 1996g).

Health promotion is also part of a shift toward preventative care rather than curative systems (e.g., the WHO Ottawa Charter [WHO 1986] and the European Community Strategy on Public Health, (CEC 1995b)), which will demand better information on health needs and health education and training—to which ICT could contribute.

Studies of health status (e.g., epidemiological studies) depend upon compiling, analyzing, processing, and communicating a wide range of health data—information on environmental and behavioral factors and determinants of the population's health, trends in health development, monitoring and surveillance of health outcomes, follow-up of health behavior, health information and education of people, and training of experts (Loslier 1996). Modern ICT enables mapping, imaging, and visualizing such complex data sets (Elliott et al. 1996).

ICT and multimedia also provide new possibilities for public information, health education, counseling, and self-learning. Visualization methods can make such information more concrete, comprehensible, and attractive for users (Kajander and Konttinen 1996). ICT can also permit a wider participation in health decision making, for example, the European health promotion network in occupational health, which raises awareness (Rantanen 1995).

The World Health Organization (WHO) is critical of the slow progress that was made in the 1980s and the early 1990s in developing health information systems, expressing concerns about lack of coverage, lack of future orientation, and unnecessary information overload, as well as the low relevance and usability of the information communicated. The main problem is that existing information systems were developed as stand-alone systems that had no capacity to share information. Also, the data are for resource allocation and not for the performance of health care or health needs. A new approach is proposed for the development of integrated information systems and for the redesign of informational content in target 35 of the European HFA Strategy (WHO 1993). It proposes integrated regional health information systems such as the WHO/EURO electronically networked WHONET.

"Seamless" Care

Seamless care (fig. 8.2) implies that when a client contacts any part of the health service system at any level, the input and processing of health information starts immediately. It is available to all who are involved at the right time in an appropriate way, and duplicate entries are minimized. After the therapeutic or other service process is completed, the information is stored and secured appropriately for future use.

Seamless care means a process orientation starting from the client's first contact with the health care system and continuing to the solution of the client's health problem. Continuity of care processes and elimination of information gaps are the most frequently recognized requirements for seamlessness, high quality, and efficiency of service performance (Vuori 1982). Seamless care means that health organization culture should become more open and communicative in addition to developing technically and organizationally.

The reality is different. Europe's fragmented mixture of public, private nonprofit, and private health service systems makes commitments to universal service provision in health care quite difficult to achieve (e.g. CEC 1995b; WHO 1993). About half of the E.U. member states have identified distinct gaps and inequalities in the coverage and in the integration of health service coverage related to cultural, socioeconomic, geographical, and policy factors (WHO 1994b).

A broad reorganization of health services is needed to adapt the service systems for processing and using substantially more information, for transferring information efficiently without geographical limits, and for making effective use of competences in any part of the health service network, as well as follow-up and evaluation of health service activities (Knauth 1996; Ministry of Social Affairs and Health 1996; Willcocks and Currie 1996).

ICT and the Cost-Effectiveness of Services

No comprehensive, systemwide analysis is available either from the United States or from Europe on the net cost-effectiveness or cost-benefit impact of ICT (Ministry of Social Affairs and Health 1996; U.S. Congress OTA 1995). This reflects the difficulty of calibrating changes in immaterial and subjective input and, particularly, output variables. Also, there is difficulty in isolating the changes that are specific to ICT.

Of the studies that exist, a cost-benefit analysis published by the U.S. Office of Technology Assessment showed that the implementation of electronic data interchange and health care financing administration software may save up to 1.8 percent of medical insurance–based health care costs (U.S. Congress OTA 1995). Also, some individual tasks in service provision (e.g., in nursing) have been improved with the help of ICT. But investments in ICT constitute only 1.4–3.0 percent of the total health budgets in most member states (Kajander and Konttinen 1996).

Some have argued that an economic appraisal is not decisive for the implementation of ICT and that other aspects, such as quality and accessibility, are more important (U.S. Congress OTA 1995). Indeed, some experts consider cost savings an unrealistic objective, stressing that the appropriate aim is *cost-effectiveness*—qualitatively better services for clients provided with the help of ICT without unreasonable increases in cost (Ministry of Social Affairs and Health 1996; Rinde et al. 1993).

Overall, presently available evidence indicates that expectations for ICT have been overoptimistic (U.S. Congress OTA 1995; McLaren and Ball 1995). But the effects need to be clarified by longer-term evaluations (Kajander and Konttinen 1996). Further development of this field is also warranted in view of both the foreseeable increase in demand for health services by aging populations and the growing costs of health care in all European countries

Consequences for Workers and Patients

The Health Care Workforce

The health sector is a major employer. In Finland, health services represent 8 percent and social services 5 percent of the workforce. In the United Kingdom, the National Health Service is the largest single employer in the country. Despite public budget constraints health is undoubtedly an area of growing demand. Thus savings in health care costs are being sought through ICT-related reductions in administrative personnel (U.S. Congress OTA 1995).

The effect of ICTs on the health sector will be similar to its effect on the workforce in general (see above). For instance, removing the health worker from direct contact with the patient is similar to removing industrial operators to a separate control room. And automating routine tasks eliminates many clerical positions (U.S. Congress OTA 1995).

Some manual jobs are likely to disappear. The numbers of professional staff will rise as new ICT experts are recruited to support frontline health workers (Ministry of Social Affairs and Health 1996). Also, restructuring existing jobs could improve efficiency. For example, nurses spend about one-fifth of their time on direct nursing tasks. Eliminating their secondary tasks with the help of ICT may improve their nursing performance (WHO 1994b).

ICT can also support health workers through better real-time and stored information and improved quality and efficiency of care through better control of events, information, documentation, imaging, and visibility of both anatomical and health function. The information is processed and represented so that decision making on diagnosis and treatment is easier and safer (Rantanen 1996a). On the other hand, with vast possibilities for monitoring, measuring, storing, and communicating data, it will be necessary to agree on what information is important and what can be left out.

Clearly meeting these new demands will require new training (see target no. 36 of the European Health for All). The new demands on health workers parallel those of ICT work in other sectors (U.S. Congress OTA 1995; Lareng 1996; Schreiber and Birmingham 1996). Special competences and skills are needed in information-intensive health work. For instance, general practitioners will have to communicate without releasing protected data. Some universities in Sweden have established new expert curricula for medical technology and cognitive sciences, although more moves in this direction are needed.

Impacts on Patients

New developments in health care systems have dual effects on patients. The scope and level of individual care are expected to be rise substantially. Treatments are likely to be better targeted and controlled, less invasive, and generally safer. Services will also be more geographically and temporally accessible. Nevertheless, new risks arise as medical services go increasingly on-line and self-help medicine proliferates.

Improving and expanding services in outpatient care, population-oriented activities, and prevention activities (Kajander and Konttinen 1996) might include the following:

- home care and follow-up (with ambulatory follow-up and control more chronically ill, handicapped, and elderly patients can receive care at home)
- remote monitoring of the general environment and alarm systems against hazardous substances, physical factors, and emergency situations
- self-care (may reduce care costs but appropriate quality assurance systems are needed to avoid incompetent, ineffective, or even hazardous practices)

Such client-oriented services allow people to take responsibility for their own health and reduce the institutionalization of long-term patients. They may be cheaper because they require less direct involvement of health personnel.

Many self-use technologies are emerging, including electronic health cards, devices for self-monitoring and self-care, and technical decision aids and educational and instruction packages on health care. For instance, diabetics use ICT-based blood glucose monitoring equipment and automatic insulin pumps. Many such instruments produce records to allow long-term follow-up and modification of insulin therapy. Remote transfer of readings to a clinic may facilitate monitoring of treatment. Applications could also be developed for bronchial asthma, high levels of cholesterol, or arterial hypertension.

Other areas of experimentation include the development of smart homes with automated, remotely controlled appliances, on-line communication, and the monitoring of patient activities and vital functions. The new technologies enable continuous tracking and thus raise the quality of care substantially compared to periodic checkups at the health center.

ICT-intensive medical practice generates information that can be used to inform and involve the client. For example, access to health information can be given to disabled people or people with communication difficulties (e.g., minority language groups). Such systems integrating sound, text (in different languages when necessary), images, and video are under development in CEC programs such as HELIOS, TIDE, and COST (Ekberg 1996).

Proliferation of information on medical matters, however, could lead to confusion and contradiction (Consultation on Health in the IS 1996). Electronic multimedia "home physicians" are entering the market, but will clients have the competence to use them? For instance, people affected by a particular disease might, through searching the Internet, achieve a level of knowledge about the disease that exceeds their GP's. But they do not have the wider range of knowledge need to interpret specific health information. Here nongovernmental organizations (NGOs) might cooperate with the health sector to disseminate accurate information on-line or off-line (WHO 1993).

Finally, on-line medical practices, in which the physician is at some distance from the patient, may affect the patient's cooperation and trust. Health service is based on the client's confidence in the physician and is founded on legislation concerning health personnel and ethical codes of professions. Trust is promoted when health care providers and clients participate in all aspects of service delivery. On-line medical practice radically changes the entire patient–physician or patient–nurse relationship, but little research is available about it. The right of the patient to be informed and to be given an opportunity to actively participate in all medical decisions is strongly emphasized in the World Medical Association Lisbon Declaration of the Patients' Rights (1995) and by national legislation (Pierce 1996). Clearly, available legislation and guidelines should be reviewed for possible amendments that would make them apply also to the information society.

Research on experiences in ICT-based health care is scarce and urgently needs to be expanded. Many issues have to be resolved: privacy, liability, safety, the consequences of operational failures and emergencies, long-term sustainability, family concerns, and human contacts. It is essential to guarantee accurate user instructions and adequate training (Kajander and Konttinen 1996). Overall, therefore, ICT for home care should be developed cautiously with well-planned and evaluated experiments.

ETHICAL ISSUES AND CONFIDENTIALITY

Medical Ethics and ICT

Health care is critically dependent on the trust that individuals and society place in the ethical standards of health service providers. The Council for International Organizations of Medical Sciences (CIOMS) and WHO consider respect for the human rights of the patient and the client to be central imperatives (CIOMS 1997). The new technologies raise new ethical issues that have not been completely identified but encompass concern for the confidentiality and privacy of personal health information (HLEG 1996).

Medicines, instruments, and alternative health care practices that are not properly tested or validated and numerous instructions concerning lifestyles or behaviors that carry health implications are already being disseminated or sold on the Internet. Unlike printed media, Internet content is not the legal responsibility of its contributors and distributors. Thus the burden of ensuring the correctness of information lies on the recipient. The rapid growth of such activities creates an urgent need to examine the situation and to find solutions to these problems.

The feasibility of previous ethical guidelines cannot be taken for granted and thus the following ethical points remain to be clarified:

- the ethics of the new telematics-based patient-physician relationship
- the ethical principles that pertain to treating patients from remote sites without personal contact
- the issues concerning ICT-assisted self-care, home care, and remote controls
- the principles governing all personnel involved in health care provision (e.g., technical personnel)
- the ethics of network-based communication, particularly in regard to protecting privacy and confidentiality
- the ethics of research and development experiments using ICT
- the issues of misinformation in ICT information channels (e.g., the Internet)

As with other new technologies (e.g., molecular biology and genetics; Bankowski and Capron 1991), ICT in health care requires a careful review of practices in view of ethics and, if necessary, the preparation of guidelines for new practices. WHO also emphasizes the need to follow the resolutions of the Council of Europe on basic human rights concerning new developments of the European social environments (Council of Europe, Basic Human Rights).

Confidentiality

Health service planning depends on data from environmental, behavioral, and even genetic determinants of health and the occurrence of health outcomes and diseases in individuals and populations. It needs quick and easy availability of information during the actual (and often emergency) operation of services, good searchability, and accessibility to multiple users at any time. It also needs secure, long-term storage of information. Such information is also prerequisite for drawing scientifically sound conclusions for the targets of health policies and programs, thus serving both collective and individual health interests (Ministry of Social Affairs and Health 1996). But all these requirements are subject to the overriding concern for the protection of confidential personal health information. Although ICT-based data systems provide effective services in responding to most of the above-mentioned demands, they simultaneously generate a number of questions on data protection, confidentiality, and data security.

The confidentiality of health data is regulated by the E.U. Directive 95/46 (CEC 1995c) on the protection of individuals with regard to processing of personal data and on the free movement of such data. The expanding use of ICT in health care, including telemedicine services, has given rise to several new liability issues. New actors—those who provide and maintain technology and of its maintenance—also play a role in confidentiality issues.

Although such data has been protected by regulations in the past, the following new challenges are associated with ICT-based information systems:

- deliberate or inadvertent mistakes and misuse and abuse of information
- technical problems such as lack of security, errors, malfunctions, system failures

In summary, then, the national implementation of Directive 95/46 and its full implementation by all member states is necessary for its effectiveness in practice. This applies particularly to the safe transfer of data between countries (Blume 1996). New liability issues have arisen in the implementation of ICT in the health sector (U.S. Congress OTA 1995). The indirect contact that occurs between health experts and patients through ICT is a new setting that has so far generated little in the way of practical and research experience. Another problem of liability is the compressed nature of information provided through telematic transfer; it may be not be sufficiently detailed to permit reliable diagnosis and treatment.

CONCLUSION

We expect growing ICT use to produce a broadly positive effect, provided that it is carefully implemented. This means making sure that that it is used safely and ergonomically, investing in training, protecting confidentiality of health information, and observing ethical principles.

ICT has both positive and negative effects on health systems (table 8.2). The positive impact is better health information and expanded health education and health promotion. The population has ready access to health information sources and can consult health experts on the Internet, which substantially improves people's access to health information.

Table 8.2 SWOT Analysis of the Impact of Implementation of ICT on Health and the Health Sector

Strengths	*Weaknesses*
• Possibility of expanding the coverage of services for all • Higher quality of services for all through teleconsultations and medical technology • Reduction of the need for patient transport and expert travel through telemedicine • Better information on health and its determinants and on performance of health services • Better cost-effectiveness, not necessarily cost reduction	• Polarization of users and nonusers • Sedentary and unreal lifestyles • Disappearnace of certain occupations and certain competences • Occupational health problems of information-intensive work • Information overload, irrelevant information, and misinformation for users

Opportunities	*Threats*
• Still much potential for the improvement of coverage and quality of services and organization of seamless care through networking • Potential for reduction of costs as long-term perspective • New professional developments for users • Better possibilities for prevention, health promotion, and citizens' own action • Special services for underserved groups (disabled, elderly, etc.)	• High vulnerability of technology and programmed systems due to technical or human failures • Intentionally destructive behavior, information, or actions within the system or with the help of the system • Productivity paradox; wide-scale investments without visible health or economic benefits • Too technology-driven development irrespective of the population's real needs leading to low acceptance of technologies • Violation of confidentiality or ethical principles

The negative impacts of ICT include a more sedentary lifestyle. The intensive use of video screens can result in psychophysiological and sensory overload. Changes in daily routine among heavy users may also be unhealthy. Misinformation, along with unhealthy behavior, products, and lifestyles, may also affect the health of a small part of the population. Better training and awareness raising are needed to avoid such adverse effects.

Occupational complaints associated with ICT include symptoms in the shoulder and neck, hand and arm, lower arm and hand (carpal tunnel syndrome), and eye strain caused by the intensive use of visual displays. Psychological problems result from information overload and high performance demands, especially when combined with time pressures and inappropriate work organization. Most of these problems can be prevented with appropriate ergonomic planning and attention to work design. It is important to make sure that workers are properly trained and supported, especially when ICT is being introduced.

ICT will play an important role in providing information to aid planning, performance measurement, and better integration of seamless care. Current estimates do not indicate that ICT will lead to lower costs but suggest that it will help improve the cost-effectiveness of care.

ICT will have an impact on employment, with organizational restructuring leading to the disappearance of some manual categories of health personnel. The competence of all categories of health personnel must be strengthened by ICT training as part of professional development.

An important implication of ICT is greater participation by clients and patients in managing their own health and treatment. More and better information, home-based treatment, and attention to special needs are all expected to make a positive contribution. But everything depends on the proper design and training of clients in the use of ICT-based health services. On the other hand, self-help medicine could lead to a depersonalization and mechanization of the human contact that lies at the heart of much of the health services. Since this development may leave some people behind, special efforts may be needed to meet the service needs of such groups and should be developed.

On the legislative framework, the rights and responsibilities of workers, employers, patients and health care personnel, and new professional groups will need to be reexamined; new regulations are needed that protect confidential data and define liability in cases of inadvertent or advertent technical failures.

Finally, further research is needed on the health and social impact of the information society, including the impact of ICT on health and on health services. A particular line of research could be the critical evaluation of health and economic impact of ICT-intensive health care and the development of methods for assessment of services using such new technologies. Overall, though, we would underline once again that the impact (both economical and social) of the information society in the health sector depends less on the technology and more on its implementation, including design, conditions of use, and competence of the users.

NOTE

The authors warmly thank Miikka Rantanen, student in technology, for assistance in collection of appropriate reference material, especially that compiled with the help of Internet.

9

Information and Communication Technologies in Distance and Lifelong Learning

Gill Kirkup and Ann Jones

Lifelong learning is a vital element of the emerging information society. But a "lifelong learning society" must be open. It should be accessible to people wishing to train or retrain in sought-after skills and it should help alleviate the "creative destruction" accompanying the introduction of information and communication technology (ICT). It should contribute to the quality of life of disadvantaged groups. Ultimately, it should contribute to the personal, social, and cultural development of all citizens.

Open and distance learning (ODL) is the foundation of any affordable system of lifelong learning, since it is eminently suited to the needs of working citizens.[1]

> Open Learning arrangements enable people to learn at the time, place and pace which satisfy their circumstances and requirements. The emphasis is on opening up opportunities by overcoming barriers that result from geographical isolation, personal or work commitments or conventional course structures which have often prevented people from gaining access to the training they need. (Manpower Services Commission 1984, 7)

THE HISTORICAL ROLE OF MEDIA IN MASS EDUCATION

Any discussion of ODL must center on ICTs, since they are so often viewed as the solution to many problems inherent in text-based open and distance learning. Indeed, it is among the ODL community in particular that research and expertise on a variety of media for teaching has developed. However, it is worth recalling that attempts to incorporate various media into educational programs, to enhance education as well as to make it more widely available beyond the classroom, are as old as the media themselves. Cheap print, broadcast radio, television, film, audio recordings on tape and disk, and telephone communication have been used with different degrees of success in a variety of educational circumstances (Tiffin and Rajasingham 1995). The nearly one hundred years experience of teaching the use of mass media offers lessons that are relevant to finding an appropriate role for new ICTs.

Mass education using mass media began in nineteenth-century Europe, driven by popular movements to widen educational provision. The majority of the population was excluded from postsecondary institutions such as universities because selection criteria were restrictive. In some countries widely scattered populations could not be served by face-to-face methods, even at school level. In those days, distance education relied on the postal system and cheap printing, a technology that was available, affordable, and acceptable to all literate people.

Commercial print publishers and educational institutions first collaborated to produce self-study course materials in 1912, when the University of Wisconsin and McGraw-Hill commissioned special texts for publication and sale on the open market. These cheap study materials and texts were also available to face-to-face institutions. Such copublishing is now a major source of income for publishers and their academic partners.

As communication technologies have developed, educators have always sought to apply them, perhaps waxing a bit overenthusiastic about their potential: "It is no imaginary dream to picture the school of tomorrow as an entirely different institution from that of today, because of the use of radio in teaching" (from the University of Iowa in 1927, quoted in Watkins 1991, 25).

It has not always been feasible to rely on postal services for teaching, especially for people with low levels of literacy or among transient populations, and educational broadcasting (radio and TV) has served as an alternative. The first educational radio broadcasting that took place failed under pressure from commercial radio, but beginning in the 1920s, the British Broadcasting Corporation (BBC) developed an extensive program of educational radio for adults. It was targeted at adult study groups and included accompanying texts. From the 1950s the proportion of BBC airtime awarded to structured adult education was very small (Dodds 1991), and small, if significant, amounts of programming on BBC TV have been given to educational programs.

A. W. Bates (1995) distinguishes between instructional television and educational broadcasting. Instructional television usually supports a specific program of study. Educational broadcasts are informative programs for the general viewer, without assessments or accreditation. The widespread ownership of videocassette recorders (VCRs) has expanded the possibilities of educational broadcasting at night, as there is less pressure to compete for viewers with commercial channels. In the United Kingdom (from 1996), the BBC named the hours between 2:00 A.M. and 5.00 A.M. the "learning zone." During these hours many instructional programs are broadcast, with students programming a VCR to record while they sleep. In a similar system in Italy, from 1992 to 1995 the Consorzio Nettuno transmitted, late at night, over 2,000 hours of university lectures (Garito 1995). This is a more cost-effective way of providing television programs than distributing recorded cassette tapes.

Digital broadcasting and "video on demand" may increase opportunities to provide instructional television by eliminating the competition for airtime with commercial programs. It may be that instructional broadcasting is entering a period of customization that will fit the individualized model of Western adult learning better than ever before. It will be able to offer better "choice" about what to study, the time and pace of learning, and also which media to use. Experiments are now taking place to associate educational broadcasts with Internet sites, where students can get more information or leave messages for the television producers.

Funding the production of high-quality educational media is difficult for most educational providers—large- or small-scale providers of education and training, publicly funded system or private. Neil (1981) distinguished between a "whole system control model" and those that are "embedded into communities of educational agencies" (cited in Moore 1991). In the whole system model the institution has control over its finance, examinations, accreditation, curriculum, and instructional services. Generally, producing and integrating multiple media for education has been most successful in whole control model systems. Educational consortia, by contrast, have found it difficult to fund media with high capital costs.

Budgetary constraints in industrialized countries have shifted funding away from large, autonomous educational institutions. Cooperative arrangements between institutions (sometimes involving private industry) are now more common, stimulated by encouragement to expand the range of media used for teaching and training. This has increased the number and variety of organizations that are producing and delivering ODL (Open Learning Directory 1996).

Many open learning programs in the United Kingdom in the 1990s have combined vocational instruction with low-level ICT training. This opens a way to integrate ICT skills and ODL as a step toward the learning society. However, this will not be possible where traditional literacy and numeracy is wanting, such as among refugees and guest workers, who are often outside mainstream educational provision. Here, the use of audiocassette tapes and pictorial flip charts in supervised local study groups remains the best educational model.

The Open University United Kingdom (OUUK) is an example of a successful provider of open learning for adults. It has made use of a broad range of media from its inception. The OUUK has always benefited from its association with the BBC for both production assistance and access to broadcasting "slots." OUUK was one of the first nationally funded ODL institutions. It is now one of the few with enough resources to produce integrated multiple media and student support and assessment on a national scale, putting the OUUK at the forefront of new media developments. Institutions lacking funding sources may enter into association with a commercial developer, with the risk of downgrading pedagogical priorities. Otherwise, they use materials developed elsewhere.

The European market for new educational media is very depressed and rather underdeveloped. For example, U.K. CD-ROM sales of nonbusiness applications for 1995 show that educational CDs accounted for only 2.2 percent of sales, in spite of representing 17 percent of the titles available. By comparison, "shoot-em up" games accounted for 24 percent of sales despite making up 11 percent of the available titles (table 9.1). The educational niche is significantly less profitable than the entertainment market, even as educational radio and TV are less profitable than commercial broadcasting. Many commercial publishers have withdrawn resources from multimedia production because of low return on investment.

Meanwhile, establishing new institutions on the whole system control model (e.g., OUUK) now seems impossibly expensive. Collaborative models must be established in ways that provide access to the resources and skills necessary for high-quality educational media production. Better use might be made of existing national ODL providers as lead bodies in more extensive networks.

Old media may be more cost-effective and educationally effective after all. M. Van Kekerix and J. Andrews (1991) make the controversial point that it is hard to find clear-cut evidence that new media help students learn any better than "correspondence" text: "Media are mere vehicles that deliver instruction but do not influence student achievement any more than the truck that delivers our groceries causes changes in our nutrition" (p. 144).

Such an assertion introduces a refreshing skepticism into overly enthusiastic discussions about the potential of ICTs. Research on mixed media teaching indicates that the integration and method of using them contribute to success and to students' perceptions of the utility. Collis (1996) refers to work by Bentley et al. (1992) in which adult distance learners were asked to rank the various media in terms of their perceived educational effectiveness. Television used alone was ranked as least useful, but when it was combined with a printed text and tutor support it was ranked as third most useful.

Bates (1995) listed six criteria to be used in selecting any media: student access; cost; teaching and learning; interaction, user friendliness, and control; organizational issues; novelty; and finally speed. He listed all the media in use by the early 1990s and rated them on these criteria (table 9.2). Bates also attempted a comparative costing of educational media. At the lowest end of the range he called the production costs of one hour's face-to-face teaching "one unit." In comparison, the production of one hour of computer-mediated communication (CMC) costs between two and five units, one hour of high-quality television, twenty to fifty units, and one hour's interactive multimedia, fifty to one hundred units.

Media-based materials are too expensive to be developed by individuals, or by departments, or even by individual institutions. To be economically feasible, they must be made available, and used by larger numbers of students than any one institution could possibly muster before the materials are out of date. . . . Campus-based teaching institutions cannot turn themselves overnight into media-based teaching institutions. Moreover, they do not have sufficient numbers to justify in-

Table 9.1 Sale of CD-ROM Games by Genre (U.K.), 1995 (estimate)

Genre	% of Sales	% of Titles
Shoot 'em ups	23.9	11.0
Graphical adventure/role playing	20.2	14.0
Strategy games and puzzles	14.1	8.0
Sports simulations	12.5	14.0
Flight/ship/submarine simulations	10.2	11.0
Fighting games	10.0	8.0
Racing games	6.1	11.0
Edutainment/infotainment	2.2	17.0
Platform games	0.4	3.0
Other	0.4	1.0

Source: Durlacher Research 1995.

Table 9.2   Strengths and Weaknesses of Different Teaching Technologies for ODL

	One-way Media						Interactive Media					
	Print	Radio	Audiocassette	Educational broadcast TV	Prerecorded TV	Videocassettes	Computer-based learning	Multimedia	Audio-conferencing	Live interactive TV	Video-conferencing	Computer mediated conferencing
Accessibility	★★★	★★★	★★★	★★	★	★★★	★★	★	★★★	★	★	★★
Cost effective for many learners	★★★	★★★	★★★	★	★★★	★★	★	★	★	★	★	★★★
Cost effective for few learners	★★	★	★★	★	★	★	★	★	★★★	★	★	★★★
Good for presenting material	★★	★	★★	★★★	★★	★★★	★★	★★★	★	★	★	★
Good for skills transfer	★★	★	★★★	★★	★★	★★★	★★	★★★	★★	★	★★	★★★
Interactivity of learning materials	★	★	★★★	★	★★	★★★	★★	★★★	★	★	★★	★★
Social Interactivity	★	★	★	★	★★	★	★	★	★★★	★★	★★	★★★
Organizational	★	★★	★★★	★	★★	★★	★	★	★★★	★★	★★	★★★
Speed	★	★★★	★★	★	★	★	★	★	★★★	★★★	★★★	★★★

Source: Adapted from Bates (1995).
Note: ★★★ = good; ★★ = average; ★ = poor.

house production of materials, so there will always be a need for inter-institutional collaboration. . . . The two key criteria for selecting specific areas of the curriculum for development are that topics must be taught widely, and widely acknowledged to present difficulties for students. (Laurillard 1993, 182)

NEW ICTs IN MASS EDUCATIONAL PROGRAMS

Two developments have the potential to transform education and training in the radical way required to produce effective learning societies. One is the increasing availability and variety of functions of ICTs and the other is the priority accorded to lifelong learning. These developments interact to produce an enthusiasm about ICTs among educational policy makers because of their potential to expand educational access and modes of delivery. Educators and politicians also see the potential for ICTs to improve the quality and range of resources for students and to help deal with increasing numbers of students while resources decrease. For example, Mason and Kaye (1990) see ICTs as making possible:

> the breaking down of conceptual distinctions between distance education and place-based education. The changing of traditional roles of faculty, administrative and support staff, adjunct tutors. And the provision of an opportunity, which never existed before, to create a network of scholars, "space" for collective thinking, and access to peers for socialising and serendipitous change." (Paulson 1992, 56)

The authors are referring in particular to telematics (telecommunications plus computers), but other new developments such as hypertext, multimedia, and desktop publishing (DTP) also contribute to this change.

Hypertexts and Multimedia

According to one definition, hypertext is "a computer-based software system for organizing and storing information to be accessed non-sequentially and constructed collaboratively by authors and users" (Jonassen 1991, 83). The information can consist of text, diagrams, pictures, video sequences, and sound. It is a much more flexible and less constrained medium than text alone. The information is structured in a way that allows multiple paths to be made through the material. Rather than progress linearly, the user navigates by clicking on an "active" word. The program then calls up the item to which it has been linked. In theory, thousands of links can be made, and once the learner has moved to another screen via a link, she has new options for making further moves.

The educational potential of hypertext systems has generated a great deal of excitement. Instead of being sequential and booklike, a hypertext system is like a museum or an art gallery in which the learner decides which avenues to explore and what links to make. It has been argued that the lack of linearity can make hypertext very learner centered and thus well-suited to independent learning.

Interest in hypertext is now subsumed within more recent interest in multimedia and the World Wide Web. The Web is a global hypermedia system that comprises separate pieces of information (text, pictures, video, or sound) held on computers in different locations, electronically linked through "hardwired" telematics systems and conceptually linked through a hypertext structure. In theory, anyone with a computer can be linked to the system through the local telephone network and thus gain access to all information in the system. In practice, access is often limited due to the slowness in the system in downloading data, especially when many users are on line. As more Web pages are including graphics and sound, many users find that their personal computers cannot access more hi-tech pages.

There are also conceptual and pedagogical issues at stake. For example, unless navigational aids are provided, learners can easily get lost in complex data structures. Returning to the art gallery metaphor, curators have understood this problem for many years. Most art galleries offer text and audio guides, often in the form of a linear "tour." As with many tools for independent learning, experience and expertise may be necessary to make best use of such applications. Laurillard (1993, 126) comments that:

> browsing, or scanning, or hunting down a piece of information from an extensive resource all play a rather small part in learning academic knowledge. The learner is likely to . . . need help with discerning the structure and through it the meaning of a particular text being studied. This is where hypertext fails to support the learner, . . . it provides no feedback. . . . It is not a stand-alone learning medium. It needs additional support from the teacher, just as library work does.

Hypertext increasingly includes sounds, video, and photographs in an extension of possibilities often referred to as hypermedia. Currently the most potentially powerful application of ICTs is a combination of the multimedia workstation with telematics. This combines the features of multimedia with the benefits of computer-mediated communication, and it is extending further to include broadcasting.

The importance of "multimedia" is that it combines traditional computer capabilities with those of other media. For example, *Analysis of Glacial Sediments* (Department of Geography, University of Southampton, United Kingdom) teaches undergraduates the techniques of analyzing glacial sediments and prepares them for their field trips. It includes some basic teaching that cannot easily be presented in text (e.g., animated images to show a glacier moving along). Students work on carefully sequenced information and test their knowledge using multiple-choice questions. In theory multimedia provides the student with more flexibility and control over content and learning, and the teacher with a wider range of resources on which to draw. It is interactive in the sense that a user can access the material presented in different ways, and the "program" can give feedback. It can also facilitate communication with other users via e-mail on in real time.

However, multimedia is too expensive for most institutions to produce. Governments have therefore encouraged consortia of educational institutions and ICT manufacturers to produce multimedia likely to have wide use. The University of Southampton program was part of a U.K. government-funded initiative (Teaching and Learning with Technology Program) to produce teaching materials for free distribution to all U.K. institutions of higher education.

There are further advantages to teamwork. Academics with no expertise in the different uses (and pitfalls) of various media can relatively easily put together a package that may look good and yet be of little pedagogical value. Courseware development teams, on the other hand, (see Laurillard 1993) can call on complementary skills and knowledge. For example, teams of specialists from different areas develop OUUK courses (e.g., broadcasting, educational technology, typographic design) as well as the academic subject specialists and computing.

Less ambitious than multimedia are the computer-assisted learning packages that have been available for many years. Students can access them either in educational institutions or at home. The educational benefits of these kinds of programs (simulation and tutorial) derive mainly from the feedback that students obtain (either on their answers to questions or their attempts to, say, carry out modeling) and the motivational power of computers themselves.

There are, however, a number of educational concerns about the use of both hypertext and multimedia, aside from the problems of navigating through hypertexts and the Web. It is not clear that computer-aided learning or multimedia makes appropriate educational use of the media. Is the computer being used to do something that could be done better another way? Much "multimedia" is essentially presentational. It lacks the interactivity that was argued to be so important (e.g., Laurillard 1993). High-quality visuals, combined with sound and movement, can make such applications very appealing, but the media may not be well exploited. Video may serve just as well and is far less expensive. Also, many multimedia packages are limited to exploring a database or encyclopaedia. Although electronic encyclopaedias can include much more information than printed versions, this does not in itself give them additional educational value.

A further criticism of multimedia, paradoxically, is that in losing linearity (a potential strength) it also loses narrative structure and coherence. Plowman (1996, 92) argues that:

> although Interactive Multimedia (IMM) Programmes superficially appear to combine media with which we are already familiar, such as film, television and books, the "reading" or interpreting skills we have acquired from exposure to these

conventional media are not directly transferable. We are not yet accustomed to the new forms of text engendered by the combination of media and our narrative expectations can be confused and thwarted.

In a large evaluation of interactive media in English and Welsh schools, Plowman and Chambers (1994) found that children apparently were unable to make sense of the program without considerable teacher intervention. Interestingly, another study—of adults using simulations rather than interactive media but in a context in which they could control their learning—also suggests that there may be a threshold of guidance that is needed in experimental learning situations (Riebler and Parmley 1995).

Research and evaluation of the educational use of multimedia is growing, but much is still unknown about its educational use or its recognized problems (such as navigation). It is crucial that we continue to evaluate students' use of educational multimedia in order to gain a better understanding of the role it can best play.

Telematics

In the 1980s computer-mediated communication (CMC) was viewed as the most important ICT application in education because it allows dialogue between learners and teachers. CMC uses computers linked through the telephone network and via satellites to provide new forms of communication: machine to machine and user to user. It allows both real-time and time-independent communication between individuals, among and between groups, and to organizations and databases outside education. Telematics can therefore support individualized learning, enhance collaborative learning, and encourage the sense of community that many students look for when they study.

In addition to e-mail facilities, computer conferencing systems allow designated groups of users to share databases of previous messages. Students and teachers (and sometimes nonacademic subject experts) are organized into groups for computer conferences. These can be based on topical interest groups or on membership in a particular tutorial group. Conferences can be "closed" so that only named individuals can contribute, or they can be open to any participant. Until recently, conferencing has been text based and has depended on a degree of literacy (traditional and technological) in students. It is therefore of little use in teaching basic literacy and life skills or for populations with low literacy skills. Also, "conferences" usually operate in only one language, which restricts the opportunity for international networking. However, nontextual forms that could overcome such barriers (e.g., digital video) have also been experimented with (below).

The Open University in the United Kingdom (OUUK) pioneered the European use of large-scale computer conferencing for postsecondary education (Mason and Kaye 1990). Conferencing is now established on a variety of courses (Mason 1994), including a foundations of technology course with around 4,500 students. A recent example is an international course on telematics that uses computer conferencing as the main medium, along with two textbooks and a small number of face-to-face meetings.

Many other providers are also using telematics. For example, the Dutch Open University (OuNI) is increasingly using telematics as part of a revised model for tutoring (Gastkemper, Schlusmans, and Speelman 1995). Current applications of telematics in both the OUUK and the OuNI allow students to get feedback on programs by e-mail, to work on assignments collaboratively, to send in work using computer conferencing, and to obtain individual support through e-mail and computer conferences. In the United States, Turoff (1997) reported on the experimental use of computer conferencing and video to create a virtual classroom at the New Jersey Institute of Technology. Over half of the students felt that it enabled them to complete more courses per semester than would otherwise have been possible and the majority felt that the virtual classroom improved the convenience of course access, access to their professors, and the quality of learning. There were some problems, however. The increased demand for access put pressure on the system, causing slowdowns.

Synchronous media such as audiographics and video conferencing are being used increasing, especially by dual-mode universities for delivering lectures to remote sites. This can provide real-time interactivity without lengthy travel (e.g., Cole et al. 1997). As Mason (1995) points out, however, teachers often resort to what they know best, lecturing, when using video conferencing and audiographics systems. Although this remains an efficient way of transmitting information, the impact of the lecture suffers when it is transferred to these new media. Students find it difficult to concentrate for an hour on information coming from a relatively small screen.

Currently, the cost of desktop multimedia machines is too high for many homes, and there it limits the potential for dialogue and interaction. Large-scale ODL institutions such as the OUUK, whose quality lies in delivering individual learning and whose students study at home, are therefore not making much use of such media, despite its extensive use of networking in general. However, as with all new technologies, it is important to experiment with case studies in order to build up expertise for the time when the technology becomes more widely available.

The European Commission has funded projects on telematics applications of all sorts, including education. One experiment, ELNET: The European Business and Languages Learning Network, provided an electronic network for business studies students in universities in the United Kingdom, France, and Germany to produce cross-cultural learning in a "virtual educational establishment" (i.e., to replicate some of the learning of an educational exchange visit) (Davies 1994).

Telematics can also support students with disabilities by allowing them to experience access and communication levels equal to their able-bodied peers (Coombs 1993). One project, however, at the Norwegian State Institution for Distance Education (NFU) (Nilsen 1995) uses telecommunications to support people who are blind or partially sighted in their use of personal computers. The SynsIT project is developing a two-way communication system so that users can have ready access to expert knowledge via a bulletin board system, support when errors occur via special software, and distance education via the video telephone.

Other dual-mode universities are experimenting with CMC to extend adult and continuing education to "off-campus students" (Silvennoinen and Kerttula 1994) and in the United Kingdom (Pincas 1995).

School networking is practiced widely (Veen et al. 1994), and experiments are taking place with equipment that is not yet available but may be in the near future. For example, demonstrations are being carried out at the Apple Research Laboratory to explore pedagogic uses of new technologies. One of these is the Multimedia Bulletin Board Research project on how technology might facilitate inquiry in science (Woolsey and Bellamy 1997). Here, school students and experts collaborated over networks, using digital video to share observations and ask questions. Prototype software was used to display video messages of pupils' questions about the weather. Messages were sent to San Francisco Exploratorium scientists who annotated them or sent back new messages containing relevant movies or descriptions of simple experiments that the children could conduct in the classroom. One benefit reported by the teachers was that it reduced their isolation and supported them by giving them access to experts.

Evaluation of these projects has demonstrated that both students and teachers need to learn new skills to interrogate distant information systems and to communicate with each other using the network. In many existing cases, educational providers have simply adapted or added some telematics onto face-to-face or other ODL provision, whereas what is needed are materials designed for the strengths and weaknesses of the particular medium (Paulson 1992). To be fully effective, ICTs need to be fully integrated into courses. The technology does not in itself contribute to improved education. In regard to computer-mediated communication generally, however, there is agreement about crucial issues, including scalability and tutor involvement, the structuring of activities, and changing the role of the learner and teacher.

Scalability and Tutor Involvement

There are fewer examples of computer conferencing being used with very large numbers of students (e.g., over 1,000), but it is clear that the potential number of messages for both students and tutors to deal with could easily become unmanageable. The OUUK often combines tutorial groups so that two or three tutors are on-line for particular conferences, but conferencing clearly does not reduce tutor involvement. In most cases, the time needed for tutor input is underestimated (Pincas 1995).

Structuring Activities

Much of the literature on computer conferencing stresses the importance of structuring activities to maximize the likelihood of students becoming involved. There are different ways of doing this. For example, Pincas (1995) comments that tutors need to structure the environment quite carefully. The use of conferencing as part of a Masters included having the students meet face-to-face at the beginning of each term. Some students felt that their contributions were ignored and others were unhappy with the uneven level of contributions—both common issues in conferencing. In this case a tighter structure was adopted in which the tutor paired students so that each member of a pair commented on the other's answer to a task; this strategy proved very successful.

Changing the Role of Learner and Teacher

One argument for the increased use of computer conferencing (see Pincas 1995) is that it is consistent with the current shift from teacher- and knowledge-centered methods to student-centered ones. However, as Mason (1995) has pointed out, although the role of the teacher is changing (to resource, facilitator), there is little evidence that it is diminishing. Indeed, telematics combined with resource-based learning requires explicit training and support.

Desktop Publishing

Desktop publishing (DTP) may be the invisible revolution in education. For many educational providers, text remains the core teaching medium. DTP offers institutional providers and teachers a potential revolution in the way texts are produced, and it does so using a technology that remains invisible to the student. DTP is the use of computers to integrate text and graphics in an electronic form, which is then produced instantly on paper. The power of desktop personal computers combined with page layout programs and quality laser printing makes it possible to produce teaching and learning texts with high-quality print and page design without accessing the skills of printing professionals. This has a number of potential benefits (Lefrere 1994). The production time of text design and the costs of design are reduced. The possibility of experimenting with layout makes it possible to improve the quality of materials and update or revise them rapidly and efficiently. Course texts can be produced on demand by a laser printer, and they can be individualized for different groups of students. DTP material can be designed to be distributed as hypertext or multimedia, as well in printed form, allowing students to print off the parts they need.

Properly trained academics could produce the texts, although it might be better to rely on the skills of DTP professionals (Balser and Sturmer 1993). As with multimedia production, multiskilled teams will usually produce the best material. Already one of the problems with the expansion of ODL to traditional situations is that some institutions presume that ODL texts are simply lecture notes and reading lists from conventionally taught courses, bound with assessment material and sold to students. Ease of production has led to some very poor quality printed ODL. It can be argued that this problem, like the use of poor-quality multimedia, arises among teachers who use new ICTs as a "bolt on" to traditional curricula or as a solution to resource problems.

Issues for Teachers

As we have seen, ICTs may be seen as a "technological fix" to the pressure of too many students and too few resources. However, ICTs are likely to increase rather than reduce the teaching load. In one case study (John Moores University, United Kingdom) the move to ODL required staff time, training, and, perhaps most importantly, a shift in culture. Additional requirements to teach via CMC, often outside of class hours, involve extra time that is always underestimated (e.g., Mason 1995). Some of the less interactive teaching (satellite and tele-teaching) that is intended to reach mass audiences and to function as a stand-alone teaching package poses the real threat of making the teacher redundant.

In a climate of increased claims on teachers' time and increased pressure on costs, some teachers are suspicious (or at best ambivalent) about the use of new technologies. The Higginson Report, produced by the Learning and Technology Committee set up by the Further Education Funding Council (FEFC 1995) in the United Kingdom, documented the current and potential use of technology in the further education sector. It noted that many teachers are "suspicious that computers and resource centers are being used to drive down teaching hours with the principle aim of saving money" (p. 13).

However, there have also been more positive reactions. It has been widely argued that the use of ICTs as information-providing resources in schools can enable the teacher to step out of the more traditional "teaching" role and become more of a colleague and guide (e.g., Fraser et al. 1990). Such changes can be empowering, allowing the teacher and students more "equal" roles as more equal partners in learning. But they also require teachers to give up power and status. It is possible that ICTs have a much higher status than teachers or education itself in the eyes of children and young adults. A closer association with ICTs could therefore raise the status of teachers and teaching. Other evaluations suggest that the introduction of technology into the classroom often sparks a reevaluation and definition of the whole activity of teaching and learning:

> Meaningful use of technology in schools required far more than just dropping technology into classrooms. Teachers implemented what amounted to a change in the learning culture at the sites. The greatest changes in student advances occurred in classes where teachers were striving to modify their traditional roles and beginning to seek a balance between the appropriate use of direct instruction strategies and collaborative, inquiry-driven knowledge construction strategies. (Dwyer 1995, 1)

Clearly, as with many innovations, ICTs have not been adopted in teaching to the extent that was predicted. This is true across all sectors of education. The reasons for the lack of up-take are not clear but are likely to be a complex interaction of predictable factors such as access, training, and resources and the culture and infrastructure of the institution. It is also likely that teachers will make their own cost-benefit analyses and decide whether an investment in ICTs will help deliver their particular curriculum objectives. Hurley (1992) notes, for example, the overriding importance of "perceived usefulness" in determining the use of technology. Research is now being carried out on the reasons for the use and the lack of use of ICTs in education at many different levels (see, e.g., Robertson et al. 1995; Cuban 1986; Barnard 1997) and should result in better information about barriers to adoption.

ISSUES FOR THE PROVIDING ORGANIZATION

Earlier, we discussed Neil's distinction (Neil 1981) between the "whole system control model" and systems that are "embedded into communities of educational agencies," arguing that less well resourced (and centrally organized) institutions may be at a disadvantage in making use of different media. In some countries (e.g., the United Kingdom) a new mechanism has been introduced recently for ensuring "quality" in both HE and school education—competition. Laurillard (1993) argues that this development leads to inefficiencies because resources are limited and competition leads to repetition of effort and could eventually lead to poorer education for all. Many European governments have attempted to counter this to some extent by allocating special funds to consortia of institutions to develop courseware for free distribution within the sector. Other developments, where money follows institutional assessment or status, will tend to ensure that the best resourced institutions stay well resourced while others stay poor. There is, therefore, a differential access to ICTs by institutions—consistency in educational quality. ICTs are expensive, require expensive infrastructure (such as an ISDN cable and technical support), and may require certain skills in their users (e.g., literacy in a variety of media). This tends to make their use, and relevance, more likely in wealthy institutions and regions.

In the near future multimedia packages may be produced and distributed, fulfilling a function similar to that of DTP software for conventional text. Indeed, many authoring packages are now promoted as enabling a teacher to produce a multimedia package on her own PC using her own resources. However, such packages are not likely to reach the high standards of media production that students now expect from commercial multimedia, and they may unfortunately also embody very simplistic educational principles (since these are the easiest to design around). They may also involve a duplication of effort. High-quality teacher-produced multimedia is likely to be rare. Because educational multimedia has proved unprofitable for commercial producers, the educational sector cannot rely on commercial producers to supply a wide range of good educational multimedia products. Governments must find other ways to promote educational production.

RESPONDING TO DIVERSE NEEDS:
ODL AND ICTs IN EDUCATION

At the beginning of this chapter we argued that ODL offers one route toward the establishment of a lifelong learning society. We have also pointed out that it will need to respond to the diverse needs of different areas. For example, in the European Union, as we have noted, student numbers have grown considerably without any corresponding increase in resources. This has led to many universities becoming dual mode, teaching via ODL methods and using ODL materials.

Such institutions, and also schools trying to teach larger classes, are attracted by ICTs, which can play a part in more learner led independent study. Because ODL will play a role in delivering the learning society and because it has a track record in producing and evaluating materials for independent learning, many of the lessons of ODL are applicable in considering the new ICTs. The strengths of ODL can be summarized as follows:

- flexibility in place and time of study
- flexibility in pace of study (although if the course is assessed, there may be assignment deadlines)
- no requirements for prior study or qualification (open access systems)
- modular and flexible materials

B. Lisewski (1994) is one of a number of education writers to argue that adult students will have to engage in more independent study and that institutions will have to make greater use of ODL. He described the Open Learning Pilot Project at the Business School at Liverpool John Moores University (LJMU), United Kingdom, which attempts to do just this. LJMU introduced an ODL version of one of its courses. At the time, the student population was becoming more heterogeneous with an increase in mature students with a much wider range of experience than traditional school dropouts. Tutors were also becoming responsible for much larger numbers of students.

Students received four modules in an ODL format, complemented by study guidance briefing sessions and a "surgery" support system. Each nine-week module was divided into three equal study periods, each with a briefing session in the first week and an "hour" surgery in weeks two and three. Much of the content was fixed. Students worked at a set pace, submitted coursework, and wrote an exam at the end of each module.

However, this arguably more student-centered approach conflicted with students' expectations. An evaluation highlighted the students' (thwarted) expectations for a weekly lecture; they also wanted tutorials. They found the

learning materials difficult and wanted greater guidance. Some students, especially mature students, enjoyed the time available to self-organize and greatly
appreciated the increased choice. Others found the greater freedom and responsibility difficult. Interestingly, therefore, this integrated style of course did
not suit the heterogeneous population for which it was designed. The course
designers also felt that the materials were not interactive enough. Lisewski
(1994) commented that "students not only need to be shown how best to use
the learning medium but also require guidance in independent study, time management techniques and the ability to reflect critically on their own learning
practices" (p. 18).

The use of resource-based learning is increasing and has been defined as
"open access, self-directed learning from a large information source" (Taylor
and Laurillard 1995). Evidence from a resource-based learning course at the
Open University (Macdonald and Mason 1997) suggests that students are able
to adapt their study patterns to the demands of resource-based learning. But a
minority of students continued to have difficulties with selective reading and
in selecting information from a vast range. Given that this is in a context in
which there was considerable support, such support is clearly necessary. In using the CD-ROM, for example, students were managing to get by because of
the relatively small size of the database but lacked skill at searching. Students
in this study were fairly evenly divided about whether they liked resource-based
learning, but several students mentioned the difficulty of managing the quantity of information.

Freeman, Robertson, and Thorne (1995), also in the United Kingdom, discussed Sunderland University's strategic approach in embracing ODL material as a step toward becoming a virtual university. Sunderland's experience is
consistent with Lisewski's: a move toward the use of more independent learning materials requires considerable support, and mature students have greater
confidence in this approach. Their technology strategy involves a large student
computing literacy program as well as CAL (computer-assisted learning) and
multimedia.

In view of the effort and support that went into the LJMU project and its
limited success, the success of ODL packages cannot be assumed. There is now
an extensive body of critical work on the weaknesses of ODL, including its
inability to offer dialogue in the manner of face-to-face Socratic tutoring, the
inflexibility of content and study method, the isolation and individualization
of the student, and the reality of its "openness." Any discussion about the use
of new ICTs to develop the learning society modeled from existing ODL approaches must, therefore, concentrate on how ICTs can overcome the weaknesses of ODL without undermining its strengths.

Ensuring That Interaction Occurs Whenever Possible

One of the problems of many current models of ODL is the limited possibility for dialogue, both between teachers and learners and among groups of learners (as we saw earlier, many uses of multimedia allow for very little interaction). The extent of the dialogue will largely depend on the range of media and technologies used. For example, programs broadcast on radio involve one-way communication, whereas an audio teleconference allows dialogue to occur. Bates (1995) gives a useful summary of the strengths and weaknesses of different technologies for ODL that includes their interactivity (table 9.2). Students need dialogue with their teachers and with other students in order to consolidate and check on their own learning. Thus in most structured ODL systems regular student assessment, often in some correspondence mode, is central to providing at least formative feedback to the students. Such dialogues allow the students to assess their learning and to be part of a community of students, they allow the institution to assess how well it is achieving its teaching objectives, and they allow students to comment on the quality and content of courses. Any system in which feedback is curtailed or delayed is less than optimal.

In arguing for more dialogue in ODL, Evans and Nation (1989) propose that adult students play a greater part in designing the content of their own education. They assert the importance of the "open text" in democratic education and see, as an aim, that students should become "collaborative developers of their own courses through critical reflection." Interestingly, critical reflection is a good example of the type of benefit that students may experience in using CMC, which at its best fosters a community of scholars who engage in debate and support each other's learning.

The speed of feedback available via CMC can be used to make student assessment more useful and reduce the dropout rate. Students can submit assessment materials electronically to a human tutor or to a computer-based system and receive feedback on performance either instantly (using the computer-based system) or quickly (using the human-based system). Computer-based assessment can now be made more widely available. For example, Iskandar and Romiszowski (1995) discuss their proposals for the research and development of both multimedia and CMC networks and voice mail tutorial systems, building on the success of audio feedback on assignments.

The Structure and Packaging of Learning Materials

Traditional ODL materials are highly structured and thus teacher centered, allowing little flexibility for students to have different educational objectives or different learning styles. They cannot easily take into account the full range of learners' needs. The linear structure of a transmitted television program, for example, permits very little flexibility for learners; even a programmed learning text that offers students different routes through the material is directive and presumes a limited set of routes and the same final goal for each student. On the other hand, an educational situation that the teacher leaves relatively unstructured and is rich in opportunities for dialogue can encourage more flexible individual and group learning. However, too little structure may leave the unsophisticated learner in particular to struggle and fail. This is one area in which ICTs have failed to learn lessons from ODL. Educational interactive CD-ROMs are often acclaimed as interactive learning packages, whereas in reality they are unstructured resource packages that offer information but no guidance, no teaching, and no assessment. Since different learners have different needs for support and independence, it is difficult to design a large-scale system that is optimal for all potential students.

Individualization and Isolation

Young (1988) has argued that the move toward home-based or work-based education and training reflects and promotes similar social trends toward the individualization of society. We have moved from public to private transport, from cinema to TV, and most recently from family viewing to individual viewing in homes with multiple TV sets. But ICTs are perhaps only accelerating a process that began with mass literacy and cheap book production. Adult education, much more than higher education, has been directed at groups and communities rather than individuals, and it has made more use of study groups. It is not necessary for educational ICTs to have as their target the individual student; they may be aimed at student or community groups. However, it is more often argued that the strengths of ODL lie in enabling the isolated individual to engage in a structured program of study. This individual focus has come in for criticism. Keddie (1980), for example, considers individualism the dominant ideology of adult education in the United Kingdom and one, she argues, that promotes an abstract, fragmented view of the learner instead of giving emphasis to a social and historical context.

ICTs also have a history of being individually based. Indeed, most of the advantages claimed for early computer-based learning material were based on their being adaptive to individual needs, for example, by giving feedback based on learner performance and allowing learners to work at their own pace. More recently, however, there has been considerable interest and research into the *collaborative* use of computers. This use includes collaborating with computers (e.g., CMC), groups working together with computers, or physically distant individuals using ICTs to work together in real time (e.g., video conferencing). Such collaboration has particular advantages for distant learners in that it can create "virtual communities" of learners while colocated learners can benefit from discussing their learning and their project. For schoolchildren there is some evidence that group work with computers offers particular benefits (e.g., Bennett 1987; Galton 1989) and that when children are working together with a computer, they are collaborating and not just working alongside each other. Researchers have been looking at children working with computers in pairs or small groups to investigate the factors that contribute to or hinder such success. Part of the context of this is increasing acceptance of the assertion that cognitive development and learning is socially located (see, e.g., Crook 1994). As we have seen, the collaborative use of computers has also increased in higher and distance education, for example, in the use of computer conferencing, and this is consistent with the increasing emphasis on social interaction, which is occurring in adult as well as children's learning, and an increasing recognition of the importance of the context of learning.

Openness

A final criticism of ODL is that, ironically, it is often not very open. "Every kind of openness associated with distance education seems to have its opposite side, a tendency to closure" (Harris 1987, 3).

Similarly ICTs, although appearing to offer great potential for reducing inequalities and opening up education, can also close it down for particular social groups. We noted above that particular ICTs can support students with disabilities. Although telematics can relieve difficulties in traveling and allow working from home, its use, as Harris suggests, brings other difficulties. For example, the increasing use of visual, icon-based systems has made life harder for students with visual disabilities.

More generally, the use of ICTs brings with it certain "requirements" that restrict its use. For example, the fact that computer conferencing has typically been text based means it depends on a degree of literacy (both traditional as well as technological) from students. It is therefore of little use for teaching basic literacy and life skills or for populations with low literacy skills. Also, "conferences" usually operate in only one language, which restricts the opportunity for international networking. Multimedia usually requires the acquisition of expensive equipment, typically, a high specification computer with good screen resolution and a lot of memory. There are therefore serious concerns about the extent to which this medium is truly "open." Davidson (1996, 155–156) expresses the same concern about the use of information technology in distance education:

> There is much rhetoric about the need for everyone to become information technology literate and skilled. Perhaps we should first ask who can afford this technology, what will it be used for, who will benefit by its use and who will not. These questions are particularly pertinent for institutions designed to help people learn.

Most of these concerns about openness are issues for learners: the extent to which a range of factors may restrict use of ICTs for particular groups of learners. In order to discuss the use of computers for adult education in particular we need to examine empirical data about the accessibility of this technology in our populations.

OPENNESS AND ACCESSIBILITY OF NEW MEDIA

For learners the first issue with respect to any educational medium is their access to it. Although some educational ICT applications are institutionally based, others rely on students' private provision for access. When an educational system is "open" in the sense that its mission is to reach all classes of society, especially those people who have had less formal education than the majority, then the technologies it uses must be easily accessible to these groups. United Kingdom data from the early 1990s on the domestic ownership of information technologies demonstrates that there is still a relationship between access to technologies, and wealth and lifestyle (fig. 9.1).

In 1994 only 24 percent of U.K. households owned a computer (HMSO 1995). Figure 9.1 shows ownership among households, with members in economically active age groups, of four major ICT devices: video recorder/player, audio compact disk (CD) player, unspecified personal computer, and telephone. Ownership of computers was low for all employment groups. Of concern also is a significant social inequality with respect to household electronics, with 50 percent of professionals having access to some form of computer in the household and less than 10 percent of the economically inactive.

Estimates of home penetration of multimedia computers for 1997 (EITO 1998) show that there is a significant difference between the countries of the European Union in the scale of this penetration.

Figure 9.1   U.K. Households with ICT (1992–1993)

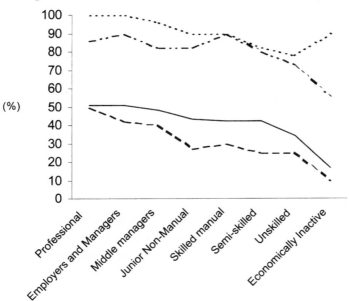

······· Phone –·–·– Video ———— CD player – – – – PC

Source: Kirkup and Jones 1995.
Note: "CD player" refers to audio compact disc player.

Table 9.3   Penetration of Home Multimedia PCs (1997)

	Percent of Households with PCs	*Percent of PC Owning Households with Multimedia PCs*
United States	37	53
Japan	26	46
United Kingdom	23	28
Germany	21	37
France	19	32
Italy	13	29
Spain	11	no data

Source: EITO (1998).

The United States generally leads in overall PC penetration rates, but within Europe there are significant differences, with Spain and Italy having only half the penetration rate of the United Kingdom.

The Internet is seen (e.g., Collis 1996) as the main revolutionary educational application with respect to home connection. But a U.K. survey (ITC 1997) found only 3 percent of the sample with home Internet access, rising to 8 percent in the twenty- to twenty-four-year-old age group. Even with fast growth, recent international comparisons indicate that on-line households remain a minority, with penetration rates for 2000–2001 projected as 38 percent (United States), 14 percent (United Kingdom and Germany), and 10 percent (France) (Spectrum Strategy Consultants/DTI 1998).

Some training programs presume that students can use employer equipment at times when it is not being heavily used for business. Increasingly, employers are refusing to allow employees to use work equipment to run any software not specifically related to the business or to allow external communication activities linked to the Internet. (In some companies employees face instant dismissal if they are found to have disks on their person while on work premises.)

These access issues, compounded by the expense and difficulty of producing good interactive multimedia and a reduction in the human interactions of learning, could lead to learning environments that are impoverished, particularly with respect to the needs of some students for support from a human facilitator in their learning. Models of distance education based on the "independent" student (regardless of the media involved) have been criticized as perhaps the most unsuitable educational form for disadvantaged adults:

> If distance education is based essentially on self-learning, to what extent is it inherently accessible to the most disadvantaged sections of the public? Is self-learning not a form of education that implies a degree of independence which these sections of the population lack? (Seabright and Nickolmann 1992, 25)

One particular group of disadvantaged adults does seem to have gained significantly through new media applications. Students with physical disabilities have been able to take advantage of ODL systems and related media to pursue education that was previously inaccessible to them. Those whose disabilities give them limited mobility, such as spinal injuries (Michael and Welkin 1990), can simply use ICT technology to study at home. Others, whose disabilities involve communication, hearing, vision, or speech, can often obtain materials in alternative media and submit assessment using alternative media. Resources can be provided specifically to support such students. For example, text materials are available at no extra cost on audiocassette for students with visual disabilities, as well as materials in large print or in electronic form that can be speech synthesized (Vincent 1983). More recently, developments in electronic publishing and compact disc technologies can be exploited to give further choice of media for students whose disabilities preclude the use of books. However, these alternative media forms need funding, and hard-pressed institutions may find it difficult to justify this expenditure for a small subpopulation of their students.

A CASE STUDY OF DISADVANTAGE

One group of students who have now been studied thoroughly with respect to their access to and use of ICTs in education is women. Socioeconomic and gender inequalities compound a difficult situation for adult women (Kirkup et al. 1995; Silverstone 1994). Surveys of U.K. distance education students (at the OUUK) have demonstrated that women students, among a student population with much better access than the national population to personal computers, had significantly poorer access than men studying the same subject. The gender gap has remained roughly constant at 10 percent, showing no sign of narrowing during an eight-year period even though a smaller gender gap for access to VCR equipment closed (see fig. 9.2).

OUUK students who had access to personal computers at home were asked questions designed to elicit more information about the locus of control of this equipment (i.e., who had first call on it, who made decisions about it). Men students were twice as likely as women to report themselves as the decision makers with respect to the choice of whether to buy equipment; women were seven times more likely to report their spouse as the main decision maker. In terms of their own use of the equipment, men were more than twice as likely as women students to report using it every day, whereas women were more likely to use it once or twice a week or less. When respondents were asked about the use made by spouses, this difference was even greater with women students being four times more likely than male students to report their spouse as using the equipment daily. The fact that computing equipment in a household "belongs" to a male rather than a female is further confirmed in response to a question about upgrading equipment. Women students overwhelmingly did not know when equipment would be upgraded or replaced because, it can be presumed, the equipment was not primarily for their use. Access to PCs is much lower for women students whenever this has been measured and at whatever educational level, from primary school to higher education. Also, when it exists, the quality of access is lower than that of male students (Kirkwood and Kirkup 1991; Kirkup 1993; Jones, Kirkup, and Kirkwood 1993; Kirkup and von Prümmer 1997).

With VCRs men and women may have similar access "in theory," but research by Gray showed men feeling more competent in using VCR technology and being more likely than others to operate the programmable features, as well as organizing and archiving off-air recording (Gray 1992).

An early analysis of the PC industry has showed how, in the United Kingdom at least, PCs were designed and marketed for a male leisure industry (Haddon 1988). Any review of educational research journals demonstrates consistent findings from schoolchildren in a range of different countries. Girls have less experience with ICTs, both qualitatively and quantitatively, at home and at school, than boys and feel less confident with the technology at any point in their school career. Busch (1995) studied students' sense of self-efficacy with computers (self-efficacy is defined as the self-confidence that one has the ability to carry out a certain task, or skill) and wrote that

female students are found to have less self-efficacy with regard to complex computing tasks than their male counterparts, they have less computer experience in programming and computer games, they are less encouraged by friends and parents, and they have less access to a home computer. . . . male students are part of a social network that is more concerned about computers, and where the use of computers gives them a higher social status. (P. 155)

Figure 9.2   Ownership of VCRs and PCs

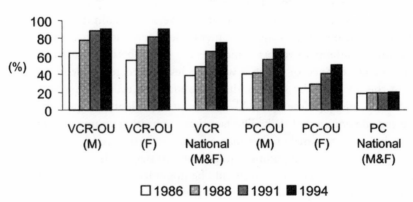

Source: Kirkup and von Prümmer 1997.

The debate about inequality in CMC is an interesting one. It has sometimes been assumed that if it were possible to give women and men equal access to CMC technology, the gender inequalities that are well recorded in face-to-face interactions would be less evident in electronic interactions when the gender of participants was not immediately obvious. However, gender is "performed" in language. Work on the discourse of CMC (e.g., Taylor, Kramarae and Ebben 1993) demonstrates that women can be silenced in this medium. Herring (1993), who looked in particular at the gendered strategies of male and female academics in academic computer conferencing, concluded,

> Rather than being democratic, academic CMC is power based and hierarchical. This state of affairs cannot however be attributed to the influence of computer communication technology; rather it continues pre-existing patterns of hierarchy and male dominance in academia more generally, and in society as a whole.

The more public domain of the Internet, Web site and news groups, gives the appearance of a gendered medium (Kramarae and Kramer 1995). Surveys measuring access to the Internet show a range of male–female ratio from 2 to 1 to 10 to 1. Mayers (1997) suggests that the 2 to 1 figure may be an indication of potential access—people who possess a log-on code; but 10 to 1 is an indication of actual use. All surveys show that men spend more time using the Internet than women. Rather than a global village (as argued by Anthony 1994), the Internet is a global male middle-class white suburb. A 1995 ITC survey of the United Kingdom reinforces this. Only 7 percent of the U.K. population had any access to the Internet; users were more likely to be male, professional, white collar, skilled, and aged 15 to 34 (ITC 1995).

Once on the Internet the communication differences become apparent:

> In studies of Internet discussion groups, researchers have found that men contribute consistently more than women. In fact when women contribute more than 30 percent on the conversation, they are perceived by the online community to be "dominating" the discussion. Even in feminist forums, where women are ostensibly most interested and expert men consistently dominate the conversation. . . . In a study of the newsgroup alt.feminism . . . men contributed 74 percent of the postings, women 17 percent and 9 percent were of unidentifiable gender. (Wylie 1995, 4)

One of the most worrying aspects of the Internet for European educators must be that it does not embody the kinds of values promoted in educational institutions. The language and social behavior evident on the Internet is very different from what is expected of a classroom or seminar. Although the education and employment sectors have developed strong institutional policies to restrict pornography and sexual harassment, both have become a particular problem on the Internet (Canon 1995). Institutions are now starting to see harassment complaints being made about student and staff activities on electronic communications, and a number of criminal proceedings have been brought against (usually male) staff for the transmission of pornographic material. Institutional harassment codes don't usually include telematics as a special area. They probably should. The atmosphere of much of the Internet exhibits a very gendered form of masculinity that would be unacceptable in most educational arenas. Some excellent Web sites do exist to disseminate information that is useful to women, for example, and others are being developed as support networks for women. But these sites, both in their tone and scarcity, are more reminiscent of "alternative" rather than mainstream publication.

Apart from issues of access and control over financial and material resources, the use of ICTs also depends on whether they accommodate students' life circumstances and learning styles and whether they are considered effective for achieving students' learning goals. Survey data from the Fern Universitat (FeU) in Germany suggest that women who have experience with using a given ICT are less inclined to judge the technology as "highly effective." For these students it was computer conferencing that had the narrowest gender gap, although neither men nor women rated it as the most effective medium (see fig. 9.3).

It seems that women judge the usefulness of ICTs by higher or at least different standards. Von Prümmer and Kirkup carried out a large-scale survey of students at the OUUK and the FeU (Kirkup and von Prümmer 1990). They argued from their empirical data that they could identify differences in the preferred learning styles of men and women that made them respond differently to different ODL methods. Women valued the opportunity for face-to-face contact with other students and staff more than men, although roughly the same proportions of men and women reported feeling isolated as distance students, which was a problem for 24 percent of the men, compared with 40 percent of the women.

Can multimedia be incorporated into educational systems in a more "women-friendly" fashion? Turkle and Papert (1990) have argued that the domination of the computing profession by men has led to a privileging of particular styles of thinking that are not the styles preferred by women. Unfortunately Turkle watched women students drop out of computing programs not because they were not learning how to program to carry out assignments but because they were constantly being told that their preferred styles of working and programming were not the "proper" ones.

Figure 9.3   Ratings of ITC Effectiveness by Users

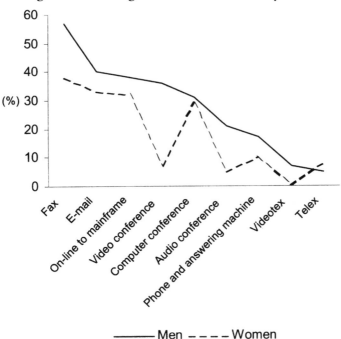

Men ——— ———— Women

Source: Kirkup and von Prümmer 1997.

As far as educational software design is concerned, Huff and Cooper (1978) argued some years ago that software designers have an implicit notion of the student for whom they are designing: a male. This is important with respect to multimedia and the notion of different learning routes. Any system can only support effectively those learning routes and learning styles that the designer has prepared for. If those are the routes and styles of a particular kind of student, having more of them will still not cater for a varied student body but will simply give the same types of students many options.

This case study of gender inequality in educational ICT applications and use shows that students must not be viewed as a homogeneous body. The positive benefits of ICT applications to students with physical disabilities can be compared and contrasted with disadvantages faced by women. Less research has been carried out on access issues among other disadvantaged or minority groups. If ICTs in education are seen as a way of reaching previously educationally disadvantaged groups, research and policy needs to be directed specifically at the particular needs of these groups (Kirkup 1996).

THE INFORMATION SOCIETY: THE CYBERNETIC SOCIETY

On one level, the computer is a tool. It helps us write, keep track of our accounts, and communicate with others. Beyond this, the computer offers us both new models of mind and a new medium on which to project our ideas and fantasies. Most recently, the computer has become even more than tool and mirror: we have stepped through the looking glass. We are learning to live in virtual worlds. We may find ourselves alone as we navigate virtual oceans, unravel virtual mysteries, and engineer virtual skyscrapers. But increasingly, when we step through the looking glass, other people are there as well (Turkle 1995, 9).

Some of the newest, most radical thinking about computer systems does not see information as their most important attribute. The "information" they contain and transmit, it is argued, is becoming transparent to the user. In this view, ICTs become, in Turkle's words, "mirrors" for us to see ourselves in. For Haraway (1991), our intimate relationship with them makes us "cyborgs." ICT systems are ways of developing new social groupings and new ways of relating to others, both human and machine. The many possible functions of ICTs in education that we have described can be seen as a cybersystem offering this kind of intimate relationship as people engage in learning.

We have not discussed ICTs as the *content* of lifelong learning. Theorists like Turkle see an understanding of the role of ICTs in human relationships and culture as the important ICT skills, not information manipulation. Education needs to develop new cyber/social communication skills so that ICTs can be used to optimize social cohesion and personal development rather than fracture it. This must become a part of all major education programs.

The extended discussion of gender differences in learning styles and in styles of human communication more generally is there to illustrate the negative impact ICTs can have if their interface and operation is modeled on only one cultural style and access to them is restricted to specific groups. The human/ social success of ICTs must be measured in how flexible they are in lending themselves to a diversity of cultural needs and worldviews.

This chapter has adopted a critical position that is based on the authors' disappointment over many years that the information society utopias painted by the policy makers have been far removed from the empirical experience of the citizen, as student, worker, or community member. Technologies per se do not change social structures. They simply reproduce or amplify social and cultural systems and structural inequality unless interventions are made. The educational system that has been planned by many European governments for over a century now is itself an intervention that challenges the reproduction of social inequality and seeks to support personal development, as well as economic and cultural development through the appropriate education of its citizens. There are real dangers for social cohesion, as well as the economic development of Europe, in getting it wrong with the new media. The benefits of getting it "right" are likely to produce positive changes of which, as yet, we have only an initial sketch.

NOTE

1. "Openness" and "distance" are not necessarily connected. Face-to-face teaching can be "open" in respect to entry qualifications, as indeed it is in most traditional adult education. Distance education, on the other hand, can be very selective in its students, in particular at university and professional levels.

10

Information and Communication Technologies and Everyday Life: Individual and Social Dimensions

Leslie Haddon and Roger Silverstone

In recent years a body of qualitative and case study research has begun to accumulate showing that users, consumers, and citizens are not just passive recipients of technology but actively engage in defining and giving meaning to information and communication technologies (ICTs). A central theme of this work is that ICTs only become meaningful in use: they are socially shaped.[1] Only through the meanings that are constructed by producers, by those who market or regulate them, and by those who consume them do they have any significance. ICTs mean different things to different people, and these meanings will change and often will conflict. For these reasons, a number of underlying themes inform our analysis:

- *ICTs are seen as both objects and media*: ICTs are doubly articulated into everyday life as machines and as media of information, pleasure, and communication.
- *ICTs are seen as material and symbolic objects*: ICTs are bought and used not just for what they can do but also for what they stand for, aesthetically, in claiming social status or in claiming membership in a group or subculture.
- *ICTs are embedded in time and space*: the consumption and use of ICTs influence, and are influenced by, location in time and space. Globally, they connect and disconnect. Locally, they can raise flexibility and control.

- *ICTs involve users both actively and passively*: users can increasingly interact with ICTs, but even the "passive" use involves choices and discrimination.
- *ICTs shift boundaries between public and private spaces*: ICTs provide new opportunities for citizenship and for surveillance, as well as new opportunities for networking; but they also promote increased isolation.

These relationships are multiple and dynamic, operating both inside and outside the home—historically, sociologically, economically, and culturally. Without a mature and sociologically sensitive understanding of the present we will misunderstand the future. The pioneering analyses discussed below can help us avoid the traps of the utopian or dystopian thinking that still dominates many business, policy, and popular discourses.[2]

THE SPEED AND SCALE OF HOUSEHOLD ADOPTION OF ICTs

It is important to realize just how long it takes for ICTs to become fundamentally and unproblematically integrated into our lives. Recent research on the young elderly notes that they were the first phone generation. Many experienced the arrival of the telephone at an early stage in their life, often first encountering it at work, and as a result became entirely comfortable with it at home (Haddon and Silverstone 1996a). Many of their own parents, those we might call the older elderly, however, are often still not totally at ease with the phone, even though they may have used it much of their adult lives. They do not have the relatively developed and relaxed phone manner of their children nor do they use it in as many ways.

More medium- and short-term changes can be seen in inelasticities of spending and time use. A recent Belgian study shows how in the medium term there is only a limited redistribution of the spending of household income across broad categories of goods and services (Punie 1995).[3] For example, between 1980 and 1992, spending on clothes and food, alcohol and tobacco was slightly down while durables, leisure, and telecommunications expenditure rose. In the shorter term there is considerable inelasticity, meaning that new goods or services have to compete for the household budget. Punie takes the U.K. experience with CDs to illustrate what this inelasticity can mean for a particular product. Although CDs have successfully ousted records, no increase took place in audio-related spending. Moreover, since CDs are more expensive than records, people acquired fewer of them and had smaller audio collections.

The Belgian research also charts changes in the domestic time budget. Despite rises in overall leisure time over the last thirty years, the ratio of time spent at home or away has remained remarkably constant at around 60 to 40. This finding should make us wary of claims (or fears) that we are becoming increasingly home-centered and that home-centered activities will dominate our time in the future. Instead there is a substitution effect. People find new reasons for going out and making social contact. The study discovered less time spent at the theater, movies, and football matches but more on holidays, outings, and going to restaurants and cafes. As with income spending, we may change the details of how we organize our lives, and the technologies and services we use may change in the medium term. But the underlying broad patterns of living do not change either so radically or so readily.

More evidence relevant to questions about the speed and degree of take-up of domestic ICTs comes from the penetration patterns of the technologies that have found their way into the home. Only occasionally does a product experience a startling short-term success. Examples, such as the radio boom of the 1920s and the PC boom of the early 1980s, were significantly related to the symbolic nature of these products. More commonly, even successful ICTs like the CD or the VCR take over a decade to go from launch to mass market. Teleshopping and telebanking have been around for at least that long without achieving a mass-market breakthrough.

Furthermore, changes in the practices of everyday life often linger behind the mere acquisition of new technologies. ICTs have to find a place in the routines and rhythms of the home environment. We are often slow to change such habits, including our habits of media and communication use (Thrall 1982; Silverstone 1995). For example, it took over a decade for most people to switch from the habit of watching one TV channel all evening to switching from channel to channel (Dutton 1995). This suggests real problems for new media like interactive TV or new communications technologies such as video telephony because they entail significantly new behavior (cf. Silverstone and Haddon 1996).

In the 1980s a number of writers evaluated claims on whether an "information revolution" was leading us to a totally new "information society" (Winston 1989; Winner 1989; Lyon 1988). They pointed out that in many respects the introduction and adoption of technological change, and its consequences, were neither as rapid nor as radical as the term "revolutionary" implied. Current evidence on ICTs in the home would support the caution such writers were showing, especially in the short to medium term.

THE SYMBOLIC NATURE OF ICTs AND THE PROCESS
OF DOMESTICATION

There is a growing literature on the consumption of goods and services in general (Bourdieu 1986; Douglas and Isherwood 1980; Featherstone 1991; McCracken 1990; Miller 1987) that focuses on the significance of food, clothes, furniture, or domestic architecture for identity, lifestyle, and taste. We may "need" food and clothes to sustain our bodies, but when we make particular choices between goods there is often much more involved than just considerations of physical survival. Such insights have more rarely been applied to technologies or ICTs, although histories of the early years of now familiar technologies discuss this symbolic dimension.[4]

One approach to these issues considers innovation a process of "domestication" (Silverstone, Hirsch, and Morley 1992; Silverstone 1994b; Lie and Sorenson 1996). The household initially confronts new ICTs as strange and maybe even frightening. The process of acceptance (and indeed resistance) is a matter of making the new technologies familiar. They must be accommodated within the complex structures and patterns of everyday life inside and outside the home. This process may involve some degree of negotiation or even conflict among household members over spending priorities or the control over the spaces and times of the household. In crossing the threshold and as they become integrated into the domestic culture of the family, the meanings of ICTs change. Of course, the arrival of a new ICT might be wholly or partially resisted. Some people continue to feel ill at ease with the role of television in their life, especially in regard to their children. They can be wary of letting in any more equipment that could threaten to increase the amount of TV watching, such as cable, VCR, or the second TV. Similarly, there are fears of "addiction" to interactive video games and Internet use. Particular technologies, perhaps above all the PC, are far from being domesticated. The PC is innately complex and tests the skill and competence of households.

Once ICTs are in the home, the further process of their domestication involves choosing where to put them and deciding how to use them. This relates to aesthetic considerations or to strategies for displaying technologies as well as functional requirements. For example, teleworkers might arrange their equipment to show that they are serious workers (Haddon and Silverstone 1993).

The location of ICTs in the home may also reflect strategies to control them. Placing the telephone or the television in shared or private spaces has consequences for who uses them and how. The daily and weekly pattern of use is equally significant. Broadcast schedules divide up the day, providing temporal markers for home-based single parents and the elderly (Randell 1990). TV watching can be a way to pass the time. On other occasions time has to be set aside from other obligations to use ICTs. It is therefore important to appreciate how consumption involves other household members; those with more power than others formulate rules about access and use. Who is allowed to use the PC and under what conditions? Is there a limit to TV watching? How much is the phone used and what are "unnecessary" calls? Of course such rules may be broken or resisted. Teenagers may commandeer the phone or illicitly view banned horror films. In other words, the home is a place with its own moral economy, but a moral economy that is often contested and is subject to renegotiation.[5] It is in this setting that ICTs are placed and given meaning.

Clearly, there is a range of questions to ask about the consumption of ICTs beyond their "usefulness," questions that actually address their social and symbolic significance. Policy and market makers too should be aware that ICTs have a double life and that the social world is not a neutral space across which technologies and services pass without change and resistance.

The recent history of the home computer boom, and the failure of home automation technologies across Europe to take off, offer revealing, if rather different, examples of how social factors intrude into the innovation process.[6] The example of the home computer illustrates how in practice wider media and institutional discourses and policies can have a significant bearing on the fate of new ICTs. Meanwhile home automation provides a good example of a product being developed in an area already rich in symbolism, where the images influence the product's development and reception. Moreover, images are contested. There is not necessarily one single or dominant discourse.[7] Crucial battles have to be fought over this world of public images.

Both producers and policy makers need to be sensitive to this dimension in their presentations, announcements, documents, promotional activities, demonstration projects, and general contact with the media. In addition to monitoring sales figures or surveys of usage, they need to pay attention to this whole question of symbolism, such as sudden and perhaps unexpected public concerns.[8]

ICTs AND PERCEPTIONS OF REALITY AND IDENTITY

The history of technological innovation, especially that of ICTs, is one of anxiety and concern as well as hope and expectation. The present generation of

ICTs is no exception. Contemporary concerns focus on three discrete but interrelated areas: social isolation, addiction, and influence. They are interrelated by a common theme that sees in technology a dehumanization: a threat to the comfortable and necessary familiarities of face-to-face interaction and to the ability to control through the measure of lived experience our relationship to the world and to other people in it. Indeed, research on media innovation throughout the century has been driven by concerns about the vulnerability of individuals and societies to media control.

Isolation

Concerns have reemerged about the effects of ICTs on our relationships with each other and on our participation in the family and in wider social life. New risks of isolation result from a withdrawal from participation in public space (e.g., by teleworkers) or for those who by virtue of age or disability are vulnerable to isolation and marginalization.

Ithiel de Sola Pool's (1977) description of the double life of technology in his discussion of the telephone is clearly important here. He recognized that the phone had the power both to connect and to disconnect—to bring people together electronically while maintaining the distance between them. All ICTs have this double life. Recent research on teleworkers (Haddon and Silverstone 1993; Huws 1993) and the elderly (Haddon and Silverstone 1995) has shown how ICTs mediate social life. They both isolate and compensate for that isolation. For example, the elderly use the phone to maintain links with dispersed relatives. Social life also mediates the effects of technology. For example, those who feel more isolated as a result of their involvement with IT may compensate by reinforcing or developing social networks (family, neighborhood, friendship, or work).

There are similar concerns for the family as a whole. The arrival of multiple TV sets and video recorders, not to mention the radio, the Walkman, and the music center, has encouraged many commentators (e.g., Young 1990) to bewail the resulting social fragmentation and dislocation. It is obvious that such technological individuation is significant, enabling household members to control their own media spaces and to create private worlds of media consumption and electronic communication. For example, parents worry about their children's exposure to TV content and use of the phone. But are ICTs undermining family life? Research suggests that such fears are exaggerated.

The history of the mass media, especially television, depicts the media as providing a hearth for the family (Frith 1983; Scannell and Cardiff 1991). Even the dispersion that follows from owning multiple TV sets may be functional, for example, by enabling teenagers to "leave" the family safely (Morley and Silverstone 1990). With the arrival of a new dominant set connected to satellite or cable (Moores 1988) the family hearth is recreated. It is also important to point out that there are more fundamental and powerful forces affecting family life, such as unemployment and changing social values and moralities. These need to be taken into account before a balanced conclusion about the effects of new ICTs can be reached.

Addiction

Each new media innovation brings fears of addiction, as some early adopters and users become completely obsessed. There will always be a ready flow of examples, particularly of children (television addicts, computer addicts). A substantial body of research explores these issues and offers evidence that addiction is both common and harmful (Winn 1977). Yet there is a fine line between creativity and addiction (Silverstone 1994b), and intense relations even with supposedly passive media suggest that such relationships can be creative (Turkle 1984; Fiske 1987; Ang 1985). People who develop such relationships are likely to have had equally intense involvement in other activities (Shotton 1989). Perhaps it is a truism to point out that although ICTs can offer intensely seductive worlds, only a few particularly vulnerable individuals are unable to control their relationship with them.

Influence

There has been a long history of concerns over ICT effects on our perceptions of the world; for example, how violence on television might influence children's behavior, how computer games might distort our sense of reality, how computers might change our perceptions of what it is to be human. However, the methodological problems to be overcome in order to isolate television as an independent variable have proved to be almost insuperable. Considerations of the context of use, the time scale of influence, the nature and definition of television violence, the complex nature of narrative and performance, the differences between real and fictional representation, as well as the definition of what can be considered violent social behavior, all contribute to a research problem that has yet to be conclusively resolved and may never be (Cumberbatch and Howitt 1989).

Interesting and important research on the long-term effects of certain kinds of representations has been conducted in the United States (Gerbner at al. 1986). But the findings have not been replicated elsewhere and the confidence with which researchers have claimed that heavy users of television have a different, distorted, and often more anxious view of the world than light viewers has been widely criticized (Morgan and Signorielli 1990).

Elsewhere, some contemporary thinking has moved beyond a concern with specific effects of media, in relation to violence or pornography, for example, to a concern with a media-engendered hyperreality of multiple simulations. The increasingly pervasive mass media are seen by these writers (see Baudrillard 1983) as replacing a world of lived experience, offering in its stead an infinity of refracted symbols isolating all who consume media from any other reality.

ICTs IN THE HOUSEHOLD

Gender and ICTs

The household is a complex and differentiated social and cultural, as well as an economic and political, environment. This complexity ramifies still further once attention turns to the differences related to gender, age, health, and impairment. One particularly strong demonstration of how ICTs can become gendered and how men and women experience them differently has been provided by feminist research offering a range of analyses.

These differences emerge in the consumption as well as production of ICTs. Innovation is not just a matter of engineering. The design of a new technology involves a whole range of actors in defining the intended characteristics of a new technology or service (Silverstone and Haddon 1996). Hardware designers, industrial designers, marketers and advertisers, software publishers, content and service providers, magazine retailers and distributors contribute to the final, but still contested, meaning of a new ICT (Cawson, Haddon, and Miles 1995; Silverstone and Haddon 1993). At all these levels we find examples of actors giving particular gender connotations to ICTs (Cockburn 1992).

Research has examined the ways in which gendered images of potential end users inform the innovation process. Specifically it has considered the extent to which women's interests are considered in their specification and design (Berg 1990) and has shown how much design assumes a male user. This can relate to the strength required to operate a technology (Cockburn 1992), to the technical knowledge that it is assumed the end user possesses, and to the genres and modes of action in software, such as interactive games (Skirrow 1986; Haddon 1993). ICTs can also acquire meaning from the places in which they are located. For example, the first public interactive game machines were installed in public arcades—male-dominated locales (Haddon 1993).

Analysis has become increasingly subtle, discussing both the ambivalence and the ambiguities in the design and content. They also allow for the fact that the gender connotations of technologies can and do become modified over time. In a recent advertising campaign in the United Kingdom British Telecom attempted (apparently with some success) to persuade men to use the phone more like women. This suggests that public education, as well as design–related policies, could allow women to engage more freely with new technologies and services.

Gender bias, however, is not limited to production and design. Considerable research, originally based on the study of the use of television in the home, has illustrated the extent of male appropriation of ICTs (Morley 1986). This can be seen as an expression of traditional male and female roles and responsibilities. Many writers point out that women are still more likely to take on the main responsibility for housework and child care. Whereas home can be more of a site of leisure for men, it is a site of work for women (Gray 1992). This has a variety of ramifications. The attention that women give to TV tends to be more fragmented as they simultaneously go about other jobs (Morley 1986) and they feel guiltier when indulging themselves in the consumption of programs (Morley 1986; Gray 1992). When acquiring ICTs, a key consideration of theirs is how it is going to help with everyday pressures (Meyer and Schultze 1995). Also, women find it harder to justify time spent experimenting, or "playing," with new ICTs such as computers (Haddon 1990). In fact, some studies have indicated that women are wary of getting involved in some ICTs, like the VCR, to avoid assuming the additional work of recording items for other people (Gray 1992). The main communications medium toward which women are favorably disposed is the telephone (Martin 1988; Rakow 1988; Moyal 1989). Here, women's conventional responsibility for maintaining family links and social circles is a key reason for acceptance.

It is clear from research (Cowan 1989; Wacjman 1991; Haddon and Silverstone 1996b) that there are fundamental aspects to the inequalities of gender in the family. Both control over and quality of space and time have been seen as having significant implications for women. Haddon and Silverstone (1996b) have discussed the notion of *temporal capital* as a way of identifying time as a crucial resource in the management of everyday life. It is clear that not only are there differences in the amount and quality of time that households can mobilize but that both the amount and the quality of "free time" are profoundly gendered. Similar differences can be seen in access to and control over space, perhaps most dramatically in the comparison of male and female teleworkers (Haddon and Silverstone 1993).

The household superimposes new meanings on the public definitions of ICTs. Insofar as the moral economy of a household is structured through gender difference, ICTs have to be fitted in and consumed in accordance with existing routines and rituals, responsibilities and conflicts. At one level, the implications are difficult to assess, since there is a strand of feminist writing that has been very critical of the ways in which males are often assumed enthusiastically to embrace technology and technical change (McNeil 1987). On the other hand, there have also been numerous concerns about women and girls being "left behind" in terms of emerging forms of ICT literacy. While the gender processes that occur in the home are less addressable by state policy compared with those around production, sensitivity to how domestic consumption is shaped may at least inform policies to make ICTs more accessible.

ICTs and Age

The Young Elderly

Many of the current generation of young elderly (aged 60–74) have taken early retirement (Laczko 1989; Laczko and Phillipson 1991). As many have accumulated savings and will benefit from occupational pensions, increasing numbers of young elderly are relatively economically comfortable. Some are experiencing a decline in physical strength that can make them feel more vulnerable and less secure, leading them to adopt a more home-centered existence. For others, however, a longer life expectancy combined with an early exit from the workforce means many years of good health and fitness. Others adopt a very active life to replace work—studying, doing voluntary work, joining clubs, and sitting on committees (Haddon and Silverstone 1996a). Yet others turn more to family, supporting their adult children, looking after grandchildren, or even caring for their own parents.

The telephone seems very important to this group. For the more active the phone is very significant in managing their commitments and many have actually noted their dependency on it. For the more home centered, the phone is a significant for keeping in touch with family and friends. For widows and widowers, the phone can become very significant for social contact, especially with geographically dispersed adult children.

Regarding ICTs, they are willing to accept fairly straightforward extensions of the familiar, such as modern or additional handsets and some cordless phones. Many possess multiple TVs, TVs with teletext, remote controls, and VCRs. The openness to incremental innovation, however, does not extend to radically new

ICTs, such as PCs. Yet there are always some technology enthusiasts and some who have used ICTs while still working.

Overall use of new ICTs depends not just on functionality but on presentation and packaging. First, it should feel familiar. For example, familiarity with the remote control means that more remote control devices in the home would not be alien. Second, it should be useful for current activities. For example, many in this group travel frequently and use teletext and radio for travel information. New ICTs that relate to their increasing involvement in activities outside the home (e.g., in the community or in hobbies) are also likely to be accepted.

The Older Elderly

Across Europe the elderly population is growing, including the older elderly (75+). Although percentages vary, many of the older elderly are women and a substantial proportion lives alone. In general, older elderly people have limited income, especially the women, since they have benefited less from occupational pensions. Demographic and other factors have increasingly limited the number and availability of female relatives in their middle years that have traditionally cared for this age group (Cullen and Moran 1991). New and innovative policies will be needed to sustain care levels as this population grows.

However, various researchers and advocacy groups for the elderly have stressed that aging should not be conceptualized solely as a problem. Living independently also involves a consideration of quality of life. Recently, greater attention has been given to assisting this age-group, as well as the young elderly, to realize opportunities, develop life interests, and contribute to the community. ICTs are often seen as having a role to play.

Reflecting the long-standing state interest in keeping the elderly in their own homes, the main technologies to receive attention have been "aids to living" that enable the elderly to carry out daily routines in their home and medical- and security-related technologies. Examples include a range of low-level aids including home automation (Gann and Iwashita 1995), remote medical monitoring and diagnostics, and personal alarms. Manufacturers of these specialized products have in part shown an interest in the elderly market because the costs of the products are often paid for by health insurance or welfare schemes (Mollenkopf 1993). Mainstream consumer electronics firms have been less interested in this market, in part because of the stigma associated with the elderly. In general, both the elderly themselves and their support groups have had very limited involvement in actual product development (Mollenkopf 1993).

Such groups have only recently begun to consider technologies that might facilitate socioemotional support and social participation in the community, especially through telecommunications.

Overall, despite an emerging "silver market" across Europe, as the numbers of relatively affluent elderly expand, there are still considerable barriers to their acceptance of innovations. As for other groups, symbolism can be as important as functionality. Therefore, design, presentation, and the strategies by which technologies are introduced are significant (Mollenkopf 1993). Above all, there are concerns that applications such as teleshopping, telemedicine, and tele-monitoring could become technological fixes leading to a loss of human contact (Cullen and Moran 1991).

Health, Impairment, and Disability

Health, impairment, and disability issues are by no means unique to the elderly. Many elderly undergo only minor degradation of faculties, and the prospects for later cohorts of elderly appear even brighter to the extent that they led healthy lives when younger. However, within this age-group there are many who are starting to experience health-related problems and lesser or greater degrees of impairment.[9]

Compare the situation of the young (i.e., preretirement age) disabled and the older, retired disabled. For the young disabled or those with a medical condition work is still a consideration, and indeed there are attempts to use ICTs to enable them to participate in the labor force through teleworking (Haddon 1991). Of course there are a number of dilemmas with this "technological" solution to increasing disability. The first concerns the risk of social isolation. The second concerns the wider issue of whether they should be segregated in discrete and dedicated institutions or integrated into an able-bodied world. Also, employers would have to develop appropriate work practices to cater for disabled workers. But there are advantages in teleworking that can make it appealing for some disabled, for those who have absolute mobility problems or find traveling to work fatiguing. Teleworking also facilitates control over the layout of the work environment. One problem for disabled outside the home can be the positioning of the items with which they work. They might also be able to control the pace of work to suit their capabilities. In these cases, telework could be attractive if it allows the maintenance of social contact and facilitates distance learning.

For disabled people who are retired work is not an issue, but social isolation and participation are. As noted in the discussion of the young elderly, given the chance, many lead active lives and engage with the outside world, friends, and family. Can new ICTs, especially communications technologies, play a role here? Within the home, intelligent home systems can supplement existing technologies to provide "aids to daily living" (Gann and Iwashita 1995). Various forms of alarms to provide a sense of security as well as help in emergencies and ICTs to monitor medical conditions have also received some attention. On the other hand, to the extent that any such aids symbolize dependency, they are sometimes resisted (Haddon and Silverstone 1996a). Even here, it is important to look to questions of functionality and usefulness and to ask what ICTs mean to people, as well as to be sensitive to how they are represented to those who might make use of them.

Finally, can new ICTs and services be designed in such a way that they do not actually create barriers to use for those with impairments? "Inclusive design" sets out to be usable by as many people as possible (Barker, Barrick, and Wilson 1995). It avoids designing in barriers to people with impairments. In fact, it is argued that sensitivity to the requirements of those with disabilities can produce design solutions to benefit everyone. For example, many people with reasonable sight may tolerate poor lighting. But they too may benefit from lighting adapted for the extra requirements of people with poorer vision. Similarly, with ICTs, design improvements could clearly be made in graphical displays or programming controls (e.g., on heating systems).

The experience of these groups, especially those defined by their age or stage in the life cycle, is varied (Haddon and Silverstone 1996a; Büchner 1990; Meyer and Schulze 1994). Values, competence, and needs change depending on past experiences with technology. Thus generalizations across cohorts or predictions about the behavior of future cohorts on the analysis of present ones are risky unless attention is given to the skills and expectations that different groups carry with them as they move through life.

Household Composition

Apart from research on the elderly and ICTs (Kordey 1993; Wald and Stückler 1991 on the telephone; Williamson 1994; Tulloch 1989; Randell 1990 on TV) the vast majority of research on the consumption of domestic ICTs has focused on nuclear families despite the fact that, in northern Europe at least, they now constitute a minority of all households. Even surveys that segment the market at different points in the life course (e.g., Dordick and LaRose 1992) often assume a progression through a nuclear family stage. This does not do justice to the diversity of household forms, each with their own dynamics, that people can experience at some point in their lives. Attention to this diversity is increasingly a precondition for research in this field.

We can point to a U.K. study of single-parent households as one of the few attempts to look at other forms of household and try to understand the particular ways in which ICTs become, or do not become, part of everyday life (Haddon and Silverstone 1995).

In the United Kingdom one in seven children live in single-parent families at any one moment while a third of all children are part of a single-parent household at some time in their childhood. These patterns reflect a more general breakup and re-formation of both partnerships and families (Bradshaw and Miller 1991). Many, usually female, single parents live on social security payments and/or part-time work, although not all. They form a substantial portion of all households classified as poor. This relative and absolute poverty is related to household composition as a consequence of the costs and constraints of child care without the daily support of a second parent. There are, sometimes, positive dimensions to this experience. Single parents are relatively free, within their own homes, of the conflicts and the compromises of an unsatisfactory relationship. However, the absence of a second adult can create particular constraints, demands, and household dynamics. Many single parents describe feeling trapped at home in the evening because there is no one else to look after the child. Organizing the logistics of child management, such as getting someone to pick a child up from school, can be more complicated for just one parent.

As a group single parents can be seen to have a potentially high demand for ICTs, but rarely sufficient resources to acquire them. For example, the phone is a vital social lifeline for many single parents trapped in the home and it can, and often does, take on great significance as a tool for organizing and coping with daily life. What other ICTs could have a similar role? The mobile phone has been mentioned as an aid to checking up on, and organizing, children (Rakow and Navaro 1993). TV can also play a more significant role for single parents than for households with partners in the sense of providing companionship, filling time, and occupying children when there is no other parent to do so. ICTs already have, both actually and potentially, a significant role in such households, yet it is becoming increasingly clear that the costs of access are likely to prohibit any but the most basic levels of access.

Two more general points can be made about household composition, first, its fluidity (Haddon 1995c). For example, where a family has broken up, children can find themselves spending time in more than one household. And when the children are visiting the other parent, their homes do become, for a time, single-person households. When both parents find new partners, binuclear families are created. The number of children present at any one time in these households will vary depending on the domestic arrangements between previous partners. Finally, in such households adults may be present only part of the time, as when some single parents spend weekends or part of the week in the home of a boyfriend or girlfriend.

Children (or indeed adults) spending time in two different households therefore are highly likely to experience different rules and regulations, or different regimes of access to ICTs. One parent in one household will allow the children to watch particular TV programs while the other, in a second household, prohibits such viewing. Access to new technologies will, similarly, vary. Traveling between homes may mean that equipment will be duplicated in the different households or carried between them.

The second point is that household composition is dynamic: people pass through different types of household at different times. Most of us experience living alone at some point. And then couples spend years together after their children have left home. Transitions between households can be traumatic and involve major readjustments, many of which can involve new demands on ICTs. For example, for single parents the phone often takes on a crucial role as a lifeline to supporting networks in the period immediately after the dissolution of a relationship and the resulting upheaval.

There are clear implications here for both niche and mass markets for ICT. Above all there is a need to recognize how markets change with the ICT experiences of different cohorts and demographic evolution.

HOUSEHOLDS AND THE OUTSIDE WORLD

The Relationship between Home and Work

ICTs have become central in mediating private and public worlds and in changing the boundaries between them. Here again interrelated dynamics of social and technical change have to be pursued in identifying the implications of ICTs' role in everyday life. In this regard, the workplace is important not just as a place for learning skills relating to new technology but as a place in which new ICTs and services gain general visibility. Even if they are not used personally by all staff, they become familiar. It is possible to appreciate their usefulness and drawbacks. One learns to feel at ease with them in that setting, just as the young elderly became used to the phone in part through work. Thus, for the unemployed (but also for those caring for children at home or the retired elderly) the absence of work can mean the absence of contact with a whole range of ICTs. Once again there is the possibility of exclusion from the information society.

It also follows that the commitment to paid employment outside the home will shape the amount of time available to use PCs, watch television, or participate in other ICT-based leisure activities. It will have a bearing, too, on when people can be contacted by phone or are free to contact others. Moves to more flexible working hours, to shift work in organizations operating a twenty-four-hour day, and to telework all mean more varied times to access ICTs. Technologies such as the VCR and the answering machine have enabled people to cope better with being out of synchronization with more mainstream leisure times. These trends could make other "time-shifting" technologies increasingly attractive, which could deliver messages, information, and entertainment on demand.

Finally we can point to the implications of changing patterns of work in the home and, in addition to telework, to the growing number of second jobs and "overspill work" that is brought home as a result, often, of pressures within the formal working environment. Mobile work often entails being on the road and periodically returning to an employer's premises, using the home as a base. Two consequences follow. The first is that with work entering the household, the boundaries between home and work blur and therefore need to be more consciously managed, sometimes through the adoption of new ICTs sometimes through changes in the patterns of use of existing ICTs. The second is that work brought home introduces ICTs into the home, which then find a domestic role. These last two points can be explored further through a case study of telework.

There are many types of teleworking, and many experiences of the phenomenon. An executive or professional in control of his or her work and accessing distant databases is far removed from a low-paid typist working at a home-based word processor, unsure when the next work will come and having to respond to clients on short notice. For some, telework is wonderful and provides great freedom. For others it is just another life phase that enables them to manage their circumstances better. For yet others it is the only viable option (Haddon and Silverstone 1993).

Haddon and Silverstone (1993) have shown how work entering the home can change the experience of existing ICTs. The best example concerns the phone. Where a second work line is not justifiable, as in the case of some self-employed clerical teleworkers, the domestic phone takes on an additional role as a work tool, and rules concerning its use have to be renegotiated. Household members, including children, have to learn how to answer appropriately or when not to answer at all. Issues arise over blocking social calls at times when they might interfere with work calls. And the whole sound regime of the home often has to be reviewed, with teleworkers deciding where the phone is to be relocated and controlling domestic background noise in an attempt to create a good impression of their working environment when taking calls from prospective clients and employers. This last example also provides an instance when ICTs can come to the rescue, as the answering machine, fax, and e-mail all enable the control of communication, the protection of privacy, and the display of status.[10]

Telework can also introduce new ICTs into the home, and the discovery of new domestic applications follows. Once in the home, teleworkers and other family members gain familiarity with the technology and experiment and develop their competencies and awareness of its possibilities. Apart from finding new uses for computers, innovative practices include using a home-based fax machine to contact distant relatives and the photocopier for school projects. Teleworking households, then, may not necessarily be early adopters of future leisure-oriented ICTs, but they are more likely to be early adopters of those that have a work-dimension and therefore are significant in the discovery of their domestic applications.

Families, Networks, Communities, and Mobility

Social and geographical mobility have increased in the latter half of this century. The consequences of this mobility have long been noted by British researchers examining the transformation of inner-city working-class communities (Young and Wilmott 1957). German research on the unemployed has charted the historical changes that have led to new patterns of geographical settlement, namely, suburbanization and the breakup of local working-class communities (Häussermann and Petrowsy 1989; Williams 1974; Silverstone 1997a). Migration from country to country, as well as from city to suburb and to rural locations, has involved the progressive fracturing of established communities and networks and has led to increasing isolation, particularly of the elderly (Meyer and Schulze 1995).

Community formation is, of course, an ongoing process. New communities form, maybe different in nature from previous ones, when people move to a new area. Despite a decline for many in the intensity of face-to-face contact, much interaction is often maintained, even though people are now located at a greater distance from each other. The cars, public transport, and, perhaps principally, the telephone have helped maintain social links despite geographical dispersal, within extended families and across generations. This has contrary implications for any new media in a similar role, since any substitution will have to demonstrate substantial advantages if it is to shift deeply engrained habits and skills.

Unpaid commitments outside the home (e.g., volunteer work) can also have a role in the diffusion of ICTs for all generations, including the young (Büchner 1990). Such activities include administration and other forms of production. For example, PCs may be used to create school reports, make tickets for sports matches, update records for hobby groups, or handle official correspondence on behalf of clubs; the telephone is useful in organizing outings and other events, arranging speakers and players, or calling meetings (Haddon 1995c). In these situations ICTs enhance the capacity of individuals to function in nonhome environments, although later uses in, and for, the home may follow, as in the case of telework. This potentially important route for ICTs into the household is often neglected.

Community has become a buzzword in discussions of the information society. Information and communication technologies are often seen as a panacea offering, through their various electronic networks, the opportunity for communities to be created and otherwise marginalized and disenchanted citizens to reclaim their right to participate in an energized and revitalized public sphere (cf. Reingold 1994).

Research has begun to confront these often utopian fantasies, based on the limits of the electronic version of community (Aufderheide 1992) and on their role in supporting existing "real" ones (Hollander and Stappers 1992). Research conducted in the United Kingdom on teleworkers (Haddon and Silverstone 1993) has identified the various ways in which social networks emerge or are reinforced to compensate for threats to, or the loss of, community (a work community) that can accompany the move to teleworking.

Yet community and communities must be a central focus of attention. The capacity of broadcasting in its heyday to create a sense of national community (Scannell and Cardiff 1991), building on the role the press had previously in "constructing" community (Anderson 1983), is well established even if it is sometimes exaggerated and romanticized. New ICTs, especially based around the Internet, clearly offer a number of different routes to (and ways of) creating networks that could be considered communities, especially as they sustain informal and real-time communication between the like-minded, albeit on a global rather than a local scale. To what extent these networks are in any sociological sense communities is of course the open question. Can they survive and contain conflict? What mechanisms do they have to survive beyond the lives of any individual participant? How can they be sustained, given the electronical capacity to participate in the network without ever declaring one's true identity? How can they be effective, given inevitable constraints on access? These are questions that have yet to be answered.

On the other hand, shared interest is clearly the basis for new electronically mediated communities to form. Bulletin boards and buddy lines provide the mechanisms for (as well as being the product of) attempts to create alternative communities based around a single interest. Correlatively, existing communities based in a shared culture or ethnicity are being reinforced by and through distinct appropriation of the products of mass culture or new forms of media delivery (Gillespie 1995). Here it is possible to point to the role ICTs may have in strengthening existing communities by providing cultural resources for shared activities that would enable the construction of distinct identities (Miller 1992) and by offering a new infrastructure for its ongoing support.

The issue of mobility and the role of mobile technologies in everyday life is the subject of little published research, and thus we offer a few general and intuitive observations. Even in relation to work, mobility and mobile ICTs appear in several guises. The growing number of full-time mobile workers and those who move between sites and meetings for some of the time are increasingly supported by mobile communications and mobile PCs. Work-related commuting has also led some professionals to utilize mobile ICTs to make more productive use of traveling time. Meanwhile "overspill" work brought home to complete after the working day may make use of portable ICTs, such as laptop PCs, which can be brought from the workplace. We noted earlier in the discussion of telework that ICTs acquired for work are often used for nonwork purposes, and certainly some research suggests that the early use of mobile phones for work purposes helped to open up one route to a mass consumer market (Wood 1993).

Leisure activities are also increasingly being supported (or indeed disturbed) by mobile ICTs as public spaces are occupied by private individuals converting what is generally public to something immediately private through their connection to a Walkman or a mobile telephone. In this context the car, much ignored too in ICT research, is significant as being more than just a vehicle or mode of transport. Its ICT infrastructure, in-car entertainment, mobile phone, and perhaps passengers with their personal stereo or mobile hand-held game console, helps this mobile space become an extension of the home environment. Similarly, the portability of such ICTs enables people to set up their own supporting technological infrastructure, to extend home and to customize new space when they are away, be it on holiday, in second homes, or in different households.

We do not yet have a framework for evaluating the social and cultural implications of such developments, but we can at least ask whether in some sense these developments might in the longer term create new forms of dependency. Do we develop a greater sense of security when we carry something familiar with us that, specifically with mobile communications, we can use to reach out and contact others at any moment? Do we use what is otherwise relatively unproductive travel time more intensely because it is possible to carry this infrastructure with us? More specifically, do mobile communications create new forms of surveillance as employers or families expect phone carriers to be continuously contactable and to maintain a link with home or the workplace? On the other hand, do mobile phones support new just-in-time lifestyles that will help us cope with stress by enabling us to organize our lives on the move? There are a number of key issues here that demand further research.

Household Resources: The New Haves and Have-nots

Concerns have been voiced about a two-tier information society (e.g., CEC 1994) in which existing elites and professional classes would have almost limitless access to all that ICTs can offer. Those at the margins (the unemployed, single parents, the elderly, the ethnically oppressed, the regionally distant, the rural) would find it increasingly hard to gain the resources necessary (even with falling costs of entry) to access the new technologically driven and increasingly technologically dependent culture. Yet voicing concern is only part of the story. Very little research has been conducted that addresses these issues directly. And considerations of disadvantage, when they are visible, tend to be limited to issues related to the lack of financial resources. To be sure, the elderly and the disabled, as potentially disadvantaged groups, are increasingly being targeted as likely to benefit from new ICTs. But the approach is based on the assessments of physical and material needs rather than cultural values and competencies. As a result, innovation is technologically driven rather than sociologically sensitive.

The new forms of disadvantage are highlighted in a German study (Häussermann and Petrowsy 1989) that demonstrates the importance of the phone for the unemployed in suburban settings. These writers note the greater consumer-oriented lifestyle, greater dependence on the market, and hence greater dependence on income from formal employment (as opposed to what households could self-produce). At the same time, in a parallel way to the arguments about children, the unemployed are also more likely nowadays to move in social networks that are at some distance from them and are based on common interests and lifestyle rather than neighborhood.

Under conditions of long-term mass employment, informal networks and active job seeking by the unemployed are becoming more significant routes to finding work than attendance at job centers. The phone helps job seekers keep up with social networks. Work opportunities are often identified by personal acquaintances should a vacancy occur, and informal inquiries may lead to the job seeker's being contacted by potential employers. The phone is also important for sorting out pensions and other benefits and finding out what documentation to bring to social security interviews. Meanwhile the phone can be vital for the quasi-self-employed in managing to get employment in the informal economy. On the consumption side, the phone can help in finding out about special offers when trying to manage on a reduced income. It can help as a psychological support, especially given the greater stigma that has accompanied the breakup of supporting communities and the individualized experience of unemployment. Finally, the phone is important for setting up meetings. The unemployed may have time to spare, but they must plan and synchronize it with others. It is often via the phone that people are invited to social events such as coffee gatherings, sports, or family celebrations. Anyone who lacks a phone could easily drop out of society.

This study also has a wider salience. The researchers make the general point that although the phone has enabled geographical relocation and new forms of social networking, it has at the same time become a necessary condition for maintaining these networks and patterns of contact. The more widespread the phone has become, the more difficult it is to be without one. The authors argue that the phone is nowadays important for citizenship and make a case for the state provision of phones and perhaps some state support for the costs of usage.

This is an important study that raises broader issues extending beyond the phone as an increasingly essential technology and beyond the particular circumstances of the unemployed. A recent study of single parents (Haddon and Silverstone 1995; cf. Silverstone 1994a) dramatically highlighted the inability of many to obtain anything beyond the most basic information and communication technologies. Maintaining even a basic level of electronic access to mass culture, information services, and social networks can generate economic stress. Beyond economic or financial disadvantage there is the risk of wider and even more significant exclusion from participation in contemporary society.

Lack of economic resources is of course a crucial determinant of exclusion in an increasingly market-based society and will become increasingly punitive in societies whose commitments to universal access in telephony and to public service in broadcasting are being weakened daily. Nevertheless, disadvantage has to be measured culturally as well as economically. It requires an assessment of skills and competencies, as well as the espousal of particular values needed to enable individuals to become full members of a society whose structures and supports increasingly are mediated electronically.

This raises two kinds of questions. The first is whether there are technologies that are likely to assume the same kind of essential status—essential to both person-to-person and person-to-institution communication as well as essential for gaining the information necessary for effective action and participation in society as a whole. For example, networks like the Internet may become a major way to access work or education. Not to have access, or not to have the ability to access, such networks would be a disadvantage. If cable companies offering free or cheap calls or other messaging systems in the local area resulted in community services being offered through these channels, being unable to afford access to cable would mean being excluded.

The second group of questions focuses on the particular problems faced by distinct social groups—problems of such scale and chronic intensity that ICTs are never even close to being seen as relevant to their circumstances. For example, in a study of single parents (Haddon and Silverstone 1995) it became clear that limited income often meant that anything beyond very basic ICTs such as the phone or television lay beyond the horizon of many single parents. They were completely preoccupied with the struggle to survive—to provide basic shelter and nourishment as well maintain basic social needs. Even those who were able to create a home, a personal space for their family, and participate in social networks and leisure activities outside the home had minimal interest in the information society, and perhaps justifiably so.

In such cases, even the improbable capacity of governments to underwrite or subsidize access to the electronic culture is unlikely to be sufficient to enable the disadvantaged to participate. With priorities lying elsewhere and basic skills and competencies being denied to them, they are going to need much more by way of incentive and support than merely financial inducements. For such groups participation in contemporary culture is as much a function of their ability to access a wide range of television programs and channels as it is to access an information service. The capacity to discuss what was seen last night on television is as important a route into society as the ability to electronically access information offered by the local social services.

CONCLUSIONS AND CONSEQUENCES

Increasingly, the end user and social aspects of the information society are being recognized in policy statements (see, e.g., the discussion by Ducatel, Webster, and Herrmann in the chapter 1 of this volume). But the implications of that recognition are rarely discussed and little consideration is being given either in policy or research as to how to alter the situation. This problem is likely to persist until we have developed a more mature understanding of the social and cultural factors that currently affect the use of ICTs in everyday life. Above all, we have to realize that the role of the domestic consumer is not just a passive one involving the resigned acceptance of innovation at the end of a long process of technical development. On the contrary, policies and markets must actively engage users in the innovation process.

User "activity" is of course complex. It is the product of social and psychological factors. It changes through time. It is a symbolic as well as a material process, involving judgments of status and aesthetics as well as usefulness and functionality. It is not determined by any single factor, and it is especially not determined by the mere availability of the latest gee-whiz ICT. This is difficult but essential to understand.

The first major implication of these arguments is the need for more and better research. Although research and technological development programs now tend to acknowledge social and cultural factors in technological change, they still mostly separate such research from the core business of getting technical results.

Likewise in policy development, access to, and participation in, the emerging information society is constrained by a complex array of social and cultural factors, not all of which are reducible to questions of material resources. The threats and realities of exclusion on the basis of language and culture, ethnicity, location, age, and gender, as well as disability, conspire to undermine any dreams of universal access or public service that must underpin any effective attempt to draw whole societies into a new age. Change is slower than often anticipated and certainly more uneven. The reverse salients are human, not technical. This suggests a need to underwrite innovation in key areas based on social policy objectives rather than leave all to the leadership of the market. It also suggests that this subsidy should not ignore access to existing forms of media that are vulnerable to the spread of market forces, for example, cable or satellite television. Access to technologically more advanced and, on the face of it, more socially necessary forms of information is also essential. Clearly, resources will need to be found to provide public access, and once again not just access to public information sites. Electronic mail and cultural consumption, as well as market participation (virtual consumption), are key foci for the emerging information society, with many depending on public kiosks or cybercafes for at least initial entry and participation.

It follows, finally, that those planning new electronic services will need to keep their heads. Technologies change faster than people. The staggering growth of the Internet notwithstanding, there is little in the way of a demonstrated need for new forms of consumption. This, together with a persistent lack of physical access and personal competence, will keep domestic markets for ICTs fragile and uneven (Silverstone 1997b).

NOTES

1. Much of the social-shaping literature has concerned itself with the process of design and production, arguing against a technologically determinist position from the perspective of the institutional and wider social processes that define and frame how a new technology will appear. The inevitable consequence has been to downplay or entirely ignore the continued shaping of technology in use (Cockburn 1992).

2. The stress on the consumer is one that is increasingly being shared by the ICT industry. Policy makers are also beginning to recognize that taking the consumer into account at an early stage is essential in the research and development of new technologies and services as well as at the point of market launch. There are a number of reasons, including increasing competitiveness in less regulated markets (e.g., telecommunications), the struggles of a converging industrial structure to define a new market (e.g., multimedia), and an increasing fragmentation of consumer tastes in a market that is both expanding and changing rapidly (a shift across the sector from hardware to software and services).

3. While the data for other European countries may vary, it is likely that many of the trends will have a more general validity.

4. On radio see Douglas 1986, Forty 1986; on TV, Spigel 1992; on the telephone, de Sola Pool 1977, Marvin 1988; on the VCR, Keen 1987; and on the computer, Haddon 1988, Skinner 1994.

5. For a discussion of the household as a "moral economy" and its relevance to the consumption and use of ICTs, see Silverstone 1994b. See also other research on ICTs, such as home computers and Minitel in Norway (Lie and Sorenson 1996; M. Aune 1992; Berg 1994a, 1994b). This form of analysis sensitizes researchers to themes that they might investigate when exploring how a new ICT might be perceived, received, or resisted and to household conflicts that might emerge from it.

6. See for the U.K., Haddon 1995a, 1995b, Haddon 1988, Haddon and Skinner 1991, Skinner 1994; on the Netherlands, Presvelou 1986, Nissen and Riis 1989; on Norway Aune 1992; and on France Jouet et al. 1991.

7. In Philips's launch of CD-i, staff, advertisers, retailers, and supporting magazines

presented the product in different ways and for different motives (Silverstone and Haddon 1993).

8. For example, all Danish audiotext services were shut down because of a public outcry about sex hotlines (Christoffersen 1994). British Telecom at one point ejected some users because of fears that political issues being discussed on their network might provoke adverse media publicity (Cawson et al. 1995).

9. Disability is a continuum; only 10 percent of registered blind are totally without sight.

10. Haddon and Silverstone (1993) found that many self-employed teleworkers, especially professionals, would use the answering machine or an answering service specifically to create an impression of working from an office or to disguise the fact that they were not, for fear of losing their credibility as either client or consultant.

11

Computer-Aided Democracy:
The Effects of Information and Communication
Technologies on Democracy

Pierre Chambat

For twenty years, with the diffusion of informatics into society, the study of information and communication technology (ICT) and democracy has grown considerably. One theme of such work concerns the transformations of the social structure implied by the passage to the "communication society." Since the first analyses of the postindustrial society (Touraine 1969; Bell 1973), the development of ICTs has been associated with the decline of the industrial society, with the emergence of the new middle classes and with the erosion of class conflict as the motor of political dynamics (Lasch and Urry 1994). A second theme treats the technological characteristics of ICTs—interactivity, digital networks, images on the screen—which break with the old technologies of print publishing and audiovisual materials around which democratic political life has been organized since the end of the nineteenth century.[1] This "technological revolution" is comparable to the printing revolution at the end of the fifteenth century (Eisenstein 1991; Martin 1988). If it leads, following the work of Innis and then McLuhan, to an examination of the impacts of technology on social and political practices, it ends up, for want of sufficient perspective, in a very deterministic vision, neglecting the long process of social adoption. Third, ICTs represent more than an agent of political transformation. New media constitute at the same time a window display and a place of debate for specialists and citizens. The Internet, where there are multiplying

259

experiments and forums relevant to electronic democracy, constitutes a crucial place for the understanding and evaluation of new practices.[2] This is a clear example of the notion of reflexivity associated with ICTs (Giddens 1994; Beck, Giddens, and Lasch 1994).

Yet assessing the impacts of ICT on democratic political systems is a delicate exercise. It should not ignore the effect of general acceptance of political domination on the political regime and of the fairly generalized situation of political apathy. Whether democracy is restrained by the political or the institutional dimension or is understood as an ensemble of social relations that feed the civil society, ICTs can be seen as either a remedy for the failings of representative democracy or as the means to institute a true democracy (Barber 1984; Grossman 1995). Sociologists have noted that emerging technologies, because they are becoming commonplace and to a degree increasingly measurable, have given rise to an overestimation of their impacts (Flichy 1991; Scardigli 1995). Dealing with the relations between ICTs and democracy, the discourse tends to reduce politics to communication. It evokes two images for reference: Orwell or Athens (Donk, Snellen, and Tops 1995). However, the social adoption of ICTs is slow and complex (Perriault 1989; Flichy 1995). As they become commonplace, as in the case of telematics in France, it is necessary to be sensitive to differences between the intentions of the designers and the dreams of the pioneers. That is why, above all else, it is necessary to pose questions in the light of outcomes, even if they are themselves still based on experimental situations.

The modern tradition of political theory since Locke and Montesquieu has associated preference for the representative form of government with the physical impossibility in modern states of assembling the people in the agora in order to make collective decisions. The contrast between antique democracy, which was direct and based on bodily presence and speech, and modern representative democracy, based on physical distance and written publicity, is rooted in the evidence of an insurmountable material difficulty linked to the sheer size of nation-states (Finley 1976, 1985). Although the audiovisual media are disappointing, ICTs, interactive and structured in a network, could permit the realization of an electronic agora (Nora and Minc 1978; Sola Pool 1983; Dertouzos and Moses 1983; McLean 1989). As yet, however, evidence does not totally confirm this hope. The analysis of the impact of ICTs has to be nuanced to avoid too strong a division between direct democracy and representative democracy and should consider their complementarity in a process of "ongoing democracy" (Tehranian 1990; Fishkin 1991; Slaton 1992; Rodota 1999; Rousseau 1996).

ICT AND POLITICAL INSTITUTIONS

Unlike the audiovisual media, ICTs have not yet made very significant inroads into the political institutions of democracy, at least in Europe, where, incidentally, scientific literature on the subject is still fairly limited. The representative democracies remain profoundly marked by a history of political struggle, which is the source of traditions enshrined in legal statute; the elevated status of these traditions in the hierarchy of norms and their symbolic power make them difficult to change. In addition, ICT is entering at the fringes through the computerization of certain aspects of the electoral process and open access to public information.

The electoral process was one of the first political domains to be computerized: ICTs are used to draw up electoral rolls and then add up polling results. By contrast, the heart of the democratic process, the poll itself, is little affected, most probably because of the symbolic overtones attached to the voting ritual with its the polling booth and ballot box.[3] Only in very specific institutional contexts, within representative bodies, especially parliaments and regional or local assemblies, have electronic voting procedures been developed for purely instrumental reasons. By contrast, teledemocracy remains highly marginal and diverse. Although the themes of "computer democracy" or "push-button democracy" are already well established, and are associated with Manichaean ideas, their use remains largely experimental (Arterton 1987; Donk, Snellen, and Tops 1995). The technological and political obstacles encountered are numerous, especially where the vote is cast from home. Technological options have to take account of inequalities and differences in equipment, identification of the voters and verification of their entitlement to vote, confidentiality of votes, and the likelihood of disputes.[4] Teledemocracy, in fact, is presented as a Trojan horse of direct democracy, aimed at destabilizing the rationale of representative democracy. In reality, different problems present themselves: who should pose the questions? how should televotes and public debates be linked? what consequences will be derived from the results? The positions adopted by populist leaders in favor of the people having a direct say on the problems of society, combined with statements favoring the use of ICT to facilitate such participation (Ross Perot, Newt Gingrich,[5] and Jean-Marie Le Pen, for example) are not conducive to progress in this area. This may lead to the manipulation of public opinion by populist leaders on the model of the TV evangelists (Bruce 1990). Teledemocracy, the modern form of the referendum (Hamon 1995), in this context appears to be questioning the role of parliamentary institutions, the lobbies, and the media, as well as potentially strengthening the executive branch and promoting the personalized exercise of power. During this phase of political crisis in Western democracies, the technological question reveals the extent to which the representative mechanisms rest on a paradox, namely, that popular participation in the form of voting translates in practice into the delegation of power to elite social groups, in contrast to the antique democracy of Athens, which opted for rotation of tasks and the drawing of lots (Manin 1995; Hansens 1991).

At the institutional level, the introduction of ICT preserves the core functions of political institutions. The implementation of the principle of open government through the organs of the democratic constitution has remained largely embedded in the traditional communication media of written documents and oral debate. The introduction of audiovisual methods into parliaments, and above all in the courts, has met with a great deal of reticence and remains strictly regulated (Franklin 1992). By contrast, ICT could play a significant role in one key area, namely, in the provision of information to the political authorities and especially to parliaments and beyond that to the evaluation of public policies. Simulation facilities, which would enable parliamentarians to evaluate and visualize the effects of government proposals and measures, would be a means whereby parliaments could enhance their capacity to exercise control over the actions of the government. The U.S. Congress does this, notably in the technical and budgetary domains, through the Office of Technology Assessment and the Congressional Budget Office.

By contrast, transparency is considered one of the foundations of democracy, which audiovisual media have not satisfied. Thus informing citizens is one the privileged domains of ICTs. They are sometimes associated with forms of on-line participation and result in the following consequences: the formation and illumination of public opinion, the growth of participation, influence on the political agenda, and the control of elected representatives. The notion of "open government" or the "network state" means giving citizens easy access to public information by means of networks of terminals, preferably multimedia ones. Easy navigation via hypertext links offers access to constitutional texts, laws and directives, parliamentary debates, official reports, statistics, speeches by officials, libraries, and so on. It is an objective of the "national information infrastructure" promised by the Clinton administration (IITF 1993) and the Bangemann Report (CEC 1994a) in Europe. Such information provision is sometimes accompanied by the consultation of users and the organization of policy forums, especially in election periods.[6] Thus the experiments stimulated since Minnesota in 1994 have centered on elections. The experiment in California provides a large amount of policy information, while the Government

Information Service launched in July 1994 in the United Kingdom offers open forums to citizens on issues of public interest from transport congestion to European monetary union. At the same time it provides information on the delivery of electronic services to citizens.[7]

The thirteen American experiments analyzed some time ago by Arterton (1987) show that the prospect of influencing a decision does not significantly increase participation (35 percent in the best case), in phone-in referenda in particular. The causes of this relative failure are primarily sociological and relate to political apathy, which the introduction of ICT cannot itself alleviate. The question arises here of the association between the political uses of these instruments and the political debate itself, especially in the audiovisual media associated with these experiments (Fishkin 1991). The best results, as it happens, are recorded in experiments that place far greater emphasis on the confrontation of opinions than on the management of the decision-making process. These results should be understood in relation to the relatively rudimentary technologies used: telephone, television, and the press. The Internet is perhaps more attractive because of its enhanced functionality and its user-friendliness (e-mail, newsgroups, hypertext links, multimedia) and accessibility to the citizen (Slaton 1993). In this regard, it would be useful to study the French case as a comparison of the failure of civic telematics in the 1980s and the more recent emergence of French public sites on the Internet.[8] The conception of robust services—accessible, up-to-date, and offering different levels and modes of access—has to reconcile the quality of information with its accessibility and avoid (1) promoting institutions and (2) simply digitalizing written information. But it would be an illusion to suppose that the accessibility of public information by itself would motivate households to buy ICT equipment, especially the disadvantaged or the apathetic. "Open government" should be seen not just as facilitating the daily life of citizens but also as reinforcing their competencies and ability to act via sites that are open and attractive. One cause of citizen disaffection is the imbalance between an abundance of information and a weak ability to act in relation to the range of mediators animating political and social debate.

STATE MACHINERY AND PUBLIC ACTION

The introduction of ICT has been more successful in the machinery of government, where it has become a key element in public administration and decision making. ICTs constitute an improvement in the provision of public services—the "modernization of the public service" (Epstein 1990; Chambat '1990)—thereby strengthening the legitimacy of democratic regimes shaken by the crisis of the welfare state.

The use of ICTs is primarily a means to an end, aimed at adapting the bureaucratic organization of the state to a competitive environment in a complex society. During a phase marked by scarcity of budget funds this recourse to technology is first and foremost aimed at generating efficiencies by rationalizing tasks. It aims to transfer repetitive operations to machines, improve services to users, simplify and speed up filing procedures, and, it is hoped, increase the job satisfaction and involvement of civil servants by upgrading their work. The computerization of municipal authorities and other administrative activities fundamentally represents the Taylorization of administrative work, even if it applies to such widespread fields as employee payrolls, accounts, land registries, planning permission databases, forensic police records, and post office automation.

ICT also accompanies the introduction of modern management methods such as information management systems, automated catalogues, analytical accounting, and customer-supplier relations between services. Often the aim is to invoke cost controls and accounting comparisons between quite different services from road maintenance to the treatment of homogeneous groups of patients in accordance with the principles of product-line management, as is fashionable in American hospitals. ICTs are a better means of identifying unprofitable activities, defining priority objectives, adapting means to ends (particularly in human resource management), and evaluating results. Technological modernization is also a means of ensuring continuity of service by circumventing possible staff-related problems, such as strikes and reductions in working hours. Service points can be open twenty-four hours a day, thanks to on-line services and automatic dispensers; transport can be automated and operational support systems can provide travel information. It is a long-awaited opportunity to transform the occupational structure and the professional culture; by transferring technical operations to machines, it releases employees for other more profitable activities centering on relations with users or customers.

Rationalization of the use of urban supply networks is a third field of application of ICTs (DIV, OECD, and URBA 2000 1992). It ranges from investment planning through the creation of models to real-time monitoring of the provision of the product or service and includes computerized housekeeping and remote monitoring of the urban network infrastructures such as water and sewerage, district heating, roads, and traffic. It also involves the management of customer services on the telecommunications model by offering services such as remote meter reading and bill payment, thereby achieving a simultaneous individualization of provision and industrialization of its production. ICTs ultimately make it possible to envisage better coordination of the urban networks thanks to cross-sectoral applications permitted by geographical information systems. Communications networks become "networks of networks," intelligent networks, and monitoring service networks (Beniger 1986; Bressand and Distler 1985).

Customer satisfaction is the proclaimed objective of official statements on modernization. But the main function of ICT is to manage equipment and services through real-time knowledge of the wishes or behavior patterns of the public and hence adjusting, without delay, the supply of services and their pricing (e.g., by computerizing school kitchens). Where they simplify administrative formalities, such as entering customs declarations on-line, they also entail the imposition of certain costly tasks to the user. They also require a minimum level of technological culture, for instance, by requiring that university inscriptions be done on-line using Minitel in France. Although not negligible, the improvements remain largely symbolic. Despite an image of modernization, it still remains for ICTs to make a complete transition from the back office to the front office.[9] Although necessary to the modernization of public services, the introduction of ICTs cannot be passed off as a miracle formula to achieve administrative reform.

The pure and simple vision of substitution of technologies driven by an accountancy-based vision of paperless offices and canned education must be abandoned (Perriault 1996). The diffusion of a communication tool does not operate through the superimposition of technological possibilities but by a transformation of services taking into account the skills of the providers and the needs of the users (Warin 1993). Organizations do not automatically decentralize. They lack appropriate expertise, attention to non-ICT related factors, commitment in terms of policy and personnel, strategic planning, and project follow-up. After all, innovation often lies less in technological modernity than in the transformation of organizational patterns. In France, the educational system and the impossibility of harmonizing emergency services, in contrast to the countries of northern Europe, are examples of resistance to change within existing structures. Similarly, the introduction of the "electronic bracelet" as an alternative to imprisonment for petty criminals, especially on grounds of cost, modifies the divisions of responsibility between police and justice. However, since the public services are integrated into complex systems involving various operators, the regulation needed for the implementation of public policies involves increasingly horizontal and contractual relationships that overcome the obstacle of administrative fragmentation and corporatism.[10]

Beyond the state machinery, public action itself is affected. Technological transformations are encouraging a redefinition of the respective areas of competence of the public and private sectors and are intensifying competition by a redefinition of supply and the entry of new actors. Public intervention, which has occupied a strong position since the development of the welfare state, is in effect disqualified. Driven as much by the internal dynamics of economic change within the sector as by external pressures, especially the single European market, the search for efficiency, in the name of the entrepreneurial model, leads to a questioning of public organizations and their roles. Often the result is the disengagement of the state and its retreat to the sole functions of regulation, authority, and strategy setting. But this development toward the Anglo-Saxon concept of public utilities comes into conflict with the French institutional conception of public service, linked to the idea of equal treatment and state control, especially in the large public networks (Chambat 1990; Stoffaes 1995a, 1995b; Walrave 1995). The setbacks experienced in France (with the *plan calcul*, the *plan câble*, *domotics*, high-definition TV, or the *Image plan* for the promotion of cartoons), the European dimension of the problems and the stakes involved make the perpetuation of public intervention in its traditional forms a less credible option. "High-tech *Colbertism*" (Cohen 1992) seems to be outdated, especially in the domain of ICTs. Public intervention is hampered by its inability to anticipate the uses of technology, to impose them a fortiori, and to reproduce the success of national scale on-line services, such as the French Minitel, that have failed to transcend national frontiers and are now rendered obsolete by the Internet (Bouwman and Christoffersen 1992).

ICTs AND CIVIL SOCIETY

ICTs and Public Space

One of the major problems identified by political pundits is the crisis of representation formed by growing individualism in society. Freedom of expression has been translated into practice by the delegation of the exercise of this right to organs—parties and media—that institutionalize the plurality of opinion and provide vertical communication in a democracy. On this point, the possibility has also been mooted of a democracy without representation, based on exchanges between individuals that are mediated by communication machines, particularly at the local level, where voters are better able to control and contextualize the information conveyed by ICT (Hermes 1989; Paillart 1995). Contrary to the hopes of teledemocracy or electronic communities entertained by some people, however, the networks can be opaque as well as transparent (Vitalis 1995; Delmas and Massit-Follea 1995).

Accompanying the decline of traditional militantism (Perrineau 1995), the professionalization of the political career has been reflected in politicians' use, to differing degrees, of specialists trained in political marketing (Gerstle 1993; Kaid, Gerstle, and Sanders 1991). The combination of television, computer, and telephone has been changing the ways in which politicians fulfil their mandate, transforming them from representative leaders of opinion to brokers of opinions. The effectiveness of political communication has increased through the systematic use of ICTs in the form of telephone surveys, selective mailing, publicity spots, and the use of e-mail opinion polls. The result is heightened targeting of specific groups of voters as if they were consumer groups for different goods. At the same time, the function of the political parties is eroding, including the horizontal communication function whereby messages are relayed to the various social groups and professional milieus (by "leaders of opinion"), the function as a mouthpiece and rallying point for demands, the function of structuring opinions by identification, and even the function of selecting leaders. Politics increasingly is seen as a communication enterprise and its defeats are presented as failures of communication. Consequently, political discourse addressed to the community of citizens as the expression of a hierarchy of problems, enshrined in a party program, as the definition of a collective vision of the future in the form of a project, is tending to degenerate into a juxtaposition of single-issue measures responding to the expectations and specific interests of the various groups. The political struggle is assuming an ever more strategic dimension at the expense of ideological debate (Dahlgren and Sparks 1993; Breton 1992). The utility of ICTs should therefore reside in their ability to foster debates based on political action.

In the media, ICTs increase the logic of competition and render partially obsolete the struggle between the public and private sectors that is characteristic of pluralism (Miege 1990; Keane 1991; Dahlgreen and Sparks 1993; Achille and Ibanez Bueno 1994). Concern for circulation or audience figures, and the need for speed and spectacle are also changing the conditions of production and delivery of information and affect the credibility of the media. Moreover, the proliferation of specialist channels and the fragmentation of the viewing public tend to erode the civic function of the audiovisual media: grouping people together and providing information about the political community. Under pressure from new forms of TV-watching behavior (e.g., channel surfing), the new media of cable, satellite, and video games, and competition, the main-stream channels once watched by the majority of the public will see their au-diences gradually disappear. It is now possible to avoid political broadcasts during electoral campaigns or practice selective exposure. Fragmentation of the pub-lic is exploding the traditional idea of the "general public" characterized by a mixture of groups, readerships, audiences, and social backgrounds (Wolton 1990). Electronic forums only partially compensate for this effect.

Beyond the straightforward electronification of the media, their profile has changed considerably, as heralded by telematics (Pailliart 1991, 1995; Chapignac 1995). The information chain is being radically altered as the function of server is emerging, an interface between supply and demand and the custodian of the right of access whose task is to reroute the desired information to each cus-tomer. This fragmentation leads to the notion of "self-media" characterized by the production of services that are highly targeted (e.g., a custom-made news-paper, the *Daily Me*) thanks to "intelligent agents" (Gilder 1990; Negroponte 1995). The rationale of differentiation thus results in an abandonment of the debate on legitimate and acceptable content and, in more general terms, the public problems created by the neutralization of conflicts that technology brings—video, encryption, CD-ROM, and so on. With the "violence chip" the confrontation of judgments in the public realm is eclipsed by the coexistence of tastes and interests provided by technology. This makes it highly unlikely that the body of citizens will ever form a political community constituent of a com-munal world and a shared common knowledge.

Last, ICTs change the geographical scope of the media and consequently alter the construction of collective identities. The globalization of information flows enlarges the group of people concerned, beyond the national political community. The liberal reasoning that regards data as merchandise joins forces with the propensity of ICT to transcend national frontiers. This weakens the power of the state and the consistency of the public realm. Increasingly, lob-byists and pressure groups drive the national public debate. Dominant and worldwide multimedia groups have also emerged with their own agendas and cultural predispositions. Protective statutory constraints are being circumvented, as demonstrated in the problems associated with controlling erotic satellite channels in Europe, faxes in China, or the satellite channels broadcasting from the Maghreb countries to France. The Internet provides the most celebrated evidence that communications are beyond national government control and that censorship, whether it be of extremist groups or dissidents, is increasingly ineffective.

Meanwhile, people's dependence on foreign resource centers is growing and national identity is gradually losing its cultural dimension, which is illustrated by campaigns to promote national heritage. Political sovereignty in the cultural field is retreating before the power of the market. Whether it is a modern manifestation of cosmopolitanism or an expression of domination by the cultural industries, globalization is challenging the preconception that underlies the classical argument on the influence of the media as the fourth branch of government: under the aegis of a paternalistic state, a collective identity, membership in a national community, and territorial sovereignty are synonymous concepts. The public realm shaped by ICTs tends to dissociate itself from the political scene that focuses on collective decision making, effectively separating debate from decision—the two aspects of deliberation.

ICTs therefore invite us to analyze more effectively the swing from party democracy to public democracy (Manin 1995). With ICTs, politics is moving away from the institutionalized electoral time frame, from its accustomed setting in the mass media, and from issues that find their way onto the agenda as a result of the competition between the government and the media. The numerous examples of public participation in the media facilitated by ICTs show ever more clearly the political importance of public opinion: expressing opinions becomes a form of engagement (Verba 1996). Opening up to ordinary members of the public may counterbalance the feeling among citizens that a widening chasm exists between themselves and the political professionals. This direct voice makes it possible to debate problems in society without the views of the experts stifling the testimony of ordinary citizens (Livingstone and Lunt 1994; Yankelovitch 1991). In a more general sense, by lowering the cost of political participation, ICTs offer fairly apolitical people and laypeople the possibility, or the illusion, of having an immediate influence on political decision making. The tension involved in expressing a view is reduced because people can log their opinion by replying to an opinion poll, sending e-mail, or signing an Internet petition. Whether this use of ICT will lead to increased numbers of ordinary people expressing their opinion or to a growth in conformism and stereotypes as suggested in the notion of a "spiral of silence" (Noelle-Neumann 1993) is not known. Or perhaps it will encourage the most committed extremists to express themselves. Here again, it is the systems of actors and, in reaction, the users of ICTs that will be determinant.

ICTs and the Social Bond

The strength of democratic life lies in the social communication that facilitates the passage from sociability to citizenship, from private concerns to public problems. It was on this point that the effects of ICT on democracy were first considered as they relate to civil society (Nora and Minc 1978; Claret,

Laperriere, and Peladeau 1988). But in France the power of utopian visions and indifference to their uses has proved to be a barrier to teleservices (Théry 1994; Breton 1994; Dard et al. 1995) and above all to telework presented as a panacea to spatial management (Rozenholc, Fanton, and Veyret 1995).

The first question to be asked concerns the tendency to withdraw into the private sphere (cocooning) and its relation to a narcissistic individualism that would open the door to a form of government consisting of a paternalistic (if not authoritarian) administration of societies, a process analyzed by Tocqueville and developed by Bellah (Bellah et al. 1985). Interest in the Internet, in the United States especially, openly aims to compensate for the loss of a sense of community. By contrast, other European writers regard "teleaction" that encourages inertia as a destroyer of sociability and civic virtues (Virilio 1990).

Beginning with the decline of urbanism (understood as the articulation between sociability and citizenship), analysts seek to find out if ICTs amplify or compensate for the anomie and growing indifference in the megalopolis (Ascher 1995). On the one hand, ICTs can contribute to the maintenance of urban qualities in delivering services to all inhabitants or in making compatible the diverse uses of public space (Mitchell 1996).[11] It can control the entrance of private cars, enhance security by means of surveillance cameras in car parks around sports stadia or in the public transportation network. It can use giant video screens to make public entertainment more spectacular. It can facilitate housework and upgrade daily life for the disabled and the dependent elderly, as well as expedite their access to services (Conte 1988). The implementation of these services raises considerable difficulties, especially in relation to the users (Dard et al. 1991, 1995).

Conversely, the generalized use of technology could ultimately erode the public realm or lead to segregation. The first point is that the devitalization of social life could be reinforced by the proliferation of automatic devices. The diffusion of surveillance devices and the privatization and control of collective areas may eliminate intermediate areas in which people can meet one another. Although security is the prerequisite of people's liberty to come and go, and hence of their autonomy, the trend toward the security control of people could accentuate the fragmentation of urban space. For example, we see buildings "turned inward," surveillance cameras in department stores and shopping centers, and access cards for residential complexes, leisure facilities, and places of work. It could also privatize and commercialize collective facilities through reserved parking, privatize security, and heighten reliance on insurance mechanisms. Technology, by dispensing unequal rights of access, is liable to give substance to a trend toward "spatial discrimination" and segregate the population to avoid undesirable social intermingling, as seen in the growth of "gated communities" in contemporary American towns (Trilling 1992).[12] Having failed to create an urbane atmosphere in the city, communications technology would then bring urban amenities into the home.

Electronic communities have been forming for twenty years; thanks to interactivity and networks, there could be a resurgence of social life operating at a distance. A similar point was often emphasized in connection with cable TV in the United States from 1963 onward, then in Canada, and finally in Europe (Communications 1974; Proulx 1988). At the present time this hope is focused on the Internet and its scope for the liberating creation of virtual communities (Reingold 1994). Since Community Memory was established in Santa Monica at the start of the 1970s, various local civic networks have been set up—Civic Networks, Community Networks, FreeNets, Public Electronic Networks (Santa Monica), and so on—offering citizens electronic conferences on subjects of local interest.[13] The issues centered on solutions to technological adaptation, the accessibility of these forums, the choice of themes of debate, but also the effects of decisions and participation. These forums mobilized isolated citizens rather than groups, concerned individuals rather than the indifferent majority, around the relations between ICTs and inequalities. In this regard, the higher rate of growth of the Internet should not create an illusion of community. It remains above all an elite phenomenon that is no substitute for direct forms of sociability.[14]

The debate, renewed with each new technological innovation, dwells on the artificiality of community at a distance and on the specificities of the linkages woven by computer-mediated communication (Shields 1996; Calhoun 1991).[15] Research into the uses of media technologies shows the limits of technological determinism. Computer-mediated communication does not simply substitute communication mediated by machines for face-to-face communication. Nor, on the other hand, is the technology neutral; it creates inequalities, at least in its initial phase.[16] The technical networks cannot create durable social networks but can lead to their consolidation; the "groups" constituted through on-line exchanges remain largely "virtual." With the progressive acceptance of ICTs a shift in emphasis occurs, from mastery of the media and fascination with the technology to relational and content issues ("Dix ans de vidéotex" 1989). Technological mediation cannot take the place of personal contact but can play an essential role in keeping people in touch between meetings.

By contrast, ICTs can be a quite significant resource for new social movements in the cultivation of their identities and the essential mobilization of sympathizers to work on public opinion. In France, for instance, nurses, students, long-distance truck drivers, homosexuals, ecologists, and others have made sustained use of ICT as a major element in campaigns to mobilize opinion.[17]

The intensive use of ICT—Minitel, answering machines, computers, and fax—is transforming the methods of collective protest. These systems encourage unconventional and less costly forms of participation, such as protests, petitions, and flaming. They make it easier to found groups and to lower overheads; they encourage subjective expression by individuals and hence the integration of that subjectivity into their struggle. Although such mobilization work is generally emphasized as a characteristic feature of such groups, it has scarcely been studied.[18] The mobilization of these groups contrasts with the removal of subjectivity in traditional political militancy. It is based on an approach that emphasizes a common identity, relates subjective experience to objective conditions, and is engaged in by means of horizontal communication deriving from shared social codes. In France, for example, activist students and nurses have used electronic communication and truck drivers have used CB radio to disseminate information and explain the background, scope, and aims of the action. More than as a means of disseminating ideology on the lines of the Internet piracy practiced by the neo-Nazis, ICTs were used to offer an instant platform, to organize the struggle, and to prepare an appearance in the realm of the public media. Immediately available information is a key resource in collective action. It permits rapid organization by disseminating slogans, objectives, and forms of action. ICT also compensates to some extent for a low level of institutionalization or for the dispersal of citizens. More than the creation of permanent organizations based on the classical mechanisms of representation and delegation of spokesmanship and of power, the challenge is to raise solidarity and to facilitate access to public opinion by the expedient of the media, thanks to the speed and power of the mobilization. These forms of action do not dispense with the movement's obligation to state its case in the public realm, but they prepare the case and its presentation.[19]

The last point at issue concerns the impact of ICT on individual and collective liberties. Democracy depends on the accessibility of public information as a control by the people on the exercise of power and on respect for privacy. The right to information and the right to privacy are threatened by the commercialization of information and by state control. The commodification of public information could endanger the fact of its accessibility in the name of the copyright protection of databases and those that use them while on the other hand, sensitive information touching private life becomes more and more the object of information capture and processing without the knowledge of subjects and in violation of protective regulations on secrecy, especially as concerns banking and medical information (Ribault 1988; Ojti 1992; Gandy 1993; CNIL 1993, 1994).

Beyond freedom of expression, which has to be reconciled with other rights, one of the challenges for individual privacy lies in the tracking and tracing of informatics use. Even daily behavior, recorded using Internet cookies that track visits to Web sites, is monitored, as is the interconnection of records, the growth of information, and their real-time accessibility. Private individuals are threatened with the invasion of their privacy or run the risk of having that privacy turned against them, whereas their own access as citizens to useful information is subject to its being reprocessed by private bodies obeying other precepts than those of democratic debate. The increase in the marketing of data intensifies business secrecy and administrative inscrutability. But conversely, the compartmentalization of data files is liable to deprive states of some of their weapons in the struggle to protect citizens and to suppress crime, especially in the fight against tax evasion or money laundering. In this way, the public realm and public action risk being emptied of part of their substance, with the public debate being based, as in the debate on the social impact of economic options, on partial, obsolete, or scarcely manageable data. Thus a redefinition of information as a public good as much as an effective protection of sensitive information is essential.

A problem arises here that a number of writers, following Michel Foucault, have called the "surveillance society" (Giddens 1994; Agre 1994). Raised in connection with the establishment of the major public data banks and databases in the 1970s (Vitalis 1981), this problem assumes new dimensions and new forms with the circulation of both private and public data over the networks (Gandy 1991). The U.S. clipper chip debate on the scrambling of information and public control of the Internet testify to the acuteness of the problem, as does the development of commerce on the Web and the practice of commercial profiling of Internet surfers with which it is associated.[20] In this respect, as previously with on-line communication in France, the pornography issue is at best an anecdote and more often a red herring. It is the inequality of powers between the individual or citizen and the organizations, public or private, with large technological systems at their disposal that really constitutes the threat to liberty (Gras 1993; Joerges 1988; Joerges and Braun 1994). More generally, the development of surveillance technologies seeks to compensate for the lack of effectiveness of democratic procedures, as is shown in France by video surveillance in public spaces (Ocqueteau and Pottier 1995) or their use as preventative measures in the United Kingdom (Cahiers de la Sécurité Interieure 1995). The protection of private life is not assured by individual access to personal data alone—it requires democratic control of the structure of databases and their users. As is cited time and again, especially in workplaces (International Labor

Organization 1993), we observe a gradual switch from a repressive legal system that protects liberties insofar as it punishes transgressions of the law after the event toward a preventive system. The new system is more dangerous and more insidious in that it seeks to define a priori the potential risks, determine potential sources of danger, and normalize behavior patterns. That is why, beyond the modification of the institutional balance, some writers do not hesitate to advance the hypothesis that ICT is starting to transform the ways in which power is exercised. Either it improves the processes of social control or, by the way in which communication dominates the political decision making systems, it makes politics invisible (Beniger 1986; Deleuze 1990).

CONCLUSION

Can the diffusion of ICTs take place without a democratic debate on the challenges of technological choices? The problem is to know what types of society we are engaged in constructing, with which technologies of communication. In this regard, two conflicting models give rise to two conceptions of democracy and liberty: consumer preferences and the decisions of the representatives of the people. In the liberal model, the question of the effects of technologies reflects the individual preferences of consumers, which neutralizes them as a public concern. The free market and competition relies as a model of democracy on the sovereignty of free choice. The other voluntarist model, in the name of challenges and impacts of ICTs and in particular the effects of polarization linked to their commercialization, places at the forefront the collective responsibility for the construction of society and locates the legitimacy of public action in the pursuit of the general interest. Thus, whether ICTs are diffused by the state or by the market, as with other technology choices, is linked to the representation given to the mode of delivery to users, in other words, to the priority given to citizenship or consumer (Vitalis 1994).

Essential changes in our societies seem to be the result of techno-economic decisions taken by private or public–private actors (Beck 1992). Constrained by the phenomenon of "path dependency," policy acts at best afterward to legitimate decisions already taken or to reduce undesirable outcomes. The traditional conception of politics in democracy as forming an expression of collective will and flowing from a public debate on the problems of an interested community is empty of meaning. Many factors intervene. The "side effects" are less visible and identifiable than for other technologies (e.g., biotechnology) because they concern social relations. Consumers constitute a latent group, difficult to mobilize; the social classes that could carry the debate and make an impact on the political agenda are more accepting of the modern technology because they are the main users (Freeman and Mendras 1995). Also, the abundant debate on the multimedia and the "information superhighway" is revealed as a self-fulfilling prophecy (Neveu 1994).

The prevailing perspective of market development supported placing information superhighways on the political agenda. Beyond the economic objectives, minimal public intervention seems needed to improve the physical rather than the cultural accessibility of ICTs and to narrow the gap between the "information rich" and the "information poor." The public authorities can (should?) support the development of multimedia resource centers in public places, encourage the wide adoption of informatics equipment, and promote an information culture in the population.[21] Tackling inequality opens a field for the creation of new services. Local public facilities can reduce the unequal access of different households to equipment, especially networked computers and access to on-line services. The second responsibility of public authorities is to stimulate large-scale debate on the challenges for society created by the diffusion of ICTs and the technological choices to be made, which it can achieve by a proliferation of experiments to introduce users to technical systems and services and thus to their evaluation. From the point of view of challenges to democracy, the object should be less to test technical and commercial feasibility or market reaction than to provide evidence of the forms of adoption and enhancement of citizenship for all (Vitalis 1995).

These two responsibilities bring to the fore the notion of "universal service" that confronts policy makers. Is the information superhighway not a matter above all of connecting existing networks and making technological development a matter of economic competitiveness, seen as the promotion of networks in place of markets? The notion that underlies the process of deregulation, which is currently rubbing out the borders between informatics, audiovisual media, and telecommunications, evokes universal service. But it is used as Theodore Vail, president of AT&T in 1908, used it: interconnection for the operators rather than the public services is the meaning of accessibility for all the users of the network. This evolution poses a policy question about the level and form or regulation that should be established in Europe.

NOTES

1. J. F. Abramson, C. Atherton, and G. R. Orren identify six characteristics of ICTs that seem worth noting for the analysis of their political impact. (1) The growth of quantity and accessibility of information. (2) The acceleration of the collection, storage, and distribution of information. (3) The growing possibility of controlling

information. (4) The possibility of targeting information at recipients. (5) The decentralization of the use of information. (6) Interactivity between senders and receivers. These new technologies demand a review of the legal framework of liberties defined for the media (Sola Pool 1983).

2. A number of experiments are being performed by researchers in political science, sociology, and communication, who, in fact, have a tendency to overestimate their significance. Nevertheless, they represent useful, especially bibliographic, resources: Phil Agre, editor of the Network Observer http://dlis.gseis.ucla.edu/people/pagre/tno.html; Paul Baker, compiler of Community Networks: An Online Guide to Resources at George Mason University http://mason.gmu.edu/~pbaker/1cnindex.html; CNC Magazine http://www.december.com/cmc/mag/current/toc.html; Kimberley Gregson http://www.gspa.washington.edu/trust/links/cyberd.html and http://memex.lib.indiana.edu/hrosenba/www/Research/commnet/us.html; Steven London (Electronic Democracy) http://www.west.net/~insight/london/; Doug Schuler (Seattle Community Network) http://www.scn.org/ip/commnet/index.html.

3. Belgium has already experimented with electronic voting by magnetic cards on 6,000 voting machines, and France has announced an electronic voting project involving smart cards on 100 voting machines.

4. These problems indirectly corroborate experiences with interactive television; technological implementation is more delicate than anticipated (Lafrance 1994).

5. See Newt Gingrich's foreword to Alvin and Heidi Toffler's *Creating a New Civilization: The Politics of the Third Wave* (1995).

6. The 1996 U.S. presidential elections saw a flowering of Internet sites; see Greenman and Miller (1996).

7. Minnesota E-Democracy http://www.e-democracy.org; California Voter Foundation http://www.calvoter.org; Politics on the Web, Project Vote Smart http://www.vote-smart.org. The European Commission has a European Digital Cities Project http://www.ispo.cec.be. Finland (http://www.minedu.fi) and the Netherlands are pioneering countries in Europe (in particular Amsterdam since January 1994 with De Digitale Stad Amsterdam http://www.amazed.nl/dpd/index.html). In France the district of Parthenay launched with the support of the EU in 1996 a digital city project http://www.district-parthenay.fr/sommaire.htm. For Barcelona, see http://www.bcnet.upc.es/democ.html. Teledemocracy Action News + Network à l'Université d'Auburn records a number of experiments: http://www.auburn.edu/tann/. On freenets, see the site of the National Public Computing Network http://nptn.org.

8. In France the 15 May 1996 circular of the prime minister required each public administration to create an Internet site by 31 December 1997.

9. Telecommunication and computer equipment in France has grown noticeably along with the perception that the usefulness and efficiency of ICTs has improved. Despite remarkable successes (such as applications in police forensics and technology) there have also been failures: the halting of the Ministry of Justice computerization; the Socrates system of railways; the resistance to the health card from certain groups of medics. In addition there were many false hopes and developments in cable, and local telematics developed more slowly than expected (see Atoll 1992; Commissariat Général du Plan 1992).

10. The municipality of Salangen in Norway has established (with the help of Richard Watson, professor of management at the University of Georgia) an interesting experiment of informatizing communications between elected representatives and administrative services in order to improve the efficiency of decision making. For a description and an evaluation of the project. see "Telecommunication within the Local Public Sector" http://www.tft.tele.no/foutos-eng/projects.htm.

11. This is also one of the themes of European projects on the information society. Elsewhere, experiments with "wired cities" proliferate that are worthy of comparison: Grand Prairie (Alberta) http://www.city.grande-prairie.ab.ca/homepage.htm#CyberCity_Initiative; Stockholm http://www.stockholm.se; Parthenay and Metz (France) http://www.mairie-metz.fr:8080.

12. Also Paris and certain secure districts of Brazilian metropolises are so affected. There is a risk of insidious discrimination in schools or school life on the basis of databases on punctuality and attendance, grades, and health.

13. The network NPTN accounted for 380,000 users in 1995, according to Doug Schuler, who recorded more than 300 sites and more than 200 in development.

14. If the inequalities decline, the different studies of Internet users underline the overrepresentation of white, urban males of high educational and income levels. Elsewhere, the telephone after a century of diffusion remains exclusive. The lagging of France is sometimes attributed to the weak take-up of microcomputers in households, as well as to the reluctance of stakeholders in telematics.

15. See the study by Neil K. Guy, "Community Networks, Building Real Communities in a Virtual Space?" Master's thesis, Simon Fraser University, British Columbia, July 1996. See also *CMC Magazine* and Smith and Kollock (1997).

16. Marc Smith, a sociologist at UCLA, has carried out an ethnographic study of the Web inspired by the paradox of the engagement in collective action identified by Mancur Olson. Smith notes that 50 percent of the messages emanate from 1 percent of participants (70 out of 7,000 people). Others have criticized the sexism of Internet norms.

17. Work on the difference between telematics, or fax and the Internet for mobilization action, is in an early stage. See Gingras (1996) for a presentation of the issue of Internet et l'action collective.

18. See the work of Doug Schuler or Mark Boncheck, who concentrate on the costs of collective action (grassroots in cyberspace). On nursing in France, see Kergoat (1994). On the CB, see Jaffrin (1994).

19. Conversely, however, as has been shown by the university matriculation procedure using the RAVEL on-line system, the method may splinter the target body and tend to dissolve solidarity by obscuring the problems likely to mobilize people. In the example cited, it took the intervention of traditional student organizations, communicating through the media, to mobilize the excluded applicants by assembling them at the university buildings where matriculation was taking place. Another example, the visibility of the struggle of the Zapatatists of Chiapas (on the Internet and other media) has been preceded by years of militant work in the population.

20. On the Web, the Communications Decency Act of February 1996 has released a protest campaign (Blue Ribbon Campaign) and a debate on freedom of expression. This underlines questions about the legal nature of the Internet (is it the Garden of

Eden or a state of nature) and of the foundations and possibilities of control (by the state or ethical codes).

21. This is the meaning of the state of the nation address by President Clinton on January 1997, and the televised declaration by President Chirac on 10 March 1997. In France, first 170 and then 74 projects of public interest were announced in October 1995 and March 1996, such as Parthenay and Metz (see note 11).

References

Achille, Y., and Bueno J. Ibanez. 1994. *Les télévisions en quête d'avenir.* Grenoble: PUG.

Agdestein, S., and M. Roemer. 1991. "Good Health at a Modest Price: The Fruit of Primary Care." *World Health Forum* 12: 428–431.

Agre, P. 1994. "Surveillance and Capture: Two Models of Privacy." *Information Society* 10.

Allan, J. 1995. "Crossing Borders or Footloose Multinationals?" In *A Shrinking World? Global Unevenness and Inequality,* edited by J. Allan and C. Hamnett, pp. 55–102. Oxford: Oxford University Press/Milton Keynes.

Allen, B. 1990. "Information as an Economic Commodity." *AEA Papers and Proceedings* 80, no. 2: 268–273.

Amin, A., and N. Thrift, eds. 1994. *Globalisation, Institutions, and Regional Development in Europe.* Oxford: Oxford University Press.

Analysys. 1995. *The Costs and Funding of Universal Service in the United Kingdom: Final report to OFTEL.* Cambridge, U.K.: Analysys.

Anderson, B. 1983. *Imagined Communities: Reflections on the Origin and Spread of Nationalism.* London: Verso.

Andreasen, L., et al., eds. 1995. *Europe's Next Step: Organizational Innovation, Competition, and Employment.* Ilford, U.K.: Frank Cass.

Ang, I. 1985. *Watching "Dallas."* London: Methuen.

Antonelli, C., and R. Marchionatti. 1996. *The Technological and Organisational Change in a Traditional Industry: A Marshallian Approach.* PREST Discussion Paper. Manchester, U.K.: Manchester University.

Aoki, M. 1988. *Information, Incentives, and Bargaining in the Japanese Economy.* Cambridge: Cambridge University Press.

Aronsson, G., and A. Sjögren. 1994. *Samhällsomvandling och arbetsliv: Omvärldsanalys inför*

279

2000–talet [Change of society and working life: Analysis of the development of environment toward the twenty-first century]. Solna: Arbetsmiljöinstitutet. In Swedish.

Arvanitaki, K., and M. Stratigaki. 1994. "Computerisation in Greek Banking: The Gendering of Jobs and Payment Practices." In *Bringing Technology Home: Gender and Technology in a Changing Europe,* edited by C. Cockburn and R. Furst-Dilic. Milton Keynes: Open University Press.

Ascher, F. 1995. *Métapolis.* Paris: Odile Jacob.

Aterton, F. 1987. *Teledemocracy: Can Technology Protect Democracy?* London: Sage.

Atoll Association. 1992. *Informatique, nouvelles technologies, et gestion locale.* Paris: La Documentation Française.

Aufderheide, P. 1992. "Cable Television and the Public Interest." *Journal of Communication* 42, no. 1: 52–65

Aune, M. 1992. *Datamaskina I hverdagslivet: En studie av brukeres domestisering av en ny teknologi, hovedoppgave.* Trondheim, Norway: University of Trondheim.

Axelsson, B., and G. Easton, eds. 1992. *Industrial Networks: A New View of Reality.* London: Routledge.

Balser, K., and H. Sturmer. 1993. "Desk Top Publishing." Paper presented at the 1993 EDEN Conference, East/West Dialogue in Distance Education: Changing Societies, Technology, and Quality, Berlin, 10–12 May.

Bankowski, Z., and A. Capron, eds. 1991. "Genetics, Ethics, and Human Values: Human Genome Mapping, Genetic Screening, and Gene Therapy." Paper presented at the Twenty-Fourth CIOMS Round Table Conference, Geneva, Switzerland.

Bannock, G., and M. Daly. 1994. *Small Business Statistics.* London: Paul Chapman.

Barber, B. 1984. *Strong Democracy: Participatory Politics for a New Age.* Berkeley: University of California Press.

Barker, P., J. Barrick, and R. Wilson. 1995. *Building Sight.* London: HMSO.

Barnard, B. 1995. "Merger Mania." *Europe,* November, pp. 22–24.

Barnard, J. 1997. "Factors Affecting Uptake of CAL in Further Education." Paper presented at the CAL 1997 Conference, Exeter, U.K., 23–26 March.

Bates, A. W. 1995. *Technology, Open Learning, and Distance Education.* London: Routledge.

Baudrillard, J. 1983. *Simulations.* New York: Semiotext(e).

Baumol, W. 1989. "Is the United States Becoming an Information Economy?" In *Productivity and American Leadership.* Edited by W. Baumol, E. Blackman, and E. Wolff. Cambridge: MIT Press.

Beck, U. 1992. *Risk Society.* London: Sage.

Beck, U., A. Giddens, and S. Lasch. 1994. *Reflexive Modernisation.* Cambridge: Polity.

Beesley, M., and B. Laidlaw. 1995. "Development of Telecommunications Policy." In *The Regulatory Challenge,* edited by M. Bishop, J. Kay, and C. Mayer, pp. 309–335. Oxford: Oxford University Press.

Bell, D. 1973. *The Coming of Post–Industrial Society: A Venture in Social Forecasting.* New York: Basic.

Bellah, R., et al. 1985. *Habits of the Heart.* New York: Harper & Row.

Belt, V., et al. 1999. "Work Opportunities for Women in the Information Society: Call Centre Teleworking." Final report to the European Commission, CURDS, University of Newcastle, Newcastle, U.K.

Belussi, F. 1992. "Benetton Italy: Beyond Fordism and Flexible Specialisation: The Evolution of the Network Firm Model." In *Computer Aided Manufacturing and Women's Employment: The Clothing Industry in Four EC Countries.* Edited by S. Mitter. London: Springer-Verlag.

Beniger, J. 1986. *The Control Revolution.* Cambridge: Harvard University Press.

Benjamin, R., and R. Wigand. 1995. "Electronic Markets and Virtual Value Chains on the Information Superhighway." *Sloan Management Review,* Winter, pp. 62–72.

Bennett, N. 1987. "Cooperative Learning: Children Do It in Small Groups—or Do They?" *Educational and Child Psychology* 4: 7–18.

Bentley, Q., et al. 1992. "Learners Deserve Better: Improving the Quality of Educational Television." In *Aspects of School Television in Europe,* edited by M. Mayer, pp. 322–328. Munich: K. G. Saur.

Berg, A. 1990. "He, She, and I.T.: Designing the Home of the Future." In *Technology and Everyday Life: Trajectories and Transformations.* Edited by K. Sorensen and A. Berg. Trondheim: Norwegian Research Council for Science and Humanities.

Berg, A. 1994a. "Technological Flexibility: Bringing Gender into Technology." In *Bringing Technology Home: Gender and Technology in a Changing Europe.* Edited by C. Cockburn and R. Dilic. Buckingham, U.K.: Open University Press.

Berg, A. 1994b. "The Domestication of Telematics in Everyday Life." Paper presented at the COST 248 Workshop: The European Telecom User, Lund, Sweden, April 13–14.

Bergqvist, U. 1984. "Video Display Terminals and Health." *Scandinavian Journal of Work, Environment, and Health* 102: 1–87.

Berne, M. 1997. "French Lessons: The Minitel Case." In *The Social Shaping of Information Superhighways: European and American Roads to the Information Society,* edited by H. Kubicek, W. Dutton, and R. Williams, pp. 96–116. Frankfurt: Campus Verlag; New York: St. Martin's.

Bessant, J. 1995. "Networking as a Mechanism for Enabling Organisational Innovations: The Case of Continuous Improvement." In *Europe's Next Step: Organisational Innovation, Competition, and Employment,* edited by L. Andreasen et al., pp. 253–270. London: Frank Cass.

Biehl, D., et al. 1982. *The Contribution of Infrastructure to Regional Development: Final Report to DGXVI.* Brussels: Commission of the European Communities.

Blankaert, H. 1995. "Effects of ICT on Individual Firms." Discussion paper prepared for the EC High Level Expert Group on the Information Society, Brussels, 30 August.

Bliesener, M.–M. 1994. "Outsourcing als mögliche Strategie zur Kostensenkung." In *BFuP* April.

BLS. 1997. "BLS Projections to 2006." *Monthly Labor Review,* November. Special issue.

Blume, P. 1996. "Implementation of the European Data Protection Directive: The View from Denmark." *Journal of Information, Law, and Technology.* Available at: http://elj.warwick.ac.uk/elj/jilt/dp/1danish.

BMWi. 1996. *Info 2000: Deutschlands Weg in die Informationsgesellschaft.* Bonn: Bundesministerium für Wirtshaft.

Boddy, M., T. Rees, and D. Snape. 1995. *Vocational Training and Labour Markets.* Working Paper no. 126. Bristol, U.K.: University of Bristol, School for Advanced Urban Studies.

Boden, D., and H. L. Molotch. 1994. "The Compulsion of Proximity." In *Nowhere,* edited by R. Freidland and D. Boden, pp. 257–286. Berkeley: University of California Press.

Bosch, G. 1995. "Flexibility and Work Organisation." In *Social Europe* [January Supplement]: *Report of the Expert Working Group.* Luxembourg: Commission of the European Communities.

Bourdieu, P. 1986. *Distinction: A Social Critique of the Judgement of Taste.* London: Routledge & Kegan Paul.

Bouwman, H., and M. Christoffersen. 1992. *Relaunching Videotex.* Dordrecht: Kluwer.

Braczyk, H.–J., P. Cooke, and M. Heidenreich, eds. 1996. *Regional Innovation Systems.* London: UCL Press.

Braczyk, H.–J., G. Schienstock, and B. Steffensen. 1995. "The Region of Baden Württemberg: A Post–Fordist Success Story." In *Industrial Transformation in Europe.* Edited by E. Dittrich, E. Schmidt, and R. Whitley. London: Sage.

Bradshaw, J., and J. Miller. 1991. *Lone Parent Families in the UK.* Department of Social Security Research Report, no. 6. London: HMSO.

Bressand, A., and C. Distler. 1985. *Le prochain monde.* Paris: Seuil.

Breton, P. 1992. *L'utopie de la communication.* Paris: La Découverte.

Breton, P., and S. Proulx. 1989. *L'explosion de la communication.* Paris: La Découverte.

Breton, T. 1994. *Les téléservices en France.* Paris: La Documentation Française.

Bridges, W. 1995. *Jobshift.* London: Allen and Unwin.

Bruce, S. 1990. *Pray TV.* London: Routledge.

Bryne, J. 1993. "The Virtual Corporation." *Business Week,* 2 February, pp. 37–41.

Brynjolfsson, E., and L. Hitt. 1995. "Information Technology as a Factor of Production: The Role of Differences amongst Firms." *Economics of Innovation and New Technology* 3: 183–201.

Büchner, P. 1990. "Das Telefon im Alltag von Kindern." In *Forschingsgruppe Telefonkommunikation, Telefon und Gesellschaft.* Vol. 2. Berlin: Volker Spiess.

Busch, T. 1995. "Gender Differences in Self–Efficacy and Attitudes Towards Computers." *Educational Computing Research* 122: 147–159.

Cahiers de la Securite Interieure. 1995. "Les technologies de sécurité." *Cahiers de la Securite Interieure* 21, 3d trimestre.

Calhoun, C. 1991. "Indirect Relationships and Imagined Communities: Large–Scale Social Integration and the Transformation of Everyday Life." In *Social Theory for a Changing Society.* Edited by P. Bourdieu and J. Coleman. Boulder: Westview.

Canon, M. 1995. "Life in the Big City: Internet Concerns." *MacUser* 7, no. 5: 17.

Capello, R. 1994. *Spatial Analysis of Telecommunications Network Externalities.* Aldershot, U.K.: Avebury.

Cappelli, P. 1995. "Rethinking Employment." *British Journal of Industrial Relations* 33, no. 4: 563–602.

Carey, J., and J. Quirk. 1989. "The Mythos of the Electronic Revolution." In *Communication as Culture: Essays on Media and Society,* edited by J. W. Carey, pp. 113–141. Boston: Unwin Hyman.

Camagni, R., ed. 1991. *Innovation Networks: Spatial Perspectives.* London: Belhaven.

Carroll, G. 1994. "Organisations . . . The Smaller They Get." *California Management Review* 37, no. 1: 28–41.

Castells, M. 1989. *The Informational City.* Oxford: Basil Blackwell.

Castells, M., and P. Hall. 1994. *Technopoles of the World: The Making of Twenty-first Century Industrial Complexes.* London: Routledge.

Catinat, M. 1998. "The 'National Information Infrastructure' Initiative in the United States—Policy or Non–Policy? Part One." *Computer and Telecommunications Law Review* 43: 68–86.

Cawson, A., L. Haddon, and I. Miles. 1995. *The Shape of Things to Consume: Bringing Information Technology into the Home.* London: Avebury.

CBS. 1995. *Automatiseringsstatistieken, 1993–1995.* Heerlen: Statistics Netherlands.

CEC [Commission of the European Communities]. 1990. *Directive on the Minimum Safety and Health Requirements for Work with Display Screen Equipment 90/270/EEC.* Basic Human Rights. Luxembourg: CEC.

CEC. 1991. *STAR: Programme Report.* March. Brussels: CEC.

CEC. 1993. *Growth, Competitiveness, and Employment: The Challenges and Ways Forward into the Twenty–first Century.* Luxembourg: CEC.

CEC. 1994a. *Europe and the Global Information Society: Recommendations to the European Council.* Brussels: CEC.

CEC. 1994b. *Competitiveness and Cohesion: Trends in the Regions.* Fifth Periodic Report on the Social and Economic Situation and Development of the Regions in the Community. Brussels: CEC.

CEC. 1994c. *Business Startups in the EC: Support Programmes.* Berlin: CEDEFOP European Centre for the Development of Vocational Training.

CEC. 1994d. "The Internet and the European Information Industry." *Information Market Observatory IMO.* IMO Working Paper no. 94/3. Luxembourg: CEC.

CEC. 1994e. "Biomed 2 Work Programme." *Biomedical and Health Research.* December, DG XII. Brussels: CEC.

CEC. 1994f. *Telematics Applications Programme, 1994–1998, European Commission.* DGXIII–C. Luxembourg: CEC.

CEC. 1995a. *Small and Medium-Sized Enterprises: A Dynamic Source of Employment, Growth, and Competitiveness in the European Union.* Report presented by the EC for the Madrid European Council. Brussels: European Council.

CEC. 1995b. *Strategy on Public Health CEC/V/F/1/04/95.* Luxembourg: CEC.

CEC. 1995c. *Directive 95/46/EC of the European Parliament and the Council of 24 October 1995 on the Protection of Individuals with Regard to the Processing of Personal Data and on the Free Movement of Such Data.* Luxembourg: CEC. Available at: www2.echo.lu/legal/en/dataprot/directiv /directiv.html.

CEC. 1996a. *First Report on Economic and Social Cohesion.* COM 96 542 Final. Luxembourg: CEC.

CEC. 1996b. *Enterprises in Europe.* Fourth Report. Luxembourg: CEC.

CEC. 1996c. *Equal Opportunities for Women and Men in the European Union, 1996.* Annual Report. Luxembourg: CEC.

CEC. 1996d. *Living and Working in the Information Society: People First.* Green Paper. Brussels: CEC.

CEC. 1996e. *Employment in Europe, 1996.* Luxembourg: CEC.

CEC. 1996f. *Trends in Health Telematics in the European Union.* Edited by D. Preston. Version 1.5. Telematics Programme Committee, EC Fourth Framework Programme. Luxembourg: CEC.

CEC. 1996g. *Report from the Commission to the Council, the European Parliament, the Economic and Social Committee, and the Committee of the Regions on the State of Health in the European Community.* Luxembourg: CEC.

CEC. 1997. *Panorama of Industry.* DGIII. Luxembourg: CEC.

Chambat, P. 1990. "Service Public et Néolibéralisme." *Annales* 3 (May–June).

Chapignac, P. 1995. "Préfigurations de la Presse Électronique: Les Leçons de la Télématique." Paris: La Documentation Française.

Chesbrough, H., and D. Teece. 1996. "When Is Virtual Virtuous?" *Harvard Business Review*, January–February, pp. 65–73.

Christoffersen, M. 1994. "User Needs and Telecommunication Service Provision in Denmark." Paper presented at the International Working Conference on Home-Orientated Informatics, Telematics, and Automation, Copenhagen, 27 June–1 July.

Christopher, M., and A. Braithwaite. 1994. "Managing the Global Pipeline." In *The Challenge of International Business.* Edited by S. Segal-Horn. London: Kogan Page.

CIOMS. 1997. Council for International Organizations of Medical Sciences: International Conference on Ethics, Equity, and the Renewal of WHO's Health–for–All Strategy, Geneva, Switzerland, 12–14 March 1997.

Claret, H., R. Laperriere, and P. Peladeau. 1988. "Une Démocratie Technologique?" Québec, ACFAS/GRID. *Les Cahiers Scientifiques* 63.

Clematide, B., and C. Ager–Hansen. 1996. "Et feolles begreb om kvalifikationer?" Mimeo. Dansk kvalifikationer, Dansk Teknologisk Institut, Center for Arbejsdliv.

Clower, D. M., J. M. Hoffman, and J. R. Votaw. 1996. "Role of Posterior Parietal Cortex in the Recalibration of Visually Guided Reaching." *Nature* 383: 618–621.

Club de Bruxelles. 1995. "The Future of Telematics Services for SMEs." Background paper prepared for the Future of Telematics Services for SMEs, Brussels, April 25.

CNIL. 1993–1994. *13e et 14e rapport, Commission Nationale De L'Informatique et des Libertes.* Paris: La Documentation Française.

Cockburn, C. 1992. "The Circuit of Technology: Gender, Identity, and Power." In *Consuming Technologies: Media and Information in Domestic Spaces.* Edited by R. Silverstone and E. Hirsch. London: Routledge.

Cohen, E. 1992. *Le Colbertisme High Tech.* Paris: Hachette.

Cole, U., et al. 1997. "Delivering a Distance Education Course Using Technology: The Needs of the User." CAL 1997 Conference, Exeter, U.K., April.

Collis, B. 1996. *Tele–Learning in a Digital World: The Future of Distance Learning.* London: Thomson Computer Press.

Commissariat Général du Plan. 1992. *Comité interministériel de l'evaluation des politiques publiques, l'informatique de l'état.* Paris: La Documentation Française.

"La communication par câble." 1974. Editorial. *Communications* (Paris) 21.

Connor, H. 1995. "Graduates: Shortage or Glut?" In *Future Skill Demand and Supply: Trends, Shortages, and Gluts,* edited by H. Metcalf, pp. 33–44. London: PSI.

Consultation on Health in the Information Society. 1996. Minutes of the meeting of the Consultation on Health in the Information Society Related to the Work of the High–Level Expert Group HLEG on the Social and Societal Aspects of the Information Society, Luxembourg, 4 September 1996.

Conte, M. 1988. *Téléalarme aujourd'hui télécontact demain.* Paris: CTNERHI.

Cooke, P., and K. Morgan. 1993. "The Network Paradigm: New Departures in Corporate and Regional Development." *Environment and Planning D* 11: 543–564.

Coombs, N. 1993. "Global Empowerment of Impaired Learners: Data Networks will Transcend Both Physical and Distance and Physical Disabilities." *Educational Media International* 301: 23–25.

Coriat, B., and R. Bianchi. 1995. "Swatch: A European Response to the Japanese Challenge." In *Europe's Next Step: Organizational Innovation, Competition, and Employment,* edited by L. Andreasen et al., pp. 59–78. London, U.K.: Frank Cass.

Cornford, J., S. Ó Siochrú, and A. Gillespie. 1996. *Regulation and the Supply Side.* Vol. 4 of *An Assessment of the Social and Economic Cohesion Aspects of the Development of an Information Society in Europe, Report to DGXIII and DGXVI of the Commission of the European Communities.* Brussels: CEC.

Cornish, S. 1995. *Product Innovation and the Spatial Dynamics of Market Intelligence: Does Proximity to Markets Matter?* Department of Geography Working Papers. New York: University of Buffalo Press.

Council for Economic Advisers. 1996. *Job Creation and Employment Opportunities: The United States Labor Market, 1993–1996.* Report by the Council of Economic Advisers with the U.S. Department of Labor. Washington, D.C.: Office of the Chief Economist.

Cowan, R. 1989. *More Work for Mother.* 2d ed. London: Free Association.

Cox, T., and E. Ferguson. 1994. "Measurement of the Subjective Work Environment." *Work and Stress* 8: 98–109.

Cronberg, T. 1997. "Reshaping the Danish Information Society: 1984 and 1994." In *The Social Shaping of Information Superhighways: European and American Roads to the Information Society,* edited by H. Kubicek, W. Dutton, and R. Williams, pp. 117–131. Frankfurt: Campus Verlag; New York: St. Martin's.

Cronin, F. J., et al. 1991. "Telecommunications Infrastructure and Economic Growth: An Analysis of Causality." *Telecommunications Policy* 156: 529–535.

Cronin, F. J., et al. 1993. "Telecommunications Infrastructure Investment and Economic Development." *Telecommunications Policy* 176: 415–430.

Crook, C. 1994. *Computers and the Collaborative Experience of Learning.* London: Routledge.

Crow, D. 1996. *Virtual Reality and Cybersickness.* Available at: www.csclub.uwaterloo.ca/u/dccrow/KIN_416.html#Vestibular.

Cuban, L. 1986. *Teachers and Machines: The Classroom Use of Technology since 1920.* New York: Teachers' College Press.

Cullen, K., and R. Moran. 1991. *Technology and the Elderly: The Role of Technology in Prolonging the Independence of the Elderly in the Community Care Context.* Work Research Centre and Ekos, FAST report FOP 295, Dublin.

Cumberbatch, G., and D. Howitt. 1989. *A Measure of Uncertainty: The Effects of the Mass Media.* London: John Libbey.

Curran, J., and R. Blackburn. 1994. *Small Firms and Local Economic Networks: The Death of the Local Economy?* London: Paul Chapman.

Curran, J., R. Blackburn, and M. Klett. 1994. *Small Firms in Services: The 1994 Survey.* Kingston University, Small Business Research Centre.

Dabinett, G., and S. Graham. 1994. "Telematics and Industrial Change in Sheffield." *Regional Studies* 286: 605–617.

Dahlgren, P., and C. Sparks, eds. 1993. *Communication and Citizenship.* London: Routledge.

Damper, R., M. Tranchant, and S. Lewis. 1996. "Speech versus Keying in Command and Control: Effect of Concurrent Tasking." *International Journal of Human–Computer Studies* 45: 337–348.

Dard, P., et al. 1991. *Minitel et gestion de l'habitat: La domotique en question.* Paris: CSTB.

Dard, P., et al. 1995. *Réseaux de communication et services résidentiels.* Paris: CSTB.

David, P. 1990. "The Dynamo and the Computer: An Historical Perspective on the Modern Productivity Paradox." *AEA Papers and Proceedings* 80, no. 2: 355–361.

Davidoff, F., et al. 1995. "*Evidence–Based Medicine*: A New Journal to Help Doctors Identify the Information They Need." *British Medical Journal* 310: 1085–1086.

Davidson, T. 1996. "Distance Learning and Information Technology: Problems and Solutions in Balancing Caring, Access, and Success for Students." *Distance Education* 16, no. 1.

Davies, D. 1994. "ELNET—The European Learning NetWork." In *Telematics in Education: The European Case,* edited by W. Veen et al., pp. 249–259. De Lier, Netherlands: Academic Book Centre.

Deleuze, G. 1990. *Pourparlers.* Paris: Editions de Minuit.

Delmas, R., and F. Massit–Follea, eds. 1995. *Vers la société de l'information.* Paris: Editions Apogée.

Denbigh, A. 1994. "UK Telecottages." *Managing Information,* April, pp. 34–37.

Den Brinker, B., and P. Beek. 1996. "Reading with Magnifiers." *Ergonomics* 39: 1231–1248.

Den Hertog, J., and P. Schröder. 1989. "Social Research for Technological Change: Lessons from National Programmes in Europe and North America." MERIT 89-028, University of Limburg, Maastricht.

Dertouzos, M., and J. Moses. 1983. *The Computer Age: A Twenty-Year View.* Cambridge: MIT Press.

Dertouzos, M., R. Lester, and R. Solow. 1989. *Made in America.* Cambridge: MIT Press.

Dillon, A. 1994. *Designing Usable Electronic Text: Ergonomic Aspects of Human Information Usage.* London: Taylor & Francis.

DIV, OECD, and URBA 2000. 1992. *Villes et technologies nouvelles.* Paris: OECD.

"Dix ans de vidéotex." 1989. *Réseaux* 37 (November).

Dodds, T. [1985] 1991. "The Development of Distance Teaching: An Historical Perspective." In *Distance Education: A Review,* edited by J. Jenkins and B. Koul, pp. 6–12. Delhi: Indira Gandhi National Open University/National Extension College.

Donk, W., I. Van De Snellen, and P. Tops. 1995. *Orwell in Athens: A Perspective on Informatization and Democracy.* Amsterdam: IOS Press.

Dordick, H., and R. LaRose. 1992. *The Telephone in Daily Life: A Study of Personal Telephone Use.* Philadelphia: Temple University Press.

Dostal, W. 1995. "Die Informatisierung der Arbeitswelt—Multimedia, offene Arbeitsformen, und Telearbeit." *Mitteilungen aus der Arbeitsmarkt- und Berufsforschung* 28, no. 4: 527–543.

Douglas, M., and B. Isherwood. 1980. *The World of Goods: Towards an Anthropology of Consumption.* Harmondsworth, U.K.: Penguin.

Douglas, S. 1986. "Amateur Operators and American Broadcasting: Shaping the Future of Radio." In *Imagining Tomorrow: History, Technology, and the American Future of Radio.* Edited by J. Corn. Cambridge: MIT Press.

DRI Europe. 1997. *Europe in 2001: Economic Analysis and Forecasts.* Final Report for European Commission. Brussels: DRI Europe.

DTI [Department of Trade and Industry]. 1994. *Study of the International Competitiveness of the UK Telecommunications Infrastructure.* Report for the Department of Trade and Industry prepared by Robert Harrison, PA Consulting Group. London: DTI.

DTI. 1995. *Fixed Radio Access: Increasing the Choice: A Consultative Document from the Department of Trade and Industry.* London: DTI.

DTI. 1996. *The Information Society Initiative.* London: DTI.

Ducatel, K. 1996. "Introduction: Work Organisation and Successful Organisation." *Futures* 28, no. 2: 99–101.

Ducatel, K., et al. 1999. *Information and Communication Technologies and the Information Society Panel Report.* Futures Project Report 03, EUR 18730EN, IPTS–JRC, Sevilla.

Ducatel, K., ed. 1994. *Employment and Technical Change in Europe: Work Organisation, Skills, and Training.* Aldershot, U.K.: Edward Elgar.

Dul, J., P. deVlaming, and M. Munnik. 1996. "A Review of ISO and CEN Standards on Ergonomics." *International Journal of Industrial Ergonomics* 17: 291–297.

Dunning, J. 1993. *The Globalization of Business: The Challenge of the 1990s.* London: Routledge.

Durlacher Research. 1995. *A Survey of the Video and Computer Games Industry.* London: Durlacher Research.

Dutton, W. 1995. "Driving into the Future of Communications: Check the Rear View Mirror." In *Information Superhighways: Multimedia Users and Futures.* Edited by S. Emmott. London: Academic Press.

Dwyer, D. 1995. "Learning from the Twenty-first Century: Lessons from Apple Classrooms of Tomorrow." In *Proceedings of ICCE '95.* Edited by D. Jonassen and G. McCalla. Charlottesville, Va.: AACE.

Eason, K. 1996. "Implementation of Information Technology in Working Life." In *Work in the Information Society,* edited by J. Rantanen, S. Lehtinen, and P. Huuhtanen, pp. 71–78. People and Work Research Reports, no. 8. Helsinki: Finnish Institute of Occupational Health.

EFER [European Federation for Entrepreneurship Research]. 1995. *Europe's 500: Dynamic Entrepreneurs, the Job Creators.* Ghent, Belgium: EFER.

Eisenstein, E. 1991. *La révolution de l'imprimé à l'aube de l'Europe des premiers temps modernes.* Paris: La Découverte.

EITO. 1995. *European Information Technology Observatory 1995,* Frankfurt.

EITO. 1998. *European Information Technology Observatory 1998,* Frankfurt.

Ekberg, J. 1996. "Social and Health Services in the Information Society." In *Work in the Information Society,* edited by J. Rantanen, S. Lehtinen, and P. Huuhtanen, pp. 79–83. People and Work Research Reports, no. 8. Helsinki: Finnish Institute of Occupational Health.

Elliot, P., et al. 1996. *Geographical and Environmental Epidemiology: Methods for Small–Area Studies.* Oxford: Oxford University Press.

Elson, D. 1989. "The Cutting Edge: Multinationals in the EEC Textiles and Clothing Industry." In *Women's Employment and Multinationals in Europe.* Edited by D. Elson and R. Pearson. London: Macmillan.

ENSR [European Network for SME Research]. 1995. *Third Annual Report.* European Observatory for SMEs. Zoetermeer, Netherlands: EIM.

ENSR. 1996. *Fourth Annual Report.* European Observatory for SMEs. Zoetermeer, Netherlands: EIM.

EPOC Research Group. 1997. *New Forms of Work Organisation: Can Europe Realise Its Potential?* Dublin: European Foundation for the Improvement of Living and Working Conditions.

Epstein, J. 1990. *Public Services: Working for the Consumer.* Luxembourg: Office for Official Publications of the European Communities.

Ernst and Young. 1996. *Business–Related Services and Local and Regional Development.* Report to the European Commission. Brussels: European Commission.

European Real Estate Monitor. 1992. London: Healey & Baker.

European Round Table. 1995. *Education for Europeans: Towards the Learning Society.* Brussels: European Round Table of Industrialists.

Eurotecnet. 1995. *Key/Core Competencies: Synthesis of Related Work Undertaken within the Eurotecnet Programme, 1990–94.* Luxembourg: European Commission.

Evans, T., and D. Nation, eds. 1989. *Critical Reflection on Distance Education.* Lewes, U.K.: Falmer.

Ewbank Preece. 1993. *STAR: Special Telecommunications Action for Regional Development: Community–Level Evaluation.* Executive Summary. Brighton: Ewbank Preece.

Falzon, P. 1990. "Human–Computer Interaction: Lessons from Human–Human Communication." In *Cognitive Ergonomics: Understanding, Learning, and Designing,* edited by P. Falzon, pp. 51–60. Computers and People Series. London: European Association of Cognitive Ergonomics/Academic Press.

Fay, R. 1996. *Enhancing the Effectiveness of Active Labour Market Policies: The Role of— and Evidence from—Programme Evaluations in OECD Countries.* Labour Market and Social Policy Occasional Papers, no. 18. Paris: OECD.

Featherstone, M. 1991. *Consumer Culture and Postmodernism.* London: Sage.

FEFC [Further Education Funding Council]. 1995. *The Higginson Report.* London: FEFC.

Fernström, E., and M. Ericson. 1996. "Upper–Arm Elevation during Office Work." *Ergonomics* 39: 1221–1230.

Financial Times. 1996. Editorial. 6 February, p. 10.

Financial Times. 1996. Editorial. 18 March, p. 9.

Finley, M. 1976. *Démocratie antique et démocratie moderne.* Paris: Payot.

Finley, M. 1985. *L'invention de la politique.* Paris: Flammarion.

Finnish Institute of Occupational Health. 1995. *Hyvä "direktiivin" mukainen näyttöpäätetyöpaikka* (Good visual display unit workplace according to the EC directive). Helsinki: Finnish Institute of Occupational Health.

Firpo, K. 1994. Online Commuting Big Benefits for Business And Employees." *PC World,* 12 May, p. 32.

Fischer, U., G. Späker, and H.-J. Weissbach. 1994. *Neuere Entwicklungen bei der sozialen Gestaltung von Telearbeit.* Dortmund.

Fishkin, J. 1991. *Democracy and Deliberation.* New Haven: Yale University Press.

Fiske, J. 1987. *Television Culture.* London: Methuen.

Flichy, P. 1991. *Une histoire des télécommunications modernes.* Paris: La Découverte.

Flichy, P. 1995. *L'innovation technique.* Paris: La Découverte.

Florida, R. 1995. "Towards the Learning Region." *Futures* 275: 505–526.

Forester, T., ed. 1980. *The Micro–Electronics Revolution.* Oxford: Basil Blackwell.

Forty, A. 1986. *Objects of Desire: Design and Society, 1750–1980.* London: Thames & Hudson.

Frances, J., and E. Garnsey. 1995. "Re–Engineering the Food Chains: A Systems Perspective on UK Supermarkets and BPR." Paper presented to the Workshop on Critical Studies of Organisations and Management Innovations, Brussels, May.

Frankenhaeuser, M. 1994. "Psychosocial Factors and Occupational Health." In *New Epidemics in Occupational Health,* edited by J. Rantanen, S. Lehtinen, and R. Kalimo, pp. 64–71. People and Work Research Reports, no. 1. Helsinki: Finnish Institute of Occupational Health.

Franklin, B. 1992. *Televising Democracy.* New York: Basic.

Fraser, R., et al. 1990. "Learning Activities and Classroom Roles with and without the Microcomputer." In *Computers and Learning.* Edited by B. Boyd–Barrett and S. Scanlon. Reading, Mass.: Addison–Wesley.

Freeman, C., and L. Soete. 1994. *Work for All or Mass Unemployment: Computerised Technical Change into the Twenty-first Century.* London: Pinter.

Freeman, C., and H. Mendras, eds. 1995. *Le paradigme informatique.* Paris: Descartes & Cie.

Freeman, R., S. Robertson, and M. Thorne. 1995. "First Steps towards the Virtual University." In *One World, Many Voices.* Edited by D. Sewart. Selected Papers from the Seventeenth World Conference of the International Council for Distance Education. Oslo: ICDE.

Frenkel, S., et al. 1998. *Beyond Bureaucracy? Work Organisation in Call Centres.* New South Wales: Centre for Corporate Change.

Frezis, H., D. Herz, and M. Harrigan. 1995. "Employer–Provided Training: Results from a New Survey." *Monthly Labor Review,* May, pp. 3–17.

Friis, C. 1997. "A Critical Evaluation of the Danish National ICT Strategy." *Economic and Social Review* 28, July, pp. 260–276.

Frith, Simon. 1983. "The Pleasures of the Hearth." In *Formations of Pleasure,* pp. 101–103. London: Routledge & Kegan Paul.

Fundesco. 1994. *Las tecnologias de la informacion y su impacto en la Pequena y Mediana Empresa.* Madrid: Fundesco.

Galton, M. 1989. *Teaching in the Primary School.* London: David Fulton.

Gandy, O. 1993. *The Panoptic Sort.* Boulder: Westview.

Gann, D., and S. Iwashita. 1995. *Housing and Home Automation for the Elderly and Disabled.* Brighton, U.K.: University of Sussex, Science Policy Research Unit.

Garito, M. A. 1995. "The Role of Television in Teaching and Learning Processes." In *Multimedia and Distance Learning for Science and Technology,* pp. 239–272. Rome: Garamon.

Garnham, N. 1997. "Europe and the Global Information Society: The History of a Troubled Relationship." *Telematics and Informatics* 144: 323–327.

Gastkemper, F., K. Schlusmans, and A. Speelman. 1995. "A Revised Model for Tutoring and the Growing Use Of Telematics." In *One World, Many Voices.* Edited by D. Sewart. Selected Papers from the Seventeenth World Conference of the International Council for Distance Education. Oslo: ICDE.

Gawith, P. 1995. "Moving with the Currencies." *Financial Times,* 6 October, p. 11.

Gerbner, G., et al. 1986. "Living with Television: The Dynamics of the Culturation Process." In *Perspectives on Media Effects.* Edited by J. Bryant and D. Zillman. Hillside, N.J.: Lawrence Erlbaum.

Gerstle, J. 1993. *La communication politique.* Paris: PUF.

Ghaffari, E. 1995. "Trends in American Small Business." Personal communication with authors, 15 November.

Gibbs, D., and B. Leach. 1994. "Telematics in Local Economic Development: The Case of Manchester." *Tijdschrift voor economische en sociale geografie* 853: 209–223.

Giddens, A. 1994. *Les conséquences de la modernité.* Paris: L'Harmattan.

Gilder, G. 1990. *Life after Television.* New York: Norton.

Gillespie, A., and J. Cornford. 1995. "Network Diversity or Network Fragmentation? The Evolution of European Telecommunications in Competitive Environments." In *European Transport and Communications Networks,* edited by D. Banister, R. Capello, and P. Nijkamp, pp. 319–332. Chichester: John Wiley.

Gillespie, A., and K. Robins. 1989. "Geographical Inequalities: The Spatial Bias of the New Communications Technologies." *Journal of Communications* 393: 7–18.

Gillespie, A., M. Coombes, and S. Raybould. 1994. "Contribution of Telecommunications to Rural Economic Development: Variations on a Theme?" *Entrepreneurship and Regional Development* 6: 201–217.

Gillespie, A., R. Richardson, and J. Cornford. 1995a. *Review of Telework in Britain: Implications for Public Policy.* Report for the Parliamentary Office of Science and Technology and the Economic and Social Research Council, CURDS. Newcastle: University of Newcastle Press.

Gillespie, A., R. Richardson, and J. Cornford. 1995b. "Information Infrastructures and Territorial Development." Background paper prepared for the OECD Workshop on Information Infrastructures and Territorial Development, Paris, 7–8 November.

Gillespie, A., et al. 1984. *The Effects of New Information Technology on the Less–Favoured Regions of the Community.* Studies Collection, Regional Policy Series, no. 23. Brussels: CEC.

Gillespie, M. 1995. *Television, Ethnicity, and Cultural Change.* London: Routledge.

Gingras, A.–M. 1996. "Internet et démocratie: Quels usages pour quelle politique?" Communication to the Congrés de la Sociéte Française des Science de la Communication, Grenoble, 15 Novembre.

Gjerdling, A. 1996. *Organisational Innovation in the Danish Private Business.* DRUID Working Paper 96–16. Aalborg, Denmark: Aalborg University, Faculty of Business.

"Global Communications for Health." 1996. *SatelLife News* 13 (Fall).

Goddard, J. 1991. "New Technology and the Geography of the UK Information Economy." In *Cities of the Twenty-first Century: New Technologies and Spatial Systems,* edited by J. Brotchie et al., pp. 191–213. Melbourne: Longman Cheshire.

Goedhard, W., ed. 1992. *Aging and Work.* OCOH Scientific Committee "Aging and Work." Den Haag: CIP-Gegevens Koninkluke Bibliotheek.

Gore, A. 1996. "Basic Principles for Building an Information Society." *International Information Communication and Education* 15, no. 2: 226–228.

Gott, M. 1995. *Telematics for Health: The Role of Telehealth and Telemedicine in Homes and Communities.* Dublin: European Foundation for the Improvement of Living and Working Conditions.

Gras, A., and S. Poirot–Delpech. 1989. *L'imaginaire des techniques de pointe: Au doigt et à l'oeil.* Paris: L'Harmattan.

Gray, A. 1992. *Video Playtime: The Gendering of a Leisure Technology.* London: Routledge.

Greenman, B., and K. Miller. 1996. *Net Vote.* New York: Wolff.

Grossman, L. 1995. *The Electronic Republic: Reshaping Democracy in the Information Age.* Middlesex, U.K.: Viking Penguin.

Gupta, S., C. Wantland, and S. Klein. 1996. *Cyberpathology: Medical Concerns of VR Applications.* Available at: www.webmed.com/mi/cyberpath.html.

Haddon, L. 1988. "The Home Computer: The Making of a Consumer Electronic." *Science as Culture* 2: 7–51.

Haddon, L. 1990. "Researching Gender and Home Computers." In *Technology and Everyday Life: Trajectories and Transformations.* Edited by K. Sorensen and A. Berg. Trondheim: University of Trondheim.

Haddon, L. 1991. *Disability and Telework.* Martlesham, U.K.: British Telecom Laboratories.

Haddon, L. 1993. "Interactive Games." In *Future Visions: New Technologies on the Screen.* Edited by P. Hayward and T. Wollen. London: British Film Institute Publishing.

Haddon, L. 1995a. "The Home of the Future Today: The Social Origins of the Intelligent Home." In *Soziale und oekonomische Konflikte in Standardisierungsprozessen.* Edited by J. Esser, G. Fleischmann, and T. Heimer. Frankfurt/Main: Campus.

Haddon, L. 1995b. "Home Automation: Research Issues." Paper presented at the second EMTEL Workshop, Amsterdam, 10–11 November.

Haddon, L. 1995c. "Information and Communication Technologies: A View from the Home." Paper for the PICT International Conference on the Social and Economic Implications of Information and Communications Technologies, Westminster, London, 10–12 May.

Haddon, L., and R. Silverstone. 1993. *Teleworking in the 1990s: A View from the Home.* SPRU/CICT Report Series, no. 10. Brighton, U.K.: University of Sussex.

Haddon, L., and R. Silverstone. 1995. *Lone Parents and Their Information and Communication Technologies.* SPRU/CICT Report Series, no. 12. Brighton, U.K.: University of Sussex.

Haddon, L., and R. Silverstone. 1996a. *The Young Elderly and Their Information and Communication Technologies.* SPRU/CICT Report Series, no. 13. Brighton, U.K.: University of Sussex.

Haddon, L., and R. Silverstone. 1996b. "Television, Cable, and AB Households." Report for Telewest PLC, Graduate Research Centre in Culture and Communication, University of Sussex.

Haddon, L., and D. Skinner. 1991. "The Enigma of the Micro: Lessons from the British Home Computer Boom." *Social Science Computer Review* 9, no. 3.

Hahn, H., et al. 1995. *Arbeitssystem Bildschirmarbeit.* Schriftenreihe der Bundesanstalt für Arbeitsschutz, Forschunganwendung, no. 31. Dortmund: Bundesanstalt für Arbeitsschutz.

Hall, C. 1995. "The Entrepreneurial Engine." OECD Industry Committee Working Party on Small and Medium–sized Enterprises High Level Workshop on SMEs: Employment, Innovation, and Growth, Washington D.C., 16–17 June.

Hammer, M., and J. Champy. 1993. *Reengineering the Corporation.* New York: Harper Business.

Hamon, F. 1995. *Le référendum.* Paris: LGDJ.

Hansen, S., et al. 1990. "Telecommunications in Rural Europe: Economic Implications." *Telecommunications Policy* 14: 207–222.

Hansens, M. 1991. *The Athenian Democracy in the Age of Demosthenes.* Oxford: Oxford University Press.

Haraway, D. 1991. *Simians, Cyborgs, and Women: The Reinvention of Nature.* London: Free Association Books.

Hardy, A. 1980. "The Role of the Telephone in Economic Development." *Telecommunications Policy* 44: 278–286.

Harker, S. 1995. "The Development of Ergonomics Standards for Software." *Applied Ergonomics* 264: 275–279.

Härmä, M. 1995. "Sleepiness and Shift Work: Individual Differences." *European Sleep Research* 42: 57–61.

Harris, D. 1987. *Openness and Closure in Distance Education.* London: Falmer.

Harrison, B. 1994. *Lean and Mean: The Changing Landscape of Corporate Power in the Age of Flexibility.* New York: Basic.

Hart, H. 1995. "Promotion of Improvements in Work Organisation and Working Conditions." Discussion paper, National Institute for Working Life, Stockholm, September.

Häussermann, H., and W. Petrowsky. 1989. "Die Bedeutung des Telefons für Arbeitslose." In *Telefon und Gesellschaft,* edited by U. Lange, 1:116–134. Berlin: Volker Spiess.

Healey and Baker. 1992. *European Real Estate Monitor.* London: Healey and Baker.

Heim, W. 1994. "Outsourcing: Wettbewerbsfaehiger durch optimale Nutzung der Potentiale von Zulieferern." *IO Management* 63, no. 7–8: 28–33.

Henley Centre. 1996. "The Future of Work in London." Report prepared for the London Training and Enterprise Council, London.

Hepworth, M. 1989. *Geography of the Information Economy.* London: Belhaven.

Hepworth, M. 1994a. "The Information Economy in a Spatial Context: City States in a Global Village." In *Information and Communication in Economics.* Edited by R. Babe. Norwell, Mass.: Kluwer.

Hepworth, M. 1994b. *Small Firms in Croydon: Trends and Policy.* London Borough of Croydon, U.K.

Hepworth, M., and K. Ducatel. 1992. *Transport in the Information Age: Wheels and Wires.* London; Belhaven/John Wiley.

Hepworth, M., and K. Robins. 1988. "Whose Information Society? A View from the Periphery." *Media, Culture, and Society* 10: 323–343.

Herring, S. 1993. "Gender and Democracy in Computer–Mediated Communication." *EJC/REC* 13, no. 2.

Hills, J. 1989. "Universal Service: Liberalization and Privatisation of Telecommunications." *Telecommunications Policy* 13: 129–144.

Hills, J. 1993. "Universal Service: A Social and Technological Construct." *Communications and Strategies* 10: 61–86.

Himmelstrup, K., and C. Stjern. 1972. *Livslang Laering og Uddannelse.* Copenhagen: Gyldenal.

HLEG [High Level Expert Group]. 1996. *Building the European Information Society for Us All: First Reflections Report of the High Level Expert Group on the Social Aspects of the Information Society.* Brussels: Commission of the European Communities.

HLEG. 1997. *Building the European Information Society for Us All: Final Policy Report of the High Level Expert Group on the Social Aspects of the Information Society.* Luxembourg: CEC.

HMSO. 1995. *Living in Britain: Preliminary Results of the 1994 General Household Survey.* London: HMSO.

Hochschild, A. 1983. *The Managed Heart: Commercialization of Human Feeling.* Berkeley: University of California Press.

Hollander, E., and J. Stappers. 1992. "Community Media and Community Communication." In *The People's Voice: Local Radio and Television in Europe.* Edited by N. Jankowski, O. Prehn, and J. Stappers. London: John Libbey.

Horgen, G., et al. 1995. "Is There a Reduction in Postural Load When Wearing Progressive Lenses During VDT Work over a Three–Month Period?" *Applied Ergonomics* 26: 165–171.

Howell, D. 1996. "Information Technology, Skill Mismatch, and the Wage Collapse: A Perspective on the U.S. Experience." In *OECD Employment and Growth in the Knowledge–Based Economy,* pp. 291–305. Paris: OECD.

Howell, D., and E. Wolff. 1992. "Technical Change and the Demand for Skills by U.S. Industries." *Cambridge Journal of Economics* 162: 127–146.

Hudson, H. 1995. "Universal Service in an Information Age." *Telecommunications Policy* 188: 658–667.

Huff, C., and J. Cooper. 1987. "Sex Bias in Educational Software: The Effect of Designers' Stereotypes on the Software They Design." *Journal of Applied Social Psychology* 76: 519–532.

Hukki, K., and P. Seppälä. 1993. "Tietotekniikka, työtehtävät ja ikä: Kyselytutkimus tietotekniikan käyttöönotosta" (Computerization, tasks and age: A questionnaire survey on the implementation of ICT). In *Ikääntyvä arvoonsa—työterveyden, työkyvyn ja hyvinvoinnin edistämisohjelman, julkaisuja 15.* Helsinki: Finnish Institute of Occupational Health and Finnish Work Environment Fund. In Finnish.

Hurley, J. 1992. "Towards an Organisational Psychology Model for the Acceptance and Utilisation of New Technology in Organisations." *Irish Journal of Psychology* 13, no. 1: 17–31.

Husen, T. 1974. *The Learning Society.* London: Methuen.

Husen, T. 1986. *The Learning Society Revisited.* London: Pergamon.

Huuhtanen, P. 1985. "Tietotekniikan käyttöönoton psyykkiset ja sosiaaliset ehdot ja vaikutukset" (Social prerequisites and effects of implementation of information technology). *Työterveyslaitoksen tutkimuksia lisänumero* 1: 1–242.

Huuhtanen, P. 1996. "Psychosocial Perspective to Telework: Challenges and Risks." In *Work in the Information Society,* edited by J. Tantanen, S. Lehtinen, and P. Huuhtanen, pp. 160–164. People and Work Research Reports, no. 8. Helsinki: Finnish Institute of Occupational Health.

Huuhtanen, P., et al. 1995. "Töiden koetut muutokset ikääntyvillä työntekijöillä" (Experienced changes in job contents by aging workers). *Työ ja ihminen.* Tutkimusraportti 2, pp. 20–38. Helsinki: Työterveyslaitos. In Finnish.

Huws, U. 1984. *The New Homeworkers: New Technology and the Changing Location of White Collar Work.* London: Low Pay Unit.

Huws, U. 1993. *Teleworking in Britain: A Report to the Employment Department.* Research Series, no. 18. Sheffield, U.K.: Employment Department.

Huws, U. 1994. "Teleworking: Follow-up to the White Paper." Social Europe, 3/95. Luxembourg: Commission of the European Communities.

Huws, U., S. Podro, and K. Arvanitaki. 1996. *Teleworking and Gender.* Analytical Social and Economic Research. Report to the Equal Opportunities Unit of DGV. Brussels: CEC.

Hyvä työkyky. 1995. Työkyvyn ylläpidon malleja ja keinoja (Good work ability: Models for the maintenance of the work ability). Työterveyslaitos ja Eläkevakuutusosakeyhtiö Ilmarinen.

Igarashi, H., J. Noritake, and N. Furuta. *Is the Virtual Reality a Gentle Technology for Humans?—An Experimental Study of the Safety Features of a Virtual Reality System.* http://fh.u–tokai.ac.jp/~takami/Publica...s/VR/IEICE T: E77–D: 1379–1384.

IITF [Information Infrastructure Taskforce]. 1993. *National Information Infrastructure: Agenda for Action.* Washington, D.C.: IITF/National Telecommunications and Information Administration.

Ilbery, B., et al. 1995. "Telematics and Rural Development: Evidence from a Survey of Small Business in the European Union." *European Urban and Regional Studies* 21: 55–68.

Ilmarinen, J., et al. 1996. "Habitual Physical Activity, Psychomotor Performance and Older Workers." *Nutrition Reviews* 54: S44–S52.

IMO [Informational Market Observatory]. 1995. *The Main Events and Developments in the Information Market, 1993–1994.* Information Market Observatory report from the EC to the Council, the European Parliament, and the Economic and Social Committee. Luxembourg: CEC.

Industry Canada. 1995. *The Information Highway: Avenues for Expanding Canada's Economy, Employment, and Productivity in the New World Marketplace.* Report by the Information Technology Branch, Ottawa.

Innovation and Employment. 1992. "Business Incubators and Job Creation." *CEC/ OECD Newsletter* 9, April.

Innovation and Employment. 1993. "From Global to Local: A New Perspective on Adjustment and Reform." *CEC/OECD Newsletter* 12, August.

Innovation and Employment. 1995. "The Environment and Job Creation at the Local Level." *CEC/OECD Newsletter* 18, June.

Interconnect Communications. 1994. *Digital Corporate Networks, Interconnect Communications.* Gwent, Wales: Interconnect Communications.

International Labor Organization. 1991. *Conditions of Work Digest on Workers Privacy, Parts 1–2.* Geneva: International Labor Office.

International Labor Organization. 1993. *Conditions of Work Digest on Workers Privacy, Part 3.* Geneva: International Labor Office.

INTUG News. 1996. Editorial, *INTUG News*, April, p. 3.

Ireland, J. 1994. *The Importance of Telecommunications to London as an International Financial Centre.* Subject Report 18. The City Research Project. London: London Business School/Corporation of London.

Iskandar, H., and A. Romiszowski. 1995. "Alternative Technologies for Tutorial Support to Distance Learners: The Case of the Indonesian Open University." In *One World,*

Many Voices. Edited by D. Sewart. Selected Papers from the Seventeenth World Conference of the International Council for Distance Education. Oslo: ICDE.

ISSC [Information Society Steering Committee]. 1997. *Information Society Ireland: A Strategy for Action.* Dublin: Information Society Steering Committee/Forfas.

ITAP [Information Technology Advisory Panel]. 1983. *Making a Business of Information.* London: Information Technology Advisory Panel/HMSO.

ITC [Independent Television Commission]. 1997. "ITC Publishes Television: The Public's View 1996." News release, 3/97. London: Independent Television Commission.

Ito, Y. 1980. "The 'Johoka Shakai' Approach to the Study of Communication in Japan." *Keio Communication Review* 1: 13–40.

Jacobson, S. 1994. "The Effectiveness of the U.S. Employment Service." Draft Report for the Advisory Commission on Unemployment Insurance, Westat, Inc.

Jaffrin, S. 1994. *La tribu des cibistes.* Paris: Editions du Téléphone.

Joerges, B. 1988. *Technik im Alltag.* Frankfurt/Main: Suhrkampf.

Joerges, B., and I. Braun, eds. 1994. *Technik ohne Grenzen.* Frankfurt am Main: Suhrkampf.

Johnson, J., J. Baldwin, and B. Diverty. 1996. "The Implications of Innovation for Human Resource Strategies." *Futures* 28, no. 2: 103–120.

Johnson, L. 1982–1983. *Images of Radio: The Construction of the Radio by Popular Radio Magazines.* Melbourne Working Paper no. 4. Melbourne: University of Melbourne, Department of Education.

Jonassen, D. 1991. "Hypertext as Instructional Design." *Educational Technology Research and Development* 39, no. 1: 83–92.

Jones, A., G. Kirkup, and A. Kirkwood. 1993. *Personal Computers for Distance Education.* London: Paul Chapman.

Jones, S. G. 1995. *Cybersociety: Computer–Mediated Communication and Community.* London: Sage.

Jones, T., and V. Clarke. 1995. "Diversity as a Determinant of Attitudes: A Possible Explanation of the Apparent Advantage of Single–Sex Settings." *Journal of Educational Computing Research* 121: 51–65.

Jonscher, C. 1983. "Information Resources and Economic Productivity." *Information Economics and Policy* 2, no. 1: 13–35.

Jouet, J., P. Flichy, and P. Beaud, eds. 1991. *European Telematics: The Emerging Economy of Words.* Amsterdam: North Holland.

Juuti, P., and K. Lindström. 1995. *Postmoderni ajattelu ja organisaation syvällinen muutos* (Postmodern approach and deep-going organizational change). Työ ja ihminen. Tutkimusraportti 4. JTO–tutkimuksia Sarja 9. Työterveyslaitos, Johtamistaidon Opisto Helsinki. In Finnish with an English summary.

Kaid, L., J. Gerstle, and K. Sanders. 1991. *Mediated Politics in Two Cultures.* New York: Praeger.

Kajander, A., and M. Konttinen, eds. 1996. *Information and Communication Technologies in Health Care.* A report prepared for the STOA Unit of the European Parliament. Saarijärvi, Finland: National Research and Development Centre for Welfare and Health.

Kanter, R. 1995. *World Class: Thriving Locally in the Global Economy.* New York: Simon & Schuster.

Kaplinsky, R. 1995. "Patients as Work in Progress: Organisational Reform in the Health Sector." In *Europe's Next Step: Organisational Innovation, Competition, and Employment,* edited by L. E. Andreasen, et al., pp. 287–304. London: Frank Cass.

Karlsson, C., B. Johannisson, and D. Storey, eds. 1993. *Small Business Dynamics.* London: Small Business Dynamics/Routledge.

Karvonen, E. 1997. "Projecting a Positive Image of the Information Society: A Rhetorical Approach." Paper presented to the Thirteen Nordic Conference for Mass Communication Research, August. Oslo: ICDE.

Keane, J. 1991. *The Media and Democracy.* Cambridge: Polity.

Keddie, N. 1980. "Adult Education: An Ideology of Individualism." In *Adult Education for Change.* Edited by J. Thompson. London: Hutchinson.

Keen, B. 1987. "Play It Again, Sony: The Origins and Double Life of Home Video Technology." *Science as Culture* 1.

Keen, P. G. W. 1991. *Shaping the Future: Business Design through Information Technology.* Cambridge: Harvard Business School Press.

Kennedy, C. 1996. "The Incredible Shrinking Economy." *Director,* April, pp. 62–68.

Kergoat, D. 1994. "De la jubilation à la déréliction: L'utilisation du minitel dans les luttes infirmières, 1988–1989." In *Les coordinations de travailleurs dans la confrontation sociale,* pp. 73–101. Futur Antérieur. Paris: L'Harmattan.

Kern, P., and W. Bauer. 1995. "New Tools for Designing Workplaces." In *People and Work,* edited by J. Rantanen, S. Lehtinen, and P. Huuhtanen, pp. 104–110. Helsinki: Finnish Institute of Occupational Health

Kerst, C. 1995. "Qualifizierte unternehmensbezogene Dienstleistungen." In *Neue Organisationsformen in Verwaltung und Dienstleistung.* Edited by H.–J. Brazcyk et al. Stuttgart: Kohlhammer Verlag.

King, A., et al. 1996. *The Health of Youth: A Cross–National Survey.* WHO Regional Publications, European Series no. 69. Copenhagen: World Health Organization, Regional Office for Europe.

Kinnunen, U., and T. Parkatti. 1993. *Ikääntyvä opettaja—kuormittuneisuus ja terveys työssä. Ikääntyvä arvoonsa—työterveyden, työkyvyn ja hyvinvoinnin edistämisohjelman julkaisuja* (Aging teacher—work load and health at work]. 8 Työterveyslaitos ja Työsuojelurahasto, Helsinki.

Kirkup, G. 1993. "Equal Opportunities and Computing at the Open University." In *Key Issues in Open Learning.* Edited by A. Tait. Harlow: Longman.

Kirkup, G. 1996. "The Importance of Gender." In *Supporting the Learner in Open and Distance Learning.* Edited by R. Mills and A. Tait. London: Pitman.

Kirkup, G., and A. Jones. 1995. "Diversity, Openness, and Domestic Information and Communication Technologies." In *One World Many Voices.* Edited by D. Seward. Proceedings of the Seventeenth World Conference for Distance Education, Birmingham, U.K., June 26th–30.

Kirkup, G., and C. von Prümmer. 1990. "Support and Connectedness: The Needs of Women Distance Education Students." *Journal of Distance Education* 5, no. 2: 9–31.

Kirkup, G., and C. von Prümmer. 1997. "Distance Education for European Women: The Threats and Opportunities of New Educational Forms and Media." *European Journal of Women's Studies* 41: 39–62.

Kirkwood, A., and G. Kirkup. 1991. "Access to Computing for Home–Based Students." *Studies in Higher Education* 162: 199–208.

Kling, J. 1995. "High Performance Work Systems and Firm Performance." *Monthly Labor Review,* May, 29–36.

Knauth, P. 1996. "Work Organizations and Work Schedules in the Future." In *Work in the Information Society,* edited by J. Rantanen, S. Lehtinen, and P. Huuhtanen, pp. 84–89. People and Work Research Reports, no. 8. Helsinki: Finnish Institute of Occupational Health.

Knolmayer, G. 1994. "Zur Berücksichtigung von Transaktions- und Koordinationskosten in Entscheidungsmodellen für Make-or-Buy-Probleme." *Betriebswirtschaftliche Forschung und Praxis* 46, no. 4: 316–332.

Knüppel, L., and F. Heuer. 1994. "Eine empirische Untersuchung zum Outsourcing aus der Sicht Potentieller und tatsächlicher Nutzer." *Betriebswirtschaftliche Forschung und Praxis* 46, no. 4: 333–357.

Kordey, N. 1993. *Nutzung der Telekommuikation durch altere Menschen: Qualitative Studien in Ausgewalten Lebenslagen und Soziale Situationen.* No. 117. Bad Honnef: Wissenschaftliches Institut für Kommunikationsdienste.

Korte, W., and N. Wynne. 1996. *Telework: Potential, Penetration, and Practice in Europe.* Amsterdam: IOS Press.

Kramarae, C., and J. Kramer. 1995. "Net Gains, Net Losses." *Women's Review of Books* 12, no. 5.

Krueger, R. 1993. "How Computers Changed the Wage Structure: Evidence from Micro–Data 1984–89." *Quarterly Journal of Economics,* February.

Kubiceck, H., and W. Dutton. 1997. "The Social Shaping of Information Superhighways: An Introduction." In *The Social Shaping of Information Superhighways: European and American Roads to the Information Society,* edited by H. Kubicek, W. Dutton, and R. Williams, pp. 9–44. Frankfurt: Campus Verlag; New York: St. Martin's.

Kuruvilla, S., and C. Venkataratnam. 1996. "Economic Development and Industrial Relations: The Case of South and Southeast Asia." *Industrial Relations Journal* 27, no. 1: 9–23.

Laabs, J. 1999. "Has Downsizing Missed Its Mark?" *Workforce,* April; available at: www.hrhq.com/research.

Lacity, M., L. Willcocks, and D. Feeny. 1996. "The Value of Selective IT Sourcing." *Sloan Management Review,* Spring, pp. 13–25.

Laczko, F. 1989. "Between Work and Retirement: Becoming 'Old' in the 1980s." In *Becoming and Being Old: Sociological Approaches to Later Life.* Edited by E. Bytheway et al. London: Sage.

Laczko, F., and C. Phillipson. 1991. "Great Britain: The Contradictions of Early Exit." In *Time for Retirement: Comparative Studies of Early Exit from the Labor Force.* Edited by M. Kohli et al. Cambridge: Cambridge University Press.

Lafrance. J.–P. 1994. "La TVI, l'autoroute electronique, Internet et les superhighways de l'avenir: Vers une restructuration de l'industrie audiovisuelle." *Technologies de l'information et société* (Paris) 6, no. 4.

Langdale, J. V. 1995. "Telecommunications and Twenty–Four Hour Trading in the International Securities Industry." Paper presented to a workshop on informatics and Telecom tectonics: Information Technology, Policy, Telecommunications, and the Meaning of Space, Michigan State University, East Lansing, Mich., 20–21 March.

Lansdale, M. 1990. "The Role of Memory in Personal Information Management." In *Cognitive Ergonomics: Understanding, Learning and Designing,* edited by P. Falzon, pp.

39–50. Computers and People Series. London: European Association of Cognitive Ergonomics/Academic Press.

Lareng, L. 1996. Comments dated 21 September 1996 given on the basis of the consultation on health in the information society related to the work of the high–level expert group on the social and societal aspects of the information society, Luxembourg, 4 September 1996.

Lasch, S., and J. Urry. 1994. *Economies of Signs and Space*. London: Sage.

Laurillard, D. 1993. *Rethinking University Teaching: A Framework for the Effective Use of Educational Technology*. London: Routledge.

Lefrere, P. 1994. "The Technology and Management of Desk–Top Publishing." In *Materials Production in Open and Distance Teaching*. Edited by F. Lockwood. London: Paul Chapman.

Lehner, F. 1993. *The Future of European Industries*. Vol. 1, *New Markets, New Structures, and New Strategies*. Monitor Fast, FOP 365. Brussels: CEC.

Leppänen, A. 1995. "Mastery of Work, Well–Being, and Their Development in the Process Industry." Paper presented to the Conference on Work, Stress, and Health 1995, Washington, D.C., 14–16 September 1995.

Leventhal, L., B. Teasley, and K. Blumenthal. 1996. "Assessing User Interfaces for Diverse User Groups: Evaluation Strategies and Defining Characteristics." *Behaviour and Information Technology* 15: 127–138.

Leyshon, A., and N. Thrift. 1993. "The Restructuring of the U.K. Financial Services Industry in the 1990s: A Reversal of Fortune?" *Journal of Rural Studies* 93: 223–241.

Li, F. 1995. "Corporate Networks and the Spatial and Functional Reorganisation of Large Firms." *Environment and Planning A* 27: 1627–1645.

Lie, M., and K. H. Sorensen. 1996. *Making Technology Our Own? Domesticating Technology into Everyday Life*. Oslo: Scandinavian University Press.

Lisewski, B. 1994. "The Open Learning Pilot Project at the Liverpool Business School." *Open Learning* 9, no. 2: 12–22.

Livingstone, S., and P. Lunt. 1994. *Talk on Television: Audience Participation and Public Debate*. London: Routledge.

Lorentzon, S. 1995. "The Use of ICT in TNCs: A Swedish Perspective on the Location of Corporate Functions." *Regional Studies* 29, no. 7: 673–685.

Loslier, L. *Geographical Information Systems GIS from a Health Perspective*. Available at: www.idrc.ca/books/focus/766/loslier1.html.

Lovelock, C., and G. Yip. 1996. "Developing Global Strategies for Service Businesses." *California Management Review* 38, no. 2: 64–86.

Loveman, G. 1994. "An Assessment of the Productivity Impact of Information Technology." In *Information Technology and the Corporation of the 1990s*. Edited by T. Allen and Scott Morton. Oxford: Oxford University Press.

Luck, S. J., E. K. Vogel, and K. L. Shapiro. 1996. "Word Meanings Can Be Accessed but Not Reported during the Attentional Blink." *Nature* 383: 616–618.

Lund, R., and A. Gjerdling. 1996. *The Flexible Company, Innovation, Work Organisation, and Human Resource Management*. DRUID Working Paper, no. 96-17. Aalborg, Denmark: Aalborg University, Faculty of Business.

Lundvall, B.–Å. 1996. *The Social Dimension of the Learning Economy*. Danish Research Unit for Industrial Dynamics DRUID Working Paper, no. 96/1. Aalborg, Denmark: Aalborg University, Faculty of Business.

Lundvall, B.–Å., and B. Johnson. 1994. "The Learning Economy." *Journal of Industry Studies* 12: 23–42.

Lyon, D. 1988. *The Information Society: Issues and Illusions.* Oxford: Polity.

McCracken, G. 1990. *Culture and Consumption: New Approaches to the Symbolic Character of Consumer Goods and Activities.* Bloomington: Indiana University Press.

Macdonald, J., and R. Mason. 1997. "Information Handling Skills and Resource Based Learning." *Open Learning* 123.

McDonald, S., and R. J. Stevenson. 1996. "Disorientation in Hypertext: The Effects of Three Text Structures on Navigation Performance." *Applied Ergonomics* 27: 61–68.

Machlup, F. 1962. *The Production and Distribution of Knowledge in the United States.* Princeton: Princeton University Press.

McLaren, P., and C. J. Ball, 1995. "Telemedicine: Lessons Remain Unheeded." *British Medical Journal* 310: 1390–1391.

McLean, I. 1989. *Democracy and Technology.* Cambridge: Polity.

McLuhan, M. 1968. *Pour comprendre les médias.* Paris: Mame/Seuil.

McNeil, M. 1987. "It's a Man's World." In *Gender and Expertise.* Edited by M. McNeil. London: Free Association Books.

MacPherson, A. 1995. "Product Design Strategies amongst Small and Medium–Sized Manufacturing Firms: Implications for Export Planning and Regional Economic Development." *Entrepreneurship and Regional Development* 7: 329–48.

Mair, A. 1994. *Honda's Global Local Corporation.* London: Macmillan.

Malmberg, A. 1996. "Industrial Geography: Agglomeration and Local Milieu." *Progress in Human Geography* 20.

Malone T., J. Yates, and R. Benjamin. 1987. "Electronic Markets and Electronic Hierarchies." *Communications of the ACM* 30, no. 6: 484–497.

Manin B. 1995. *Principes du gouvernement représentatif.* Paris: Calmann–Lévy.

Manpower Services Commission. 1984. *A New Training Initiative.* Sheffield, U.K.: Manpower Services Commission.

Mantovani, G. 1996. "Social Context in HCI: A New Framework for Mental Models, Cooperation, and Communication." *Cognitive Science* 20: 237–269.

Marschan, R. 1996. *New Structural Forms and Inter–Unit Communication in Multinationals: The Case of Kone Elevators.* Helsinki: Helsinki School of Economics and Business Administration.

Marshall, J., and R. Richardson. 1996. "The Growth, Location, and Mobility of Services." Report prepared for Locate in Scotland, Edinburgh.

Marteniuk, R., C. Ivens, and B. Brown, 1996. "Are There Task Specific Performance Effects for Differently Configured Numeric Keypads?" *Applied Ergonomics* 27: 321–325.

Martin, H.–J. 1988. *Histoire et Pouvoirs de l'Ecrit.* Paris: Perrin.

Martin, M. 1988. "Rulers of the Wires? Women's Contribution to the Structure of Communication." *Journal of Communication* 12, no. 3.

Marvin, C. 1988. *When Old Technologies Were New: Thinking about Communications in the Late Nineteenth Century.* Oxford: Oxford University Press.

Maskell, P., and A. Malmberg. 1995. *Localised Learning and Industrial Competitiveness.* Berkeley Roundtable of International Economy Working Paper, no. 80. Berkeley: University of California Press.

Mason, G. 1996. "Graduate Utilisation in British Industry: The Initial Impact of Mass Higher Education." *National Institute Economic Review* 156: 93–103.

Mason, R. 1994. "Computer Conferencing and the Open University." *The Computers in Teaching Initiative File* 17 (July): 5–8.

Mason, R. 1995. "Synchronous and Asynchronous Media for Distance Teaching." In *One World, Many Voices.* Edited by D. Sewart. Selected Papers from the Seventeenth World Conference of the International Council for Distance Education. Oslo: ICDE.

Mason, R., and T. Kaye. 1990. "New Paradigms for Distance Education." In *Online Education: Perspectives on a New Environment.* Edited by L. Harasim. New York: Praeger.

Massey, D., P. Quintas, and D. Wield. 1992. *High-Tech Fantasies: Science Parks in Society, Science, and Space.* London: Routledge.

Masuda, Y. 1981. *The Information Society as Post–Industrial Society.* Washington: D.C.: World Future Society.

Masuda, Y. 1996. *East and West Dialogue and the Global Information Society.* School of Social and International Studies Working Papers, no. 5. Sunderland, U.K.: University of Sunderland.

Mayer, R. 1990. *Information et compétitivité.* Paris: La Documentation Française.

Mayer. 1996. Mayer Computing Services Web site: http: /yaron.clever.net/quest.shtml.

Meacham, D., and C. Wilkin. 1990. *Distance Education as Rehabilitation.* Australia and South Pacific External Studies Association, no. 9. Redfern, New South Wales, Australia.

Meharg, T. 1994. "TELEMATIQUE in Northern Ireland." Paper presented at the European Conference on Telematics, Crete, 24–26 October 1993. Brussels: Commission of the European Communities.

Meyer, S., and E. Schulze. 1994. *Alles automatisch: Technikfolgen für Familien: Engsschnittanalysen und zukunftige Entwicklung.* Berlin: Edition Sigma.

Meyer, S., and E. Schulze. 1995. "Smart Home in the 1990s: Acceptance and Future Usage of Private Households." Paper presented at the second EMTEL Workshop, Amsterdam, November 10–11.

Miege, B., ed. 1990. *Médias et communications en Europe.* Grenoble: PUG.

Mill, U., and H. Weissbach. 1992. "Vernetzungswirtschaft." In *ArbYTE: Modernisierung der Industriesoziologie?* Edited by T. Malsch and U. Mill. Berlin: WZB.

Millard, J. 1995. "The Role of Telematics in Rural Development: With Examples from Denmark." Paper presented to the Finnish FORADA Seminar on Telecommunications Strategy for Rural Areas, Seinajoki, 23–24 November.

Millard, J., et al. 1995. *Ad–Employ: Employment Trends Related to the Use of Advanced Communications.* Synthesis Report, TeleDanmark Report to DGXIII. Brussels: CEC.

Miller, D. 1987. *Material Culture and Mass Consumption.* Oxford: Blackwell.

Miller, D. 1992. "'The Young and the Restless' in Trinidad: A Case of the Local and the Global in Mass Consumption." In *Consuming Technologies: Media and Information in Domestic Spaces.* Edited by R. Silverstone and E. Hirsch. London: Routledge.

Ministry of Social Affairs and Health. 1996. *Finnish National Strategy for Utilization of Information and Communication Technologies (ICT) in Social and Health Services.* Helsinki: Ministry of Social Affairs and Health.

Ministry of Research. 1994. *Info–Society 2000.* Copenhagen: Ministry of Research.

Mitchell, W. 1996. *City of Bits.* Cambridge: MIT Press.

"The Mittelstand Meets the Grim Reaper." 1995. *Economist,* 16 December, 57–58.

Mitter, S. 1991. "Computer-Aided Manufacturing and Women's Employment: A Global Critique of Post-Fordism." In *Women, Work, and Computerization: Understanding and Overcoming Bias in Work and Education*. Edited by I. V. Eriksson, B. Kitchenham, and K. G. Tijdens. North-Holland, Amsterdam.

Mollenkopf, H. 1993. "Technical Aids in Old Age: Between Acceptance and Rejection." In *Arbeitsgruppe Sozialberichterstattung*, pp. 93–106. Berlin: Wissenschafts–centrum Berlin.

Molnar, K. K., and M. G. Kletke. 1996. "The Impacts on User Performance and Satisfaction of a Voice–Based Front–End Interface for a Standard Software Tool." *International Journal of Human–Computer Studies* 45: 287–303.

Moorcraft, S., and V. Bennett. 1995. *European Guide to Teleworking: A Framework for Action*. Dublin: European Foundation for the Improvement of Living and Working Conditions.

Moore, M. 1991. "International Aspects of Independent Study." In *The Foundations of American Distance Education*. Edited by B. Watkins and S. Wright. Dubuque, Iowa: Kendall/Hunt.

Moore, N. 1998. "The British National Information Strategy." *Journal of Information Science* 245: 337–344.

Moores, S. 1988. "'The Box on the Dresser': Memories of Early Radio and Everyday Life." *Media, Culture, and Society* 10, no. 1.

Morgan, K. 1992. "Telematics and Regional Development: Conference Report." Paper presented at the Telematics Conference, Kells, Northern Ireland, 30–31 May.

Morgan, K. 1995. *The Learning Region*. Papers in Planning Research, no. 157. Cardiff, Wales, U.K.: Department of City and Regional Planning/University of Wales College of Cardiff.

Morgan, M., and N. Signorielli, eds. 1990. *Cultivation Analysis: New Directions in Media Effects Research*. London: Sage.

Morley, D. 1986. *Family Television: Cultural Power and Domestic Leisure*. London: Comedia.

Morley, D., and R. Silverstone. 1990. "Domestic Communication: Technologies and Meanings." *Media, Culture, and Society* 12, no. 1.

Moss, M. L. 1992. "Telecommunications and Urban Development." In *Cities and New Technology*, pp. 147–158. Paris: OECD.

Moss, M. L., and A. Dunau. 1986. "Offices, Information Technology, and Locational Trends." In *The Changing Office Workplace*, edited by J. Black, K. Roark, and L. Schwartz, pp. 171–182. Washington, D.C.: Urban Land Institute.

Moss, M. L., and A. Dunau. 1987. "Will Cities Lose Their Back Offices?" *Real Estate Review* 171 (Spring).

Moyal, A. 1989. "The Feminine Culture of the Telephone: People, Patterns, and Policy." *Prometheus* 7, no. 1.

Mueller, M. 1993. "Universal Service in Telephone History: A Reconstruction." *Telecommunications Policy* 175: 352–370.

Murray, A. C., D. M. Jones, and C. R. Frankish. 1996. "Dialogue Design in Speech–Mediated Data–Entry: The Role of Syntactic Constraints and Feedback." *International Journal of Human–Computer Studies* 45: 263–286.

NACFAM. 1996. *U.S. National Skills Standards Project for Advanced Manufacturing*. Washington, D.C.: National Coalition of Advanced Manufacturing/U.S. Department of Labor.

Naisbitt, J. 1994. *Global Paradox: The Bigger the World Economy, the More Political Its Smallest Players.* New York: William Morrow.

Neathey, F., and J. Hurstfield. 1995. *Flexibility in Practice: Women's Employment and Pay in Retail and Finance.* Research Discussion Series no. 16. London: Industrial Relations Services.

Negroponte, N. 1995. *L'homme numérique.* Paris: Robert Laffont.

Neil, M. 1981. *The Education of Adults at a Distance.* London: Kogan Page.

Nelson, K. 1986. "Labour Demand, Labour Supply and the Suburbanisation of Low Wage Office Work." In *Production, Work, and Territory: The Geographical Anatomy of Industrial Capitalism,* edited by A. J. Scott and M. Storper, pp. 149–167. Boston: Allan & Unwin.

NERA [National Economic Research Associates]. 1993. *Regional Telecommunications Investment Requirements and Financing Perspectives to the Year 2000 for Objective 1 Regions.* Report to DGXIII of the Commission of the European Communities, Brussels.

NERA. 1995. *OECD Wage Subsidy Evaluations: Lessons for Workstart.* Final Report for the Department of Education and Employment. London: NERA.

Netherlands Economic Institute/Ernst and Young. 1993. *New Location Factors for Mobile Investment in Europe: Final Report.* Regional Development Studies 6. Brussels: CEC.

Neveu, E. 1994. *Une société de communication?* Paris: Montchrestien.

Nexus Europe. 1995. *Initial Results 2: Preliminary Report from the Study on Social and Economic Cohesion Aspects of the Development of an Information Society in Europe.* Dublin: Nexus.

Nexus Europe, CURDS, and Culture and Communications Studies. 1996. *An Assessment of the Social and Economic Cohesion Aspects of the Development of an Information Society in Europe.* Vol. 5, *Synthesis and Recommendations.* Final Report to DG XIII and DG XVI of the Commission of the European Communities. Dublin: Nexus Europe.

Nilsen, S. E. 1995. "Distance Education via Telecommunications for People Who Are Blind or Partially Sighted." In *One World, Many Voices.* Edited by D. Sewart. Selected Papers from the Seventeenth World Conference of the International Council for Distance Education. Oslo: ICDE.

Nissen, J., and U. Riis. 1989. "Computer Captivated Youth: A Swedish Picture." Paper presented at the Children in the Information Age conference, Sofia, Bulgaria, May.

Noelle-Neumann, E. 1993. *The Spiral of Silence: Public Opinion, Our Social Skin.* Chicago: University of Chicago Press.

Nohria, N., and R. Eccles. 1992. "Face–to–Face: Making Network Organizations Work." In *Networks and Organizations: Structure, Form, and Action,* edited by N. Nohria and R. Eccles, pp. 288–308. Boston: Harvard Business School Press.

Nonaka, K. 1991. "The Knowledge Creating Company." *Harvard Business Review,* November-December.

Nora, S., and A. Minc. 1978. *L'informatisation de la société.* Paris: Points–Seuil.

NTIA [National Telecommunications and Information Administration]. 1995. *Falling through the Net: A Survey of the "Have Nots" in Rural and Urban America.* Washington, D.C.: NTIA. Updated in 1998.

NUTEK. 1995. *Telematics Profile: Sweden.* Stockholm: NUTEK.

Nygård, C.–H., L. Eskelinen, and S. Suvanto. 1991. "Associations between Functional Capacity and Work Ability among Elderly Municipal Employees." *Scandinavian Journal of Work, Environment, and Health* 17 (suppl) 1: 122–127.

O'Connell, T., and N. Kennedy. 1994. "Dublin's International Financial Services Centre: A Review." *Quarterly Bulletin, Central Bank of Ireland* 4 (Winter): 47–64.

Ocqueteau, F., and M.–L. Pottier. 1995. *Vigilance et sécurité dans les grandes surfaces.* Paris: IHESI/L'Harmattan.

OECD [Organization for Economic Cooperation and Development]. 1992. *Schools and Business: A New Partnership.* Paris: OECD.

OECD. 1993a. "Active Labour Market Policies: Assessing Macroeconomic and Micro-economic Effects." *Employment Outlook,* June, pp. 39–80.

OECD. 1993b. *The Public Employment Service in Japan, Norway, Spain and the United Kingdom.* Paris: OECD.

OECD. 1994. *Employment Outlook July 1994.* Paris: OECD.

OECD. 1995. *The OECD Jobs Study: Implementing the Strategy.* Paris: OECD.

OECD. 1996a. *Technology, Productivity, and Job Creation.* Paris: OECD.

OECD. 1996b. *OECD Jobs Strategy: Enhancing the Effectiveness of Active Labour Market Policies.* Paris: OECD.

OECD. 1996c. *The Public Employment Service in Denmark, Finland, and Italy.* Paris: OECD.

OECD. 1996d. *Lifelong Learning for All.* Paris: OECD. Meeting of the Education Committee at Ministerial Level, 16–17 January.

OECD. 1996e. *The Public Employment Service in Austria, Germany, and Sweden.* Paris: OECD.

OECD. 1996f. *Mapping the Future: Young People and Career Guidance.* Paris: OECD.

OECD. 1997a. "Use of Information Networks and Their Impact on Organisational Structures: Firm–Level Evidence from Japan." In *IT Outlook 1997,* pp. 67–73. Paris: OECD.

OECD. 1997b. "Information Technology Scoreboard." In *IT Outlook 1997,* pp. 13–66. Paris: OECD.

OECD. 1999. *The Economic and Social Impacts of Electronic Commerce: Preliminary Findings and Research Agenda.* Paris: OECD.

Oftel. 1995. *Universal Telecommunications Service: A Consultative Document on Universal Service in the UK from 1997.* London: Oftel.

OJTI. 1992. *Commercialisation des données publiques: Observatoire juridique des techniques de l'information.* Paris: La Documentation Française.

Open Learning Directory. 1996. *Pergamon Open Learning.* Edited by Richard Taylor. Oxford: Pergamon.

Ó Siochrú, S., A. Gillespie, and L. Qvortrup 1995. *Advanced Communications for Cohesion and Regional Development ACCORDE.* Final Report to Commission of the European Communities. Dublin: Nexus.

Osterman, P. 1994. "How Common Is Workplace Transformation and Who Adopts It?" *Industrial and Labor Relations Review* 472: 173–187.

Pailliart, I. 1991. *Les processus d'iinnovation dans la fonction d'edition: Le cas des services télématiques municipaux.* Grenoble: GRESEC rapport de recherche au plan urbain.

Pailliart, I., ed. 1995. *L'espace public et l'emprise de la communication.* Grenoble: ELLUG.

Parker, E., and H. Hudson. 1995. *Electronic Byways: State Policies for Rural Development through Telecommunications.* 2d ed. Washington, D.C.: Aspen Institute Rural Economic Policy Program.

"Passage to India Brings Savings for Data Logic." 1994. *Computing,* 5 May.

Paulson, M. 1992. *From Bulletin Boards to Electronic Universities: Distance Education,*

Computer–Mediated Communication, and Online Education. Research Monograph no. 7 of the American Center for the Study of Distance Education, College of Education, Pennsylvania State University.

Pearson, R., and S. Mitter. 1993. "Employment and Working Conditions of Low–Skilled Information–Processing Worker in Less Developed Countries." *International Labour Review* 1321: 49–64.

Pekkola, J., and P. Ylöstalo. 1996. *Information Work and the Labour Markets.* Työpoliittinen tutkimus, no. 159, 1–62. Helsinki: Ministry of Labor.

Penn, R., and D. Sleightholme. 1995. "Skilled Work in Contemporary Europe: A Journey into the Dark." In *Industrial Transformation in Europe.* Edited by E. Dittrich, G. Schmidt, and R. Whitley. London: Sage.

Perednia, D. A., and A. Allen. 1995. "Telemedicine Technology and Clinical Applications." *Journal of the American Medical Association* 273: 483–488.

Perriault, J. 1989. *La logique de l'usage: Essai sur les machines à communiquer.* Paris: Flammarion.

Perriault, J. 1996. *La communication du savoir à distance.* Paris: L'Harmattan.

Perrineau, P. 1994. *L'engagement politique: Déclin ou mutation?* Paris: Presses de la Fondation Nationale des Sciences Politiques.

Philips, D. 1995. *Spatial Consolidation: Replacement Outsourcing of Corporate Information Systems.* Department of Geography Working Paper. New York: University of Buffalo Press.

Phillips, A., and B. Taylor. 1980. "Sex and Skill: Notes Towards a Feminist Economics." *Feminist Review* 6: 79–88.

Piccoli, B., et al. 1996. "Viewing Distance Variation and Related Ophthalmological Changes in Office Activities with and without VDUs." *Ergonomics* 39: 719–728.

Picot, A., R. Neuburger, and J. Niggl. 1995. "Ausbreitung und Auswirkung von Electronic Data Exchange: Empirische Ergebnisse aus der Deutschen Automobil- und Transportbranche." In *Managementforschung,* edited by G. Schreyögg and J. Sydow, 5: 47-106. Berlin: Empirische Studien.

Pierce, P. F. 1996. "When the Patient Chooses: Describing Unaided Decisions in Health Care." *Human Factors* 38: 278–287.

Pincas, A. 1995. "Assuring Quality in Higher Education by Computer Conferencing." In *One World, Many Voices.* Edited by D. Sewart. Selected Papers from the Seventeenth World Conference of the International Council for Distance Education. Oslo: ICDE.

Pine, B. 1993. *Mass Customization: A New Frontier in Business Competition.* Boston: ABS Press.

Piore, M., and C. Sabel. 1984. *The Second Divide: Possibilities for Prosperity.* New York: Basic.

Plowman, L. 1996. "Narrative, Linearity, and Interactivity: Making Sense of Interactive Multimedia." *British Journal of Educational Technology* 27, no. 2: 92–105.

Plowman, L., and P. Chambers. 1994. "Working with the New Generation of Interactive Media Technologies in Schools: CD–i and CDTV." *British Journal of Educational Technology* 252: 125–134.

Pollert, A. 1988. "Dismantling Flexibility." *Capital and Class* 34.

Porter, M. 1990. *The Competitive Advantage of Nations.* London: Macmillan.

Presvelou, C. 1986. *Households, the Home Computer, and Related Services in the Nether-*

lands: *Attitudes, Trends, and Prospects.* FASR Report no. 95. Wageningen, the Netherlands: University of Wageningen.

Probert, B., and A. Hack. (n.d.) *Remote Office Work and Regional Development: The Australian Securities Commission in the La Trobe Valley.* Melbourne: CIRCIT.

Proulx, S., ed. 1988. *Vivre avec l'ordinateur: Les usagers de la micro–informatique.* Montreal: Vermette.

Punie, Y. 1995. "Media Use on the Information Highway: Towards a New Consumer Market or Towards Increased Competition to Win Round the Consumer." Paper prepared for the PICT International Conference on the Social and Economic Implications of Information and Communications Technologies, Westminster, London, 10–12 May.

Pyke, F. 1994. *Small Firms, Technical Services, and Inter–Firm Cooperation.* Research Series, no. 99. Geneva: International Institute for Labor Studies.

Quelch, J., and L. Klein. 1996. "The Internet and International Marketing." *Sloan Management Review,* Spring, pp. 60–75.

Qvortrup, L. 1986. *Social Experiments with Information Technology and the Challenges of Innovation.* FAST Occasional Papers, no. 114 Rev., September.

Qvortrup, L., and A. Bianchi. 1996. *Barriers to and Strategies for Effective Participation in the Information Society in the Cohesion Regions.* Volume 3 of *An Assessment of the Social and Economic Cohesion Aspects of the Development of the Information Society.* Report to the European Commission, DGXIII and DGXVI. Brussels: CEC.

Rakow, L. 1988. "Women and the Telephone: The Gendering of a Communications Technology." In *Technology and Women's Voices.* Edited by C. Kramerae. London: Routledge.

Rakow, L., and P. Navaro. 1993. "Remote Mothering and the Parallel Shift: Women Meet the Cellular Phone." *Critical Studies in Mass Communication* 10, no. 2.

Randell, E. 1990. "Switching on at 60–Plus." In *The Neglected Audience.* Edited by J. Willis and T. Wollen. London: BFI.

Rantanen, J. 1995. "The Finnish Approach to Workplace Health Promotion." Report of the Workshop on Workplace Promotion, European Network, to the Federal Institute for Occupational Safety and Health (BAU), Dortmund, 20–21 June.

Rantanen, J. 1996a. "Human Technology Interface: Problems and Challenges." In *Work in the Information Society,* edited by J. Rantanen, S. Lehtinen, and P. Huuhtanen, pp. 90–100. People and Work Research Reports, no. 8. Helsinki: Finnish Institute of Occupational Health.

Rantanen, J. 1996b. "Demands of the Information Society for Working Capacity and Competence." Paper presented to the Telework Congress: Change and Challenge for Europe, Luxembourg, 26–28 June.

Rees, T., and W. Bartlett. 1996. "A Market in Adult Guidance? Trends in the UK, Germany, and France." Paper presented at the ESRC Learning Society program seminar Choice and Markets, University of Bristol, 17–18 September.

Rees, T., W. Bartlett, and A. Watts. 1996. "Adult Guidance and the Learning Society: Marketisation of Guidance Services in the UK, France, and Germany." Paper presented to the conference of the European Commission's Year of Lifelong Learning, University of Newcastle, November.

Regourd, S. 1992. *La télévision des Européens.* Paris: La Documentation Française.

Reingold, H. 1994. *The Virtual Community.* London: Secker & Warburg.

Reynolds, S. 1996. "Interactive Television as a Tool for Distance Education in Europe." In *Lifelong Learning, Open learning, Distance Learning.* Edited by J. Frankl and B. O'Reilly. Proceedings of the fifth European Distance Education Network (EDEN) Conference, Pointiers, France. Oslo: EDEN.

Ribault, T. 1988. "Rapport de mission aux États–Unis pour le groupe de travail sur les systèmes électroniques d'information." Paris: Commissariat General du Plan.

Richardson, R. 1994. "Back Officing Front Office Functions: Organisational and Locational Implications of New Telemediated Services." In *Management of Information and Communication Technologies,* edited by R. Mansell, pp. 309–335. London: Aslib.

Richardson, R. 1995. "Teleservices and Economic Development: A Case Study of Ireland." Mimeo. CURDS, University of Newcastle.

Richardson, R. 1996. "Telematics and Training and Human Resource Implications." Paper presented to Tyneside Training and Enterprise Council, Gateshead, February 13.

Richardson, R. 1997. "Network Technologies, Organisational Change, and the Location of Employment: The Case of Teleservices." In *The Economics of the Information Society,* edited by A. Dumort, T. Fenoulhet, and A. Onishi, pp. 194–200. Luxembourg: CEC.

Richardson, R., and A. Gillespie. 1996. "Advanced Communications and Employment Creation in Rural and Peripheral Regions: A Case Study of the Highlands and Islands of Scotland." *Annals of Regional Science* 30: 91–110.

Richardson, R., and J. N. Marshall. 1996. "The Growth of Telephone Call Centres in Peripheral Areas of Britain: Evidence from Tyne and Wear." *Area* 283: 308–317.

Riebler, L. O., and M. W. Parmley. 1995. "To Teach or Not to Teach? Comparing the Use of Computer–Based Simulations in Deductive versus Inductive Approaches to Learning with Adults in Science." *Journal of Educational Computing Research* 134: 359–374.

Riegler, C. 1995. "Process Support and Productive Structures for Work and Development: Swedish Experiences." Discussion paper presented at the Swedish Institute for Work Life, Stockholm, 15 September.

Rinde, E., I. Nordrum, and B. J. Nymo. 1993. "Telemedicine in Rural Norway." *World Health Forum* 14: 71–77.

Robertson, I., et al. 1995. "Computer Attitudes in an English Secondary School." *Computers and Education* 24, no. 2: 73–81.

Robinson, P. 1996. "The Role and Limits of Active Labour Market Policies." Paper presented at the Conference on Unemployment, European University Institute, Florence, April 12–13.

Rodota, S. 1999. "La souveraineté au temps de la technopolitique: Democratie électronique et démocratie représentative." In *La Democratie Électronique.* Edited by S. Rodota. Paris: Apogée.

Roessner, J., et al. 1993. *Tracking High Technology into the Twenty-first Century: Indicators for Twenty-eight Countries.* Technology Policy and Assessment Center. Atlanta: Georgia Institute of Technology Press.

Rosenbrock, H. H., ed. 1989. *Designing Human–Centred Technology: A Cross–Disciplinary Project in Computer–Aided Manufacturing.* London: Springer–Verlag.

Rousseau, D., ed. 1995. *La democratie continue.* Paris: LGDJ.

Rozenholc, A., B. Fanton, and A. Veyret. 1995. *Télé–travail, télé–economie: Une chance pour l'emploi et l'attractivité des territoires.* Paris: IDATE/DATAR.

Rubery, J., M. Smith, and C. Fagan. 1995. *Changing Patterns of Work and Working–Time in the European Union and the Impact on Gender Divisions.* Brussels: CEC.

Salmela, M. 1996. "Irti ajasta" (Detachment from time—Internet users). *Helsingin Sanomat,* October 27, D1–2. In Finnish.

Sassen, S. 1991. *The Global City.* Princeton: Princeton University Press.

Sassen, S. 1994. *Cities in a World Economy.* Thousand Oaks, Calif.: Pine Forge.

Saxenian, A. 1991. "The Origins and Dynamics of Production Networks in Silicon Valley." *Research Policy,* 20 October.

Scannell, P., and D. Cardiff. 1991. *A Social History of British Broadcasting.* Vol. 1, *1922–1939.* Oxford: Basil Blackwell.

SCANS [Secretary's Commission on Achieving Necessary Skill]. 1991. *What Work Requires of School.* Washington, D.C.: SCANS.

Scardigli, V. 1992. *Les sens de la technique.* Paris: PUF.

Schneider, D. 1995. "Kern oder Rand." *Mitbestimmung,* September, pp. 18f.

Schreiber, A., and W. Birmingham. 1996. "Editorial: The Sisyphus–VT initiative." *International Journal of Human–Computer Studies* 44: 275–280.

Screen Digest. 1995. Editorial. October, pp. 216–240.

Seabright, V., and F. Nickolmann, eds. 1992. *Distance Education in Europe: Studies and Recommendations by the Council of Europe.* Strasbourg, France: Council of Europe.

Seden, M. R. 1996. "Home Resource–Based Learning in Structural Engineering." In *One World, Many Voices.* Edited by D. Sewart. Selected Papers from the Seventeenth World Conference of the International Council for Distance Education. Oslo: ICDE.

Senge, P. 1990. *The Fifth Disciple: The Art and Practice of the Learning Organization.* New York: Doubleday.

Sengenberger, W., G. Loveman, and M. Piore. 1990. *The Reemergence of Small Enterprises.* Geneva: International Institute for Labor Studies.

Senker, P. 1992. "Automation and Work in Britain." In *Technology and the Future of Work,* edited by P. Adler, pp. 89–110. Oxford: Oxford University Press.

Servan-Schreiber, J. 1967. *Le défi Américain.* Paris: De Noël.

Sheth, J., and A. Parvatiyar. 1995. "The Evolution of Relationship Marketing." *International Business Review* 4, no. 4.

Shields, R., ed. 1996. *Cultures of Internet.* London: Sage.

Shotton, M. 1989. *Computer Addiction: A Study of Computer Dependency.* London: Taylor & Francis.

Silvennoinen, H., and E. Kerttula. 1994. "The TOMU Project." In *Telematics in Education: The European Case,* edited by W. Veen et al., pp. 39–49. De Lier, Netherlands: Academic Book Centre.

Silverstone, R. 1994a. *Future Imperfect: Media, Information, and the Millenium.* PICT Policy Research Paper, no. 17. Uxbridge, U.K.: Brunel University.

Silverstone, R. 1994b. *Television and Everyday Life.* London: Routledge.

Silverstone, R. 1995. "Media, Communication, Information, and the 'Revolution' of Everyday Life." In *Information Superhighways: Multimedia Users and Futures.* Edited by S. Emmott. London: Academic.

Silverstone, R. 1997a. *Visions of Suburbia.* London: Routledge.

Silverstone, R. 1997b. "New Media in European Households." In *Exploring the Limits: Europe's Changing Communication Environment,* pp. 113–134. Berlin: Springer-Verlag.

Silverstone, R., and L. Haddon. 1993. "Future Compatible? Information and Communications Technologies in the Home: A Methodology and Case Study." Report prepared for the Commission of the European Communities Socioeconomic and Technical Impact Assessments and Forecasts, RACE Project 2086, SPRU/CICT, University of Sussex.

Silverstone, R., and L. Haddon. 1996. *Television, Cable, and AB Households.* Report for Telewest plc. Sussex: Graduate Research Centre in Culture and Communication.

Silverstone, R., E. Hirsch, and D. Morley. 1992. "Information and Communication Technologies and the Moral Economy of the Household." In *Consuming Technologies: Media and Information in Domestic Spaces.* Edited by R. Silverstone and E. Hirsch. London: Routledge.

Sinden, A. 1995. "Telecommunications Services: Job Loss and Spatial Restructuring in Britain, 1989–1993." *Area* 27, no. 1: 34–45.

Sinden, A. 1996. "The Decline, Flexibility, and Geographical Restructuring of Employment in British Retail Banks." *Geographical Journal* 162, no. 1: 25–40.

Skinner, D. 1994. "Computerised Homes: Visions and Realities." In *Proceedings of the International Working Conference on Home Orientated Informatics, Telematics, and Automation.* Edited by K. Bjerg and K. Borreby. Conference held in Copenhagen, June 27–July 1. Copenhagen: University of Copenhagen.

Skirrow, G. 1986. "'Hellivision': An Analysis of Video Games." In *High Theory/Low Culture.* Edited by C. McCabe. Manchester, U.K.: Manchester University Press.

Slaton, C. 1992. *Televote: Expanding Citizen Participation in the Quantum Age.* New York: Praeger.

Smith, A. 1995. "New Technology and the Process of Labour Regulation: An International Perspective." In *Workplace Industrial Relations and the Global Challenge.* Edited by J. Belanger, P. Edwards, and L. Haiven. Ithaca, N.Y.: ILR Press/Cornell University Press.

Smith, M., and P. Kollock, eds. 1997. *Communities in Cyberspace.* Berkeley: University of California Press.

Smith, S., and D. Wield. 1987. "New Technology and Bank Work: Banking on IT as an 'Organisational Technology.'" In *New Perspectives on the Financial System.* Edited by L. Harris. London: Croon Helm.

de Sola Pool, I. 1977. *The Social Impact of the Telephone.* Cambridge: MIT Press.

de Sola Pool, I. 1983. *Technologies of Freedom.* Cambridge: Harvard University Press.

Sorensen, K. 1994. *Technology in Use: Two Essays on the Domestication of Artefacts.* STS–Arbeldsnotat 2/94, Centre for Technology and Society. Trondheim: University of Trondheim.

Spectrum Strategy Consultants/DTI [Department of Trade and Industry]. 1998. *Moving into the Information Age: International Benchmarking Study 1998.* London: DTI/HMSO.

Spigel, L. 1992. *Make Room for TV: Television and the Family Ideal in Postwar America.* Chicago: University of Chicago Press.

Spirduso, W. 1995. *Physical Dimensions of Aging.* Champaign, Ill.: Human Kinetics.

Spirduso, W., H. MacRae, and P. MacRae. 1988. "Exercise Effects on Aged Motor Function." *Annals of the New York Academy of Sciences* 515: 363–375.

Stanback, T. 1981. *Services: The New Economy.* Totowa, N.J.: Alanheld, Osmun.

Stanback, T., and T. Noyelle. 1982. *Cities in Transition.* Totowa, N.J.: Alanheld, Osmun.

Stanworth, J., and C. Stanworth. 1989. "Home Truths about Teleworking." *Personnel Management,* November, pp. 48–52.

Statistics Finland. 1997. www.stat.fi/tk/yr/tietoyt.htm.

Stewart, T. 1995. "Ergonomics Standards Concerning Human–System Interaction: Visual Displays, Controls, and Environmental Requirements." *Applied Ergonomics* 26: 271–274.

Stoffaes, C. 1995a. *Services publics: Questions d'avenir.* Paris: Editions Odile Jacob.

Stoffaes, C. 1995b. *L'Europe de l'utilité publique.* Paris: Editions ASPE.

Stopford, W., and S. Strange. 1991. *Rival States, Rival Firms: Competition for World Market Share.* Cambridge: Cambridge University Press.

Storey, D. 1994. *Understanding the Small Business Sector.* London: Routledge.

Storper, M. 1995a. "The Resurgence of Regional Economies, Ten Years Later: The Region as a Nexus of Untraded Interdependencies." *European Urban and Regional Studies* 23: 191–221.

Storper, M. 1995b. "Regional Economies as Relational Assets." Paper prepared for the Association des Science Régionales de Langue Française, Toulouse, 30 August–1 September.

"Sun Life Finds Success in India." 1993. *Computing,* 28 October.

Suvanto, S., et al. 1991. "Performance Efficiency and Its Changes among Aging Municipal Employees." *Scandinavian Journal of Work, Environment, and Health* 171: 118–121.

Taloustutkimus Oy. 1996. *Verkon käyttö leviää nyt työpaikoilta* (Widening of the Internet use spreads through workplaces: Fourth survey on Internet users in Finland). Available at: www.toy.fi/uusia/internet.html. In Finnish.

Tanner, K., and D. Gibbs. 1997. "Local Economic Development Strategies and Information and Communications Technologies." In *Innovation Networks and Learning Regions,* edited by J. Simmie, pp. 196–210. London: Jessica Kingsley.

Taylor, H., C. Kramarae, and M. Ebben. 1993. *Women, Information Technology, and Scholarship.* Bloomington: University of Illinois Press.

Taylor, J., and D. Laurillard. 1995. "Supporting Resource-Based Learning." In *Information Technology and Society.* Edited by N. Heap et al. London: Sage.

Taylor, P. 1996. "As Costs Fall, Corporate Interest Rises Rapidly." *Financial Times,* 3 April, IT sec., p. xii.

Tehranian, M. 1990. *Technologies of Power.* Norwood, N.J.: Ablex.

TEKES. 1995. *Finland: A Pioneer in Telematics Applications.* Helsinki: Finnish Value Relay Centre.

"Teleworking." 1994. IDS Study 551. London: Incomes Data Services.

Théry, G. 1994. *Les autoroutes de l'information.* Paris: La Documentation Française.

Thompson, H. 1995. "Pay Is on the Increase for Call Centre Staff." *Call Centre Europe* 6: 25.

Thrall, C. 1982. "The Conservative Use of Modern Household Technology." *Technology and Culture* 23, no. 2.

Tiffin, J., and L. Rajasingham. 1995. *In Search of the Virtual Class.* London: Routledge.

Toffler, A. 1980. *The Third Wave.* London: Collins.

Toffler, A., and H. Toffler. 1995. *Creating a New Civilisation: The Politics of the Third Wave.* Paris: Fayard.

Toppinen, S., and R. Kalimo. 1996. "Generalized and Professional Sense of Competence in Computer Professionals and Others." In *Work in the Information Society,* edited by J. Rantanen, S. Lehtinen, and P. Huuhtanen, pp. 202–205. People and Work Research Reports, no. 8. Helsinki: Finnish Institute of Occupational Health.

Touraine, A. 1969. *La société post–industrielle.* Paris: De Noël.

Trilling, J. 1992–1993. "La privatisation de l'espace publique en Californie." *Annales de la Recherche Urbaine* (Paris), December 1992–March 1993, pp. 57–58.

Tringham, M. 1996. "Giving the Web a Spin." *Engineer,* March, 2–3.

Tulloch, J. 1989. "Approaching the Audience: The Elderly." In *Remote Control: Television, Audience and Cultural Power.* Edited by E. Seiter et al. London: Routledge.

Turkle, S. 1984. *The Second Self: Computers and the Human Spirit.* London: Granada.

Turkle, S. 1995. *Life on the Screen: Identity in the Age of the Internet.* New York: Simon & Schuster.

Turkle, S., and S. Papert. 1990. "Epistemological Pluralism: Styles and Voices within the Computer Culture." *Signs: Journal of Women in Culture and Society* 161: 128–157.

Turoff, M. 1997. The Virtual Classroom and the Virtual University at New Jersey Institute of Technology. See http://eies.njit.edu/~turoff/

Tyson, L. D'Andrea. 1992. *Who's Bashing Whom?* Princeton: Institute for International Economics.

UNCTAD [U.N. Conference on Trade and Development]. 1994. *World Investment Report 1994: Transnational Corporations, Employment, and the Workplace.* New York: UNCTAD.

U.S. Census Bureau. 1998. *Statistics about Small and Large Businesses.* Available at: www.census.gov: 80/www/smallbus.htm.

U.S. Congress. Office of Technology Assessment. 1995. *Bringing Healthcare Online: The Role of Information Technologies.* OTA–ITC–624. Washington, D.C.: GPO.

U.S. Congress. Office of Technology Assessment. 1995. *The Technological Reshaping of Metropolitan America.* Washington, D.C.: GPO.

U.S. Department of Labor. 1993. *An Annotated Bibliography of High Performance Work Systems.* Washington, D.C.: U.S. Department of Labor.

U.S. Department of Labor. 1995. *What's Working and What's Not?* Washington, D.C.: Office of the Chief Economist, U.S. Department of Labor.

Van der Horst, R. 1995. "The Role of SMEs in Networking and Subcontracting." Paper presented at the EUROSME 95 Conference, European Union Finance for SMEs, Brussels, 16 May.

Van Eijnatten, F. 1993. *The Paradigm That Changed the Workplace.* Stockholm: Swedish Centre for Working Life.

Van Kekerix, M., and J. Andrews. 1991. "Electronic Media and Independent Study." In *The Foundations of American Distance Education,* edited by B. Watkins and S. Wright, pp. 135–157. Dubuque, Iowa: Kendall/Hunt.

Van Offenbeek, M. A. G., and P. L. Koopman. 1996. "Information System Development: From User Participation to Contingent Interaction among Involved Parties." *European Journal of Work and Organizational Psychology* 5: 421–438.

Veen, W., et al., eds. 1994. *Telematics in Education: The European Case.* De Lier, Netherlands: Academic Book Centre.

Verba, S. 1996. "The Citizen as Respondent: Sample Surveys and American Democracy." *American Political Science Review,* March.

Vincent, T. 1983. "Home Computing for the Visually Handicapped." *Teaching at a Distance* 23: 24–29.

Virgo, P. 1995. *Riding the Whirlwind: The 1995 IT Skills Trends Report.* Sidcup, Kent: Institute for the Management of Information Systems.

Virilio, P. 1990. *L'inertie polaire.* Paris: Christian Bourgois.

Vitalis, A. 1981. *Informatique et libertés.* Paris: Economica.

Vitalis, A. 1994. *Médias et nouvelles technologies: Pour une socio–politique des usages.* Rennes: Editions Apogée.

Vitalis, A. 1995. "Contrôle politique et démocratisation des technologies nouvelles." Paper presented to a Council of Europe seminar on electronic democracy, Paris, 23–24 March.

Vuori, H. 1982. "Quality Assurance of Health Services." *Public Health in Europe 16.* Copenhagen: World Health Organization, Regional Office for Europe.

Wacjman, J. 1991. *Feminism Confronts Technology.* Oxford: Polity.

Wald, R., and F. Stickler. 1991. *Telekommunikation und altere Menschen.* No. 62. Bad Honnef: Wissenschaftliches Institut für Kommunikationsdienste.

Walrave, M., ed. 1995. *Les réseaux de services publics dans le monde.* Paris: Editions ASPE Europe.

Wang, E. 1997. "Taiwan's Strategies for IT–Led Development and NII: A Longitudinal Study." In *Annual Pacific Telecommunications Conference,* 1: 277–286. Honolulu: Pacific Telecommunications Council.

Warf, B. 1995. "Telecommunications and Knowledge Transmission." *Urban Studies* 322: 361–378.

Warin, P. 1993. *Les usagers dans l'evaluation des politiques publiques.* Paris: L'Harmattan.

Watkins, B. 1991. "A Quite Radical Idea: The Invention and Elaboration of Collegiate Correspondence Study." In *The Foundations of American Distance Education.* Edited by B. Watkins and S. Wright. Dubuque, Iowa: Kendall/Hunt.

Watts, A. 1991. "The Impact of the 'New Right': Policy Challenges Confronting Careers Guidance in England and Wales." *British Journal of Guidance and Counselling* 193.

Webster, J. 1995. "Networks of Collaboration or Conflict? Electronic Data Interchange and Power in the Supply Chain." *Journal of Strategic Information Systems* 41: 31–42.

Webster, J. 1996. *Shaping Women's Work: Gender, Employment, and Information Technology.* London: Longman.

Webster, J. 1998. "The Talents of Women in the Knowledge Economy: Technological Work and Women's Prospects." Paper presented to the Rationalisation, Organisation, and Gender conference, Dortmund, 8–11 October.

Wedderburn, K. 1995. *Labour Law and Freedom: Further Essays in Labour Law.* London: Lawrence & Wishart.

Weinkopf, C. 1997. "Information and Communication Technologies in Job Placement and Advice." Report for the High Level Expert Group on the information society, mimeo. Gelsenkirchen: Institut für Arbeit und Technik.

Weißbach, H.-J. 1997. "Europaeische Integrationsmuster und kulturelle Voraussetzungen des Managements in der Informationsgesellschaft." In *Jahrbuch Arbeit + Technik*, edited by Werner Fricke, pp. 122–131. Bonn: Dietz Verlag.

Westerman, S., D. Davies, and A. Glendon. 1995. "Age and Cognitive Ability as Predictors of Computerized Information Retrieval." *Behaviour and Information Technology* 14: 313–326.

Westlander, G., and E. Viitasara. 1995. "Evaluation of an Ergonomics Intervention Programme in VDT Workplaces." *Applied Ergonomics* 26: 83–92.

What Is Wrong with Your Head-Mounted Display? 1993. Edinburgh Virtual Environment Laboratory, originally published as *CyberEdge Journal* monograph September–October 1993. Available at: www.cyberedge.com/4a7c.html.

Wheeler, J., and R. Mitchelson. 1991. "Information Flows within the World System of Cities: The Role of Major Metropolitan Centers." Paper presented to the Regional Studies Association Conference, New Orleans, November.

Whitefield, A. 1990. "Human–Computer Interaction Models and Their Roles in the Design of Interactive Systems." In *Cognitive Ergonomics: Understanding, Learning, and Designing*, edited by P. Falzon, pp. 7–25. Computers and People Series. London: European Association of Cognitive Ergonomics/Academic Press.

WHO [World Health Organization]. 1986. *Ottawa Charter for Health Promotion*. Copenhagen: World Health Organization, Regional Office for Europe. Available at: www.who.dk/policy /ottawa.htm.

WHO. 1993. *Health for All Targets 1993: The Health Policy for Europe*. Copenhagen: World Health Organization, Regional Office for Europe.

WHO. 1994a. *Health in Europe: The 1993/1994 Health for All Monitoring Report*. WHO Regional Publications European Series, no. 56. Copenhagen: World Health Organization.

WHO. 1994b. "Implementation of the Global Strategy for Health for All by the Year 2000." In *Report on the World Health Situation,* vol. 5, *European Region.* Copenhagen: World Health Organization, Regional Office for Europe.

WHO/FIMS [International Federation of Sports Medicine]. 1995. "World Health Organization and International Federation of Sports Medicine Committee on Physical Activity for Health: Exercise for Health." *Bulletin of the World Health Organization* 73: 1356.

Willcocks, L. P., and W. L. Currie. 1996. "Information Technology and Radical Reengineering: Emerging Issues in Major Projects." *European Journal of Work and Organizational Psychology* 5: 325–350.

Williams, G. 1997. "Three Lines of Production." *Higher,* 7 February, pp. 1–2.

Williams, H. 1994. *AIM–Project A 2011: Framework for Telemedicine Services in Europe.* Brussels: CEC.

Williams, H., and J. Taylor. 1991. "Information Technology and the Management of Territory by Firms." In *Cities of the Twenty-first Century: New Technologies and Spatial Systems,* edited by J. Brotchie et al., pp. 293–305. Melbourne: Longman Cheshire.

Williams, R. 1974. *Television: Technology and Cultural Form.* London: Fontana.

Williamson, K. 1994. *Drinks on the Phone at Five O'Clock: Telecommunication and the Information and Communication Needs of Older Adults.* Melbourne: Royal Melbourne Institute of Technology.

Wilson, M. 1994. "Offshore Relocation of Producer Services: The Irish Back Office."

Paper presented at the conference of the Association of American Geographers, Florida, March.

Wilson, M. 1995. "Press 1 for Reservations: Information Technology and the Location of Airline Operations." Paper presented at the conference of the Association of American Geographers, Chicago.

Winn, Marie. 1985. *The Plug-in Drug: Television, Children, and the Family*. Harmondsworth, U.K.: Penguin.

Winner, L. 1989. "Mythinformation in the High–Tech Era." In *Computers in Human Context: Information Technology, Productivity, and People,* edited by T. Forester, pp. 82–96. Oxford: Basil Blackwell.

Winston, B. 1989. "The Illusion of Revolution." In *Computers in Human Context: Information Technology, Productivity, and People,* edited by T. Forester, pp. 71–81. Oxford: Basil Blackwell.

Witz, A. 1992. "The Gender of Organisations." In *Gender and Bureaucracy.* Edited by M. Savage and A. Witz. Oxford: Blackwell.

Wobbe, W. 1991. *Anthropocentric Production Systems: A Strategic Issue for Europe.* APS Research Paper Series, vol. 1, FOP245. Brussels: Commission of the European Communities.

Wolff, E. 1995. "Technology and the Demand for Skills." *STI Review* 18.

Wolton, D. 1990. *Eloge du grand public.* Paris: Flammarion.

Womack, J., D. Jones, and D. Roos. 1990. *The Machine That Changed the World.* New York: Rawson Associates.

Wood, J. 1993. "Cellphones on the Clapham Omnibus: The Lead–Up to a Cellular Mass Market." SPRU/CICT Report Series, no. 11. Brighton, U.K.: University of Sussex.

Woolsey, K., and R. Bellamy. 1997. "Science Education and Technology." *Elementary School Journal* 97, no. 4: 385–399.

World Bank. 1998. *World Development Indicators 1998.* Washington, D.C.: World Bank.

World Medical Association. 1995. "Declaration of Lisbon on the Rights of the Patient: Adopted by the Thirty-fourth World Medical Assembly," Lisbon, Portugal, September–October 1981, and amended by the Forty-seventh General Assembly, Bali, Indonesia.

Wylie, M. 1995. "No Place for Women: Internet Is a Flawed Model for the Infobahn." *Digital Media* 4, no. 8: 3.

Yankelovitch, D. 1991. *Coming to Public Judgment.* Syracuse: Syracuse University Press.

Young, M. 1988. "Education for New Work." In *Open Learning in Transition: An Agenda for Action.* Edited by N. Paine. Cambridge: Cambridge National Extension College.

Young, M. 1990. "The Future of the Family." The First ESRC Annual Lecture, Swindon.

Young, M., and P. Wilmott. 1957. *Family and Kinship in East London.* London: Routledge & Kegan Paul.

Ziegler, J. E., P. H. Vossen, and H. U. Hoppe. 1990. "Cognitive Complexity of Human–Computer Interfaces: An Application and Evaluation of Cognitive Complexity Theory for Research on Direct Manipulation Style Interaction." In *Cognitive Ergonomics: Understanding, Learning and Designing,* edited by P. Falzon, pp. 27–38. Computers and People Series. London: European Association of Cognitive Ergonomics/Academic Press.

Zuboff, S. 1988. *In the Age of the Smart Machine: The Future of Work and Power.* New York: Basic.

Index

About the Contributors

Gerhard Bosch is vice president of the Institut Arbeit und Technik, Gelsen-kirchen, Germany, and professor at the University of Duisburg, Germany.

Pierre Chambat is associate professor in political science at the IRIS Research Center (Institut de recherche interdisciplinaire en socio-economie), Université de Paris Dauphine, Paris, France.

James Cornford is a senior research associate at the Centre for Urban and Regional Development Studies (CURDS) at the University of Newcastle, UK.

Ken Ducatel is currently seconded to the Institute for Prospective Techno-logical Studies (IPTS) of the Joint Research Centre of the European Com-mission in Sevilla, Spain, from his post as senior lecturer in the Management of New Technology at PREST, the University of Manchester, UK.

Andrew Gillespie is professor of communications geography and executive director of the Centre for Urban and Regional Development Studies (CURDS) at the University of Newcastle, UK.

Leslie Haddon is currently a visiting research associate in the media and com-munications department at the London School of Economics, UK.

Mark Hepworth is a director of the Local Futures Group, London, UK.

Werner Herrmann is unit head in the directorate general for education and culture of the European Commission, Brussels, Belgium, and visiting professor at the University of Texas at Austin.

323

Ann Jones is senior lecturer in educational technology at the Institute of Educational Technology of the Open University, UK.

Gill Kirkup is senior lecturer in educational technology at the Institute of Educational Technology of the Open University, UK.

Suvi Lehtinen, is chief, Office of Information and International Affairs of the Finnish Institute of Occupational Health, Helsinki, Finland.

Jorma Rantanen, is professor and director general of the Finnish Institute of Occupational Health, Helsinki, Finland.

Teresa Rees is professor of labour market studies, at the school for policy studies, the University of Bristol, School for Policy Studies, UK.

Ranald Richardson is a senior research associate at the Centre for Urban and Regional Development Studies, the University of Newcastle, UK.

John Ryan is deputy director of the Euro Centre of Excellence, PA Consulting Group, Dublin, Ireland.

Hanne Shapiro is centre manager of the Centre for Competence Development of the Danish Technological Institute, Aarhus, Denmark.

Roger Silverstone is professor of media and communications at the London School of Economics and Political Science, London, UK.

Juliet Webster is a research fellow in the employment research unit at Trinity College, Dublin, Ireland.

Claudia Weinkopf is senior researcher in the labour market department of the Institut for Arbeit und Technik, Gelsenkirchen, Germany.

Hans-Jürgen Weißbach is professor for technology assessment at the University for Applied Sciences, Franfurt am Main, Germany, and is a former general manager of the Institut für Sozialwissenshaftliche Technikforschung, Dortmund, Germany.

DATE DUE
